SERGEI TRETYAKOV

I WANT A BABY
AND
OTHER PLAYS

I Want a Baby and Other Plays

by Sergei Tretyakov

Translated by Robert Leach and Stephen Holland

© Introduction and translations of *The World Upside Down, A Wise Man, Are you Listening, Moscow?!, Gas Masks* and *I Want a Baby* (second version): Robert Leach

© Translations of *Roar, China!* and *I Want a Baby* (first version): Stephen Holland

Book cover and interior design by Max Mendor

Publishers
Maxim Hodak & Max Mendor

© 2019, Glagoslav Publications

www.glagoslav.com

ISBN: 978-1-912894-30-7

A catalogue record for this book is available from the British Library.

This book is in copyright. No part of this publication may be reproduced, stored in a retrieval system or transmitted in any form or by any means without the prior permission in writing of the publisher, nor be otherwise circulated in any form of binding
or cover other than that in which it is published without a similar condition, including this condition, being imposed
on the subsequent purchaser.

SERGEI TRETYAKOV

I WANT A BABY
AND
OTHER PLAYS

TRANSLATED BY ROBERT LEACH AND STEPHEN HOLLAND

GLAGOSLAV PUBLICATIONS

CONTENTS

Introduction 9

I Want a Baby and Other Plays

    The World Upside Down (*Zemlya Dybom*) 33

    A Wise Man (*Mudrets*) 77

    Are You Listening, Moscow?! (*Slyshish', Moskva?!*) . . 137

    Gas Masks (*Protivogazy*) 161

    Roar, China! (*Rychi, Kitai!*) 191

    I Want a Baby (*Khochu Rebënka*) 269

    I Want a Baby (*Khochu Rebënka*) 371

Sergei Tretyakov
1892 - 1937

To the memory of
Tatyana Sergeyevna Gomolitskaya-Tretyakova

'You are not dead while there are those alive who loved you.'

INTRODUCTION

The First All-Union Congress of Soviet Writers was held in Moscow between 17 August and 2 September 1934. It was here that the nearest attempt to define 'socialist realism' as the only viable medium for Soviet literature was formulated, and the experiments of the previous decades were denounced as 'formalism'. Nearly three hundred speeches were made by writers at the Congress, including a 'substantial contribution' from Sergei Tretyakov,[1] one of the co-organisers of the conference.

Tretyakov was at the time a successful poet, playwright and film scenarist, as well as a journalist and cultural worker, and editor of the influential Russian edition of *International Literature*. He was chosen to edit the proceedings of the Congress. Yet barely three years later he was dead, an early victim of Stalin's 'Great Terror'.

On 16 July 1937 Tretyakov was arrested and accused of spying for the German and Japanese secret services. He was tortured and hauled before a 'People's Court', where he admitted the charges, explaining that he had needed the money to pay off his gambling debts. It was an ironic attempt to signal, at least to his friends and those who knew him, the absurdity of the charges: he was a well-known and vocal opponent of all forms of gambling. Less than two months later, in September, Tretyakov flung himself over the banisters of the fourth floor of Butyrka Prison, where he was being held, and was killed on the paved floor below. The authorities responded by placing nets across the stairwell of the prison. They did not inform the writer's family of what had happened.

Tretyakov's works vanished from view, like those of many other writers who suffered similar fates. Yet gradually most of the playwrights whose

---

1   Bowlt, John E., *Russian Art of the Avant Garde*, London: Thames and Hudson, 1988, p.291.

work was strangled in Stalin's Terror have since been published and their plays resurrected on the world's stages. Thus, the complete works of Isaac Babel, who was shot on 27 January 1940, were published in a handsome edition by Pan Macmillan in 2002. His best-known play, *Maria*, was actually published in *The Golden Age of Soviet Theatre* by Penguin as early as 1966, and has received several major productions across the world. The work of Daniil Kharms, who died of starvation in a prison psychiatric ward on 2 February 1942, has also been extensively published, both in individual authored volumes and in anthologies, and there have been a number of important productions of his best-known play, *Elizaveta Bam*. Nikolai Erdman, whose *The Suicide* was banned at the same time as Tretyakov's *I Want a Baby*, was arrested, but he survived and even worked productively with Yuri Lyubimov at the Taganka Theatre in the 1960s. Translations of *The Suicide*, and his earlier *The Mandate*, have been published, and in England alone they have received productions at the National Theatre and the Royal Shakespeare Theatre. Tretyakov's plays have never received comparable restoration.

EARLY LIFE

Sergei Mikhailovich Tretyakov was born on 21 June 1892 in Kuldiga, Latvia, the eldest child of a large, warm, happy family of eight children and the leader of all their games and adventures. Both his parents were teachers. His father's family were Russian, but his mother's were German and Dutch, and he spoke German – as well as Russian and Latvian (Lettish) – from an early age. In 1913 he graduated with a gold medal from Riga Gymnasium and entered the Law Faculty of Moscow University, completing his studies there in 1916.

During this period he met many of the then-notorious Futurist artists and poets, including Vladimir Mayakovsky with whom he became friends. He wrote copious amounts of poetry, only a fraction of which he published. According to Vladimir Markov, Russian Futurism's most knowledgeable critic, he was an 'urbanist,' his work showing 'the modern city both from outside and inside.' Markov describes how 'in one poem, the poet feels a gay desire to approach a female passerby; in another, an automobile ride to the beach is described in all its futurist beauty of speed; in a poem filled with images of steel, factories, railroads and construction, a paean to the strong is sung and new music is heard in the clanking of metal'. This is, concludes Markov, 'a true poetry of the interior'.² During these pre-revolutionary years, Tretyakov became acquainted with, among others, the great theatre director, Vsevolod Meyerhold, the prominent literary theorist and critic, Viktor Shklovsky, and the composer, Alexander Scriabin. Tretyakov had perfect pitch and was an excellent pianist, whose playing excited Scriabin's intense admiration.

In the whirlwind that was the 1917 Russian revolution, Tretyakov found himself first in Pugachov in central southern Russia, east of the Volga, and then in Vladivostok. Here, with other Futurists, he formed the group, *Tvorchestvo* (*Creation*), which published poetry, including Tretyakov's first collection, organised lectures and staged plays. He also met Olga Viktorovna Gomolitskaya, whom he married, and adopted her daughter, Tatyana. He became involved with the Red partisans, and only escaped capture by fleeing to China. He rejoined the *Tvorchestvo* group when the capital of the Far Eastern Soviet moved to Perm.

In the autumn of 1922 Tretyakov returned with Olga and Tatyana to Moscow. He became a contributing editor on Mayakovsky's radical journal *LEF* ('Left Front of Art') and a member of the Central Committee of the Proletkult (the organisation for proletarian culture). He and his family actually lived in the Proletkult's cramped living quarters in a side alley beside the former Morozov mansion which had been requisitioned for their cultural work. Tretyakov taught in the Proletkult's writers' workshop and joined the First Workers Theatre of the Proletkult where his friend Sergei Eisenstein was director. He also joined Meyerhold's theatre workshop, where he taught 'Text-Movement' with Meyerhold, and organised Meyerhold's Jubilee, celebrated at the Bolshoi Theatre, that year. For both these world-renowned directors he created scenes and sketches for acting practice, and it was these two who were to be responsible for producing all Tretyakov's major plays.

THE WORLD UPSIDE DOWN

The first to be staged was *The World Upside Down* (*Zemlya Dybom*), which has been variously translated as *Earth Rampant*, *Earth Prancing*, *The World*

---

2 Markov, Vladimir, *Russian Futurism: a History*, Washington D.C.: New Academia, 1992, p.112.

in Turmoil, and more. The play, in verse, deals with a peasant insurrection, and the present title deliberately echoes the thought of those agrarian revolutionaries of the English seventeenth century, the Diggers, Levellers and others, who desired to turn the world upside down but ultimately, like their counterparts in the play, failed. *The World Upside Down* was adapted from *La Nuit* by the French revolutionary syndicalist and poet, Marcel Martinet. Trotsky had admired Sergei Gorodetsky's translation of the play – 'a noble work of art' he called it – and Lunacharsky recommended it to Meyerhold. But the latter detested its vagueness, its long-windedness and its lack of humour. He asked Tretyakov to remake it. This Tretyakov did, to such an extent that he created virtually a new play.

He explained his proceedings in an article, 'Text and Speech Montage', published in the journal *Performance* at the time. Here he identified the principal weaknesses in Martinet's original as the prevalence of pathetic soliloquies, rhythmic monotony and, especially in the Russian version, too many 'filler' words serving little purpose beyond making up the line. He cut over a third of the text, reduced the five long acts to eight self-contained episodes and sharpened the verbal style, creating what he called 'semaphore speech', or 'verbal gestures.' He also introduced distinctly 'low' humour, as when the defeated Emperor proposes to make common cause with his conquerors against his own subjects, the peasants whose uprising has cost him victory. His nervousness loosens his bowels, and he is forced to sit on the chamber pot. In Meyerhold's production, at this point, the orchestra blasted out 'God Save the Tsar', and an orderly brought on the pot, which was emblazoned with the royal arms. When the business was finished, the orderly carried the pot away, holding his nose, and the exhausted Emperor was carted out in a wheelbarrow.

More significantly, perhaps, Tretyakov strengthened the structure of the play so that Ledrux, the leader of the rebels, became Mariette's son, and the parallel between Mariette and Generalissimo Bourbouze was invigorated. The struggle between the 'Black International' and the peasantry was clarified, and the implications of the action were crystallized in projected slogans, which also often contained a vicious or humorous irony. Thus, the moment of the Emperor's betrayal of his people and his unexpected need to defecate was accompanied by the slogan, 'RULE BY TERRIFYING YOUR ENEMIES'. Tretyakov asserted that 'The problem for the playwright is to lift the playgoer out of his equilibrium so that he will not leave [the theatre] serene, but ready for action.'³ Trotsky, attending an early performance, obviously agreed. Yuri Annenkov, who was there the same night, recalled:

> During one of the acts, turning by chance to Trotsky's place, I saw that he was not there any more. I thought that perhaps the performance was not to his taste, and that he had left the theatre unobtrusively. But after two or three minutes, Trotsky unexpectedly appeared *on stage* and, in the very midst of the play, the actors gave way to him. He made a short speech about the fifth anniversary of the Red Army which was very appropriate to the occasion. After a stormy ovation, the action on stage continued in the most natural way and Trotsky went back to his seat.⁴

The production was extremely successful, and on 29 June 1924 it was transformed into an outdoor 'mass spectacle' by Alexander Nesterov, Vladimir Lyutse and Mikhail Koronev and performed for the Fifth Congress of the Comintern.⁵ This version deployed a cast of over fifteen hundred performers, with military personnel appearing in lorries, cars and motorcycles. Despite rain on the day, 25,000 enthusiastic spectators watched and cheered.

A WISE MAN

While Meyerhold was working on *The World Upside Down*, Sergei Eisenstein was working on *A Wise Man*, Tretyakov's equally radical adaptation of Alexander Ostrovsky's *Even a Wise Man Stumbles*. Tretyakov transferred the action of Ostrovsky's nineteenth century comedy to the contemporary world of Paris and set it among the anti-Bolshevik émigrés. This allowed the satire to be both topical and wide-ranging: the play lampooned not only the Russian Whites, and their political plotting, but also the NEPmen, those who would make a quick killing in the period of

---

3   Nizmanov, P., 'The Soviet Theatre Today', *International Literature*, July 1933, p.140.
4   Annenkov, Yurii, *Dnevnik moikh Vstrech*, Inter-Language Literary Associates, 1966, p.61.
5   *Comintern*: the 'Communist International', an alliance of Communist Parties from many countries, founded in 1915, which held congresses and worked for the installation of Communist governments across the world.

Lenin's New Economic Policy at the expense of the Russian lower classes. It also took aim at institutional religion and hypocritical morality, as well as fashionable entertainment, and more.

Tretyakov's most original move was to make the characters not psychologically-convincing individuals, but figures who operate simultaneously on three levels. Each actor plays a role which incorporates, first, the person in the story, now modified into a conventional dramatic 'type'; second, an equivalent from the circus or popular culture; and third, a contemporary political personality. Thus, Glumov, the scheming protagonist, is also the White Clown of the circus and a NEPman on the make; Gorodulin, the villain, is a juggler and also Mussolini, the Italian Fascist leader newly come to power; Mamaev, the hypocritical moralist, is also an acrobat and Pavel Milyukov, Foreign Minister in Prince Lvov's Provisional Government; and Golutvin, the mysterious stranger, is also a silent movie detective and a double-dealing NEPman. This multiplication of roles is not arbitrary: each illuminates and resonates with the others. For example, Gorodulin's villainy, his juggling skills and his Fascism each shed ironic light on the others, Mamaev's hypocritical moralising, his acrobatics and his political chicanery cleverly complement one another; and so on.

The different levels at which the action thus operates allows the play to exhibit a fast-moving stream of comical vitality and riotous political satire. But beyond this, Tretyakov again restructured the original to sharpen its irony. In Ostrovsky's play, Mamaev encourages Glumov to flirt with his bored wife and a few scenes later Glumov begins to do just that. Treyakov, besides shortening these scenes considerably, merges them so that the audience now sees Mamaev downstage and Mamaeva on a raised level behind, and Glumov running haplessly between them: the montage thus created reinforces not only the absurdity of the action, but also the cynicism of the characters.

The play ends with an extraordinary Epilogue, which features, among other unexpected *coups du théâtre*, Eisenstein's first film, and this provides a novel reality-shattering moment. It shows Golutvin in a car heading towards the Morozov mansion, the actual theatre building where the performance is taking place, and soon after he enters the stage, still in his film costume and out of breath. A second short film includes a further illusion-smashing moment when the director himself bows to the camera. These film sequences still exist, and make amusing viewing even without knowledge of this exhilarating play, which is their context.

ARE YOU LISTENING, MOSCOW?!

A Wise Man was something of a *succès de scandale* in Moscow in the summer of 1923. It inspired Eisenstein to write his seminal article, 'The Montage of Attractions', to explain his production methods, and it encouraged him and Tretyakov to create two more plays for the Workers Theatre of the Proletkult, *Are You Listening, Moscow?!* and *Gas Masks*. Both are short, sharp melodramas with explicit political intent.

Like all of Tretyakov's plays, *Are You Listening, Moscow?!* references reality, but in an unusual way: the premiere took place on the anniversary of the Bolshevik seizure of power, 7 November 1923, and the climax of the fictional dramatic action also takes place on 7 November 1923. The author described the piece as 'agit-guignol', which implied something both agitational and cruel, perhaps horrific. And indeed there is cruelty in the vicious whipping of Kurt by Marga, and horror in the murder of Shtumm, as well as the shooting of Kurt. The denouement in a play (or pageant) within the play is another of Tretyakov's *coups du théâtre*. As the culminating triumph of the government-sponsored pageant, a *bas-relief* of the Count's illustrious forebear is to be unveiled. But when the curtain is drawn back it reveals instead a gigantic portrait of Lenin. One of the workers turns to the audience: 'Are you listening, Moscow?' – and the audience replies: 'We're listening!'

More like conventional melodrama are the characters who, initially at least, seem to function – as they should in a melodrama – as types: the Count himself is the braggart, with his muscles and his boasting; Marga is a classic courtesan, imperiously demanding slavish devotion from every male; and Shtumm, the informer, is nervous, secretive and stuttering. But they are not merely types. Tretyakov's 'typage' implies the postmodernist conception of 'performativity': these characters *perform* their types, thus giving the play a resonance which more typical melodramas never attain.

In 1926, the critic Alexei Gvozdev suggested that *Are You Listening, Moscow?!* 'was, and in the history of revolutionary theatre will always remain, a magnificent model',[6] and some features may indeed be seen as prefiguring later greater work. The central image of *Are You Listening, Moscow?!* is the cathedral wall, covered with scaffolding, which is built up further and further during the course of the play as the supposed *bas-relief*

---

6   Gvozdev, Alexei, 'A New Triumph for the Soviet Cinema', *Zhizn iskusstva*, 26 January 1926.

is constructed, only finally to reveal something quite unexpected at the climax of the play. It was a model Tretyakov was to use again, with greater sophistication, in the first version of *I Want a Baby*, where the apartment block is the central image, which is transformed in the final scene of Milda's dream. Tretyakov also develops here the ability to jump rapidly from the near-realism of the scenes involving the workers to the grotesque scenes involving the reactionary aristocrats, a technique he was to develop significantly in *Roar, China!*

GAS MASKS

The story of *Gas Masks*, Tretyakov's second agit-melodrama, was based on a newspaper report about a factory director who had spent money intended for safety equipment on drink. But its relation to reality was greatly intensified by its staging, which took place in the Kursky Voksal gasworks, the first performance being on 19 February 1924. In fact, to some extent the reality overcame the drama, as mammoth gas turbines, hissing pipes and the nauseous smell of gas distracted the audience, rather than enhancing their experience. Melodrama's relation to reality is inevitably problematic because it is a dream or fantasy form. In some ways, its settings need to be more real than reality, as seems to be the case sometimes in dreams. But the reality of the gasworks here was overpowering, and the experiment failed. The play received a mere seven performances, and of these only three took place at Kursky Voksal: the factory manager, having initially welcomed the Proletkult troupe, had soon had enough of their disruption. It was the one play by Tretyakov, which was not a success when first staged, though when it was produced in Birmingham in August 1989, the local *Birmingham Post* drama critic wrote that the production succeeded in 'bringing this long-neglected play to life,' and suggested it contained 'remarkable immediacy'.[7]

Gas Masks exemplifies Eisenstein's 'new method of structuring a show'.[8] Thus, a scene which in a genuine nineteenth century melodrama might have been no more than 'comic relief' turns out to be in Tretyakov's hands a 'montage of attractions'. An 'attraction' is any self-contained moment of theatricality, complete in itself, but interacting with other attractions

---

7   Grimley, Terry, 'Gas Masks', *The Birmingham Post*, 10 August 1989.
8   Eisenstein, S.M., *Writings 1922-1934*, trans. Richard Taylor, London: BFI, 1988, p.33.

in a montage. The montage reveals the meaning. Thus, in *Gas Masks*, the episode of Vaska and the ikons, rather than being mere comic relief, has three distinct attractions: first, the director climbs the ladder, where he perches precariously; then, Vaska runs in with the ikon which the Old Woman snatches and beats him over the head with, cheered by the other women; thirdly, there is a sudden silence among the women, and the ikons are hurled into a pile, where they become, in the Old Woman's word, 'firewood'. The subject here is religion in the officially-atheist country: the villainous director on the ladder overseeing all is an image of God; the holy ikon hits the iconoclastic worker Vaska so he stops his tricks; the crowd silently (and powerfully) turn the ikons into 'firewood'. Each 'attraction' reflects on and gains meaning from the others. Tretyakov himself felt that the final production of *Gas Masks* approached what was fast becoming a radical artistic ideal in the young Soviet state: 'industrial art'.

A NEW PHASE

After *Gas Masks*, Eisenstein moved into film and the Workers Theatre of the Proletkult began a rapid decline into extinction. At the same time, Tretyakov became increasingly involved in the ideological artistic disputes which engulfed *LEF* and other journals and literary groupings concerned with the development of literature under the new Communist state. His trenchant article, 'From Where to Where?', for example, published in *LEF*, argued that the revolution had brought *avant garde* art into everyday life. He argued that agit-art, presumably of the sort embodied in his own last two plays, was only a temporary way forward, and he vested more hope in Constructivism, which was a kind of 'industrial art'. What was necessary, he maintained, was an art which was functional and able to organise 'the human psyche through the emotions'. In a further article, 'Lef's Tribune', he met head on the abuse of the *avant garde* by the increasingly ascendant artistic and cultural conservatives. It was a battle which would continue.

In the summer of 1924, Tretyakov had left Moscow with his family to take up a one-year appointment as Professor of Russian at the University of Beijing. He brought back with him in August 1925 a film scenario about China, which interested Eisenstein but was never made, the first rough draft of his 'bio-interview', *Den Shi-hua*, various parts of which appeared in journals over the next few years, the complete work (of over

300 pages) finally appearing in 1930, a collection of poems, called *Roar, China*, and a play.

ROAR, CHINA!

The play was also called *Roar, China!*, and it was immediately accepted for production by Meyerhold. However, the 'Master' was then preparing his groundbreaking production of Gogol's *The Government Inspector*, and most of the work on *Roar, China!* was carried out by his assistant, Vasily Federov. Nevertheless, the production, which received its premiere on 23 January 1926, turned out to be an enormous success, staying in the Meyerhold Theatre's repertoire for over five years and touring Europe with the company to great acclaim. In fact, it became Tretyakov's most successful play, receiving many other Soviet productions including in the Ukrainian, Georgian, Tartar, Uzbek and Armenian languages. It was first performed in Germany in 1929, in Austria, China and New York in 1930, in England in 1931, Australia and Poland in 1932, Japan in 1933, Argentina in 1935, Norway in 1936, Canada in 1937, and India in 1942. In 1944 a group of Jews in Czestochowa concentration camp put on *Roar, China!* in Yiddish, and when Shanghai fell to the Communists in 1949, it was revived, having first been performed in the city in 1933.

Roar, China! is an epic drama based on a historical incident in which an American businessman had drowned after an argument with a local ferry boatman near where a British gunboat, *Cockchafer*, was anchored. This ship's captain was so outraged he insisted on the ferryman being executed. When he could not be found, the captain demanded that two other Chinese be executed, or else he would bombard the whole town. Two innocent Chinese were put to death. These grim events are not presented as a sort of Orientalist fantasy, with tinkling bells, stylized dragons or pagoda roofs whose edges curl upwards: they form a deliberately unblinking glare at a horrific – albeit not untypical – episode in the history of western imperialism. Nor is the evident racism which tinges the action Tretyakov's – his attitude to the Chinese is infused with the cultural assumptions of his time, of course, but his perspective is not that of most contemporary non-Chinese observers, even such 'liberal' visitors to China as Albert Einstein. It is worth emphasising that any overt racism in the play belongs to the dramatic characters, not to the author.

Tretyakov presents the events with filmic urgency. Despite the long, seemingly naturalistic stage directions, the play is structured through a series of 'links', a word Tretyakov preferred to 'Acts' because a link is complete in itself, yet gains significance when it forms a chain with other links. The relationship between them is therefore one of parataxis: they sit beside each other as independent entities, but each is firmly attached to the next. This is a refinement of Eisenstein's theory of the play as a 'montage of attractions': Tretyakov spoke of 'link montage' as opposed to the earlier form of 'collision montage'. And by chopping up each link into short scenes, he ensures that the internal dynamic never slackens.

Tretyakov focuses his play on groups of people rather than individuals, presenting the Chinese with a sort of gritty realism while the effete Europeans are seen as grotesques, ridiculous but also merciless. The dramaturgical consequences of this include, again, creating characters who are effectively de-psychologised: they are seen as 'types'. Thus, the Captain in his dazzling dress uniform is a version of the traditional theatrical braggart soldier; Cordelia is the courtesan, or vamp; while the First Boatman is the stoical cynic. The contrasting costumes function like traditional stage masks. The endistancing effect is reinforced by the relentless changes in the spectator's focus from the pristine gunboat to the ramshackle wharf where the Chinese drink tea, mend their boats and complain about their lot; and by highly stylised passages such as the opening of Scene One in the Seventh link. We concentrate on typical aspects of behaviour and relationships, not on personalities.

Yet the result is not the coolly rational response which Bertolt Brecht, for instance, sometimes advocated. Just as at the end of *Are You Listening, Moscow?!* the audience was supposed to respond, 'We're listening!', so in *Roar, China!*, the audience is expected to respond by roaring, 'China!' But there is also a sense here that this ending brings not closure, but a new beginning. By these means Tretyakov desired that 'the theatrical show' would be replaced by 'the theatrical blow'.[9] And sure enough, when Federov's production was seen in Berlin, the British Consulate General reported to the Foreign Office, the theatre was packed, and the impression created in the audience was one of mingled pity, disgust and rage. Whilst some left the building before the performance was over,

---

9   Kleberg, Lars, *Theatre As Action*, Basingstoke: Macmillan, 1993, p.85.

others shouted 'pfui England', 'pfui Europe', 'Nieder mit England', and other choice things.[10]

THE LATER 1920S

In the following years, Tretyakov moved towards film work, including supporting Eisenstein during the filming of *Battleship Potemkin* and *The General Line*, and working with him on the projected film of *Das Kapital* which was never made. In 1927 he became drama consultant to the Georgian State Film Studio in Tbilisi, for whom he scripted four films, *Eliso* (1928), *Salt for Svanetia* (1930), *Kharbadia* (1931) and *A Song About Heroes* (1932) which had music by Hanns Eisler and was directed by Joris Ivens. In addition to cultural work on state farms, which led to the publication of a number of books and short stories by Tretyakov, in January 1927 he founded *Novy LEF* (*New LEF*) to replace the original journal, *LEF*, which had ceased publication while he was in China.

I WANT A BABY

But his major work in the later 1920s was devoted to creating *I Want a Baby*, not only the author's most significant work, but one of the most remarkable plays of the twentieth century. This drama centres on Milda, a Latvian Party cadre, who wishes to further the aims of the new society being built in Soviet Russia by bearing a child with an impeccable proletarian heredity. She does not wish to burden herself with a husband, however. She lives in an overcrowded Moscow apartment block surrounded by an extraordinarily diverse cross-section of contemporary citizens from a drug-addicted poet to eager Party workers, and from violent hooligans to a grumbling 'aunty' run off her feet by the children she looks after. Milda invites a down-to-earth proletarian building worker, Yakov, to father her baby, despite the fact that he is already virtually engaged to a postal worker, Olympiada (Lipa). He is astonished by her proposal, but finally agrees, and soon Milda is pregnant. Yakov becomes sentimental at the thought of fatherhood, but Milda sends him back to Lipa. Her behaviour has aroused the ire of her neighbours, but she shrugs this off, and in a dream foresees the Soviet future when her baby will win the

---

10   Leach, Robert, *Revolutionary Theatre*, London: Routledge, 1994, p.167.

prize for the best kind of Soviet child. But her triumph turns sour when she has to share the prize with the child of Yakov and Lipa, and the next prize is won by the child of the drug addict, whose partner Milda had counselled to have an abortion. Yakov is left to salute the children in an uncanny pre-echo of Stalin himself: they are 'the heroes of the age!' The ending is thus highly ambiguous.

I Want a Baby is clearly about creating a new kind of person for the new age – making a baby means making a future. 'The play isolates and examines dispassionately the expenditure of sexual energy which has as its aim the birth of a baby,' Tretyakov asserted somewhat primly, though he added that it thereby 'aims to discredit the so-called love intrigue, that commonplace of our theatrical art and literature.' One of the methods he uses to achieve this is to present a bewildering array of love or sex partnerships – Saxoulsky seduces the naive Kitty; Barbara is infatuated with the poet, Filirinov; the Block Superintendent makes a clumsy attempt to get Milda to go to bed with him; Andryusha's attitude to Ksenichka is hopelessly romantic; she is gang-raped by a group of hooligans; and so on. Milda's own approach to sex and love is appallingly anti-septic and ingenuous. 'Up to now on stage,' Tretyakov maintained, 'love has been a spicy stimulant. The tension of it gripped the spectator, turning him into an "illusory lover". In the play *I Want a Baby*, love is put on the operating table and traced to its socially significant result.'

This suggests the author's sociological, as opposed to psychological, approach to his material. Milda herself is a typical female Communist with briefcase and leather jacket. She is interested in child-bearing, not sex. Yet she is just one among the teeming crowd of undertakers, supervisors, prostitutes, flower sellers, working women, nappy-changing fathers, drama students, drunkards and poets who form a vivid kaleidoscope of contemporary society. They are shown with an absolute lack of sentimentality, but also with a good deal of humour, and they are connected to the play's theme rather than its overt 'plot'. How can this jostling, unruly multitude, which includes Milda, conjure a happy future for the Soviet Union?

The question is asked, but not answered, and Tretyakov explained:

> I will not bow any more to plays which end with some kind of approved maxim, which emasculates any struggle towards understanding. The intrigue has been worked out, the conclusion

has been presented, and the spectators can go and put on their galoshes in peace. I think plays which stimulate in the spectator something that lasts beyond the theatre are more valuable.[11]

I Want a Baby is thus a highly unconventional play, which rejects the expected notions of theatrical naturalism. This is exemplified as early as the second scene when Saxoulsky performs an incident of extreme pathos from the Civil War to the Club Secretary. An old general lies dying in Paris, and his Bolshevik son comes to visit him. But he rejects him even on his deathbed: 'No Bolshevik's a son of mine,' he declares. 'There are no commissars in the Polyudov family. In my veins flows the blood of Catherine's court.' But at the scene's conclusion, the Club Secretary is shocked: 'Ideological claptrap!' he asserts. So Saxoulsky performs the scene again. An old general lies dying, but this time in Moscow, and his White Guard officer son comes to visit him. The old man rejects him: 'No White Guard's a son of mine. There are no tsarist cavalry captains in the Polyudov family. In my veins flows the blood of Pugachev's warriors.' The tears now are for a valiant Bolshevik, and the Secretary exclaims: 'Now that's artistically valuable and ideologically consistent.' By presenting the two scenes in exactly the same way, and achieving totally opposite responses, Tretyakov undermines the very basis of psychological drama, which readers, or spectators, expect.

Besides specific vignettes like this, Tretyakov creates a virtually unique cacophony of voices, snatches of overheard conversations, a jigsaw of apparently ill-fitting pieces, which appear to have little connection with the 'plot' of the play. But in fact they are its life blood. And because they are carefully orchestrated, they make up an endlessly-echoing context for Milda's search.

This myriad of voices prompted El Lissitzky's extraordinary designs for *I Want a Baby*, made in 1926. They entailed dismantling the conventional theatre arrangement altogether: the action was to take place on gangways, in galleries and on the stairs of a multi-storeyed, flexible construction which was transparent so that every spectator would be able to see every acting area. According to the art historian, Christina Lodder,

---

11   Fevral'skii, A., 'C.M.Tret'yakov v teatre Meierkhol'da', in Tret'yakov, C.M., *Slyshish', Moskva?!*, Moscow: Iskusstvo, 1966, pp.203-4.

'Lissitzky's model fused architectural and theatrical elements together to create a new concept of the theatrical stage and the theatrical interior.'[12]

Meyerhold accepted *I Want a Baby* for production in September 1926, and rehearsals began on 16 February the following year. But this was not a sympathetic time for such a radical venture. The struggle by Stalin's cohorts against the 'Left Opposition', notably Trotsky, was reaching its climax, NEP was being replaced by the first Five Year Plan, and the Communist Party was beginning its fight against 'spiritual NEP'. Theatres were to establish Artistic Soviets which would include trade union and Party representatives, and the central censorship agency, Glavrepertkom, was flexing its muscles. *I Want a Baby* was banned.

THE SECOND VERSION OF *I WANT A BABY*

Tretyakov undertook to completely rewrite the play, and the following year produced what is printed here as the second version of the play. The story of Milda's search for a properly proletarian father for her baby is the same, but is now given a rural agricultural setting. Milda is an agronomist, and the story is framed by discussions of crop-growing, insecticides and animal husbandry.

Gone, therefore, are the fast-changing glimpses of the stresses of everyday life in the Moscow apartment block. The peasants who people this play resemble the peasants of *The World Upside Down* more than the urban misfits and malcontents of the first version of *I Want a Baby*. Eugenics – or a crude interpretation of eugenics which Tretyakov's irony may suggest that he himself had doubts about – becomes the leading theme. Thus, the breeding of pure white rabbits by the farm lad demands Milda's attention, as does the harvesting of gherkins in the greenhouse and the growing of cabbages on peat. The prevailing conditions at the time of gestation must also be factored in, as with the native tribe where prospective parents are not allowed to drink alcohol if they wish to conceive. Milda worries about the seeding machine, while plenty of blossom in the spring may still mean very small fruits on the trees in the autumn. Finally, the baby competition at the end is infused with considerably more bite by the implicit comparison

---

12 Lodder, Christine, 'El Lissitzky's set for Sergei Tretyakov's "I Want a Child", and Constructivist Stage Design', unpublished paper given at the conference, 'Tretyakov, Brecht's Teacher', University of Birmingham, January 1989.

between humans and farm livestock – both are exhibited, with medals awarded to the finest children as to the finest piglets.

Though not so stark as the first version, and perhaps lacking some of its originality and daring, this second version of *I Want a Baby* is by no means merely a paler version of the first. It is able to link more effectively genetic heritage with female sexuality and a woman's control over her own body. And the play's ending, apparently different, is just as ambiguous. Stoneturner has invented an electric rattle, and in the final scene he leads the whole cast, Pied Piper-like, round the stage and away: 'Those who would like to give their best babies to the Soviet Union,' he cries, 'not deformed or abnormal little monkeys, but healthy, bouncing, beautiful, Soviet babies, follow me.' Brandishing his device, he goes into the heart of the kindergarten, and the crowd follows him. The alternative ending to the second version, appended here, is perhaps even more destabilising: how does it inform any view of a future society?

I WANT A BABY AND THE SOVIET CENSOR

On 4 December 1928 Tretyakov read this second version of *I Want a Baby* to the Artistic-Political Soviet of Glavrepertkom. In the debate which followed, Petrov, the representative worker from the Hammer and Sickle factory, still objected to some of the language and vulgarities such as the reference to masturbation, while the representative of the Guardians of Motherhood and Babyhood resolutely opposed any performance. Valery Pletnev, erstwhile leader of the Proletkult who had crossed swords with Eisenstein and Tretyakov years earlier, suggested slyly that the Soviet public was not yet 'ready' for a play like this. It was strongly defended by the film director, Abram Room, and the critic, Vladimir Blyum (who is referred to in Scene 6 of the first version of the play, by the way). He argued that 'Fears connected with this play are analogous to fears around Darwinism. If workers can't go to this play with their families, then their families are philistines.'[13] However, sensing which way the discussion was going perhaps, Meyerhold intervened to suggest that consideration of the play should be based on the director's concept of staging, rather than the written text. The meeting agreed, and Meyerhold and Igor Terentiev, who was hoping to direct it in Leningrad, retired to consider possibilities.

---

13   *Sopvremannaya Dramaturgiya*, No. 2 (1988), p.239.

The meeting reconvened on 15 December, when the two directors outlined their plans. They suggested that the play should be presented as a 'discussion', with the action being stopped at various moments so that the audience could ask questions and clarify dubious ideological points. At the end of each performance there would be a further discussion with the audience. Having heard these proposals for staging, Comrade Pikel of Glavrepertkom, clearly still nervous of the outcome, even if he was also hesitant to appear too dictatorial, allowed Meyerhold, but not Terentiev, to go ahead: 'The play remains banned,' he ruled. 'Comrade Meyerhold is permitted to produce the play on a trial basis. But the possibility is not closed to Comrade Terentiev to mount a production in another city. If Comrade Terentiev rehearses with another theatre, we will consider the question again.'[14]

But Meyerhold's theatre was on the brink of a complete refurbishment and the production was postponed. This was apparently because El Lissitzky's design could not be accommodated in the old Zon Theatre. Yet curiously, the second version, which was what had been accepted 'on a trial basis' by the censor, did not require Lissitzky's setting, which related to the Moscow apartment block of the first version of the play. It is therefore still not quite clear why the play remained unproduced. Furthermore, it was not until 1931 that Meyerhold actually vacated the Zon Theatre building. Then, as Stalin's political tyranny tightened, the refurbishment of the theatre turned to obfuscation, and Meyerhold's company never returned. Perhaps the fact that Igor Terentiev, the other director involved in the application for permission to perform it, was arrested in 1929 was significant for the play's non-production.

The first version of *I Want a Baby* was finally presented in Moscow in February 1990, and even then, in the dying days of Communism, it aroused fierce controversy, with some members of the Teatr u Nikitskikh Vorot Soviet still arguing that the Soviet public was 'not ready' for this play. The second version has probably never been staged in Russia.

With the failure of plans to produce *I Want a Baby*, Tretyakov tried to turn the play into a film script, but, as with the play, the film was not produced. He worked on at least two other possible stage works, one about the restructuring of the patriarchal society in Svanetia, and a second entitled *We Fill the Earth*, but neither were performed, and their texts seem lost.

---

14   *Ibid.*, p.243.

TRETYAKOV AND RURAL RUSSIA

Tretyakov's attention now was turning to rural Russia, and the implications of the collectivization of agriculture, a subject initially addressed in the second version of *I Want a Baby*. He spent time in Svanetia, a mountainous region in the Caucasian northwest of Georgia, which led to his collection of sketches and stories, *Svanetia*, published in 1928, and the semi-documentary film, *Salt for Svanetia*, directed by Mikhail Kalatozov, which was released in 1930. By then he was working with the 'Communist Lighthouse' kolkhoz (collective farm) in the north Caucasus region near the River Terek. Walter Benjamin recorded some of Tretyakov's work here: 'Calling mass meetings; collecting funds to pay for tractors; persuading independent peasants to enter the kolkhoz; inspecting the reading rooms; creating wall newspapers and editing the kolkhoz newspaper; reporting for Moscow newspapers; introducing radio and mobile movie houses; etc.'[15] His publications *Oklik* ('The Call') and *Mesyats v Derevne* ('A Month in the Country') were sketches and stories from this period, when he was seeking to expand the very definition of literature into what he called 'factography', that is, using the writer's imagination to communicate real life experiences.

TRETYAKOV AND INTERNATIONAL LITERATURE

At the same time, Tretyakov's international profile was strengthening. In December 1930 he made his first visit to Germany, lecturing on 'The Writer and the Socialist Village' and meeting many of the most prominent German left wing writers, artists and intellectuals, most notably Bertolt Brecht. At the same time, he became embroiled in the controversy between those, like himself, who advocated 'open' epic forms, such as he had developed in *Roar, China!* and *I Want a Baby*, and the more traditional forms of 'realism', advocated by Georg Lukacs, Gottfried Benn and, perhaps surprisingly, Ezra Pound, whose *Open Letter to Tretyakov* was published in the German journal, *Front*, in February 1931. *Lyudi Odnogo Kostra* ('People Caught in a Bonfire'), his 'literary portraits' of the German writers and artists whom he met at this period was published in 1936 after Hitler had secured power, and contained unique information about John Heartfield, Bertolt Brecht, Erwin Piscator, Hanns Eisler, Friedrich Wolf and others.

---

15   Benjamin, Walter, *Reflections*, New York: Schocken Books, 1986, p.223.

TRETYAKOV AND BRECHT

The Brecht connection was particularly fruitful. In 1932 and again in 1935 Brecht stayed at Tretyakov's flat in Moscow, and in 1934 Tretyakov published his translations of three of Brecht's plays under the title *Epic Dramas*. It is possible to see Tretyakov's influence on Brecht at various levels. For example, in *The Good Person of Szechuan*, Brecht echoes Yakov's flight of fantasy in Scene 13 of the first version of *I Want a Baby* when the pregnant Shen Te fantasizes: 'Come, my son, inspect your world. Here, that is a tree. Bow politely, greet him,' and so on. We might speculate, too, about the choice of the Caucasus for Brecht's chalk circle after Tretyakov's involvement with the area, though this coincidence may also be connected with Stalin's origins in Georgia. Certainly the peasants who people *The Caucasian Chalk Circle*, as well as *The Good Person of Szechuan*, derive much of their essential quality from those in *The World Upside Down, Roar, China!* and the second version of *I Want a Baby*.

Perhaps more intriguingly than any of this, the trajectory of Brecht's playwriting career followed a path which may have been marked out for him by Tretyakov. When he met Tretyakov, Brecht was writing brief agitational pieces, the so-called *Lehrstucke* like *He Who Says Yes/No* and *The Measures Taken*. These are not unlike *Are You Listening, Moscow?!* and *Gas Masks* in their structuring and intentions. It is clear that the two writers discussed dramatic form consistently over a period of years, and it was only after he met Tretyakov that Brecht moved from Communist agit-drama towards the open epic form of his later plays, the form pioneered by Tretyakov. Perhaps this was what moved Brecht later to call Tretyakov 'my teacher'.

MORE INTERNATIONAL CONNECTIONS

Tretyakov had a further, indirect effect on Brecht's developing aesthetic. In 1935 he used his Chinese connections to bring the famous Chinese actor, Mei Lan Fang, to Moscow. Mei's performance was witnessed by Meyerhold and Eisenstein as well as by Brecht, who was staying with Tretyakov at the time. After the performance, Eisenstein noted 'the principal aspect of the Chinese stage':

> Realistic in its own specific sense, capable of touching upon familiar episodes of history and legend, as well as upon social

and everyday problems of life, the Chinese theatre, nevertheless, is conventionalized in its form, from its treatment of character to the minutest detail of stage effect.[16]

The description could not only apply to Eisenstein and Tretyakov's theatre of 1923 and 1924, but also to Brecht's theatre. 'Everything put forward by [the Chinese actor] has a touch of the amazing,' Brecht wrote. 'Everyday things are thereby raised above the level of the obvious and automatic'.[17]

Tretyakov occupied a respected place in international literature by the mid-1930s. From 1934 to 1937 he served as deputy to Mikhail Koltsov, President of the Foreign Committee of the Soviet Writers Association, and he made further significant contacts in Denmark, where he was introduced to the socialist writer, Martin Anderson-Nexö, whom he made the subject of another 'literary portrait', and Czechoslovakia, which he visited with Koltsov and Alexander Fadeyev. This visit inspired what became Tretyakov's last book, the searing documentary, or 'factographic', *Strana-Perekrestok*, ('A Country at the Crossroads'), written as Hitler was threatening to invade Czechoslovakia, and published in 1937.

THE END

But that summer the clouds of despair were gathering, and Tretyakov knew it. He was taken into the Kremlin Hospital suffering from 'nervous exhaustion'. Brecht tried to encourage him in his poem 'Recommendation to Tretyakov to Get Well', which ends:

> Swim in the lake ... The water
> Which could drown you
> Buoys you up.
> Swimming you cleave it, behind you
> It comes together again.[18]

---

16 Eisenstein, S.M., 'The Enchanter from the Pear Garden', in Mei Lan Fang, *My Life on the Stage*, Holstebro, Denmark: ISTA, 1986, p.47.
17 Brecht, Bertolt, *Brecht on Theatre*, edited and translated by John Willett, London: Eyre Methuen, 1964, p.92.
18 Brecht, Bertolt, *Poems 19131-1956*, London: Eyre Methuen, 1976, p.250.

But Treyakov did not get well. He was arrested on 16 July in the hospital, and died two months later.

AND AFTERWARDS

Three months after Tretyakov's disappearance, the secret police raided the family flat. It was 4 o'clock in the morning, and they brought dogs with them. The flat was ransacked, papers seized and Olga Viktorovna was taken into custody. She was dragged out, the back of her head banging on each stone step down to the road. Here she was hurled into a car which sped off in the darkness. Tatyana, now in her early twenties, watched it retreating. She fell on her knees, and called out, 'Oh God, if you are up there, help me!'

Not much later Tatyana learned that her mother had been taken to a prison camp in far-off Siberia. She was alone. After what had happened, most of the friends and acquaintances of the Tretyakovs avoided her, even crossing the road so as not to have to recognize her. It must be recorded, however, that Sergei Eisenstein was not one of them. He continued to call her 'Baby', and did what he could to comfort her.

Olga Viktorovna was finally released in 1955, two years after Stalin's death. She immediately put in train an appeal for her husband's 'rehabilitation' and this was granted in 1956. Slowly, some of his books began to be republished in Russia, including three plays (*Are You Listening, Moscow?!*, *Gas Masks* and *Roar, China!*) in a small volume in 1966. In Germany, Fritz Mierau edited *Sergej Tretjakow: Lyric, Dramatik, Prosa*, which included German translations of *Are You Listening, Moscow?!* and *Gas Masks*, published by Verlag Philipp Reclam in Leipzig in 1972. In 1989 the Berliner Ensemble mounted a full scale production of *I Want a Baby*, directed by Gunter Schmidt, and more recently a good deal of impressive research work on Tretyakov has been done by Tatyana Hofmann and Edouard Ditschek.

I met Tretyakov's daughter at a conference, 'Eisenstein at 90', held at Keble College, Oxford, in July 1988, and she encouraged me to explore his work, especially his plays, further. She then attended a conference, 'Tretyakov, Brecht's Teacher', which I organised at Birmingham University in January 1989, at which my production of the second version of *I Want a Baby* was performed. I also directed *Gas Masks* at the Midlands Arts Centre in the summer of 1989. That same year, the Moscow theatrical journal, *Dramaturgiya*, published the first version of *I Want a Baby*, and Mark

Rozovsky, who had attended the Birmingham conference, invited me to direct it at his Teatr u Nikitskikh Vorot in Moscow. It opened in February 1990, and remained in the theatre's repertoire for more than six years. I also directed the British premiere of the first version of the play, in Stephen Holland's incisive translation, in Birmingham in 1993. Further productions followed in British and American universities. It seemed that with the fall of Communism Tretyakov was beginning to be recognized as the major force he was.

It was the dearest wish of Tatyana Tretyakova, the writer's daughter, to have at least his plays published in English. She was clear that though she was adopted by him, he had always treated her as his own daughter. She called him 'papa', and he was always affectionate and often very funny. But in 1996, in her eighties, Tatyana, who had invested great hope in a future for Russia under Boris Yeltsin, came to despair even of this new regime. She committed suicide by throwing herself from the window of her fourth floor Moscow flat.

After the early 1990s, interest in Tretyakov's work had seemed somewhat to stall. Then in 2016 I was asked to write a history of Russian Futurist theatre, and was reminded of the brilliance and subtlety of Tretyakov's plays. When Edinburgh University Press published my *Russian Futurist Theatre: Theory and Practice*,[19] I decided it was time to try to fulfil Tatyana's wish. With the strong support of Tretyakov's earlier translator, Stephen Holland, and the encouragement of knowledgeable Russian specialists, Arch Tait and Robert Chandler, I made contact with Ksenia Papazova, the sympathetic and imaginative publisher at Glagoslav Publications. The result was the book you are holding.

Robert Leach

---

19 Leach, Robert, *Russian Futurist Theatre: Theory and Practice*, Edinburgh: Edinburgh University Press, 2018.

I Want a Baby and Other Plays

The World Upside Down
(*Zemlya Dybom*)

(1923)

Adapted from Night by Marcel Martinet

Translated by Robert Leach

The World Upside Down,
Episode 8 : The body of Ledrux is brought in.
(Note the screen above the stage.)

The World Upside Down

Characters

Mariette, a peasant woman, aged 70 years
Anne-Marie, her daughter-in-law
Louis, Anne-Marie's son, aged 12 years
Ledrux, a soldier, Mariette's son, Anne-Marie's husband, Louis's father
Goutaudier, a soldier
Favrolles, a soldier
Generalissimo Bourbouze, aged 70 years
Bordier Dupatoy, People's Deputy
His Imperial Highness
Major du Hault de la Sourdiere
General Damfranchy
Attaché
Grandfather Toine
Mr Pierre, schoolteacher
Father Bayon, priest
Peasants
Soldiers

First performed at the Meyerhold Theatre, Moscow, on 4 March 1923, under the direction of Vsevolod Meyerhold.

Notes

The original title of this play, *Zemlya Dybom*, was insisted on by Tretyakov despite doubts voiced by Meyerhold. The phrase is almost untranslatable. It has been rendered here as *The World Upside Down*, but other attempts to English it have included *Earth Rampant*, *The World Prancing*, *The Earth Rebellious* and more.
    The slogans in the text, and the episode titles, are to be projected onto a screen at the back of the stage.

EPISODE 1: DOWN WITH WAR

The living room of Mariette's cottage. There are several peasants sitting down. Enter Grandfather Toine.

TOINE: Mariette, good evening. Evening, everybody.
MARIETTE: Good evening, grandfather Toine. Well? Have you heard anything?
TOINE: No. It's been three days now, still nothing, just this silence.
A WOMAN: Yes, a terrible silence has come.
　　The din of the guns, the bombs and the machine guns,
　　All the racket from those diabolical machines,
　　Has vanished.
MAN FROM THE HILLS: Everywhere – just silence. It's been three days now.
　　We've had people mad from terror,
　　Not able to eat and saying:
　　'Are any soldiers left – or are they all murdered?'
TOINE: It's been three days
　　Since anyone saw
　　Even a single soldier.
A GIRL: Only corpses, freshly dead,
　　Bloodstains yellowing on the white snow.
　　Carrion crows fly down, caw caw,
　　And peck at their lips and eyes, as if they were ripe cherries.
MAN FROM THE HILLS: And wolves come out, trotting through the snow where it's melting,
　　And gnaw and chew on the murdered soldiers.
　　(*Louis cries as a hysterical woman goes to Toine.*)
HYSTERICAL WOMAN: You pity them. It's them you pity.

> The people who brought death and murder on us,
> You cuddle in your arms their freezing children,
> And you pity them.
> I had a little girl. Dead.
> I cuddled her in my arms.
> She laid her head down on the earth,
> Her blanket was the snow,
> This terrible snow, so cold, white, white.
> What harm had she done to anyone?
> Tell me that, priest. What are you staring at?
> Is that your religion? What had she done to God?
> A little kitten. A little kitten.
> Pity? Not pity. No more of that.
> I curse that. I curse everything, everything, everything ...

MARIETTE: We didn't know about this, daughter. Forgive us.
> I feel wretched. These are great troubles.
> We all, you know, partake of
> Our own sorrow. And now your sorrow.
> It's not easy for any of us.
> I've buried my man in the earth.
> My younger son was killed.
> There's no news of the older one.
> Does she know what's happened to her man?
> Or the boy to his father?
> But all of us, those who're here, and those who've been orphaned,
> While we're alive, however wretched we are,
> We will stand by one another, each for all.

HYSTERICAL WOMAN: That's right, granny. But it's a heavy load.

TEACHER: But this will end one beautiful day.
> And on that day people will come back to life.
> They'll stand tall at work, they'll come to their senses,
> They'll wake from the bloody delirium.

TOINE: Yes, that's fine, let it end 'one beautiful day'.
> But for us, the end will have arrived earlier.

MARIETTE: I don't know how it all started.
> We are people of the earth.
> We're only used to thinking about things of the earth.
> And in other matters we used to take

> What was said in leaflets and by town people.
> But we've woken up from that.

A WOMAN: Yes, we've woken up. The earth awoke us.
> But can the earth stand this destruction?
> Destruction of people, devastation? And are we going to accept it?

MARIETTE: No, we do not accept this. We mustn't accept it.

PRIEST: No, my dear, we must. And we must lift up our prayers to God.

(*SLOGAN: Religion is the opium of the people.*)

TOINE: Quiet, priest. We don't believe in God any more. We don't believe in that.
> She doesn't believe.
> And you yourself haven't believed in it since all this happened.

PRIEST: I do believe.

TOINE: Whatever you say, holy father,
> You come here when night falls,
> To Mariette's, where we all gather.
> We can't stay at home, in our ruined houses,
> But do you stay in the church with your Lord?
> I haven't studied as much as you, father,
> And less than you, mister teacher,
> But we're all buoyed up at Mariette's just the same,
> She's stronger and better than all of us.

(*Suddenly the door is opened. Enter First Soldier.*)

FIRST SOLDIER: I come to you ... from there, the war ... I ran.
> I've brought news.
> It's over, finished.
> We're saved. You're saved, too.
> I don't come from round here, but I'm of the soil, like you.
> It's finished. I just ran.
> We all ran. Everywhere, like rivers bursting their banks.
> There was a light here with you.
> Peasants, do you hear me, do you understand, do you believe me?
> Now it's finished, it's over.

TEACHER: The end has come.

A GIRL: We're not in a dream?

MARIETTE: No no, we're in reality.

TEACHER: The soldier's standing there. Look.

ALL (*except Toine and the Man from the Hills*): The war's over. The war's
    over.
TOINE: Is it true?
MAN FROM THE HILLS: You're not lying?
MARIETTE: Don't you dare get our hopes up
    For nothing, young laddie.
FIRST SOLDIER: It's finished, I tell you, done for.
ALL: Finished.
TOINE: Truly?
PRIEST: He's not lying?
A GIRL: Look him in the eye.
LOUIS: You're telling the truth?
ANNE-MARIE: I kiss your hand for bringing this news.
A GIRL: I kiss the mud of the trenches on your greatcoat.
ALL: Thank you!
A WOMAN: For the news.
A GIRL: For the happiness.
MARIETTE: Sonny, say it again, shout it aloud,
    So we can be sure, so there's no doubt.
FIRST SOLDIER: Then listen to me. I don't know how to make speeches,
    And others'll come who'll tell it better.
    But listen.
    It was the enemy soldiers more than us who did it.
    They were more exhausted than we were,
    Even though they were winning. They'd seized our country, yes,
    But did that give them bread, or dry clothes?
    Did it save them from being wounded, or killed?
    Did it take the heat off their old folk, their wives or children?
    And did the victory explain to them
    Why they were condemned to this death in life?
    Now they were here, they didn't have the will to go on.
    So they rose up in the countryside, in the towns,
    The same as us, slaves,
    Submissive, trembling, they rose up
    Against those who commanded them: 'Go. Maim. Kill. Murder.'
(SLOGAN: *The author of war – industrial capitalism.*)
    Looking them straight in the eyes, they said: 'No!'
    That's all. Let's wake up. We're people, too.

(*During this speech, more soldiers have entered.*)
MARIETTE and MAN FROM THE HILLS (*together*): Yes yes, we're people, too.
SECOND SOLDIER: We're people, too.
>Enough of being in the knacker's yard – human butcher's meat.
>Enough of being meat, flayed worse than a bull's carcase.
>Enough of being hired to murder people who're already skint.
>Enough of this madness.
>You haven't told everything, comrade.
>Their officers, commanders, generals, their very top brass,
>Who drove them to murder and death and torture,
>They were caught, disarmed, put in handcuffs,
>And then the lot of them were stripped of their ranks.

(*SLOGAN: Down with the gold insignia of rank.*)
>Death was rammed back down their own gullets like rabid dogs.
>Now listen.
>The king of the hangmen, the leader of the leaders,
>The emperor himself, yes, the actual, real emperor,
>Was flushed out of his lair like a hunted animal.

(*SLOGAN: Peace to the cottage, War to the palace.*)
>He was chased out of his palace, even though it was locked and defended.
>He fled from one town to another, from one village to another.
>Fool and bandit, he hurried to his own army, to the army
>Which had always been loyal, but which now was in revolt.
>Then he was caught, and tied up, like a wild pig,
>Yes, yes, their emperor, emperor, emperor.

(*SLOGAN: Knock off the crown of the last of the tsars.*)
TOINE: Sonny, sonny, such amazing things
>Really are possible. They really are probable.
>And you really believe them.

PRIEST: But if this is so, friends, why, it's a revolution.
SECOND SOLDIER: Right, reverend. Call it what you want.
>Okay, a revolution. Things are blown up with words,
>They make us muddled. Perhaps that's what you're trying to do.
>It makes you want – I don't know –
>To spit. I really don't know:
>But they're not shooting at us any more.

TOINE: Can it really be that this is just their cunning?
A WOMAN: What if it's a trick?
FIRST SOLDIER: What? Cunning? A trick? No, friends,
    We're not afraid of that, we believe them.
    They've spoken to us, we personally have spoken to them.
SECOND SOLDIER: And who wants to go on with the trade of murder?
GOUTAUDIER: They won? We won? Poor woman, able only to think
    of who's won.
    We've all won – through suffering, despair, poverty,
    And death. Through thinking
    How many are dead, dead, dead.
MARIETTE: You've won today.
    You've stopped killing today.
    You've beaten death.
GOUTAUDIER: We went to them.
    They let us into their trenches.
SECOND SOLDIER: Our commander didn't dare hold us back.
    I went there myself more than once, just when I wanted to.
    They told us about themselves.
    It was like a holiday.
    We ate, danced, drank together.
THIRD SOLDIER: We've just got back from there. That's what.
    As for the emperor – they didn't need him.
    So they sent him to us. They gave him to us.
FIRST SOLDIER: What a present!
TOINE: You've said it.
MAN FROM THE HILLS: You certainly have.
TOINE: Life has started.
ALL: The war is ended. Finished. Work begins.
(*SLOGAN: The floor is yours, comrade tractor.*)
TEACHER: What more is there to say?
    Work begins.
A GIRL: Life is starting.
TOINE: And that means, you know, young people begin to work.
THIRD SOLDIER: We'll work, granddad, we'll work well. You'll see.
(*SLOGAN: Machines have conquered water, the air, under the ground;
    agricultural machines will conquer the earth.*)
MARIETTE: And my son, Ledrux, will come back.

EPISODE 2: ATTENTION!

The living room of Mariette's cottage. Mariette, Anne-Marie and Louis sit in the room. Enter Haute de la Sourdiere.

SOURDIERE: Anyone at home?
    Here's –
    What a little darling. Marvellous.
    Your house is needed by us for a little time.
    In a day or two
    We'll return it to you. Could you put your head down somewhere else
    For the next few nights?
MARIETTE: Where, mister officer?
    Our house is the only one in the region which has escaped devastation.
    People come here for a bit of company of an evening.
SOURDIERE: Granny, I am
    Colonel Haute de la Sourdiere.
    Your house now finds itself
    The Command Headquarters of Generalissimo Bourbouze
    And his staff.
    (*Enter Bourbouze and his entourage.*)
    Attention, gentlemen!
    (*Music.*)
OFFICER: Attention! Right dress.
MARIETTE: There's two women here, general, and also my grandson.
    Don't make us perish in the snow.
    We were told – the war was over.
BOURBOUZE: Oh no, they didn't really tell you that, granny.
    Who said that?

　　　　The soldiers, I bet. Oh no! Lucky men. Ah.
　　　　The chickens have flown.
　　　　And discipline, what did they say about that?
　　　　Mm? That it's slacked off, eh?
　　　　Well, granny, you're not complaining, are you?
　　　　Suits you all right, doesn't it?
　　　　Don't you know that's exactly why we're here?
　　　　It is time to finish off these scoundrels, gentlemen.
　　　　Is it not? Uh?
(*SLOGAN: How to look after your betters.*)
　　　　It's no trouble for you to grant us
　　　　This place for the briefest time? Is it?
　　　　Go out, Mr General, and unload the second automobile,
　　　　And fetch in, oh, those plans, maps, everything.
　　　　Oh, and, general, er, something to eat?
GENERAL: Cook! Unload the second automobile!
OFFICER: By the right, quick march!
　　　　(*Music.*)
MARIETTE: General, are all three of us
　　　　To go out into the snow?
SOURDIERE: Get on, get on, that's enough whining.
BOURBOUZE: Well, well, colonel!
　　　　Granny, up you get. Brr! Hm!
　　　　Just think of the fate of the country, its deliverance,
　　　　And your deliverance, you must understand.
　　　　How many of you are there, do you say? Three? No husband?
MARIETTE: Three. No husband.
　　　　My husband was killed just the other day in a bombardment.
　　　　My younger son was killed two years ago.
　　　　My elder's at the front.
　　　　What's with him, I don't know.
　　　　He's her husband, (*indicating Anne-Marie, then Louis*) and his father.
BOURBOUZE: Ah oh, ah oh, you've still got one left.
　　　　You'll manage somehow.
　　　　Gentlemen, we have to spend the night here tonight, and tomorrow,
　　　　And perhaps more nights.

>   The woman and this young fire-eater
>   Will manage somehow, won't you?
>   Well, granny, it's a bargain.
>   Good night.
SOURDIERE: Off you go, granny, off you go!
>   Good night.
>   (*Mariette, Anne-Marie and Louis go out.*)
>   Ah, general, these peasants
>   Don't understand their own good fortune.
>   They don't value your fatherly concern.
BOURBOUZE: Yes, colonel, it's what you expect from them.
>   Dear de la Sourdiere,
>   Is a little comfort impossible? (*He indicates the bottle.*)
>   Ah. Do try.
>   Brr ... hm. Goodnight.

EPISODE 3:

THE TRUTH OF THE TRENCHES

The tap room of a country inn. Soldiers sit or stand, come and go, but during the scene their numbers increase.

FIRST SOLDIER: Ah, there you are.
SECOND SOLDIER: Yes. We're all here now.
GOUTAUDIER: We'll hold a meeting. Decide what's to be done.
FIRST SOLDIER: And who's calling this meeting?
(*SLOGAN: Everyone to the meeting!*)
SECOND SOLDIER: Everyone is.
    Are you worried?
FIRST SOLDIER: Well, same as you, I'm a bit afraid
    It'll end in some new trouble.
SECOND SOLDIER: What sort of trouble?
FIRST SOLDIER: I've been in this for four years now, devil take it,
    And I've seen a lot ... funny things have happened.
SECOND SOLDIER: It's different now.
FIRST SOLDIER: We've seen the world.
SECOND SOLDIER: They don't know how to deal with us.
FAVROLLES: Look what's happening on the other side of the trenches.
    That's given 'em something to think about.
FIRST SOLDIER: Well, okay, but then what?
    It'll still carry on to its end, won't it?
THIRD SOLDIER: You believe that? Do they know whether you agree
    to that?
    Did you even know what they were doing with you?

Did they warn you in advance where you'd be the next day?
FIRST SOLDIER: They dropped dead first.
But it's all very well bragging,
We've still got to be careful.
SECOND SOLDIER: Be careful?
You've seen what's happening. It's all but over.
THIRD SOLDIER: Well, is that it? Is that all? No more to say?
VOICES: – Open the meeting. Everyone's here.
– Time to open the meeting.
– What's the matter?
– Don't make a song and dance now.
– We want to know things.
– We know. We know. We can tell.
– Make a start.
– Make – a – start.
– Who's going to speak? Time to begin.
– Favrolles! Goutaudier!
– Favrolles! Goutaudier!
– Favrolles! Goutaudier! Goutaudier!
– Well, Goutaudier, up you go. Silence!
SECOND SOLDIER: Shut your drink-holes.
GOUTAUDIER (*standing on a table*): Comrades,
We've got our guns,
Now we want our share of the power.
Murder and torture have gone on day after day.
But we can stop all that if we're united.
We've got to decide
What we're doing here, why we've come together.
Isn't it true for us,
Comrades,
That we've seen so much, and we've lived through so much,
That it's time we stood together, time
We lived like brothers?
That's all, comrades.
VOICES: – Yes.
– Agreed.
– Bravo.
– Here here.

SECOND SOLDIER: We've got to be united. Then no-one can stand in
 our way.
VOICES: – All workers are brothers.
 – Brothers.
 – We shouldn't be ordered about. That's enough of all that.
 – Down with war.
 – Down with war.
 – Down with it.
FIRST SOLDIER: What are we going to do?
FAVROLLES: Comrades, let me have the floor.
VOICES: – Go on, Favrolles.
 – Speak, Favrolles.
FAVROLLES: Comrades, Goutaudier said it true: 'We are united'.
 But here's another comrade saying:
 'That's all very fine, but what are we going to do?'
 And actually, hasn't he got a point, comrades?
VOICES: – Maybe.
 – Yes.
 – Probably.
FAVROLLES: So I ask you,
 What did they over there in the other trenches
 Find they had to do?
 They had to
 Seize the top brass –
 Tie them up and throw them out,
 The lot of them.
 Except
 They sent one special parcel
 Over to us.
GOUTAUDIER: Not true.
VOICES: – True.
 – No, not true.
 – Maybe.
 – Could be.
FOURTH SOLDIER: Favrolles has told you the truth, it's been confirmed.
 They've sent him to us.
 I've seen him – he's a
 Simple Simon.

I WANT A BABY AND OTHER PLAYS   47

He's nothing like the pictures of him, either.
I saw him.
They did, too.
It's the emperor
Himself!

FIRST SOLDIER: So it's true. I believe it.
It's an end to all the torture.

SECOND SOLDIER: Comrades, unite!

(*SLOGAN: Workers of the world, unite!*)

FAVROLLES: Comrades,
Over there they immediately understood who to make an end of first.
Now, it looks like we're worse than them.
So I'll say it again.
We still have leaders over us.
We still have these dogs running free, with muzzles off.
You haven't done badly, you've stopped being slaves,
You're not going like lambs to the slaughter any more.
But now – what? What do you think I'm really saying? That a little bit more
Must be said. And a little bit more
Must be done. And there's no time to lose.
We must strike the top brass while they're in disarray.
With one blow you could lay waste
All the crap they've shoved on you.
Revenge,
Revenge yourselves, catch them, catch them. No mercy!

VOICES: – Comrades, hey, none of that.
– He's right.
– We're not wild animals.
– They tell us to commit murder. Then they have us executed.
– While they loll in a hot bath.
– We want peace. We want truth. Here and now.
– We can't just kill 'em.
– We can't do it.

FOURTH SOLDIER: Eh, Favrolles, when you were the captain's batman,
You preferred touching your cap to being a firebrand.

FAVROLLES: That's an insult.

VOICES: Ha ... ha ... ha.
FOURTH SOLDIER: Nobody's insulting you.
    But they're obviously like us – they don't believe you.
VOICES: – No no – we trust him.
    – Cowards.
    – Yak yak yak.
FAVROLLES: Comrades.
    You don't want saving – fair enough.
    But then – don't whine later. That's all.
GOUTAUDIER: Has it got down to trading insults?
    All against all? Shame on you.
LEDRUX (*who is the 3rd Soldier*): You can argue about it, but Favrolles
    is right.
    You're being dunned. It's a great victory for them
    When we fight each other over their corpse.
    That's being lower than slaves.
    What? – Don't we even hate the boss class,
    We just go on doing their work for them,
    And meanwhile we're hating each other,
    We're hating our own strength.
    But, you know, that's what we've got – strength,
    It's alive in us. We're strong!
    (*Favrolles makes to interrupt.*)
    Favrolles, I didn't try to shout you down.
    No. I believe we are all
    Comrades and brothers.
MANY VOICES: Bravo, Ledrux. Bravo.
GOUTAUDIER: We are brothers.
    That's our truth.
VOICES: – Ledrux is right.
    – You're right, Ledrux.
    – We're with you.
FIRST SOLDIER: But what should we do? Go on.
LEDRUX: Favrolles is right, our time has come.
    And it won't come again.
    But while it's ours, we're strong.
    Not if we go wild, just because we
    Scent victory. No.

And not if we let in new leaders
Who want new epaulettes on their shoulders.
Watch out for that, comrades, watch out.

VOICES: – Down with the self-seekers.
– Self-seekers.
– Down with the self-seekers.
– Down with them.

LEDRUX: Remember – behind us is the whole country,
And all its strength,
Even though it's been cut off from us,
It doesn't know us ...
And what is 'the whole country'?

(*SLOGAN: Long live the union of workers and peasants*)

Peasants, like us.
All who live by their labour, and are in want.
Are we going to climb over them,
Like drunkards on a mounting block,
When victory is so near,
Our triumph is at hand?
But, comrades, Favrolles is not right in one respect,
And that is on the need to kill
The leaders who are in power.
What would the peasant say about that?
Or the poor in the towns?
We are a new force
Because we don't want to kill any more.
And we don't want to die.
We are against death.
We are for freedom, and life!

VOICES: Bravo!

LEDRUX: Comrades, the reign of humanity is opening!

(*SLOGAN: Forward to Communism.*)

Who is for peace?
Who is for the working class?
Stand up!

FAVROLLES: A concrete proposal.

VOICES: – Let him finish.
– He's speaking.

– Ledrux, the floor's yours. Speak.
– Go on. Speak, Ledrux.

LEDRUX: Choose one person
For every hundred.
Make a soviet. Choose people
You can trust, people
You can rely on. Then
The soviet will consider everything.
Decisions will be taken
In the name of all,
And a delegation will go,
Not to beg for favours, but
To make demands.

(*SLOGAN: All power to the soviets.*)

Already we have control of the telephone system, the telegraph and the railways.
We must despatch appeals and information across the whole country
Immediately.

EPISODE 4:

THE BLACK INTERNATIONAL

Mariette's cottage. Generalissimo Bourbouze and his entourage.

BOURBOUZE: It's disgusting.
SOURDIERE: Mr General?
BOURBOUZE: The tobacco. It's disgusting. Loathesome.
    Brr ... brrr ... hmm.
SOURDIERE: Mr General,
    Mr General,
    Mr General,
    General Damfranchy.
DAMFRANCHY: Mr General, pardon me troubling you.
    There are some thoroughly deplorable events going on.
    They may take a turn for the worse:
    There's agitation going on all over the place.
BOURBOUZE: Your information is inaccurate, general, it is inaccurate.
    They're not content, devil take 'em, my lads – not content?
    They're being naughty, what? They're naughty, that's all, devil take 'em.
    One has to shut one's eyes. They'll have to be taken in hand a bit, what?
    Victorious soldiers don't stir up revolutions.
    Don't worry, it doesn't amount to anything.
    It's a good day today, general, a magnificent day.
    We are victorious.
    Victory, general, victory.

SENTRY: Halt! Who goes there?
SOLDIERS (*escorting the emperor and his cook*): It's us.
BOURBOUZE: What's that? Go and see, go and see.
    Eh? You're the cook, eh? And what have you got?
COOK: A spring chicken.
BOURBOUZE: What's that? And who's this?
ADJUTANT: (*one of the retinue*): His highness, the emperor.
BOURBOUZE and COOK (*together*): God preserve your Majesty ...
BOURBOUZE: Brr ... hm ... brr ... hm ...
    Yoo ... yo ... Your Maj ... majesty,
    Wh ... wh ... what an honour, an honour for us, for the army and for me,
    Your majesty. Majes ... in the person of me, in the person of m ... me,
    Our whole army, our whole country salutes your highness,
    A hero even in your misfortunes.
EMPEROR: In my misfortunes. Yes, of course.
    Thank you, gentlemen. I salute you.
BOURBOUZE: Your highness ... I salute you. Allow me, yes, allow me ...
    You ... yo ... Your highness must be tired
    From this ... from the journey, from your ordeal.
EMPEROR: It was a little unexpected. And took rather a long time.
    Twenty hours in fetters.
    On both hands, gentlemen,
    And both legs. And here as well.
    (*Indicates his head.*)
BOURBOUZE: Were you kicked?
EMPEROR: No. But - sticks.
BOURBOUZE: Your majesty – not *our* army, I hope?
EMPEROR: Not yours, don't worry.
    Your troops didn't do me any harm.
    Don't worry.
BOURBOUZE: But if so ... my duty ... I am forced to ... Your highness,
    You ... you ...
EMPEROR: To take me into captivity.
BOURBOUZE: Yes, yes. You understand, of course.
EMPEROR: Of course. It's the best way out.
    I'll be safe in your hands.

But there does arise a rather big 'But'.
Now I am yours ... well, you understand ...
Who now is your enemy? The people.
Just the people, gentlemen. My people.
That is, the working class, the peasants, the soldiers –
They're getting on, you know, without me.
Well, what can you do with a rabble like that?
Ah!
But what about your own side, Mr Supreme Commander?
Is everything as all right as it should be?
Is your country content
That the war should carry on into a fifth year?

BOURBOUZE: Brr ... hm ... brr ... hm ...
Brr ... hm ... brr ... hm ...

EMPEROR: The danger threatens even you, you see.
But
What if
You, the victorious,
And I, the vanquished,
Arranged
A league of governments!

(*SLOGAN: The League of Governments against the people.*)

And then to take matters – listen – into our own hands.
It would be our business, and your business,
To start setting up various deals, if you see what I mean ...
(*He seats himself on a chamber pot.*)

(*SLOGAN: Rule by terrifying your enemies.*)

An excellent proceeding. Ahh!

BOURBOUZE: But, your highness, this business is too delicate
To communicate to ministers, the government.
The provisional government? – No!
Ah, it requires subtlety, great subtlety,
Great skill.
We are familiar with your political dexterity,
Your highness ... hm ... hm ...
Your love of peace, it's renowned.
Oh, it's unbelievable, gentlemen.
Your highness, we

        Are at your service.
        Your highness, perhaps you would like us
        To bring up ... a throne for his majesty.
EMPEROR: Not at all.
BOURBOUZE: Your majesty, you're not too tired from your journey?
        Your majesty, permit us to withdraw.
        Military duty, military duty, your highness!
        (*They go out, leaving the Emperor alone.*)
(*SLOGAN: Interval.*)

EPISODE 5:

ALL POWER TO THE SOVIETS

Two months later. The tap room, which has now become the soldiers' revolutionary headquarters. Ledrux and others are at tables, which are covered with papers, telephones, etc.

LEDRUX: How is it with the tenth army?
FIRST COMMISSAR: A telephone message.
    Generals arrested. We're in control.
    A cavalry squadron of former officers held its ground.
    We've ended their resistance.
LEDRUX: Okay. Killed?
FIRST COMMISSAR: No information.
LEDRUX: Request the information.
    We must avoid bloodshed.
    But actually, perhaps it doesn't matter.
    Our weapon is the truth, total honesty.
FAVROLLES: There are machine guns with that detachment of ours.
LEDRUX: Favrolles, learn, and understand.
    War is something we have to do.
    But we don't want to, not any more than we have to.
    We always keep in mind why we're doing what we're doing.
    When's Bourbouze being brought in?
SECOND COMMISSAR (*on the telephone*): Hello. Yes. Good. Now.
FIRST COMMISSAR: He'll be here now.
SECOND COMMISSAR: Ledrux, they're sending news from the west.
    All power over there is in the hands of the local propaganda committee.
    They're taking care of food distribution. There's no unrest.
    The peasants are with them, they're agreeing to the requisitioning…

> The Workers Committee has restored steel production …
> There's been some sabotage by the bureaucrats …
> Yes, a good reason to crush the bureaucracy …

(*SLOGAN: Education is the sword of revolution.*)

> There are two new trade union schools,
> The theatres are working. Lectures through the countryside …
> What? Very. Hello.
> The only friction's with the provisional government.
> It wants to foist its stooges on us
> When we've only just chucked them off the committees.
> They're all scoundrels, speculators, cowards …

LEDRUX: I thought so. It's beginning.

SECOND COMMISSAR (*still on the telephone*): Hello. No more flour?
> The government's threatening to stop deliveries if the committee doesn't give way.
> They're demanding that the soviet give way. Hello.
> Yes, wait, don't go away from the phone.

LEDRUX: They must struggle to the very end.

(*SLOGAN: The struggle against counter-revolutionary speculation and sabotage.*)

> They can eat maize. Let them put it in the papers,
> They can eat maize.

ALL (*those by the telephone*): Struggle on to the end.

LEDRUX: They're cowards and ditherers in the provisional government.
> As soon as pressure's applied, they back off.
> All won't be lost if we stand our ground.

FAVROLLES: But they're not scared of us.
> We'll have to come to an agreement.

LEDRUX: What? Really?
> We thought of you as one of the more bloody-minded among us.
> Tell the comrades they must hold on.

SECOND COMMISSAR (*on the telephone*): You must hold on.

LEDRUX: When will the delegate from the government
> Arrive? Tomorrow?

FIRST COMMISSAR: No, today.

LEDRUX: Okay. But we've still got time to deal with Bourbouze.
> Warn the guard not to admit him till we've dealt with Bourbouze.
> And telephone the government about what's going on in the west.

FIRST COMMISSAR: Commander's H.Q. Don't admit the delegate
    Till we've dealt with Bourbouze.
LEDRUX: Who is the delegate? Do they know him here?
FIRST COMMISSAR: Bordier-Dupatoy, a people's deputy from the old
    clapped-out assembly.
FAVROLLES: From our district.
FIRST COMMISSAR: What's he like?
FAVROLLES: Well, he's not so bad. From that lot, he's one of the better
    ones.
    Not too hard, anyway.
GOUTAUDIER: Bourbouze is coming.
    (*Enter Bourbouze, guarded.*)
LEDRUX: Come in.
    Bourbouze, first of all, you refused even to admit our delegates
    Two weeks ago
    When we wanted to negotiate an agreement with you.
    Secondly ...
BOURBOUZE: I ... didn't know ... brr ... br ...
    Gentlemen, I didn't know you were in a position to ... brr ...
LEDRUX: That's enough, Mr Bourbouze, of pretending to be
    simpleminded.
    That kind of put-on stupidity is convenient, but we don't believe
    it.
    There's too much blood on you, Bourbouze.
    You've always taken freedom for granted, haven't you?
    But now, it's all over. We're arresting you.
BOURBOUZE: Brr ...
LEDRUX: Take him away. (*Bourbouze is led out.*)
    What next for him? Comrades, you have the floor.
FAVROLLES: There's one very neat solution.
    It seems to me he should be taken to the trenches on the other side:
    They despatched their top person to us under guard. We'll send
    them this fat swine.
GOUTAUDIER: No, send him to the government.
SECOND COMMISSAR: Oh no, never.
FIRST COMMISSAR: You know what the government would do?
SECOND COMMISSAR: I saw what it did in the west.
LEDRUX: The best way out is to execute him. Now.

>   I know the danger of creating a martyr,
>   But still, what are we fighting for?
>   Fifteen million martyrs are under the ground.
>   Before them, this buffoon is nothing.
>   He's an old fool, and I'll take his blood upon myself.

GOUTAUDIER: But we can't be the ones to judge.
LEDRUX: We can conduct a trial today, in the name of the people.
FAVROLLES: Aha, a dictatorship!
(*SLOGAN: Long live the dictatorship of the proletariat.*)
LEDRUX: The masses will approve such a measure now.
>   A fortnight ago the execution of Bourbouze would have
>   Roused threequarters of the country against us.
>   A week from now it could rouse half the army against us
>   And they'd hand us over to the government.
>   But today it will terrify the cowards.
>   The door to the capital is open to the true leaders of the people.
>   The provinces are liberated and no-one can tie the army's hands.
>   I vote for his death.

FAVROLLES: Send him over to the trenches on the other side.
LEDRUX: Never! No!
>   Send Bourbouze to them, so they can return him to our government?
>   I vote he's put to death.

FIRST COMMISSAR: Who votes for his death?
>   Put up your hand who votes for his death?
>   (*Only a few hands go up.*)

LEDRUX: Okay. But I just hope that isn't a vote
>   For other people to be put to death.
>   (*Soldiers run in, followed by Bordier-Dupatoy.*)

SOLDIERS: – Long live the people. Hurray ...
>   – Long live the revolutionary army. Hurray ...
>   – All power to the soviets. Hurray ...
>   – Long live Ledrux. Hurray ...

DUPATOY: I knew, comrades, soldiers, that in coming to you
>   I was coming to the very heart of the revolution ...

FAVROLLES: Long live the delegate.
DUPATOY: Dear colleagues in struggle, you who set it going,
>   Heroic leaders of the heroic armies,

           Thank you for the brotherly and simple way
           In which you have honoured an old fighter like me
           In the name of the country and the government who've sent me.
(*SLOGAN: Down with the ministers of the capitalists.*)
           I express our gratitude and our thanks to you all.
           And above all, as I'm sure everyone agrees,
           Our thanks go to
           Our young comrade-leader – Ledrux.
LEDRUX: Comrade, we're just getting on with the next task.
           Each of us expects to work, and to make sacrifices.
           There's no call to glorify any one of us individually.
           Now's not the time for relaxation and applause.
           We have just arrested Generalissimo Bourbouze,
           And the traitors to the people, his generals.
           In the provinces the working class are organising,
           They've taken power. But what then?
           What do you think?
           That therefore justice has already begun her reign on earth?
           It'd be nearer to the truth
           To say that nothing has yet been accomplished.
           D'you imagine the whole gang of the old rulers
           Has just resigned? That their claws are suddenly trimmed?
           Look, from under new masks
           They're getting ready to trade in human lives again.
           Watch out! Of course,
           You won't easily become again
           A flock of sheep for the shearing.
           Today we are strong.
           But that's exactly why we mustn't sleep,
           Why we must carry on, why
           With pickaxes in our hands
           We must demolish the old way of life
           And build our own new world
           Through labour, and with truth.
(*SLOGAN: We will build a new world.*)
           The provinces are calling for help.
           Comrades, beyond the trenches are our brothers,
           Swindled by this treacherous provisional government.

We have no time to lose.
To work, comrades. To work
In your committees and your party cells,
To work in the villages.
(*SLOGAN: Labour will bring mastery of the world.*)
To strengthen the connection between the town and the country,
To work in the workshops and factories. Enough of talk. To work.
Citizen, I think you must have already filled your quota,
Since you have time to visit the army.
Report back to your colleagues
That you found the people here working to some purpose.
Tell them – in everything, they're ready.
DUPATOY: Comrade Ledrux, my friend,
I'm one the first to applaud your red-blooded speech.
I agree wholeheartedly with comrade Ledrux.
Other people might flatter you, and say
That after your glorious and hard-won achievements
It's time to rest, relax.
But not Ledrux. He's a leader you can be proud of.
So all I've got to say, in my simple but honest way, is,
Yes, times are hard, but still there's joy for everyone,
For all who work and who are united in defence of freedom.
I'm glad to learn that Bourbouze,
That monster of oppressive tyranny, has been arrested,
The whole government is gladdened.
Comrades, let there be no little clouds between us.
The whole country is beginning to rally round the government,
Yes, the whole country, comrades, is unshakeably, enthusiastically united.
And the government acknowledges it is bound
Indissolubly to its heroic revolutionary army.
Comrades, it has proved this.
Of course, I know there have been rumours, they've probably reached here,
Slanders invented by jealous minds,
Dreaming in their despotic brains of a hateful dictatorship.
But we have dispelled those clouds from our sun.
In these matters, the government has

Shown its good faith by its gratitude to the troops,
Not one of whom has it forgotten.
Yes, I know that people say that we're a government
Composed only of civilians, people who made their piles out the war.
But, comrades, there are civilians and civilians,
And those at the top of the government,
All of them, including me, are the honest friends of the soldiers,
All of them, including me, are counting the hours
Till the armies can be discharged.
We are ending the business you have so happily begun.
That's all I wanted to say.
But I just have one request to add:
I'd like to visit the graves
Of those who perished serving the revolution,
I'd like to honour them.
(*SLOGAN: Down with the grave-diggers of the revolution.*)
They are the heroes, who for our sake
Went to their graves, to give life to their heirs.
(*Exit Bordier-Dupatoy and soldiers.*)
SECOND COMMISSAR: It was a mistake not to have arrested him in time.
LEDRUX: Mm. Not everything is lost yet.

EPISODE 6: SHEARING THE SHEEP

The living room of Mariette's cottage. Peasants sitting about.

A PEASANT: They got into the cellar.
     Our keg was buried there.
     They drank the whole lot.
FIRST PEASANT WOMAN: Scoundrels.
SECOND PEASANT WOMAN: They're all swine. Scum.
FIRST PEASANT WOMAN: Worse than those on the other side.
TOINE: Monsieur Bordier Dupatoy said
     We should go to him with our complaints.
PEASANT: We need a government.
TOINE: We've got one.
FIRST PEASANT WOMAN: Yes, and we'll soon see what it's made of.
SECOND PEASANT WOMAN: But that young man that's just arrived,
     What's he called? – The Attache
     Of Monsieur Bordier Dupatoy,
     It seems to me you can deal with him.
OLD WOMAN: How soon will he be here?
FIRST PEASANT WOMAN: Probably somebody with a complaint
     Detained him.
SECOND PEASANT WOMAN: Or one of those scoundrels
     You have to stand on ceremony with.
OLD WOMAN: And they dare to say that there are those among us
     Who support these hooligans.
     But give them enough time, the priest said,
     And they'll smash their own skulls.
FIRST PEASANT WOMAN: It's Mariette. She's completely mad.
     All the mischief comes from her.
     And you sang her praises.

(*Enter the Attaché.*)
ATTACHÉ: Well, good people, and what do you want?
ALL: Mr Attaché ... Mr Attaché ... Mr Attaché ...
ATTACHÉ: Not all at once.
FIRST PEASANT: We were here first.
ATTACHÉ: Very well, then, you speak.
SECOND PEASANT: Hey, we've come further than you.
ATTACHÉ: Now then, friend, it'll be your turn soon.
PEASANT: The soldiers have turned everything upside down.
    They've pinched our apples,
    And drunk up everything that was in the keg.
ATTACHÉ: So. Okay. We'll see. Their names?
PRIEST: Excuse me, Mr Attache,
    But we look to you to compensate us for our losses.
    Here's our delegate.
    (*Enter Bordier Dupatoy.*)
ATTACHÉ: Ah, my superior. Sir,
    There are very many complaints.
DUPATOY: Friends, everything's going on fine.
    I can certainly promise you
    That soon everything will be completely sorted out.
    I know how bitter have been the days
    You've lived through ...

EPISODE 7:
THE STAB IN THE BACK OF THE REVOLUTION

The tap room of the country inn. A few commissars, including Ledrux, are working resolutely, with papers, telephones, etc. We are aware of discontented crowds outside, whose shouts can sometimes be heard.

FIRST COMMISSAR: There's still no let-up. They warned us
    How those devils would be able to twist everything.
    The delegates are clever as poison, too,
    They'll be able to control things brilliantly
    When everything's gone mouldy.
A VOICE: Oho.
SECOND COMMISSAR: What's to be done?
GOUTAUDIER: What's to be done?
    The soldier masses are dissolving.
    They're not fulfilling the orders of the committee,
    They've gone off into looting and anarchy.
    It seems to be turning out that we rose up against death
    So we could become the purveyors of new types of death.
VOICE: Things are splitting apart.
FIRST COMMISSAR: In the end, only one death
    Really matters. Our own.
    Down with being victorious.
VOICE: Ha ... ha ...
FIRST COMMISSAR: It's all been just too much. Five years of war,
    Then these last three months ...
    I can't go on living like this.
VOICE: Serves you right ...
SECOND COMMISSAR: To die? Alone?
    No, those renegades are going to die with us. Before us.

        I'm also waiting for death.
        To die.
        It'd be bitter for me on my own,
        But if I snuff it along with some of their dead bodies …
VOICE: You couldn't if you tried.
FIRST COMMISSAR: Revenge? That's not the answer.
        We made our first mistake,
        Perhaps you could say, committed our first crime,
        When we rose up, but didn't complete the victory.
        Now – to fall asleep, to sleep, to sleep.
SECOND COMMISSAR: So, like I said – what's to be done?
VOICE: Drink, little bird … drink.
SECOND COMMISSAR: Death? Done for?
        It's never too late to win, to turn things round.
(*SLOGAN: Keep in step with the revolution.*)
        In other words, now is the time to step up the struggle.
        We can still win the prize.
VOICE: Not on your life.
GOUTAUDIER: Poor young fellow.
THIRD COMMISSAR: Shut up. The bomb under the provisional government
        Is ready to go off at any minute.
        And you're losing hope.
        You've already given up. But listen to the news:
        The comrades in the capital are hurling themselves into the attack.
VOICE: Tell us another.
THIRD COMMISSAR: Two districts, two whole districts,
        Are already in their hands.
        Wake up!
        Victory can still be ours!
VOICE: A likely tale.
LEDRUX: Yes, two whole districts fell to us this morning.
        And it's now clear
        That these districts have been cleaned out with machine guns,
        All resistance smashed.
        Anyone still holding out tomorrow
        Is going to be court martialled and shot.
VOICE: Oh yes?

LEDRUX: To teach the bourgeoisie a lesson.
 But it's late, too late. Or else – too early.
 (*The crowd outside is getting closer and noisier.*)
VOICE: What do you think?
FOURTH COMMISSAR: Ledrux, Ledrux,
 You're beginning to doubt.
VOICE: He's a dictator.
LEDRUX: This is a revolt.
 But we'll face it without batting an eyelid.
 Well, what are you waiting for? You out there,
 Don't just wheeze like drunken old women, beg for death,
 Wail about revenge, cackle about victory.
VOICE: Cut it out.
LEDRUX: Do you really need to hide from the truth?
 We, on the other hand, will be absolutely faithful
 To our only friend: the naked truth.
VOICE: Aha. Truth in whose eyes?
GOUTAUDIER: What's to be done?
VOICE: Clear off to the devil's mother.
LEDRUX: Wait.
VOICE: Wait yourself.
LEDRUX: Don't ever
 Expect it, but
 Miracles do happen.
VOICE: If you're a miracle-worker.
LEDRUX: Wake up!
 Be ready for anything.
 Wait.
VOICES: – Let's go home, lads,
 – Let's go home.
GOUTAUDIER: Miracles with them? I don't think so.
LEDRUX: Listen, men, you're probably
 Ready for anything.
VOICE: Ready to pack it in.
LEDRUX: With no regrets?
 Listen. Let each one of us
 One by one
 Go out

> Into the masses.

VOICE: To hell with these dogs of agitators.

LEDRUX: To the crowds,
> To that crowd out there.

VOICE: Death to Ledrux.

LEDRUX: Everyone – in groups.

VOICE: There's no-one to tell them.

LEDRUX: Make them listen to reason, tame them,
> They're like wild beasts. We can
> Wake those people up, they're
> Human beings, they're
> The same as us.

VOICES: – Fling him into the trenches.
> – Let's go home – let's go home.

VOICE: To the firing squad with these commissars!

(*Enter Favrolles.*)

FAVROLLES: What's happening? Is it death?

FIRST COMMISSAR: To you first.

VOICE: The world's unclean.

FAVROLLES: Oh, is it?
> I don't think so.

VOICE: Chuck out the committee men.

FAVROLLES: Louse.
> That won't help.
> But we can still save ourselves. Surrender.
> Let's go, comrades, let's surrender together.

(*The crowd rushes in, shouting.*)

VOICES: – Time's up.
> – To the firing squad. Death.
> – Goodnight. Down with them. Kill them.
> – Flog him. Death to Ledrux.
> – Kill him.

LEDRUX: Comrades.

VOICES: We're not comrades.

LEDRUX: Remember, if only for a spark of honesty …

FIRST CONSPIRATOR: Assassinate him!

SECOND CONSPIRATOR: Ready.

(*A shot. Ledrux falls.*)

(*SLOGAN: Look after our leaders.*)
THIRD CONSPIRATOR: This is it – for everybody.
FIRST CONSPIRATOR: Scoundrel!
GOUTAUDIER: He was honest.
SECOND CONSPIRATOR: Traitor.
SECOND COMMISSAR: Who shot first?
THIRD CONSPIRATOR: Anybody see?
FIRST COMMISSAR: He was killed on someone's orders. The government's?
SECOND SOLDIER: Fat bastards.
GOUTAUDIER: The people's best friend.
FIRST CONSPIRATOR: Muck.
THIRD SOLDIER: Muck yourself.
  (*Bordier Dupatoy enters self-importantly.*)
DUPATOY: He was a great man,
  Comrades. Maybe he made mistakes,
  Serious mistakes,
  Dangerous mistakes,
  Criminal mistakes.
  But this shouldn't stop us remembering what he really was.
  He was our comrade. He may have been guilty of some things,
  But we should pay just tribute to him, and respect his body now.
  His life, his death, even the mistakes he made,
  Teach us. He was our great comrade, but he's dead now,
  Fallen. It doesn't matter by whose hand.
  (*To the body.*) You didn't understand how events were moving.
  You were overwhelmed by the wheel of fate. But comrades,
  Forgive him, in your hearts, and in your minds.
(*SLOGAN: Down with the class traitors.*)
  I see we can agree, I see we can forgive.
  There is forgiveness,
  Even for those who have been so severely
  And so unjustly treated.
  He was a good man, my friends,
  He deserved the name of father of his soldiers,
  And he led you, comrades, to victory.
  But his own mistakes brought him low.
  We will remember this man

    And hold him dear in our hearts,
    Like a father in the hearts of his children.
    Comrades – look – who's here?
    (*Enter Generalissimo Bourbouze.*)
BOURBOUZE: Yes indeed. Yes, children, sons.
    Ah, ah. Great, heartfelt emotion.
    Loyalty, fidelity,
    And the brotherhood of a great rebellion.
    Brr ... brr ... You are the finest soldiers in the world.
(*SLOGAN: Down with imperialistic butchery.*)
CONSPIRATORS: We did our best, your worshipful.
BOURBOUZE: Now it is we who savour the fruits of victory.
    Mmm. Victory, my boys, victory.
CONSPIRATORS: Hurray ... hurray ... hurray.
DUPATOY: The generalissimo is deeply moved.
    So are we all. In his name,
    I can report to you, friends,
    The great and joyful news: the war will continue,
    It will go on
    To a victorious end.
    The government has resolved
    That the emperor himself,
    Our enemy, who must and who can pay,
    Will be returned to his own jaded and pitiful army.
    He's nothing now, a trifle. We will beat him down.
    And every one of you shall receive
    His share of the spoils.
CONSPIRATORS: We humbly thank you, your worshipful.
DUPATOY: Forward!
    Your suffering will not be in vain.
CONSPIRATORS: Humble thanks, your worshipful.
BOURBOUZE: Company – quick march.
DUPATOY: To arms! On to victory!

EPISODE 8: NIGHT

The living room of Mariette's cottage. Peasants.

MAN FROM THE HILLS: There are piles of corpses in the woods
    Lying frozen, stiff with cold,
    The bodies of our young men.
HYSTERICAL WOMAN: Blood, blood. What does the spilling of blood matter
    So it washes away all the crimes of men?
PRIEST: All the sins of men.
HYSTERICAL WOMAN: Blood.
    I am cursed. Cursed – everyone, everyone, everyone …
    I am a hungry she-wolf,
    I smell the blood,
    And a terrible beast is eating me away inside.
    And now I'm happy, I'm happy.
A WOMAN: The war goes on.
    They're chasing about, killing each other, gobbling each other up.
    But for us – it's better now. We're making them pay.
    It's those scoundrels' turn, and our men have given them a shock.
    We were just stupid before.
TEACHER: That was what those vermin did to us.
PRIEST: Our general's a good fellow. He's getting everything going again.
HYSTERICAL WOMAN: We'll skin 'em, the swine.
TEACHER: Vipers.
ALL (*except Mariette*): For the sake of our dead sons.
    For the sake of our fields.
    For the sake of our farms.
MARIETTE: For the sake of our dead sons.
    For the sake of our dead sons.

    For the sake of our new dead sons.
PRIEST: Mariette.
MARIETTE: So you'll wash away blood with blood?
TOINE: That's enough, Mariette.
    Aren't you really glad
    That our native land will be saved?
    You can't still be dreaming
    About what went on here,
    All that fantasy, that unbelievable nonsense?
LOUIS: Really, granny, was everybody happy
    When there was no war on,
    And the generals were dumped in prison?
TEACHER: Quiet, young 'un.
MARIETTE: Quiet, Louis.
    Anne-Marie, the boy's come out in a rash.
    It's too much for him to cope with.
ANNE –MARIE: He'll go to sleep now.
PRIEST: Mariette, you see, you yourself ...
MAN FROM THE HILLS: The young 'un's right.
    We were strong ...
PRIEST: Pride, Mariette ...
TOINE: We don't hold it against you, Mariette.
    You supported everybody in the bad times.
    But we're old now.
    We don't have the strength to really change things.
    Do you think that on our own
    We could actually be victorious,
    We could strike like thunder,
    When we're just nobodies, really?
    Maybe if we were still young, like they were,
    We could at least argue about it,
    But you know, they've all been killed.
WOMAN: Of course we forgive you, dear Mariette,
    But this house, and you yourself,
    Remind us too much
    Of the good times, the ideas, the hopes.
    So I'm not coming here any more.
    I won't come down this road.

        Goodbye, Mariette. God forgive you.
        Goodbye, Anne-Marie.
        (*She goes.*)
TOINE: She's got a hard heart. She's suffered
        Less than anybody.
        She's afraid of us, afraid
        Of the soldiers, and the refugees.
        She's stashed away bags of silver.
OLD WOMAN: Well ... we can come here
        Once too often,
        Tt-tt, you understand,
        We can ... that ... find ourselves in trouble ...
        In our own cottages ...
        But we all like you.
PRIEST: The house of prayer is once again open to you, my children.
        Good evening, Mariette. Good evening, my daughter.
        You know, now you can return my visits.
        And you will not scorn the House of God. Er.
        (*He goes.*)
MAN FROM THE HILLS: I'll be going, too. Goodbye, Mariette.
        I live a long way away. But don't give up on me, Mariette.
        I'll be back. But for now, I don't think there's much left
        For the likes of me round here.
        Only you. But you're the best of us.
MARIETTE: Well, goodbye then, lad, goodbye.
        I'm no better than the others, any of them.
        It's hard to tell what's true and what's not.
        And harder still to tell what's got to be done
        Now. Goodbye.
TOINE: Everybody likes you, Mariette,
        They like you a lot.
        No, don't say anything, granny.
        I'm old, too. I always needed you.
MARIETTE: Go on, then, all of you. Time to be off.
        Goodbye.
        Anne-Marie, you look tired.
        Go to bed.

(*Everyone has gone by now, leaving only Mariette, Anne-Marie and Louis.*)

ANNE-MARIE: Yes, grandmother.
Grandmother, I don't say much, but this evening
I was with you, grandmother, all the time.
I was with you in being appalled by these killings,
And I was with you when you were thinking that
Working people can't make their own lives.
I'm with you now, too.

MARIETTE: Little daughter, my dear, I know you're sharp,
You always understand.

ANNE-MARIE: Sharp? No, not always.
You see, there's something else, grandmother:
I'm frightened, I'm frightened, I'm frightened ...

MARIETTE: Hush about that, hush about it.
Don't say a word about my son.
But know, Anne-Marie:
Your son will be a leader of the people.

ANNE-MARIE: Goodnight, grandmother.

MARIETTE: Goodnight, daughter.
May the night pass safely for us.
And for everybody.
For everybody.
(*Anne-Marie goes to bed. Louis goes too. Mariette sits. Silence.*)

VOICE (*outside, quietly*): Hey!

MARIETTE: Who's there?

VOICE: Hey.

MARIETTE: Who's that?

MAN FROM THE HILLS (*entering*): Me. They met me.
They've brought ...

MARIETTE: Who?
(*The body of Ledrux is brought in.*)

SECOND COMMISSAR: Ledrux!

MARIETTE: My son! He's come back!

SECOND COMMISSAR: He died a hero. *Agents provocateurs* were
aiming for him.
He suspected what was going on. But he was chairman
Of the revolutionary committee at the front.

He was the one who held the whole thing together – our Ledrux.
(*SLOGAN: We will always honour the memory of our fighters.*)
MAN FROM THE HILLS: They stole his body. They were lucky to find you.
The murderers were preparing a magnificent funeral for him.
What a sham!
SECOND COMMISSAR: But we'll get even with them.
(*Enter Anne-Marie and Louis.*)
MARIETTE: Ah. Anne-Marie, Anne-Marie,
Ledrux has come back.
MAN FROM THE HILLS: He's your man – he's here.
It's night ... just us, and the body.
MARIETTE: I remember everything. Perhaps
It falls out right.
Thanks. You've helped.
Goodbye, children.
Let her stay with him. Goodnight.
(*They take out Ledrux' body. Anne-Marie goes with them.*)
LOUIS: Grandmother ...
MARIETTE: Little one, you're now all on your own.
I'm so old. How can the people be woken up?
Little one, you'll have to take your father's place.
(*SLOGAN: The young take the place of the old.*)
When they're stirred up next time
And the workers turn the world upside down,
Please – be fresh, be upright, be ruthless.
Tomorrow is your day.
You're young.
You'll be victorious.

A Wise Man
(*Mudrets*)

(1923)

Agit-buffoonade adapted from
Even a Wise Man Stumbles by A.N.Ostrovsky

Translated by Robert Leach, with Angela Ermarkova
and Tatyana Gomolitskaya-Tretyakova

A Wise Man, Epilogue:
"Religion is the Opium of the People."

A Wise Man

Characters

The White Clown, Yegor Dmitrievich Glumov
The Red Clown, Glafira Klimovna Glumova, *Glumov's mother*
Four other Clowns
Stage hands
Yegor Vasilievich Kurchaev, *a hussar, suitor to Mashenka*
Golutvin, *a mysterious person*
Manefa, *a fortune-teller*
Pavel Nikolaevich Mamaev, *also known as Mamilyukov-Prolivnoi,*[20] *Glumov's supposed uncle*
Cleopatra Lvovna Mamaeva, *Mamaev's wife*
Mamaev's Man
Ivan Ivanovich Gorodulin, *a Fascist*[21]
General Joseph Joffre[22]
Joffre's Servant
Adjutant
Officers
Mary Mac-Lac (Mashenka), *Turusina's niece, a stockbroker*
Princess Sofia Ignatievna Salon-Turusina, *Mashenka's aunt, a rich widow*
Grigory, *Turusina's footman*
A parrot
Granny Black) *Turusina's*
Kerenskaya*[23]*) *hangers-on*

---

20   *Mamilyukov:* Adapted from the name of Pavel Nikolaevich Milyukov, founder of the Cadet Party, Foreign Minister in Prince Lvov's Provisional Government. He emigrated after the Bolsheviks took power. In Ostrovsky's original play, Mamaev's name is Nil Fedosevich.
21   *Fascist:* Mussolini came to power in Italy in October 1922, just as Tretyakov and Eisenstein were beginning work on this play. In performance, Gorodulin should be identified with Mussolini.
22   *Joffre:* General Joseph Joffre, commander of the French Army in the First World War till December 1916, when he was promoted to Marshall and thereby removed from power.
23   *Kerenskaya:* Satirical name derived from the womanish Alexander Fedorovich Kerensky, leader of the Provisional Government which was overthrown by the Bolsheviks.

Note

In the original production, Kurchaev was played by three actors simultaneously. There was a good deal of cross-casting – for instance, Glumova, Manefa and Turusina were all played by men. The same actor played all the servants. Mamaev in the script is identified with Milyukov, but in production Eisenstein seems to have identified him with the British Foreign Secretary, Lord Curzon.

A few of the tricks and stunts from Eisenstein's original production are indicated in the following text, but a new director would be free to add to these and experiment with others. Eisenstein also used projections and small pieces of film at many points. Finally, music accompanies the action almost non-stop: without music, the play utterly fails.

'Everything should be done very quickly, and in the style of clowning. The exposition should be very clear – the plans of the émigrés, the sight of Glumov making his career, etc.' – S.M. Eisenstein.

'A gesture turns into gymnastics, rage is expressed through a somersault, exultation through a *salto-mortale*, lyricism by a run along the tightrope. The grotesque of this style permits leaps from one type of expression to another, as well as unexpected intertwinings of two expressions.' – S.M.Eisenstein.

'Pieces of action, turns, even acts are connected by different arrangements of equipment, musical interludes, dancing, pantomime, carpet-clowns.' – S.M.Eisenstein.

The setting

Alexander Levshin, who played General Joffre in the original production, described Eisenstein's design as follows:

'According to Sergei Mikhailovich's design the set ought to minimize the distance between the actor and the spectator. A construction resembling a circus ring had to be designed. A round green carpet with a red hem was halfway surrounded by the spectators' chairs. On the opposite side yellow ramps led to a small platform. On the platform they placed two ladder-like constructions with a dark cherry red, almost black, curtain hanging on them. There was another curtain under the platform, and a screen on the wall. The props included a black trick chest (the actors 'disappeared' and reappeared on the balcony), trapezes, rings for the actor playing the parrot, two yellow cylindrical columns, and a grand piano. During the performance the props were brought in and removed by stage hands.'

First performed by the First Workers Theatre of the Proletkult, Moscow, on 26 April 1923, under the direction of Sergei Eisenstein.

PROLOGUE

The circus ring. Circus music. Circus stage hands set the apparatus. Enter the White Clown, Glumov. Business. He grabs the leading stage hand.

GLUMOV: Comrade Chief Button, you have ears. Here they are. Listen, understand, and having understood, sob your heart out for me from toe to head. That is, I'm sorry – from head to toe. My mama was born Zhiropudova, the daughter of a first class merchant. You understand? My papa was a respectable pillar of the dubious commercial world. Ha ha. The eminent Bakhryabuchinsky.[24] You comprehend? And I – ee-ee-ee – I'm a victim of circumstances. What this revolution has done to me! And I'm such a well-educated person. I studied Theology. I know all about it. I always had excellent marks in Geography. In a single night I would go from Vienna to Prague, from Prague to El Dorado, and from El Dorado to the Transvaal. So when morning comes, I'm so transvaalquilized that I have to put my head under the cold tap. As for History, I know that pretty well, too. After Alexander I came Alexander II, then the third, then the fourth, then the fifth, then the sixth. After Nicholas I was the second, the third, the fourth ...
STAGE HAND: What Nicholas III? We didn't have one after the second.
GLUMOV: There were no more? Right you are, there were no more. If I had been there, I wouldn't be crying now in front of you. If he was still alive, I'd swear at you for using such filthy language that ... Well, well, don't get angry. Don't forget I'm a victim of circumstances. A victim of cruel circumstances. I studied

---

24   *Bakhryabuchinsky*: An amalgamation of the names of two well-known rich merchants, Bakhrushin, founder of Moscow's Theatre Museum, and Ryabuchinsky, a banker prominent in the counter-revolutionary bourgeoisie.

jurisprudence, I know who I can punch in the teeth, and who I can't.

STAGE HAND: So who can you?

GLUMOV: In the old days, I'd have been able to punch you in the teeth, and you wouldn't have been allowed to punch me.

STAGE HAND: But now I can punch you?

GLUMOV: And now I can't punch you and you can punch me. (*Chase.*) I was a gentleman, now I'm a zero. Less than zero, double zero. A hole. The middle of a ring doughnut.

STAGE HAND: And are there still lots of zeros like you around?

GLUMOV: Lots and lots of zeros. Just as many zeros as on Soviet banknotes. But I'm trying my best to put a one in front of my zeros. I've been dealing in rice, I've been dealing in newspapers, I've been spreading rumours, I've begged for alms in the porch of the chapel where the miracle-working ikon of the Iverskaya Virgin[25] used to be. This is me, the son of a respectable pillar of dubious commerce. What on earth brought this revolution on us? It's ruined me, foolish child that I am. Poor little child, I've been fleeced of the creases in my tail coat by the revolution. (*He cries.*) I haven't even got anything to wipe my eyes on now.

STAGE HAND: Get up, citizen, you can't wet this place.

GLUMOV: But it's from my eyes.

STAGE HAND: I'm talking about your eyes. Don't make a decent place all slimy. Go on, buzz off.

GLUMOV: How dare you, lackey?

STAGE HAND: Listen to him, jabbering French. Go on, off you go. Poor old squire, caught in revolution's fire! His toes are poking through the ends of his shoes. Perhaps I'll call a policemen.

SECOND STAGE HAND (*entering*): Mr Glumov, a parcel for you.[26]

(*Stage hands and Glumov play a clownish version of 'Pass the Parcel'.*)

GLUMOV (*enthusiastically*): ARA, ARA, ARA![27]

---

25   *The Iverskaya Virgin*: This miracle-working ikon of the Iverskaya Virgin was a particularly holy shrine and place of pilgrimage.
26   *Glumov*: At this point, Eisenstein's scenario says: 'He mispronounces the name, Glumov.'
27   *ARA.*: American Relief Agency, which supplied food to combat famine in the Volga region in 1921. A pun on 'hurrah'.

FIRST STAGE HAND: What are you shouting? You should shout 'Hooray!'

GLUMOV: Under the old regime one shouted 'Hooray!' Now one shouts 'ARA!' I'm very pleased. ARA, I'm very pleased. In honour of our American friends, let's give a Russian ARA! (*He opens the parcel and produces goods like a conjuror producing rabbits from a hat. It is American relief – e.g. milk. He chucks the wrapping paper over his shoulder like a hussar with a vodka glass.*) Citizens, help yourselves, the merchant's son Glumov, a representative of Golden Youth, is entertaining in his private mansion. Help yourself.

FIRST STAGE HAND: Listen, mister. This isn't a paper factory. Where are you throwing all that?

GLUMOV: It'll come in, it'll come in, my dear chap. Paper always comes in. It'll come in handy. (*He begins to pull out something much larger. The others help him.*) Oh dear, there's only one boot here. Oh no, bravo – here's the other. Both feet, one, two, well provided for. Socks, very nice. Trousers, no, not trousers – breeches! Breeches, little breeches, breechy-doodles. (*He pulls out the Red Clown.*) And something in the breeches, plenty in the breeches. (*Red Clown bows to the audience. Everyone is amazed.*)

RED CLOWN: Ah, here you are, my dear fellow. I need to speak to you about an urgent, important, vital, top secret ... matter. (*The Stage Hands try to overhear. The Clown topples them like dominoes.*) My dear fellow, the ornament and pride of the Russian nation, the brain of the country, support of our great sovereign motherland, shame on you! How can you stay and freeze here?

GLUMOV: You have to, if firewood's 300 million roubles a stick!

RED CLOWN: Don't you realize, they're waiting for you? You're needed there, where they've run to ... where those who remain here have gathered on the platform of culture, humanism and great national ideals ... the flower of the Russian nation. You know, of course, that in our Paris – that's a little town, it's the main town in the district of France – the question of the continued existence of the Bolsheviks has been decided. In two weeks, the Soviet regime will come crashing down. Allow me to develop the point. Thus, in two weeks it will come to an end. It's all weighed up and provided for. Burtsev[28] himself has approved it. And Martov[29] has said – 'Ahem. It's all very simple. First we take Minsk, then Smolensk, then Gzhatsk, then Kuntsevo, then Khamovnichesky, then the Arbat Gate, then, then we take the Kremlin! It's obvious!' (*He falls over.*) To cut a long story short, though, this isn't very important. The main thing is, who, in your opinion, will be the Prime Minister? (*Modestly*) None other than your humble servant. Because only I could be a Russian Iron Chancellor, because you see I'm made of metal. I have an iron fist and a leaden wit. With one glance, like Napoleon, I make women faint. Watch, young man. They faint.

GLUMOV: Not very easily, but anyway they do faint. They faint, they drop, like melons off their stalks.

RED CLOWN: Yes, well, you see, I came here *incognito*. I came to seek support. To extract it from the reservoir of what's left of the people, and in the first place to extract you. Yes, you. Don't be embarrassed about it, be grateful. Russia still needs people like you. You will come with me to Paris.

GLUMOV: It might be better for me to act from here?

RED CLOWN: Oh no, you can get a running start much better if you begin from Paris.

GLUMOV: Some people have already started – they're running in all directions.

RED CLOWN: No, if you make a running start in Russia, you bounce, like this. (*He bounces and falls over.*) You see?

GLUMOV (*indicating Stage Hand*): He saw. And me too. (*Glumov and red-haired Clown shake hands.*)

RED CLOWN: So let's swear on our noble, commercial sword. (*A formal oath on a bankbook.*) To free our tortured native country from these Herods. For the glory of our distinguished nobility, clergy and merchants, and to mend the broken peace of our congregation, and put back the altar on our living fatherland. Squeeze the people to the last drop of their blood. Pay all our debts to the heroic allies,

---

28   *Burtsev*: Vladimir Burtsev, a journalist who denounced *agents provocateurs* placed in revolutionary cells by the tsarist police.
29   *Martov*: Yulius Martov, pseudonym of Yuri Osipovich Tsederbaum, leader of the Mensheviks.

with interest. Give work to the unemployed Romanov family,[30] and at every crossroads place an old style policeman, to the greater glory of Capital. Amen. It will be, have no fear. Let's put our wives and children into pawn, till the victory of truth, the tsars and our native land is secured.(*The sobbing of four clowns is heard, off stage. They enter, tumbling and leapfrogging over the Stage Hands. They are Mensheviks.*)

THE FOUR CLOWNS (*to Glumov*): For whom will you desert us, my darling? You are our brother. (*They catch sight of the red-haired Clown.*) Kidnapper, seducer! Provocateur! Shit-stinker! Spyhole! And worse! Ruffian, mar-vicar!(*The Red Clown escapes the four by leaping onto Glumov's shoulders.*)

GLUMOV: Careful, Glumov. Use your head. We can feather our nest in Paris. (*He takes up an orator's pose.*) Brothers, the reign of the Anti-Christ is over. Here comes Savva on a white charger, and with a general's stripe down the seam of his trousers. The people are shocked, they greet him: 'Bless you, Your Highness'. The horse is pale, his name is Savinkov,[31] his hooves have struck the stones of Warsaw, he pricks up his ears and neighs on French credit. Brothers, sad is our parting, but be of good cheer, I will return, and bring with me a new, joyful, prosperous way of life. The rivers will flow with milk and honey, and the cows will die of unemployment. Civil and military freedom will be re-established, and tongues will wag merrily this way and that in a parliament elected according to the most backward system. Wait for me!

RED CLOWN: Long live the Constituent Assembly!

GLUMOV: Let's go! But how shall we go?

EVERYBODY, RED CLOWN, STAGE HANDS: How shall we go?

---

30   *Romanov family.* The royal family of the tsars.

31   *Savinkov:* Boris Savinkov, real name Ropshin, had been with Bogdanov and Lunacharsky in internal exile in Vologda in 1898 for political dissidence. He became a terrorist and leading member of the SR party, and later prominent in the Provisional Government after February 1917. He was extremely anti-Bolshevik, and led the Paris-based Russian Political Committee for the Struggle Against the Bolsheviks. In August 1924 he returned to Moscow, was arrested and sentenced to death. This was commuted, but he either committed suicide or was pushed out of an upper window in Lubyanka Prison and fell to his death. He was also a poet and novelist, best known for his novel, *Pale Horse*, published in 1917.

RED CLOWN: Pardon the indiscreet question, but are you an SR?[32] (*Glumov hesitates.*) I see you're wavering. Don't you realize that SR means Super Reliable?

GLUMOV: Yes yes yes. In that sense I am an SR.

RED CLOWN: Precisely like me. SH, that's to say ...

GLUMOV: Shit.

RED CLOWN: Nothing of the kind. – SH, Soon to be Honoured.

GLUMOV: But how shall we travel? The main thing is – speed. Don't try to shack up here.

RED CLOWN: In, in – in a sack. Yes, in a sack. (*Trying to squeeze Glumov into one of the sacks.*) The head's in – but the peripherals are out. (*The sacks are labelled by the names of prisons – Butyrka (Moscow), Kresty (Petrograd), etc.*)

STAGE HAND (*trying to squash him into the other sacks*): You can't conceal him, there's always something sticking out.

GLUMOV: You can't hide a needle in a sack – the truth will out!

RED CLOWN: You're not Ann Eedle, you're Fomka.

GLUMOV: I'm not Fomka, I'm a Junker.[33]

RED CLOWN: Stop it. I've thought of a way that'll beat everything. We'll take you as anti-parasite. We'll turn you into an anti-insect powder. (*Two red-haired Clowns bring in large mortars, labelled 'Izvestia' and 'Pravda'.*)

FIRST CLOWN: Yes, the sack's no use, let's turn him into powder. (*They put him into a huge pestle labelled 'Agit-Prop' and pound him. Music. A Stage Hand picks something up from the floor.*)

RED CLOWN: What's that?

STAGE HAND: The flies are already dying.

RED CLOWN: Is he done?

FIRST and SECOND CLOWNS: He's not crushed yet.

RED CLOWN: What's the matter? Is he made of reinforced concrete?

SECOND CLOWN: No, his head's wooden. A couple of chips flew off, but he's still in one piece.

GLUMOV: Yes, I'm a seasoned blockhead.

RED CLOWN: This is a problem. Is there a way out?

---

32   *SR*: Social Revolutionary Party, progressive, anti-Bolshevik.
33   *Junker*: This series of freely associated names covers the stage business, which is performed with grotesque clowning.

GLUMOV: An exit?
RED CLOWN: Is there a way of getting such a rascal out?
ALL THE STAGE HANDS: Yes.
RED CLOWN: What is it?
ALL THE STAGE HANDS: In his coffin.
RED CLOWN: Let's do it. (*They lift up the lid of the table, take out two funeral candles, mourning bows and crepe, three wreaths (a tyre, a life-belt and a chamber pot, all done up with black crepe), and a torch. They put Glumov in the 'coffin' (the table), close the lid, and, weeping, pick up the coffin and take it away on a toy dreadnought, also taken out of the table.*) And so, on your way, to the Heavenly Kingdom.
SONG[34]: Kiddies all come running back ... in their trousers.
    Hurriedly they call for dad ... without his trousers.
    Daddy, dad, look in our sack ... not in our trousers.
    Is it good or is it bad ... without his trousers?
    (*The Stage Hands form national frontiers. The clowns carry the 'coffin' round the stage. At the first barrier (Germany), Stage Hands stop the Clowns.*)
STAGE HAND: Raw material?
RED CLOWN: Rotten material.
STAGE HAND: Cargo specification?
RED CLOWN: Carrion for fertilizer.
    (*The Stage Hands pierce the 'coffin' with swords. There is obviously nothing alive in it. They allow the Clowns with the coffin to pass. At the second barrier (France), Stage Hands stop the Clowns.*)
STAGE HAND: Is this packaging good quality? No leaks?
RED CLOWN: Well, we're just leaking abroad. (*He gives him a bribe. Exit the other Clowns.*) We've arrived. This is home. Come out, you, dead body. (*Bending*) What if he really is dead? No, he smells. That means he's alive.
    (*He vaults the coffin and flies behind the curtain.*)

---

34   *Song:* This is a parody of a poem by Pushkin.

ACT ONE

The coffin lid opens. Glumov puts his head out.

GLUMOV: Here I am. (*He steps out. He is now dressed in the latest Paris fashion.*) Paris isn't so bad. The most important thing is – it's just like a Russian city. It's got landlords, and vodka, and caviar. Russia – but where's the Red Clown? Oy, red hair! (*The Red Clown zooms in on roller skates, dressed as a woman.*) What's this – Prime Minister, iron chancellor? Is there a head of government?

RED CLOWN: There was a head, there was a head on the top, and now the head – the head's at the bottom. (*Looking through his own legs.*) Don't be surprised. I'm not the only one with bad luck. What about Lloyd George – he was sacked, for all he quacked. Wirth[35] vanished. I'm no worse than they are, considering the situation, the state of affairs. It's the European concert.

GLUMOV: It's not a concert, it's a balalaika. Listen, and try and remember.

RED CLOWN: An ember.

GLUMOV: I want to make a career.

RED CLOWN: An ear.

GLUMOV: And every girl who wants to make a career ...

RED CLOWN: Are you a girl?

GLUMOV: Dunce.

RED CLOWN: Ponce.

GLUMOV: ... should have a mother. And a red-haired one at that. So you can be my mother.

RED CLOWN (*turning to the audience*): Is he talking to you?

GLUMOV: No, to you.

RED CLOWN: I can't do that, I haven't had any training.

---

35 *Wirth:* Karl Joseph Wirth, German Chancellor, 1921-2.

GLUMOV: Listen.
RED CLOWN: Pissin'?
GLUMOV: No! Listen to the next thing, fool.
RED CLOWN: Okay, then, I'll be your mother. (*Clips him round the ear.*)
GLUMOV: Have you gone out of your mind?
RED CLOWN: Am I your mother or aren't I? Do I have the right to punish you if you speak to me in that tone of voice? The egg teaching the grandmother to suck!
GLUMOV: Okay. You have the right. Sorry, but you'll have to write a letter to Princess Salon-Turusina, to prevent her niece marrying Kurchaev. Write that he's a red Bolshevik, a Komsomol member, and so on and so forth.
RED CLOWN (*as Glumov's mother*): Don't worry, they won't give her to him. Salon-Turusina has a dowry of 200 thousand.
GLUMOV: I have four hundred left out of a million after I took the tram.
MOTHER: Twelve gold-plated false teeth, as well as aquamarines, diamonds, agate, aspirin ... Salon-Turusina has influential relatives, they won't give the niece to you.
GLUMOV: No, mummy, they will. You know me, I'm quick, dangerous, clever. What did I do before? Speculated, sabotaged what I didn't like, supported the esteemed Kerensky. To please the Reds I scribbled off a few pamphlets, criticised the émigrés, and in general kept my eye on the main chance. No, it was fine, don't laugh at fools, one should know their weak points and use them. How do people get on? Not just by their deeds, more often by their words. Ah, in Moscow, and Petersburg, I knew how to talk to people. It was all blah-blah-blah in the Duma-ma-ma!
MOTHER: Milyukov, Maklakov,[36] Rodichev,[37]
   Sing plaintively
   Of a little Constituent Assembly
   Set up by them,
   Still-born.

---

36   *Maklakov*: Nikolai Maklakov, the tsar's Minister for the Interior, Cadet deputy in the Duma. Mashenka in this play is known as Mary Mac-Lac.
37   *Rodichev*: Fedor Rodichev, founder member of the Cadet party, deputy in the Duma.

GLUMOV: I can't be unsuccessful in this talking-shop which is Paris. Impossible, I'll adapt myself for anybody: Cadet, Fascist, Black Hundred,[38] warmonger. I'll begin with Salon-Turusina's circle. I'll squeeze everything out of it, marry her niece, and then I'll be able to climb even higher.
MOTHER: Higher?
GLUMOV: Go and write the letter.
MOTHER: God bless you.
GLUMOV: *Merci.* So, enough of vitriolic pamphlets and liberal criticisms. Let's turn to panegyrics, I'll dance to their tune and burn incense at their altars. All the bile that's stewing in my soul I'll put down in this diary, but on my lips there'll be nothing but honey. What's in here will not be for public consumption. I'll be both author and reader. I think Burtsev will pay a lot for this. (*The bell rings. Kurchaev and Golutvin enter. Kurchaev is in triplicate – three extra-polished hussars, who move and speak absolutely in unison. Golutvin skulks behind, wearing a mask, and with green electric eyes, top hat and a floor-length black cloak.*)
KURCHAEV: *Bonjour.* Ha-ood-oo-yudoo.[39] *Guten tag.*
GLUMOV: Pleased to meet you. What can I do for you?
KURCHAEV: We've come on business. (*Points at Golutvin.*) May I introduce ...
GLUMOV: I think I already know who he is. I've read Pinkerton[40] ever since I was little. Well, gentlemen, I'm short of time. What do you want?
KURCHAEV: Have you got any poems we could have?
GLUMOV: Poems? I think you might have the wrong address.
GOLUTVIN: No, this is right.
KURCHAEV: We need something pithy. He wants to start writing denunciations and lampoons under your direction.
GOLUTVIN: And you've got a diary where you detail everyone's faults.

---

38   *Cadet, Fascist, Black Hundred:* The Cadets were a constitutional rightist Liberal party; the Fascists were Mussolini's party in Italy; the Black Hundreds were a viciously racist Russian group before 1917.
39   *Ha-ood-oo-yudoo:* A literal transcription from the Russian: 'How do you do?'
40   *Pinkerton:* Fictional American detective.

KURCHAEV: So give us it, come on, give us it. (*He starts drawing on a piece of paper, which covers a circus hoop of the sort the Clown dives through.*)

GLUMOV (*ironically, to himself*): Just what I dreamed of!

KURCHAEV: You won't give us it?

GLUMOV: No.

KURCHAEV: Well, in that case, go to hell. (*He stands up.*)

GLUMOV: Have you finished your drawing?

KURCHAEV: Yes. The commissar for drains! By the way, I forgot to tell you. My aunt has fallen head over heels in love with you, she's like a cat, a tiger, a panther.

GLUMOV: What do you mean?

KURCHAEV: She saw you at the zoo. She couldn't stop looking at you, she almost wrung her neck looking at you.

GLUMOV: Whose neck? Yours?

KURCHAEV: No, her own.

GLUMOV: What a shame.

KURCHAEV: She kept on asking me, Who's that? Who's that? So have you got any poems we could have?

GLUMOV: No.

GOLUTVIN: There's no point in talking to him any more. Let's go. (*Kurchaev and Golutvin leave. Glumov looks out of the window.*)

GLUMOV: Mummy! (*Enter Glumova.*) Look. This is the person I need to become friends with.

GLUMOVA (*looking through her lorgnette*): Who's that?

GLUMOV: Our distant relative, my uncle, Mamilyukov Prolivnoi.

GLUMOVA: And who drew this picture?

GLUMOV: His dear nephew the 'smenovekhovets',[41] Kurchaev. I'd better hold onto this picture. The problem is that Prolivnoi doesn't like his relatives. He has about thirty nephews, followers of every kind of counter-revolutionary – Savinkovites, Vrangelites, Kutepovites, Romanovites, Chernovites, Martovites and other sheep, sheep. He shears them all, then he chooses one of them for his cabinet of ministers for the future Russian government, and the rest had better keep out of his way. And when he gets sick and tired of this

---

41   *Smenovekhovets:* From *Smena Vekh*, a right wing magazine.

favourite, he kicks him out and chooses another. At the moment, this Kurchaev is his favourite.

GLUMOVA: Ah, if you –

GLUMOV: Yes, it's hard, but I'll try. Oh, by the way, the aunt, Cleopatra Lvovna, seems to have taken a shine to me. Like a cat, a tiger, a panther. She's seen me somewhere. Make a mental note of it. But the most important thing just at the moment is to make friends with Prolivnoi. That's the first step in my business. Uncle will introduce me to Joffre and Gorodulin: first, he'll take me to Turusina's house, they're people of consequence, they'll provide me with a good position; and second they'll make friends for me with Salon-Turusina herself. All I need is to be introduced at that house and I'll marry her, without fail I'll marry her. Twelve false teeth, agate, aspirins ...

GLUMOVA: Maybe. But the first step is the most difficult.

GLUMOV: Don't worry about that, I've already taken it. Malyukov Prolivnoi is coming here.

GLUMOVA: How's that?

GLUMOV: No problem, everything has been arranged in advance. Mamilyukov Prolivnoi likes to look over flats. I've hooked him on that bait. (*Mamaev's man enters.*)

MAN: Pavel Nikolaevich is here.

GLUMOV: Wonderful. Here. (*Gives him a tip.*) Show him in. Mummy, go to your room now, I'll call you if I need you. (*Mamaev's man goes out and returns with Mamaev, who runs in followed – apparently pursued – by a rolling car tyre from which the air hisses out. The 'turn' ends.*)

MAMAEV (*begins to look round without taking his hat off*): This is the flat. And – it's suitable for a bachelor?

GLUMOV: Yes, I'm not married.

MAMAEV (*pays no attention to him*): It isn't a bad flat, but it's for a bachelor. Why did you want me to come here, my man?

GLUMOV: Won't you sit down, please?

MAMAEV: Thank you. Why did you bring me here? (*Gets up and goes to the other side of the room.*) Why did you bring me here, I asked you.

MAN: Sorry.

MAMAEV: You ought to know that I'm an ex-Minister, and all the old guard are friends with me.

MAN: Sorry.

MAMAEV: And that my wife, your mistress, likes to live openly.

MAN: Sorry.

MAMAEV: We need a sitting-room and there isn't one. Where's the sitting-room, I ask you.

MAN: Sorry.

MAMAEV: Where could we put all our furniture? Where? (*The furniture is brought in and placed in the room.*) It looks awful. (*The furniture is removed.*)

GLUMOV: Don't be angry with him, sir, it isn't his fault, it's mine. When I told him about this flat, I didn't know you were a family man.

MAMAEV: Do you hold the lease of this flat?

GLUMOV: Yes.

MAMAEV: Why are you renting it?

GLUMOV: I can't afford to live here.

MAMAEV: But why did you take the lease if you can't afford it? Who made you do it? Are you a Russian refugee? And now you'll have to live in one room instead of a nice big flat. You won't like that, will you? Br, brr, brr. It's like moving from Moscow to poverty-stricken Paris.

GLUMOV: No, I want to take on a bigger flat.

MAMAEV: A bigger flat? But how are you going to take on a bigger flat if you can't afford this? What rhyme or reason is there in that?

GLUMOV: Sheer stupidity.

MAMAEV: Sheer stupidity? What nonsense is this?

GLUMOV: It's not nonsense, I just am stupid.

MAMAEV: You just are stupid? This is odd, what do you mean by stupid?

GLUMOV: It's very simple. I didn't read Milyukov. Why are you surprised? Such things happen, and quite often.

MAMAEV: Well, this is certainly interesting. A man who says he's a fool. Like Shulgin.[42]

GLUMOV: Why should I wait for other people to call me stupid? What's the difference if you can't conceal it anyway?

MAMAEV: Yes, of course, it's difficult to conceal such a problem.

GLUMOV: So I'm not concealing it.

---

42   *Shulgin:* Vasily Vitalievich Shulgin, member of the Duma who received the tsar's abdication in February 1917; became a leading anti-Soviet émigré.

MAMAEV: And there's nobody who could advise you?

GLUMOV: No, there's nobody.

MAMAEV: And yet there are people who can give advice, very good advice. Martov, for example, Milyukov, Burtsev. By the way, would you like some pornographic pictures? Yes, there are worthy people, but nobody seems to listen to them nowadays. That's the way things are – Bolshevism. Everywhere.

GLUMOV and MAMAEV (*together*): Immorality, Communism.

MAMAEV: Don't tell me about it, please, I beg you. That October, it was as if someone had pierced me, here, right through. (*Points to his chest.*) And even now I feel it like some –

GLUMOV: Is this the place?

MAMAEV: Higher.

GLUMOV: Here?

MAMAEV (*holding his heart*): Higher, I told you.

GLUMOV: Excuse me, please, don't be angry. I told you I was a fool.

MAMAEV: Well, so you're stupid. That's too bad.

GLUMOV: Yes, that's the trouble, I have no-one to help me. There is mother, but she's even more stupid than me. She's the red-haired type, you understand? I'm told I've got an uncle, but I don't know anything about him.

MAMAEV: Why?

GLUMOV: Ah, well, you see, if he was poor I'd go straight to him, and kiss his hand. But he's rich. I would go to him for advice, but he'd think I was coming for money. How could I explain to him that all I want is a piece of advice, that I'm craving for a direction in life, like manna from heaven. Apparently he's a very clever person, I'd be ready to listen to him day and night.

MAMAEV: You're not as stupid as you think.

GLUMOV: Sometimes something dawns on me. It's like the sun emerging from behind the clouds. But then everything goes gloomy again. Most of the time I don't understand what I'm doing. And I haven't got anybody to ask for a piece of advice.

MAMAEV: And who is your uncle?

GLUMOV: I'm afraid I've forgotten his surname. His other names are Pavel Nikolaevich.

MAMAEV: And who are you?

GLUMOV: George Glumov.

MAMAEV: Is Bakhryabuchinsky your godfather?

GLUMOV: Yes, he is.

MAMAEV: Well, then I'm your uncle, Mamilyukov.

GLUMOV: Oh, my God, impossible! No, how can that be? Let me kiss your hand and your heart. Oops, sorry, slip of the tongue, just your hand. But, uncle, I thought you didn't like your relatives? Don't worry, we can be as distant as before. I shall never presume to come and visit you without your permission. I'm just happy to have seen you, and to have enjoyed the conversation of such a cultivated man.

MAMAEV: Oh, come and see me, whenever you need a piece of advice.

GLUMOV: Oh, thank you so much. And let me introduce you to my aged mother. She's not very bright, but she's kind, a naturally kind woman.

MAMAEV: Oh, certainly.

GLUMOV (*shouts*): Mummy! Here ... (*Glumova enters.*) Don't cry, please. (*They are both crying.*) Providence has brought our uncle, Pavel Nikolaevich, whom you wanted to meet so much.

GLUMOVA: Oh, brother, let me look at you. Just like Lloyd George? No, you're not like him a bit.

GLUMOV (*in a whisper*): Remember, mother, ssh!

GLUMOVA: Why am I supposed to shush? All I said was they're not alike a bit.

MAMAEV (*severely*): What are you whispering? Who'm I not like? I am only like myself.

GLUMOV (*to his mother*): What's the use of talking such trivialities?

MAMAEV: Well, since you've begun, you'd better tell the whole story.

GLUMOVA: I only said the picture bears no resemblance to you.

MAMAEV: What picture? Where've you got a picture from?

GLUMOVA: You see, Yegor Vasilievich Kurchaev comes to see us from time to time. He seems to be your relative as well.

GLUMOV: He's a nice jolly chap.

MAMAEV: What of it?

GLUMOVA: He's always drawing pictures of you. Show him, George.

GLUMOV: Oh, er, well, I can't think where I've put it.

GLUMOVA: Look for it properly. He only drew it a little while ago. Don't you remember he came with ... what's his name? Harry Piel.[43]

---

43   *Harry Piel:* Fictional German cinema detective.

No, not Harry Piel ... whatever his name is, he's a sort of red Pinkerton. Monsieur Bukharin[44] keeps writing about him. Kurchaev said he's drawn a picture of uncle and you could make up a caption. I heard everything you were talking about.

MAMAEV: Show me the picture, show me immediately.

(*Glumov holds up the picture in the hoop. Mamaev is completely outraged and in his fury he actually dives right through it.*)

GLUMOV: Forget it, uncle. It's not like you at all, and the caption doesn't refer to you – 'The Paris People's Commissar for Drains.' You shouldn't say things, which are going to hurt somebody else, mummy.

MAMAEV: Teach your grandmother to suck eggs. Don't listen to him, sister, you hang onto your simplicity, that's much better. You wouldn't make a caricature of me, would you?

GLUMOV: Certainly not. What do you take me for?

MAMAEV: Good, fine. You can come and see me, er, this evening. And you come, too.

GLUMOVA: Oh, no, I'm afraid you'd get sick and tired of my silliness.

MAMAEV: And from now on, Kurchaev had better keep out of my way.

(*Mamaev goes out. Glumov escorts him to the door.*)

GLUMOVA: It seems to be working. But there's still a lot for George to do. It's so hard to become a person among these donkeys.

GLUMOV (*returning*): Mummy, Manefa's coming. Be polite to her, won't you? And not just polite, try and flatter her if you can.

GLUMOVA: Do you want me to stoop to that old peasant's wife?

GLUMOV: You want me to be Prime Minister, don't you? Be in the cabinet, an iron chancellor, in the European jazz band? But you can't be bothered to lift a finger for it. Don't you realize she has an *entrée* to all the salons, because she pretends the spirit of Grigory Rasputin[45] is upon her. So White generals invite her to the Bathhouse with them, and she can wash away their sins.

MANEFA (*singing*): Doh, lah, fah – depart from vanity, depart ...

---

44   *Bukharin*: Nikolai Ivanovich Bukharin, one of the leading Bolsheviks after the revolution; shot after a show trial in 1938.

45   *Rasputin*: Grigory Rasputin, the hated monk who held almost hypnotic sway over the tsarina.

GLUMOV and GLUMOVA (*singing*): I'm departing, I'm departing, like Denikin[46] from Tula.
MANEFA: Don't be greedy, hold tight to your pocket, it's full of lechery and fraud.
GLUMOV and GLUMOVA (*singing*): I'm holding tight, I'm holding tight, like OGPU holds our sort.
MANEFA: I flew and I flew and I flew to your place.
GLUMOVA: I appreciate, I appreciate, I appreciate that.
MANEFA: I've just been with a very religious family, and they gave me ten roubles for charitable purposes. It's better to pass such gifts through holy hands, like mine, than through sinful ones.
GLUMOV (*taking out money*): Accept half a pound sterling from your servant George.
MANEFA: Blessed are those that give. It's not much, but it is sterling, so acceptable for a widow and for God.
GLUMOVA: Don't forget us in your prayers!
MANEFA: In that very religious family I was just with, they treated me with tea and coffee, not to mention the monk's favourite drink – you know, home-brewed mother's ruin. I don't mind repeating that.
GLUMOVA: Come in here, mother, I've got some all ready.
(*Manefa is led away.*)
GLUMOV: Make a note of that. Three shillings to Mamaev's man, half a pound sterling to Manefa. Also make a note of the conversation with uncle.
KURCHAEV (*entering*): Has uncle been here?
GLUMOV: Yes.
KURCHAEV: This is an intrigue, a hellish intrigue!
GLUMOV: I'm listening, carry on.
KURCHAEV: Can you imagine, uncle met me on the way here and ...
GLUMOV: And ... ?
KURCHAEV: And he ordered me not to venture into his sight again. Imagine!
GLUMOV: I am imagining.

---

46   *Denikin:* Anton Ivanovich Denikin, commander of the White forces in the Civil War, who led the retreat from Tula.

KURCHAEV: I went to Turusina's, they wouldn't receive me. They sent out some stupid hanger-on, some dependent of hers, to say that they couldn't receive me. Do you hear?
GLUMOV: I do.
KURCHAEV: Explain to me what's happening!
GLUMOV: Examine yourself, how you conduct your life.
KURCHAEV: How? I'm like everybody else, how the salt of Russia lives. Paris is on the Seine and we are in a stew. But it's not the sort you can eat, and you can't offer it to others, either. Everyone lives like that, but I'm the one who's being picked on. You can't rob a man of his position for this, deprive him of his inheritance, smash his career.
GLUMOV: Well, I know you. But I'm very careful about who I know. I want to protect myself, so I'd be grateful if you wouldn't visit me any more.
KURCHAEV: You what? Are you out of your mind?
GLUMOV: Dear uncle prefers not to see you any more and I'd like to model myself on such a thoroughly respectable man.
KURCHAEV: Ah, now I begin to understand. You'd better watch out.
(*Kurchaev shoots from his gun, exits. Glumova rushes in.*)
GLUMOV: Uncle chased him off. That's the first step finished.
GLUMOVA: And the first act, too.

ACT TWO

The stage represents Mamaev's apartment. Mamaeva and Glumova.

MAMAEVA: He's young, good looking, well educated, sweet, and he wears a striped scarf. Ahh.
GLUMOVA: And with all these merits he could still have perished unknown, Cleopatra Lvovna.
MAMAEVA: He should have fled Russia earlier. We would have noticed him earlier, I'm sure we would have.
GLUMOVA: To be noticed, you need to be either clever or rich.
MAMAEVA: You're unfair to your son. He's quite clever enough, you don't have to be that brainy. It's enough that his coat's flared and he got his hair cut on Kuznetsky Most. It's extremely painful to see a good-looking young man who's poorly dressed. I have contacts all over Paris, I'll look after him.
GLUMOVA and MAMAEVA (*together*): A Union of Bored Ladies. We want to enjoy gazing on him. Handsome young men are so rare.
GLUMOVA: Did you ever see him before today?
MAMAEVA: I'm not sure, I may have seen him in church.
GLUMOVA: I'm certain he hasn't seen you before.
MAMAEVA: How's that?
GLUMOVA: Well, he's only just set eyes on you, and suddenly there was such a ...
MAMAEVA: Yes, yes, what?
GLUMOVA: And suddenly he was overcome with such a feeling of closeness – for you. An angel, he said, she's an angel, and burst into tears on my bosom. You see, this is probably the first time in his life that he's seen such a beautiful lady as you. Where could he have seen one before? And you're so tender with him, and so indulgent ... of course, as a relative. He is in a fever, about

50 degrees. No wonder he's losing his wits. Of course, just being conscious that such a ravishingly beautiful woman is so close to you when you're so young ... He can't sleep at night, he comes home from your place, and wanders about bereft, it's a wonder he hasn't fallen over and broken an arm or a leg yet.

MAMAEVA: So he trusts you, he doesn't try and conceal his feelings from you?

GLUMOVA: That would be sinful of him. Besides, his feelings are quite innocent.

MAMAEVA: Oh, yes, absolutely. But he needs someone to guide him.

GLUMOVA: Someone to guide him, yes. If you were to be so kind, really, it would be so kind of you.

MAMAEVA: You love him very much, don't you?

GLUMOVA: He's my only child, how could I not love him?

MAMAEVA: Let's both love him together, like a collective.

(*Boxing match – who shall have Glumov? Glumova is knocked out and carried away.*)

MAMAEVA: What a chatterbox! If her son had heard what she was saying, he wouldn't have thanked her. He's so proud, so haughty and cold, and yet that's how he carries on at home. He flings himself down, flings himself down. Still, I can still arouse genuine passion in a young man. That's how it should be. I've been feeling I haven't had so many admirers recently, but that's because they've become old and stale. It's understandable, the diamonds have been sold, and the amount being invested for intervention in Soviet Russia's become extremely small. But now, at last, this. (*Glumov enters.*) Come, come here. Why are you standing over there? Nephews don't need to behave like that. (*Glumov removes his hat.*)

GLUMOV: I'm very pleased to meet you.

MAMAEVA: Be more open with me, what are you scared of? I'm not God, forgiving the dead.

GLUMOV: The OGPU.[47]

MAMAEVA: Be sincere with me. Don't forget, I'm your aunt.

GLUMOV: I would be more sincere with you, if ...

---

47   *OGPU*: The Soviet secret police, created in 1922 to supersede the Cheka, founded in 1918.

MAMAEVA: If what?

GLUMOV: If you were an old woman.

MAMAEVA: Don't talk nonsense. I have no wish whatever to be old.

GLUMOV: And I don't want you to be either. But if you were, I wouldn't be so shy. I should feel freer.

MAMAEVA: Why? Why would you feel freer if I were an old woman?

GLUMOV: Well, a young woman has plenty of other things to think about – her manicure, the dressmaker, the hatmaker, sweets, telephone conversations, the Beauty Salon. She has no time to think about her poor relations. But an old woman thinks of nothing else.

MAMAEVA: Why should you think a young woman couldn't care about her relations?

GLUMOV: Perhaps she could, but I'd feel ashamed to ask her to care about them, even to bother her with them.

MAMAEVA: Well ... if I were an old woman, what would you ask me to do for you?

GLUMOV: Well, if you were ... But you're not!

MAMAEVA: Never mind, never mind, say.

GLUMOV: No, I won't tell you. But, for example, I know you'd only have to say a word to Gorodulin, and I'd have a very good place. But, all the same, I'm not going to bother you with such requests.

MAMAEVA: Why not?

GLUMOV: Because it would be like forcing something on him, and I'm a democrat. I don't believe in violence.

MAMAEVA: So you don't want me to put in a word for you?

GLUMOV: No, I don't want you to. But even more than that, I don't want to be in your debt. How could I pay you back?

MAMAEVA: Well, how would you have paid an old woman back?

GLUMOV: If the old woman had been really kind to me, I'd attach myself to her, I'd love her, like, for example, a grandmother of the Russian revolution.

MAMAEVA: Do you think it's possible to love a young woman like that?

GLUMOV: Possible, but it's better not to. It would encourage erotic feelings, and erotic feelings are strictly forbidden.

MAMAEVA: At last!

MAMAEV'S MAN: Ivan Ivanovich Gorodulin.

GLUMOV: I'll go into my uncle's study, where the émigré cabinet is. I've got work to do.

MAMAEVA (*the footman*): Bring him in.

GORODULIN: Comradely greetings!

MAMAEVA: Very good, very good, please sit down. What wind, or what thunderstorm, has blown you to my place?

GORODULIN: The wind that's in my mind, and the thunderstorm of passion which throbs in my heart!

MAMAEVA: Thank you. It's nice to know you haven't forgotten me, when I'm all on my own, deserted, forsaken.

GORODULIN: Where is he, where's the wretch who deserted you? Show him to me. I'm in a thoroughly aggressive mood tonight, I've just come back from a peace conference.

MAMAEVA: It's you, you're the one. You should be murdered or something.

GORODULIN: Oh. Well, I wish it was someone else.

MAMAEVA: Don't worry, I've invented an exquisite punishment for you.

GORODULIN: Just let me know it, tell me what it's to be. You can't execute me without letting me know how you're going to do it. If you want to smother me in your embrace, well, I won't appeal against that.

MAMAEVA: No, I'm the one who's going to make an appeal.

GORODULIN: So you want to change roles, eh?

MAMAEVA: How could you appeal to me? You're trying to give this civilisation its next shock – fascism.

GORODULIN: Yes, yes, I'm a lion, a Leon.[48] The slogan of fascism is: Seem to be left-wing, but be right-wing in your heart. But for the ladies, I am always ...

MAMAEVA: Enough of that nonsense. I want to talk about something more serious.

GORODULIN: Yes, madam.

MAMAEVA: My nephew needs ...

GORODULIN: What does your nephew need? A little coat? A pair of pantaloons? Eau de cologne? Some little mint cakes?

MAMAEVA: You're getting on my nerves. He needs a situation.

GORODULIN: What do you want me to organise? (*He is polishing his boots.*)

---

48   *Leon*: A reference to Trotsky.

MAMAEVA: Well, obviously, a good one, at least equal to the seventeenth grade. He has a lot of ability. He's an expert.

GORODULIN: A lot of ability? What a pity. There's no call for a lot of ability nowadays. Paris is full of extremely gifted Russians. He's just one more. In Russia all such people can find situations. Lenin's one, another one's Trotsky …

MAMAEVA: You're so irritating, we shall quarrel. Just say whether you can get a situation for him.

GORODULIN: For an ordinary mortal – yes. But someone who wants to be a Prime Minister and to cope with the current of state affairs – hardly. There are altogether too many people for that in this day and age.

MAMAEVA: Fine. Yegor Dmitrievich! George! I shall leave you alone for a while, I shall wait for you in the sitting-room. Yegor Dmitrievich, Ivan Ivanovich wants to speak to you. (*She goes out.*)

GORODULIN: Are you in work?

GLUMOV: I was in work. But now I'm not, and I don't want to be.

GORODULIN: Why's that?

GLUMOV: God didn't grant me the right kind of skills.

GORODULIN: But all you need is your natural gifts and the desire to work. (*He is juggling.*)

GLUMOV: That's not what's important. The point is that it actually doesn't matter how hard you work, you'll still be a junior clerk in the Society for the Salvation of our Ruined Russia. If you want to get on in Paris, and you haven't got a protector, you're going to need something else.

GORODULIN: What do you mean?

GLUMOV: Well, you shouldn't discuss it when your boss cracks a joke, you should just guffaw with laughter. You should do all his work for him, but still pretend it's his. You should seem to have no interest whatsoever in promotion, you should attend the church memorial service to the assassinated Romanovs, and you should know how to jump up and greet the boss in such a way you're servile and not servile at the same time – like a servant greeting his master, but with a touch of nobility in it. You have to be both direct and gracious, and also you have to do it in the Russian manner. When your boss sends you for something, you need to know how to fly on air, something between a gallop, a march and an ordinary walk. Like this. (*He demonstrates.*)

GORODULIN: Excellent! I mean, everything you've said is awful, but your way of saying it is wonderful, really good. Superb, superb. You're very talented.

GLUMOV: I'm glad you like my ideas. It's a pity there are only a few people like you.

GORODULIN: The ideas are nothing. All us fascists have plenty of ideas – it's not the ideas, it's the words, and the phrases, that are so impressive. You know, you could do me a great favour.

GLUMOV: What would you like?

GORODULIN: Would you write all this down for me on a piece of paper?

GLUMOV: My pleasure. But what do you want it for?

GORODULIN: I'll tell you the truth. We're both honourable men, we can speak frankly to one another. The problem is that tomorrow I have to make a speech at the joint dinner of the groups 'Down With!' and 'Long Live!' And I simply haven't got time to prepare anything.

GLUMOV: Then, with pleasure, with pleasure.

GORODULIN: Do it for me, out of friendship.

GLUMOV: Heavens, don't mention it. Whatever you like. I'm not against work. I'll work proper, has long has I'm hable. I have honly one condition, that is, that my work is undubitously useful. I want it to enlarge the numbers of those making good, which is right and proper for the prosperity of Earth and Liberty, the Sword and the Bullet.

GORODULIN: You must put that bit down – 'to enlarge the numbers of those making good.' It's brilliant. I understand you perfectly – with your way of thinking positively, you should have a position as steward or chief clerk in a public or a charitable institution, like the Union of the Liberation or the Patriotic Co-operative for the Extirpation of Pernicious Communists.

GLUMOV: *Merci*. But no, you should give me a post where I could come into contact with the world and his wife. Give me a chance to see people's needs first hand and then I can satisfy them quickly, without making a fuss. Long live the Constituent Assembly, the Earth and Freedom. And the Constitution, 'God bless the Tsar.' Do you want me to write the whole speech for you?

GORODULIN: Why not? (*To the audience*) You see how quickly honourable men can become friends. They just have to say a couple of words to each other, and that's it. And how you can speak, how you can speak. *Mama mia!* You'll be successful just because of the way you can speak. That fool Joffre's the only one who still believes in military intervention. But there's no chance. His speeches and his methods, especially his methods, need 'communizing'. Their weapons, our victory. That's the fascist slogan. Come to my place tomorrow. I'm very pleased to have met you, very pleased.
(*Gorodulin goes out. Enter Mamev.*)

MAMAEV: Come here. Joffre came to my place yesterday because he wanted to discuss something. He's a nice old chap, and he's written something about militarism. But it needs editing, and phrasing properly. He didn't go to a 'Rabfac' school,[49] and he writes in the ancient style of Patriarch Tikhon. I've recommended you to him. In our committee he's not considered a clever man, and what he's written may well be thoroughly stupid. But when you see him, butter him up a bit …

GLUMOV: So that's what you're going to be teaching me, is it, uncle?

MAMAEV: Don't go overboard, but a little bit of flattery, twenty kopeck's worth, won't do any harm. And, er, one more, rather delicate question: what sort of relationship do you have with your aunt? (*Mamaeva becomes visible above on the platform.*)

GLUMOV: I'm a bit of a haberdasher,[50] I can dance the One-Step, I don't need to be taught manners.

MAMAEVA: Kiss my hand, your problem is solved.

GLUMOV (*runs to her*): But I haven't asked you anything.

MAMAEVA: I guessed it.

GLUMOV: Then thank you. (*He turns back to Mamaev.*)

MAMAEVA: Where are you going?

GLUMOV: I'm going home, I'm so happy. (*He returns to Mamaev.*)

MAMAEV: Well, what I'm going to say is stupid, perhaps. (*Mamaeva mimes appropriately behind him.*) She's still young and beautiful,

---

49   *'Rabfac' school*: These were schools set up by the Bolsheviks to bring their own working class supporters' level of education up to the standard required for University entrance.

50   *Haberdasher*: Glumov's attempt to impress with long words.

she doesn't need your 'manners'. You don't want to make some sort of an enemy of her, do you?

GLUMOV: I don't understand you, uncle.

MAMAEV: Well, if you don't understand, listen carefully, and you'll learn something. A woman never forgives a man who fails to notice her beauty.

GLUMOV: Yes yes yes, of course, I'm going bonkers. But I'm still not convinced. (*He runs back to her.*)

MAMAEVA: Are you happy?

GLUMOV: I'm as happy as I could be.

MAMAEVA: So you're not completely happy?

GLUMOV: What else could I want? A position for me has been found.

MAMAEVA: I don't believe you, I don't believe you. It's because you're so young that you want to show yourself to be a historical materialist, and you want me to think you're only interested in your new position and money.

GLUMOV: Cleopatra Lvovna –

MAMAEVA: That you don't love anybody. But I know, I can see it in your eyes – you're in love. Poor you, are you suffering a lot?

GLUMOV: You have no right to use such means. (*He runs back to Mamaev.*)

MAMAEV: You understand, old chap. You're a very distant relative, it's true, but still you are a relative, so you have a certain freedom which a mere acquaintance wouldn't have. Sometimes, you might seem to forget yourself (*he whistles*) and kiss her hand. Maybe you could make eyes at her – I dare say you know how to.

GLUMOV: No, I don't.

MAMAEV: You what, old fellow? Look, like this. (*He demonstrates. Glumov goes to Mamaeva and copies him.*) Like Sashenka Kerensky.[51]

GLUMOV: Really, I wouldn't dare!

MAMAEV: Well, you could practice in front of a mirror.

MAMAEVA: Who are you in love with?

GLUMOV: Please – have mercy.

MAMAEVA: Is she worthy of you?

GLUMOV: Oh God, what are you doing to me?

---

51   *Sashenka Kerensky*: 'Sashenka' is a baby's diminutive for Alexander, which was Kerensky's name. (See note 4 above.)

MAMAEVA: Can she appreciate your passionate nature, your fervent heart?

GLUMOV (*getting up, returning to Mamaev*): Even if you were to kill me, I wouldn't make so bold.

MAMAEV and MAMAEVA (*together*): Go on, my friend, be bold!

MAMAEV: But it's for my sake, don't you see, don't you get it?

GLUMOV: I still don't understand.

MAMAEV: Your aunt is a naturally optimistic woman, you see. She is hot-headed. She is quite capable of falling for any dandy. The devil take it, she might go for an artisan. Maybe even a convict. God does not bless such affairs. Who knows where they lead to? Well, now you can see where you come in. You're a member of the family, you're tried and trusted. The mouse can play, and the cat can stay away.

GLUMOV: Ha ha ha. You're clever, uncle, really clever.

MAMAEV: I hope so.

GLUMOV (*runs back to Mamaeva*): Who'm I in love with?

MAMAEVA: Yes.

GLUMOV: You!

MAMAEVA: Ahh!

(*She appears to faint. He runs back to Mamaev.*)

MAMAEV: That's it, that's it!

GLUMOV: To prevent any tittle-tattling by outsiders, perhaps you'd care to introduce me to the Salon-Turusina, so I can court her niece quite openly, and perhaps even propose to her, if you'd like me to. That way, both the mice can play, while the cat can stay away. But better not mention that to Cleopatra Lvovna, she'd be ... not jealous, but ... you know.

MAMAEV: Absolutely, I won't, no no no.

GLUMOV: When shall we go to Turusina's?

MAMAEV: Tomorrow.

GLUMOV (*makes for Mamaeva, but is caught halfway between the two*): I'm your slave for life. Punish me for my presumptuousness, but I love you. (*To Mamaev*) Forgive me!

MAMAEVA: You are forgiven.

(*Tableau.*)

ACT THREE

The scene is now General Joffre's parade-ground.

GLUMOV: I want to see General Joffre.
SERVANT: Who?
GLUMOV: Joffre.
SERVANT: You can't see him without being announced.
GLUMOV: Well, what shall I do?
SEERVANT: You'll have to wait.
GLUMOV (*gives him money*): Just like Moscow.
SERVANT: Okay, I'll announce you.
GLUMOV: Just like the old days. Keep hold of yourself, Glumov, this is the moment for General Joffre to come a cropper.
(*Joffre enters, drilling his troops to the sounds of a military band.*)
JOFFRE: Halt! Right turn! Left turn! Excellent. Good lads.
STAGE HAND: Present and correct, sir.
SONG: *An Apple.*[52]
    Eh, my apple,
      Off you roll,
        Chick, vick,
          Won't you stroll?
JOFFRE: Squad! Squad will move to the right in threes, right turn! Quick march! Squad, halt! Halt! Turn right! Quick march! Stop! Squad will move to the left in threes, left turn! Squad, halt! About turn!
SONG: *An Apple.*

---

52   *An Apple*: An adaptation of a well-known Russian round song. Tretyakov's comically revised version is given here in literal translation. In performance, an adaptation of 'Three Blind Mice' or 'London's Burning' might be preferable.

> Eh, my apple,
>> You are green,
>> I'll buy a gun
>>> And kill Lenin!

JOFFRE: Gentlemen officers, get to your places. Quick march! Church Parade!

ADJUTANT: Hats off!

PRAYER: *An Apple* (*as before*).

JOFFRE: Hats on!

ADJUTANT: Sir!

JOFFRE: Ready for the ceremonial march past.

ADJUTANT: Get your dressings!

OFFICER: All ranks, right turn! Left turn!

OFFICERS: Move to the left in threes, quick march!

JOFFRE: Thanks for organising them.

STAGE HANDS (*barking*): Woof woof woof!

(*The troops march past, with Joffre taking the salute. When they go, Glumov is revealed.*)

GLUMOV: Present and correct, your Excellency!

JOFFRE: Aha. Ready?

GLUMOV: Ready, your Excellency.

JOFFRE: What?

GLUMOV: This is a sheer revelation. It couldn't emanate from an ordinary brain, it must have sprung from a brain with epaulettes, your Excellency.

JOFFRE: Good for you, laddie. You take after Petlyura.[53] You don't speak badly.

GLUMOV: It comes from the Gospels, your Excellency.

JOFFRE: What comes from the Gospels?

GLUMOV: Well, look, for example: smash them between the eyes. Those are golden words, your Excellency. Or what about these: covet not your neighbour's ass, but you can grab his oil and coal deposits as quick as you like. What an exemplary Christian you are, your Excellency.

---

53   *Petlyura:* Semyon Vasilievich Petlyura, leader of independent Ukraine from 1917; defeated by the Red Army in 1920.

JOFFRE: Huh uh ... Give me the notebook. Blessed are the meek Germans, for they shall inherit a clout round the ear. Blessed are those Frenchmen that hunger and thirst for they shall be filled – with war reparations. Blessed are those that are persecuted for righteousness sake – that is, Bukharin and that lot – for they shall make their mark on Russia.

GLUMOV: Not 'make their mark on' – 'leave their dirty marks all over' Russia, your Excellency.

JOFFRE: Yes, they'll leave their dirty marks all over it. Man cannot live by bread alone, but by something stronger down his throat. Don't put new wine into old bottles. But it's not such a bad idea to put Communists like Monmusso[54] into gaol.

GLUMOV: That is the wisdom of the state, your Excellency.

JOFFRE: I bring on earth not peace but the sword. We've got the peace already, you see – the Peace of Versailles. But the sword is not enough, you have to have dreadnoughts. If that's not enough – howitzers and tanks. Still not enough? – Then armoured trains.

GLUMOV: Your revolver, your Excellency.

JOFFRE: If someone hits you on the left cheek, don't turn the right, belt him straight back. Long live a fighting spirit and the iron fist of militarism. (*The Marseillaise is heard.*) Good for you, Glumov!

GLUMOV: My pleasure, your Excellency.

JOFFRE: Well, you've managed that all right, what sort of reward would you like?

GLUMOV: You could make me a colonel.

JOFFRE: Wha-a-at?

GLUMOV: I'll take a town for you. One town, two towns. Well, okay – three towns.

JOFFRE: It's not enough. There's a system for promotions. You'd have to wait to become a colonel. I don't mind giving you a medal. What medal would you like, mm?

GLUMOV: The Order of the System of Saint Stanislav.[55]

---

54   *Monmusso:* The reference (deliberately absurd) is to Mussolini, and perhaps his alliance with Italian monarchy.

55   *The Order of the System of Saint Stanislav:* The Order of Saint Stanislaus was originally a Polish order of knighthood, taken over in 1831 by tsarist Russia, and abolished in 1917. This is conflated with a reference to the Stanislavsky system, still the basis for all acting styles. Stanislavsky, who was a-political, spent much

JOFFRE: I haven't got any of Stanislavsky's System left. I did have someone who could do it, but he's fled to America.
GLUMOV: Well, give me an Anna of the second degree.
JOFFRE: No, I'll give you the medal of the Honourable Legion. All the reprobates ... er, rep ... reporters on our newspapers wear it.
GLUMOV: Respectful thanks, your Excellency.
(*Joffre pins a medal to his chest.*)
JOFFRE: Well, is that all?
GLUMOV: One more request ...
JOFFRE: Shoot!
(*A Stage Hand shoots the huge cannon.*)
GLUMOV: You see, your Excellency, now I'm a champion of the right wing, the Honourable Legion, I mean, I have the perfectly honourable desire to enter into the state of matrimony. With a young lady called Mary, Miss Mary Mac-Lac, that was her father's surname, but Mary Make-Eyes by her mother's side. You'd know her as the niece of Salon-Turusina, and I'd like to ask you ...
JOFFRE: To act as your father at the wedding, yes?
GLUMOV: Yes, act as my father, that's it, your Excellency.
JOFFRE: Have you proposed to this young lady who's hooked you?
CHORUS: Why did you hook me to the kettle?
JOFFRE: I imagine you'll make something out of it, won't you?
GLUMOV: I'll get an armaments factory, your Excellency.
JOFFRE: Right.
GLUMOV: Some coal mines, oil fields.
JOFFRE: Excellent. And what will you do with the money?
GLUMOV: Well, your Excellency, our motherland must be saved from the Bolsheviks.
JOFFRE: Mmm?
GLUMOV: In order to be victorious, we shall need soldiers, transport, field hospitals ...
(*Stage Hands enter.*)
JOFFRE: Mmm?

---

time in the early years of Soviet power on tour with the Moscow Art Theatre abroad, notably in U.S.A. Joffre fails to note, of course, that Glumov's performance here would have delighted Stanislavsky!

GLUMOV: ... and of course, your victorious Excellency to take command of the triumphant campaign.
JOFFRE: Aha. I understand. Not bad. But there's just one thing. We need an agreement. I'll take the money, and get an army equipped, but I will not invade through Archangel. I'm sick of the place, and the same goes for the Crimea, and for Siberia – I'm not a fool. And I won't invade through Petersburg, or through Finland, or through Poland – no way!
GLUMOV: Your Excellency, we shall find a way.
JOFFRE: There are plenty of ways – but they're all ways out of Russia. You show me the entrance.
GLUMOV: I think the best plan might be an assault from the North Pole.
JOFFRE: I agree with you. So – you'll provide the funds?
GLUMOV: Uh huh.
JOFFRE: And then, we'll set up a joint stock company, a company to exploit the natural as well as the supernatural riches of Mary Mac-Lac, and what with one thing and another ...
GLUMOV: Our happiness, your Excellency, only depends on the matter of the wedding and your active support for it, otherwise ...
JOFFRE: God provides – you shall be a capitalist! We need people like you. You're one of us. You won't go talking to any visitors from the Soviet Commissariat for Foreign Trade, will you? (*Glumov spits three times over his left shoulder to indicate that such an idea is impossible.*) Now listen, no tricks.
GLUMOV: Will you be needing me any further, your Excellency?
JOFFRE: No.
GLUMOV: Then I'll wish you good day, your Excellency.
JOFFRE: Halt! About turn! Not a word about my propositions. You understand? I'm already using them in the Ruhr, and just waiting for some fat reparations to flow in. If you don't keep quiet, I'll do the same to you as was done to the workers in the Ruhr, understand?[56]
GLUMOV: I get it, your Excellency.

---

56   *The Ruhr*: In January 1923 French troops occupied the German industrial heartland of the Ruhr because of Germany's failure to pay First World War reparations.

(*He yawns. Stage Hands make the sign of the cross over him. Everybody sleeps.*)

CHORUS: Sleep, fighter-eagles,
        Sleep, with peace in your souls,
        You, who deserve glory and eternal peace.
        (*A signal. Morning, dawn.*)

STAGE HAND: The aunt of the bridegroom has arrived.

JOFFRE: Ah, I haven't seen you for ages, not since the Sevastopol campaign.

MAMAEVA: Since Sevastopol. Was that with Vrangel?[57]

JOFFRE: No, I mean the real one.

MAMAEVA: Well, how would I remember that? It was seventy years ago! Do you think I can remember that?

JOFFRE: Excuse me. I'm an imperialist and you're an imperialist. I imagine we're of an age. However, if you find that offensive, better turn left. I'm very pleased with your relative.

MAMAEVA: He's sweet.

JOFFRE: Uh huh. He's a naughty youngster. But he's a good boy, like Skobelev.[58]

MAMAEVA: Why?

JOFFRE: Don't you know?

MAMAEVA: Tell me, why?

JOFFRE: He's found himself a bride.

MAMAEVA: What bride? (*She faints. First Stage Hand administers an enema.*)

JOFFRE: Not just any old bride, one worth an oil well that produces endless profits.

MAMAEVA: Who? (*She faints.*)

JOFFRE: Money, shares, dividends, bonuses, coupons, cheques and banknotes, she controls half Europe. Our 'little one' will scale the heights.

MAMAEVA: Shut up, you make me sick.

---

57   *Vrangel:* Baron Peter Nikolaevich Vrangel, commander of the White Army in southern Russia, based in Sevastopol in 1920.

58   *Skobelev:* Mikhail Dmitrievich Skobelev, a highly successful nineteenth century general, who was also a fanatical Russian imperialist. He died young in 1882, leaving his political aspirations unfulfilled.

JOFFRE: And he loves her with all his soul and all his pockets. His waistcoat pockets, his trouser pockets, his jacket pockets, his coat pockets. She's an angel, he says. He even wrote a poem to her.
CHORUS: If you're an angel in the flesh,
    Take out your wallet and pay cash.
JOFFRE: Eh well ... And you and me, we can look at this happiness and sigh contentedly.
MAMAEVA: I'm not Turkey for you to pillage. I'm not the Ruhr to pay for you.
JOFFRE: All the same –
    If Joffre is going to launch a campaign
        To capture the riches of Ruhr,
    He'll bring a halter for the workers' necks,
        And he'll flay them alive eight times o'er.
    Bravo, soldier ladies, bravo.
MAMAEVA: Help! He's going to 'occupy' me! Now I'm up a gumtree.
    (*A balancing pole is brought in. She climbs the pole, which is held by Joffre, and performs suitable stunts.*)
JOFFRE: Nothing of the kind, it's just a small intervention.
MAMAEVA: Now I'm right up the pole. But I'll frustrate the marriage of Mary Mac-Lac and Glumov by hook or by crook.
JOFFRE: But, you know, now you're like Moscow, it's impossible to reach you.
MAMAEVA: Yes, now I'm as unattainable, and as dauntless, as Soviet Russia.
    (*She returns to earth, and runs out, with Joffre in pursuit.*)

ACT FOUR

The arena now represents Turusina's apartment. Turusina and Mashenka. Turusina wears a flimsy skirt and a top, which is little more than two inverted lampshades to cover her breasts. These light up or flash at moments of excitement.

MASHENKA: Let's go, aunty, let's go. Please come on.
TURUSINA: You want to see Kurchaev, but I'm not going to let you.
MASHENKA: Why don't you like him? He's the very most faithful of all Vrangel's hussars.
TURUSINA: His eyes mock me. He argues against religion. He makes fun of my holy people.
MASHENKA: Do you think they are holy?
TURUSINA: Of course. I said to him, 'Look, my old granny Black's face is shining with holiness,' and he said it was shining because she was so fat. I can't forgive him, he's an atheist, a Bukharinite. Besides, yesterday I received two telegrams.
MASHENKA: Anonymous ones?
TURUSINA: What of that? They're both about the same thing, and anyway, the handwriting's different.[59]
GRIGORY: There's pilgrims at the door.
TURUSINA: What does he call them? How does he put it? Oh yes, they're 'émigrés'. Berlin ruined them with drink, that's what he says. Make them a special trough and put the potato peelings in. Then make sure they sing 'God save your people' while they eat it. Well, listen to what this says: 'I can't choke back my fears when I think you've chosen a man like Kurchaev. He was seen coming

---

59   *The handwriting's different*: Genuine telegrams were not handwritten, of course.

out of the Soviet Office of Foreign Trade in London, arm in arm with a Soviet woman. At night Kurchaev rolls his moustache in the Soviet daily, *Izvestia*. You can see that he has betrayed our national struggle,' and so on and so forth.

MASHENKA: That's ridiculous.

TURUSINA: Are you arguing again? Very well, marry him. But remember, you'll be upsetting me very much, and it won't be any good complaining if I ...

MASHENKA: ... don't give me your investments.

TURUSINA: But the most important thing is – my blessing.

MASHENKA: Don't worry. Business, commercial transactions – they still come first. I can't risk losing those factories and mines because of a pair of spurs on a hussar's boots. Your stocks are going up – your 'Kerensky's' are proving popular in Japan, your 'Romanovs' are doing well in Washington. I don't need Kurchaev – I won't die of consumption without him – I'm no heroine out of Ostrovsky or Turgenev. Give me anyone you like, but soon – I want a good time.

TURUSINA: I like your adaptability.

MASHENKA: I'm not going to live any worse than you, aunty.

TURUSINA: God bless you, this is God's way.

MASHENKA: Absolutely. You'll be my example. One can't repent if one hasn't sinned. So first I'll sin, then I'll repent, sin and repent, sin and repent, sin and repent.

TURUSINA: Sinful words, Maria.

MASHENKA: Pardon. Here's today's Market Bulletin. The mark's going down. Angier shares are in demand, the dollar's stable.

TURUSINA: The sweet girl, how can I be cross with her? She doesn't understand what she's saying, she's just burbling. But it gets me so excited I could sneeze.

GRIGORY: Mister Gorodulin.

TURUSINA: Show him in.

GORODULIN: Comradely greetings. May I have the honour?

MASHENKA: I'm not sure. Have you got shares in metallurgy?

TURUSINA: We haven't seen you for ages.

GORODULIN: I've been busy. Europe is cracking under the weight of conferences, and our dashing fascist escapades. I've just got back from a couple of little pogroms – one in Poland, the other in Italy.

TURUSINA: You've become so important. Now one of your people is to be a Prime Minister,[60] you've forgotten about the Russian refugees, and your duty to defend the oppressed.//
MASHENKA: Gold's at fifteen dollars.
GORODULIN (*to Mashenka*): I'm talking francs. (*To Turusina*) Are you referring to that old witch who tells your fortune in the coffee grounds and who foresaw the magical restoration of the Russian tsar?
TURUSINA: What a foul way to describe her. She's a holy woman, a theosophist, the Holy Spirit has touched her.
GORODULIN: I'm not so sure about the Holy Spirit. A soldier from the Caucasian Wild Division[61] certainly touched her. Everything became clear when he was in court. She was running a brothel.
MASHENKA: I'll let you have Bryan and Putilov shares on temps.
GORODULIN: I can be your broker on temps.
MASHENKA: I'm giving 500 on differentials.
GORODULIN: I'm adding 200. (*To Turusina*) A shopkeeper was poisoned with one of her 'love potions'.
TURUSINA: Well ...
GORODULIN: He died, not from love, for quite opposite reasons.
TURUSINA: Oh, how dreadful, how can one live in this world?
MASHENKA: Who's going to buy?
GORODULIN: The owner of the Lyons velvet factory.
MASHENKA: I'm selling shares in two Lyons factories for less than they cost me.
TURUSINA: No, it's all so cruel. I've made an awful mistake. The scum, running a brothel. But I'll still carry on with my charitable work with the poor. That'll be my only consolation if you sell my Lyons factories. It's true.
GORODULIN: Genuinely holy people are rare these days.
GRIGORY: There's a holy man here.
GORODULIN: Really?
TURUSINA: Who is he?

---

60   *Prime Minister:* A reference to Gorodulin-Mussolini, Prime Minister of Italy.
61   *The Caucasian Wild Division:* A notoriously cruel division of White Guards consisting of Georgians, Armenians and others from the Caucasus region.

GRIGORY: Well, he's very ugly. He's got a wild look, and he's all hairy, like an Angoran Turk.
TURUSINA: He must be Greek.
GRIGORY: No, his nose isn't big enough for a Greek. He must be a Hungarian and a hangman, a Black Hundred.
TURUSINA: Bring him in, feed him, and ask if he needs anything else.
GRIGORY: I reckon what he really needs ...
TURUSINA: Go on.
MASHENKA: Horthy's position in Hungary looks secure.[62] I'm buying Hungarian loan stock.
TURUSINA: Buy some for me, too. Okay? (*To Gorodulin*) Can you give me some advice about Mashenka?
GORODULIN: A husband for her? I support all kinds of chains except matrimonial ones.
TURUSINA: So you can't think of anyone?
GORODULIN: I can. For you. You saw him. Glumov.
TURUSINA: Is he suitable?
GORODULIN: He certainly is. I'll lay pounds on it. He's an honest man, he doesn't gamble. (*To Mashenka*) I'm taking marks. (*To Turusina*) He's an excellent young man. Yegor Dmitrievich. I must be off. Arriva-dividend-erchi! (*He goes.*)
TURUSINA: Gone. Gone again.
GRIGORY: Mister Joffer.
TURUSINA: Joffre, I've told you. Show him in.
JOFFRE: *Vive la Russe!* You're all nervous, your hands are ice cold. They smell of something. You shouldn't tire yourself out like this ...
TURUSINA: I've asked you before not to talk to me about that.
JOFFRE: Well, well, I won't, I won't.
TURUSINA: Do sit down.
JOFFRE: I don't want to.
TURUSINA: Tea?
JOFFRE: I can't sit down. I'm going to launch a campaign in the Ruhr, but before all the battles and attacks I thought I'd make a detour to my dear old friend, my dear old girlfriend. I'm

---

[62] *Horthy*: Miklos Horthy, leader of the counter-revolutionary forces which defeated the Hungarian Soviet Government of Bela Kun in 1920. He became Regent of Hungary, and ruled until 1944.

sure you remember how close you and I were in the days of Alexander III.

TURUSINA: Oh, don't remind me. Now I'm ...

(*Grigory brings in the tea on a tray balanced on a pole. When he is near the audience, he slips, the tray comes off the pole, the tea things off the tray ... Luckily, they are empty and tied in place with strings, so they dangle just above the spectators' heads.*)

JOFFRE: But why not? Why shouldn't we remember the good old days, with their court ceremonies, their coronations, concessions, loans and our affair.

TURUSINA: *Attendez!*

GRIGORY: Madame, there's an ugly man here.

TURUSINA: Not an ugly man, a holy one. How stupid these people are. They can't even recognize Merezhkovsky.[63]

JOFFRE: There are too many of them in Paris now, and what are they stuffing their heads with? Black caviar, probably. And I must say, when you led the life of a monarchist, you were much healthier than you are now.

TURUSINA: My body may have been, but not my soul.

JOFFRE: Well, that's not my business. But you were fitter, stronger. You're still young, you know, you should live properly.

TURUSINA: I do live properly.

JOFFRE: Well, I mean, it's a bit early to become so ... sanctimonious.

TURUSINA: I asked you ...

JOFFRE: Oh yes, sorry, sorry, I won't do it again.

TURUSINA: You're such an odd man.

GRIGORY: Madame, there's an odd man here.

TURUSINA: Where did he come from? Didn't you ask him?

GRIGORY: He says he's come from far away. He started off from Vladivostok, crossed two borders, and now he's in Paris he's still trying to double-cross people.

TURUSINA: Show him to where the others are.

GRIGORY: But if they're all together, they'll split into fractions and start arguing. They'll tear each others' hair out.

TURUSINA: So?

---

63   *Merezhkovsky*. Dmitri Sergeyevich Merezhkovsky, mystical and religious novelist and poet, who was violently anti-Soviet and emigrated after 1917.

JOFFRE: You ought to ask your congregation for their passports.
TURUSINA: What for?
JOFFRE: Well, I know someone who rescued three refugees ...
TURUSINA: What of it?
JOFFRE: And all three proved to be expert engravers ...
TURUSINA: Well, so, what of it?
JOFFRE: It's a pretty shady profession.
TURUSINA: What's shady about engraving?
JOFFRE: Well, you see, they weren't engraving portraits ...
TURUSINA: Ikons?
JOFFRE: No, not ikons. Proclamations and posters for the syndicalists!
TURUSINA: They never were?
JOFFRE: Yes, they were, and when we live in a state of constant conflict ...
TURUSINA: Well, I believe in doing good for good's sake, which is just as gratifying as art for art's sake.
PARROT: Popka the fool, they spit on Popka's soul, a swastika.
TURUSINA: By the way, I wanted to speak to you about something rather important.
MASHENKA: I'm offering metallurgical and artillery shares.
JOFFRE: Now we're getting ready for a new war, the artillery ones should rise.
MASHENKA: Are you giving out contracts?
JOFFRE: Yes – three dreadnoughts, one hundred howitzers.
TURUSINA: Do you know a young man who wears pince-nez? He's the kind we need.
JOFFRE: What kind do you need? (*To Mashenka*) Forty per cent comes to me for brokerage. Bank on bread rising ... (*To Turusina*) The kind you need ... There are plenty of them ... (*To Mashenka*) I'm taking a million poods of American wheat ... (*To Turusina*) I know exactly who you need.
TURUSINA: Well?
JOFFRE: He's modest, respectful and carries himself like a sergeant-major. He's patriotic, too. He intends to subsidize our allies. Altogether, he's a good young chap.
TURUSINA: What's his name?
JOFFRE: Yegor Dmitrievich Glumov! (*Surprise.*) Damn it, he gave me his address, too. What the devil have I done with it? He has beautiful handwriting, like a regimental secretary. Handwriting like that's

only fit for military reports. Excellent calligraphy, he makes the old-style i with a dot. Take it, you might find it useful one day.

TURUSINA: Paper's always useful. Thank you, that's Providence.

JOFFRE: Don't mention it. It's an honest soldier's duty. Goodbye. Shall I come and see you again, or are you still angry?

TURUSINA: Oh, I'm always pleased to see you.

JOFFRE: All I say is, Good luck.

TURUSINA: Come again.

JOFFRE: Well, goodbye for now. (*He goes.*)

TURUSINA: Frisky old boy. A natural Frenchman, complete with moustache and spurs, and as for dancing the mazurka – he does that like a Frenchman, too. Hmm, all the same, who is this Glumov? And why do two people with completely opposite points of view both speak well of him? Ah, what a loss it was when Grigory Rasputin died, he would have made everything clear. I don't know whether Manefa will ever be an adequate substitute for him, but there is a lot of the supernatural, the metaphysical about her.

FIRST HANGER-ON: Do you want to whip out the cards now?

SECOND HANGER-ON: Whip him?

TURUSINA: Whip who? The one we seek? Are you going soft in the head? Mashenka, I've talked to my friends about your little business.

MASHENKA: And they ...? I'm giving pounds.

TURUSINA: They recommended ...

MASHENKA: Two of them? I'll take marks.

TURUSINA: No, they agreed ...

MASHENKA: Hm, I'll accept it then. But cotton's going up in London. Who is he?

TURUSINA: I don't trust them.

FIRST HANGER-ON: Shall I get the fortune-teller?

TURUSINA: Yes, do. Joffre and Gorodulin may be mistaken.

MASHENKA: But rather than find out about his spiritual condition, it'd be better to try and find out about his bank account, or call up Pinkerton from America to tell us.

TURUSINA: They're all people. Don't hold a dog by its tail. The message must come to us direct from heaven, so let's wait in the fear of God and our belief in Him

MASHENKA: Well, I don't know of a radio that can receive messages direct from heaven.
TURUSINA: Here she is. (*Sings*) Doh la fah.
GRIGORY: Manefa.
TURUSINA: You see. Please come in.
MANEFA: I went out like I was and I came in like I was. I came in, I sat down, like dough in the bowl. What are you goggling at?
TURUSINA: Oh, we're just so pleased and happy to see you, Mother Manefa.
FIRST HANGER-ON: Oh, so pleased.
SECOND HANGER-ON: Very pleased.
TURUSINA: I wanted to ask ...
MANEFA: Don't ask anything. I know in advance. The knowing one runs, but the unknowing lies down. Less a virgin, more a woman.
SECOND HANGER-ON: Right, right, right.
FIRST HANGER-ON: My goodness, my goodness, remember this!
SECOND HANGER-ON: Take it down in shorthand.
TURUSINA: We want to know the man's name.
MANEFA: It was, it was a vision. Yegor coming down the high mountain. Blond suitor or blind satyr, sweetheart or sweat-maker.
SECOND HANGER-ON: I say, it's Yegor.
FIRST HANGER-ON: But he's dark.
MASHENKA: But Kurchaev's name's Yegor, too.
TURUSINA: But you heard, you saw him in a vision – holy people don't see hussars in their visions, even dark ones.
MANEFA: No.
TURUSINA: We doubters are unsure. There are so many Yegors, blond ones, too.
MANEFA: The stranger is far away.
GRIGORY: Editing LEF.[64]
MANEFA: But the chosen one is at the gate. Get dressed, prepare yourself, the guests are coming.

---

64   *LEF*: Left Front of Art, Futurist journal of the arts under the editorship of Vladimir Mayakovsky. Tretyakov was on the editorial board, and became editor of *Novy LEF* (*New LEF*) when Mayakovsky resigned in 1928. Eisenstein's important essay, 'The Montage of Attractions', about his production of *A Wise Man*, was published in *LEF* in June 1923.

MASHENKA: When?
MANEFA: Now, this minute.
TURUSINA: Oh, mother!
MANEFA: They come with gifts.
GRIGORY: Pavel Nikolaevich Mamilyukov.
TURUSINA: Just him?
GRIGORY: No, there's a young gentleman with him, a blond one.
FIRST and SECOND HANGERS-ON: Ahh!
TURUSINA: Show them in. Well, Mashenka, my prayers have been heard.
MASHENKA: This is all so strange.
TURUSINA: Go and calm down. Come back later.
MASHENKA: I'm taking six hundred Pennsylvanias.
MANEFA: It's the end, the climax of the whole thing.
TURUSINA: Take her to the kitchen, give her some tea. You hear? Tea.
MANEFA: You'd have to be pretty desperate to want to drink tea.
TURUSINA: All right, give her whatever she wants.
MAMAEV: Sofia Ignatievna, allow me to introduce you to my nephew, Yegor Dmitrievich Glumov.
SECOND HANGER-ON: Ahh, the blond one!
MAMAEV: You'll like him.
TURUSINA: Thank you, we do already.
GLUMOV: She's in my pocket. It's bulging with money.
(*A dance – the polonaise. Everyone joins in.*)

ACT FIVE

Glumov's flat again. Glumov is writing his diary.

GLUMOV: Everything's fine. So we shall write down, how an old buffer thought he'd get hold of somewhere to be the headquarters of imperialism. That's worth a new page in my diary. Morning – at General Joffre's, and tea-time – at Princess Salon-Turusina's. The most important thing is to conceal the fact that I'm going to get married from my aunt, otherwise my whole escapade will go up in smoke! Everything's okay for now. So, sing for me, finches, siskins, canaries, pour your sweet balm on the soul of the future owner of the greatest factories in the world. Mummy, are you going to Turusina's?

GLUMOVA: Yes.

GLUMOV: You're a bit late, mummy.

GLUMOVA: They'll get sick of me.

GLUMOV: Do what? Eat till you get sick? No, you must keep in with the servants, notice everybody who comes in.

GLUMOVA: And who goes out.

GLUMOV: Give them little presents, don't spare expense. Stay by the little window, out of the way. Aim for the hangers-on – the tart Kerenskaya and old granny Black. Give them a little snuff box each for cocaine, they love that. Since they fled from Gatchina,[65] they haven't had any other consolations apart from sniffing that stuff for the illusions it gives them. Shoo! Hurry the wedding preparations along. Go on. Quick! Two snuff boxes for the big-nosed SRs. (*Mother goes out. Mamaeva approaches.*) Who's that? Cleopatra Lvovna, and in a mask. That means she's come to see me. Does she

---

65   *Gatchina:* Town south of St Petersburg, a centre of tsarism.

know or doesn't she know? Lip, curl upwards. O, what happiness, do I see you?

MAMAEVA: I haven't come to see you, I've come to see your mama.

GLUMOV (*aside*): She knows. (*To Mamaeva*) She was here, but she's just popped out.

MAMAEVA: What a pity.

GLUMOV (*aside*): She doesn't know. (*To Mamaeva*) Don't go, stay with me.

MAMAEVA: I'm so unhappy.

GLUMOV (*aside*): She knows. (*To Mamaeva*) What beast, what serpent has made you unhappy?

MAMAEVA: It wasn't a beast, it was the dentist. It's got nothing to do with serpents, it's just that the crown came off my tooth.

GLUMOV (*aside*): She doesn't know. (*To Mamaeva*) I'm not a dentist, or a Bolshevik, I don't knock crowns off tsars' coconuts – therefore it's not my fault.

MAMAEVA: Well, that's nice – 'therefore'!

GLUMOV: Well, yes, therefore I couldn't have upset you.

MAMAEVA: Do you swear?

GLUMOV: May lightning strike me.

MAMAEVA: That's not strong enough.

GLUMOV: May my ears fall off.

MAMAEVA: Not strong enough.

GLUMOV: I can't swear stronger than that.

MAMAEVA: I'm sure you can.

GLUMOV (*aside*): She doesn't know. Oil your way into the woman's favour, Yegor. (*To Mamaeva*) I am a naturally ardent knight, unbelievably passionate, wanting to be madly in love. I was languishing alone when you appeared, O unbelievably beautiful lady, and my heart started thumping in my chest like a motorbike revving up. You, O you, yes, you, you – you have stooped to me, a poor émigré who looks absolutely dreadful. You didn't push me to one side, you warmed my poor suffering heart. What could I ever desire except you?

MAMAEVA: Are you going to get married?

GLUMOV: Why ... No ... Yes ... But ... She knows.

MAMAEVA: You're getting married, aren't you?

GLUMOV: Not me. It's for them. They're marrying me for the money. (*Aside*) She knows. We'll have to try something else.

MAMAEVA: They're marrying you?

GLUMOV: Yes, I'm bound – arms, legs, lips, teeth. They're trying to make me into a proper man, they're trying to work out their political speculations on me. I'm just a humble labourer. Capital, in the shape of your husband, is trying to suffocate me. You understand, left wing ideas appeal to you.
MAMAEVA: Oh, yes, I understand. But aren't you in love with your bride?
GLUMOV: With that pig's snout? I wouldn't mind if someone chucked a brick at it.
MAMAEVA: That makes me feel a bit better.
GLUMOV: And now I'll make you completely well. Heroism, real heroism. I shall refuse to get married, for your sake.
MAMAEVA: Really?
GLUMOV: Honest to God.
MAMAEVA: You are a hero. That's really noble.
GLUMOV: I'm a knight.
MAMAEVA: A viscount.
GLUMOV: A marquis.
MAMAEVA: A hidalgo.
GLUMOV: A prince. A great ruler, descended from Rurik, founder of Russia. All this I lay at your feet. There's just one condition. I'll scupper the marriage myself. If you start interfering, it'll be the worse for you. (*Aside*) I think I've talked the old bag round.
MAMAEVA (*aside*): He's lying, that's for sure.
(*The door bell rings. Glumov goes to answer it. Golutvin enters through the window. He wears a black mask.*)
GOLUTVIN: Here I am. Come on out with you, Cleopatra Lvovna.
MAMAEVA: Aihh, who are you?
GOLUTVIN: It's me, me.
MAMAEVA: Name?
GOLUTVIN: Golutvin.
MAMAEVA: First name, middle name, single or married, occupation, are you in the armed forces, what's the number of your labour permit?
GOLUTVIN: Golutvin, no other information's necessary.
MAMAEVA: Why are you here?
GOLUTVIN: He ...
MAMAEVA: Well?
GOLUTVIN: ... is decei ...
MAMAEVA: Yes?

GOLUTVIN: ... ing you.
MAMAEVA: Your proof?
GOLUTVIN: His diary.
MAMAEVA: Where is it?
GOLUTVIN: Underneath you.
MAMAEVA: Ah yes!
GOLUTVIN: Revenge! Steal it and publish it.
MAMAEVA: Distract his attention for three minutes forty-six seconds. I must check.
GOLUTVIN: Very well. Here he comes.
 (*Glumov returns.*)
GLUMOV: That's very strange. The bell rang, but there's nobody at the door. Only a dog. But dogs can't ring bells.
GOLUTVIN (*hiccoughs*): Hic!
GLUMOV: You – here again. So it was you who rang the bell? Another trick?
GOLUTVIN: Suppose it was?
GLUMOV: What do you want?
GOLUTVIN: Three minutes conversation.
GLUMOV: My ears are at your service.
MAMAEVA: And what's written here? About my husband. Well, well, well, he deserved it, the old ass. His bride – that's me – she's 'a little minx'. And as for me ... 'an over-ripe strumpet.' Oh, I feel sick. Hold me, I'm falling.
MAMAEV (*entering*): Clepa, I'm here.
MAMAEVA: That base, mean man. Steal it and get it published.
GOLUTVIN: And then?
MAMAEV: Glumov will be exposed. Thanks to you.
GOLUTVIN: I'm at your service.
MAMAEV: That'll smash him.
GOLUTVIN: Completely. ... Do me a favour, send my top hat after me.
MAMAEV: Okay.
 (*Mamaev and Mamaeva hurry off, bumping into Turusina on their way.*)
GLUMOV (*grabs Turusina*): Where am I? In a dream? Drunk? Hypnotised? Captive?
ACTRESS WHO PLAYS TURUSINA: Excuse me, my name is ---. (*She gives her own name and hurries away.*)

GLUMOV (*calls after her*): Cleopatra Lvovna's disappeared. And my diary ... (*Golutvin hiccoughs.*) Give it back, you swine! (*Golutvin hiccoughs again.*) Come on, comrade.
GOLUTVIN: Mum is writing her memoirs. Dad is writing his dadoirs. But this man is writing ...
GLUMOV: Give me my diary!
(*Golutvin grabs his top hat and runs out, leaving Glumov alone.*)

EPILOGUE

Glumov alone.

GLUMOV: The swine, he's run off. He'll publish my diary. I'll have to be quick with the marriage, quick with the marriage. It's my only hope. (*Enter Manefa.*) You can be the priest. Move! Get yourself a censer. Fire off some prayers. (*Exit Manefa.*) I've got to get spliced before the papers come out.

(*Glumov runs out as the lights go down. A film is projected showing Golutvin escaping with Glumov's diary. He jumps from a car, rushes into a building, climbs out of a second floor window and scrambles to a parapet. From there he ascends to the top of a tower. He hangs his top hat on a pinnacle and beckons urgently, apparently into the sky. Glumov peers out of the second floor window, sees the hat, then an aeroplane, which has taken Golutvin off. Glumov is mystified. Then, a crowd of people is seen peering into the sky, an open top car arrives, and someone jumps from a passing aeroplane into the car – it is Golutvin. The car races away. Stage lights come up again. Enter Mashenka, dressed as a racing driver but in a bridal veil, followed by the three rejected suitors, the hussar, Kurchaev.*)

KURCHAEV: So you're going to marry Glumov?

MASHENKA: Yes.

(*They perform a 'separation' routine, and Mashenka sings a melancholy song, 'Marusya, your fingers, Marusya', accompanied by xylophone effects created on the hussars bell-like uniform buttons. Glumov reappears. Mashenka rushes into his arms.*)

KURCHAEV: But you're in such a hurry. This isn't 'going' to get married, it's 'rushing' to it.

(*Kurchaev departs. Enter Gorodulin, juggling.*)

GORODULIN: *Bon jour.*

GLUMOV: What do you want?
GORODULIN: A cheque for a hundred pounds for the wedding.
GLUMOV: Afterwards.
(*Enter Joffre, tumbling.*)
JOFFRE: *Salut.* A cheque for the organisation of the wedding celebrations.
GLUMOV: Afterwards, afterwards.
(*Enter Mamaev, acrobatically.*)
MAMAEV: Best of luck, (*He holds out his hand.*)
GLUMOV: Another cheque? After the ceremony, please. Ah, here she comes. (*Enter Mamaeva as a circus bareback equestrienne and with a ringmaster's whip, with the three actors of Kurchaev. Music. She comforts the three rejected suitors.*) Luckily I've managed to hoodwink aunt, so she's not only agreed to our getting married, but she's even come to the wedding, unless she's being thoroughly artful. Oh, that diary, I'm so worried about it. (*He sits, looking depressed.*)
MAMAEVA: Where are you going?
KURCHAEV: Home.
MAMAEVA: Home? You look upset. Wait. Maybe you won't have to go. Why don't you say anything? You're in love, I know. And she loves you. I'm sure she loves you. ... Don't lose hope. All sorts of surprises happen in life, ha ha ha.
KURCHAEV: You laughing cheers me up.
MAMAEVA: Why?
KURCHAEV: Cause it reminds me of a horse.
MAMAEVA: Fooey.
KURCHAEV: No, not fooey – foo-oo-oo-ey!
(*She cracks the whip, and the three 'perform' in the ring – two as horses, one as the rider. At the end of the 'turn', Manefa returns with a censer.*)
MANEFA: Oh Lord, we beseech thee ...
MAMAEVA: Coooee!
(*All gather round. The marriage ceremony begins. All sing: The priest had a dog.*[66] *Manefa performs a circus turn as a dog. Then the voice*

---

[66] *The priest had a dog*: An endless song, similar to the English: 'A dog came in the kitchen and stole a crust of bread; Then Cook up with her ladle and beat him till he was dead. Then all the dogs came running and dug the dog a tomb, And

of a newspaper boy is heard: 'Glumov leaving Paris! Glumov leaving Paris!' Glumov runs out.)

MAMAEVA: What's that?

GOLUTVIN (*enters, still masked*): Here you are. The evening paper. Special edition. *The Evening Swindler.*

MAMAEVA: Read it out.

GOLUTVIN: 'Sensation!' Listen to this. 'Two thousand times a philanderer. The diary of – a bridegroom.'

ALL: A diary? Shame on him. Scoundrel. Swine. Lout. Shame. Disgrace. (*The lights dim, the second film sequence begins. 'Glumov's Diary'. In a series of sequences, each using trick photography, the truth about each character as Glumov sees it, is revealed. The first shot is of the diary itself – a film being wound. Then, Turusina is seen. Glumov approaches her, bows, then – to please her – turns into a card house, which she kisses. Joffre stands grimly on a tank. Glumov approaches, and obligingly turns into a big cannon. Joffre is delighted. Gorodulin leans against a wall, smoking contemptuously. Glumov bows to him, then turns into a large swastika which Gorodulin spins round and dances with. Next, Mamaeva is seen on a flight of steps. Glumov exaggeratedly offers her his heart, but it is only when he is transformed into a baby that Mamaeva approaches and picks him up. Mamaev is standing on a park bench when Glumov approaches and, with a forward roll, turns into a donkey. This is just what Mamaev wants. He embraces the animal's neck, and pulls its tail, which he also kisses. Finally, Glumov is seen walking down what appear to be church steps, his pipe-smoking bride on his arm. A cross is held over them. Glumov can hardly conceal his laughter. But when Mamaev, Joffre and Gorodulin approach together with their palms outstretched for money, Glumov rejects them with a rude gesture. The film is unwound. The director takes his bow. The film is over and the stage lights go up again.*)

MANEFA: The marriage will be finished with Kurchaev as the groom. Because of the large number of bridegrooms, a mullah will conduct the service.

---

wrote upon the tombstone for the eyes of dogs to come: A dog came in the kitchen ... etc.

(*Four Stage Hands carry in a mullah on a board. He blesses the couple(s), sings 'Allah Verdi'.*[67] *Then he springs off the board to perform a Cossack dance, after which he holds up the board for the audience to see. On it is written: 'Religion is the opium of the people.' Everyone joins in a dance. Then Mashenka and the three grooms are packed into a large box, and pots are smashed against it in a parody of the ancient marriage ritual, while Gorodulin, Mamaev and Joffre sing: 'Who here is young, who here's not wed?' They are interrupted by Glumov running in, clutching a newspaper.*)

GLUMOV: Hurray, there's nothing in the paper.

ALL (*mocking Glumov*): Tally-ho! View halloo! Woof, woof, woof! Yap-yap-yap! Get out!

(*They go, leaving Glumov alone.*)

GLUMOV: So it's out! Suddenly all my limbs have turned to jelly. So much energy, so much money, laid out – all in vain. There's only one thing left: repentance. A rope. Give me that rope.

(*A rope is lowered from the ceiling.*)

STAGE HAND: You'll break it.

GLUMOV: I won't break it.

(*GLUMOV fixes angel wings to his shoulder blades, attaches himself to the rope, takes a lighted candle from a Stage Hand, and is raised towards the ceiling.*[68])

FIRST STAGE HAND: A dog's death for a dog. Give him the rope.

SECOND STAGE HAND: The sailor is sailing on his last voyage.

(*Song: 'At midnight an Angel flew across the heavens.' Enter Golutvin. Glumov sees him.*)

GLUMOV: I'll show you, you trouble-maker ... get out of the way. (*He descends.*)

GOLUTVIN: Shut up, baby.

GLUMOV: Are you calling me a baby? Hey, comrade, help me out of this noose. (*Stage Hand helps him. To Gorodulin*) Now – defend yourself. You'll be unmasked ... (*A sword fight. Glumov knocks Gorodulin down and tears a large label off his trousers. On it*

---

67   *Allah Verdi*: A parody of a Georgian Islamic chant, with overtones of Guiseppe Verdi. But there is also a pun in the stage direction: the song is to be sung 'à la Verdi'.

68   *The ceiling*: This scene is a parody of the Ascension.

is written: 'NEP'. Melodramatically throwing open his arms, welcoming him)

So – you're a Nepman!⁶⁹ Is that your game?

FIRST STAGE HAND: It's this –

(*He sings*)   I'm a market speculator,
I broke stocks and shares as well.
Even my wife and all her diamonds
For a trillion I will sell.

(*Spoken*) NEP will be vitally necessary for a long time yet, quoth someone or other.

(*Sung*)   All we need is just one day,
And we'll get to work on that.
Come to the RSFSR,
Brothers, come and start on that.

We'll be standing shoulder to shoulder,
No-one ever could be bolder.
We're the vanguard, we're ahead,
That's the way we'll smash the Red!

(*During the song, Golutvin and Glumov dance together. The Red Clown joins them.*)

SECOND STAGE HAND: And the Cheka?⁷⁰

GOLUTVIN: If the Trust doesn't betray us, the Cheka won't be any trouble. (*To Glumov*) You're obviously a fine swindler. Come and be my apprentice. You'll strut across Kuznetsky Most and everyone'll goggle.

---

69   *NEP, Nepman:* N.E.P. was Lenin's 'New Economic Policy', promulgated in March 1921; a Nepman was one who profited from its apparent step back from Communism. That Golutvin is a Nepman is a major revelation, and is played in high melodramatic style.

70   *Cheka:* Soviet Security Force – the secret police, founded in 1918, replaced by OGPU in 1922. (See note 27 above.)

GLUMOV: I don't want to be a Gogol,⁷¹ I'd rather be an Alexei Tolstoy.⁷²
All the same, I agree. We'll be allies. Maestro, let's go.
RED CLOWN: I'll go and pack my things. (*Exit.*)
GLUMOV: Well, back to Russia then. (*Golutvin ascends the tightrope and walks on it over the heads of the audience back to 'Russia'. Glumov tries to walk the tightrope, but his courage fails him.*) Oi-oo, this is a bit tricky. I'd better go round the back way. (*Exit.*)
RED CLOWN (*returns, sees the stage is empty, bursts into noisy tears*): Everybody's gone. But they've forgotten somebody.⁷³ Everybody's gone. But they've forgotten somebody. Everybody's gone. But they've forgotten somebody ... And I – and I – (*He is making a sound like a donkey: 'Ee-ore! Ee-ore!'*)
GRIGORY (*enters down the tightrope, hanging on by his teeth*): Here's the fool. And what a fool! You'll have to stay here.
RED CLOWN: You'll stay, too, then. I feel better with someone to boss me about.
GRIGORY: And I do, too. Doesn't Kuznetsky Most lead straight to the Lubyanka?⁷⁴
RED CLOWN: You know, with your masters, time'll soon be ...
GRIGORY: Soon be what?
RED CLOWN: Up! (*He throws a bucket of water over Grigory, who falls over in surprise. Then he turns to the audience*) The end!
(*He bows. At this moment fireworks explode under the seats of the spectators.*)

---

71   *Gogol*: Nikolai Vasilievich Gogol, one of the greatest of all Russian writers, best known for his play, *The Government Inspector*. The pun on 'goggle' is not as effective as Tretyakov's original: a 'gogol' in Russian is a tufted duck. Golutvin therefore actually says, 'You'll strut across Kuznetsky Most like a tufted duck.' Glumov replies, 'I don't want to be a Gogol, I want to be an Alexei Tolstoy.'
72   *Alexei Tolstoy*: A prolific author, a 'smenovekhovets' (see note 41 above) at the time *A Wise Man* was written, though afterwards he returned to the USSR and died laden with honours from Stalin.
73   *'Everybody's gone. But they've forgotten somebody'*: Quotation from Firs's last speech in *The Cherry Orchard* by Anton Chekhov.
74   *Lubyanka*: The headquarters of the secret police.

Are You Listening, Moscow?!
(*Slyshish', Moskva?!*)

(1923)

Agit-guignol

Translated by Robert Leach

Are You Listening, Moscow?!,
Act 1: Marga and the Count, left, with Kurt
and the National militia men, right.

Are You Listening, Moscow?!

Characters

Count Stal, governor of the province, landowner and factory owner
Prefect of the Police, a Fascist
Furts, leader of the Yellow Socialists
Bishop
Mr Pound, representative of the American banks
Marga, a courtesan   )
Grabbe, a poet   ) spongers on the Count
Grubbe, an artist   )
Shtumm, an *agent provocateur*
Kurt, secretary of the strikers' group
Hugo, his brother
Fred, an artist
Hubert, an actor
Tsorn, a metal worker
Elli, a textile worker
Dick, a coal miner
Guard of the National Militia
Second Guard
Other National Militia Guards
Detective
Workers

Germany, 1923

The action takes place in the square in front of the cathedral wall. The centre of the square is cordoned off by a barrier. On the left is a platform for the official party. On the right, a speakers' platform. In front of the wall, scaffolding has been erected, above which is a *bas-relief,* curtained from view.

First performed by the First Workers Theatre of the Proletkult, Moscow, on 7 November 1923, under the direction of Sergei Eisenstein.

ACT ONE

Bishop, Prefect, Furts.

BISHOP: The elections to the town council have gone brilliantly, praise the Lord! I've been celebrating a thanksgiving mass with special feeling today.
PREFECT: I wouldn't be Prefect of Police if I couldn't make sure of that. I swear by the imperial crown that our socialists are good patriots and they're supported in this by their leader, Mr Furts.
FURTS: I agree. By all that's holy, the citizens understand where the promises of those good-for-nothing Communists come from.
BISHOP: Yes, the Lord's hand was upon you when you broke up their dreams of a united front so decisively.
PREFECT: How could there be a united front with people who betray the national interest and want to demolish our industries?
POUND (*who has entered unnoticed, and now pushes himself into the conversation*): And just at the very moment when Wall Street has promised finance for the local steelworks. What a how-d'you-do. It's good to hear intelligent talk. You're a socialist, you know better than I do – without industry, socialism's not possible.
FURTS: Industry without industrialists –
POUND: I don't think we're acquainted.
PREFECT: Prefect of Police.
FURTS: Mr Pound, our guest. Representative of the Ferrous Bank.
PREFECT: Well, I don't know! Very pleased to meet you.
BISHOP (*to Pound*): You've been inspecting the Count's factories, haven't you? Isn't it the wisdom of the Lord to unite in one worthy personage landowner, manufacturer …
PREFECT: And governor.
FURTS: What did you make of the elections?

POUND: It seemed to me this place started to get sensible. And if this took root –

PREFECT: I should say! When the socialists refused to join the alliance, the whole thing began to come unstuck.

POUND: Not gaining any ground?

PREFECT: I should say! Thank God, no, and it's not the first time I've been in charge of an election. For anyone wanting to make mischief, I have some excellent, quiet, comfy and utterly isolated sanatoria. They feel as secure there as if they had a current account with the Ferrous Bank.

POUND: Ha ha!

BISHOP: They'll accrue interest and help to shore up the nation.

FURTS: Things can't work out without something like that. Otherwise there wouldn't be peaceable and fair elections. Their demagogy ...

POUND: And you're not worried about November the seventh?[75]

FURTS: Excuse me, but what do the affairs of loyal workers have to do with meddlers from Moscow?

POUND: And those who aren't loyal?

PREFECT: With respect, I've already told you.

POUND: Sorry! You've taken care of the ringleaders, a small group, but what about the rest? And actually, what about the whole mass of workers? You know there's a lot of discontent, there are problems with food supplies, poverty's growing, the unions are having an effect.

BISHOP: This'll all stop when capital begins to flow in, and industry revives.

POUND: But capital isn't going to flow into somewhere that's not stable.

PREFECT: Please don't worry about that. I swear on my honour there won't be any demonstrations.

POUND: You're certain of that?

PREFECT: Damn my eyes. All sorts of things might fall apart, but we'll stand firm as a rock.

POUND: But where are your guarantees? What are the facts? We Americans love facts.

---

75 *November the seventh*: The anniversary of the Bolshevik seizure of power in Russia.

BISHOP: Their papers have been closed down. Hundreds of workers have been laid off. What more do you want?

FURTS: There won't be any speeches. I answer for the workers.

PREFECT: That's the first thing, but for a second, our governor, Count Stal, has devised a brilliant way of providing bread and circuses.

BISHOP: But I suppose it should be, first, the circus, and then the bread. (*To Pound*) That'll be your department.

PREFECT: I can't say about that. His Excellency will say what he wants. We're waiting for him. And here he is. All correct, sir!

(*Enter Count, Marga, Grubbe and Grabbe.*)

COUNT: Greetings! Mr Pound! I'm delighted! Meet my lady friend, the fascinating Marga. Grubbe, an artist. Grabbe, a poet.

GRUBBE (*to Marga*): What an amazing place! The effect of the skyline – only your eyes can match it for purity.

GRABBE: We'll place the platform here. It'll be like in a tournament, and I'll be your humble troubadour, I'll sing verses in honour of the rose, climbing around its dried-up thorns.

MARGA: How do you know they're dried up? That's not very nice.

GRUBBE: This place couldn't be better. Over here – the Count's palace. Over there – the Count's factory chimneys. Here are the Count's coal mines. And you see the scaffolding on the cathedral wall? That's where my *bas-relief* of the Iron Count will be mounted.

MARGA: Shh! He'll do you if you blab about it before it's time.

COUNT: So what about the 'Iron Count'? Eh?

BISHOP: We're impatient to know what your Excellency has decided for everyone's happiness.

COUNT: Eh? Yes! It's an idea designed for the public good. It's the Prefect of Police's idea – amazingly clever.

PREFECT: Oh, your Excellency! It was entirely your idea. I only endorsed it.

COUNT: Eh? Yes! Of course, everyone endorsed it. They endorsed something amazingly clever. The point is that the first Count Stal, my forebear, conquered this region in the eighteenth century. He subdued the heathen inhabitants, set them to work, and converted them to Christianity ...

BISHOP: Yes, yes. He was almost a saint. Like an apostle.

COUNT: Uh-huh, not quite. Particularly if his ingenious method of improving the pedigree of the local barbarians is taken into account: the first child of the best women all had the blood of Count Stal in their veins.

MARGA: So all the local people are your cousins? How moving!

COUNT: Marga, don't start moving.

GRABBE: Oh! A charming pun!

GRUBBE: Delightfully witty!

COUNT: Some of the barbarians retreated to the hills and lived wild in the backwoods, in poverty and bitterness. The Count tried to get them to come back. He showed them the comfortable, cultured life of their subdued brothers, but they ... well, the Count's triumph was ... they laid down their arms and became loyal subjects.

GRUBBE: And they didn't rise up against the Count's rule?

COUNT: No, they submitted – never, right up to today.

BISHOP: It's obvious. I mean, did they have communist agitators then?

PREFECT: And they won't have them now, damn them.

COUNT: That's why we decided with the Prefect of Police – that is, I decided – to erect a memorial to my forebear who civilized this region. An amazing *bas-relief* created by our very own Michelangelo.

GRUBBE: Your Excellency, it's such an honour.

COUNT: And a theatrical pageant is going to be made out of the superlative patriotic ballad of our very own Shakespeare.

GRABBE: You are altogether too kind to us, your Excellency;

COUNT: A little simple entertainment. And then – beer, sandwiches ...

PREFECT: ... a strong heartfelt gesture ...

COUNT: And the upshot – I hit the bull's eye.

BISHOP: But first, we immortalise the memory of our national hero.

FURTS: And that'll encourage the working people's patriotic feelings.

COUNT: And it'll happen on no other day than – the seventh of November.

FURTS: Fuck Moscow, ha ha ha! Brilliant tactics!

MARGA: You're a dear, you're a charmer, an absolute puppy-dog.

POUND: But what was the first Count called?

COUNT: The Iron Count. Eh? Not bad?

GRABBE: Because of his superb physical strength ...

GRUBBE: ... which has been so impressively inherited by his Excellency.

COUNT: Huh. Eh? Yes. (*He rolls up his sleeves.*) Not bad muscles, eh? Fencing, hunting ...

MARGA: ... canoodling.
COUNT: In my younger day, when I grabbed somebody like that, he couldn't breathe.
BISHOP: I think even now you –
COUNT: Yes, why not? A spot of gout, but apart from that ...
MARGA: Tie my bootlace.
> (*They all throw themselves at her feet. The Count, wheezing, with difficulty, finally gets to his knees.*)

VOICES: – What!
– Marble!
– A goddess!
POUND: In a New York music hall she could make a load of money.
MARGA (*squealing and giggling*): Don't tickle! Whose are those whiskers? Count, stand up! Oh yes, the Iron Count! (*Picking him up.*) Thank me!
> (*The* agent provocateur, Shtumm, *heavily made up, enters to the Prefect. His hand shakes convulsively. He speaks conspiratorially.*)

PREFECT: Something wrong?
SHTUMM: In the gaol. They're planning to spring Tsorn this evening.
PREFECT: Okay. We'll put a stop to that. And the seventh of November – they planning anything for that?
SHTUMM: Yes.
PREFECT: A demonstration?
SHTUMM: No.
PREFECT: What then?
SHTUMM: I don't really know. There's a meeting in an hour.
PREFECT: Where?
SHTUMM: Here.
PREFECT: Seize them?
SHTUMM: Not before I know everything.
> (*Kurt walks by.*)

MARGA: Look at this handsome fellow! What pectorals – and his eyes! He's a real Iron Count!
COUNT: Marga, don't be crude!
MARGA: Get lost! Hey, laddie, laddie! Young man!
PREFECT: Ignoramus! The lady's speaking to you.
KURT: Did you want something?
MARGA: You're looking very down.

KURT: Excuse me, I'm busy.
GRUBBE: My dear fellow, it's not possible to be busy here. To be going about business in the presence of the governor and this beautiful lady.
GRABBE: Or are you dreaming about the sandwiches on the seventh of November?
(*Laughter.*)
MARGA: If you're a true gentleman, I want ...
KURT: Can I do something for you?
MARGA: I want, I want ... What do I want? I want you to kiss me here.
(*She indicates her leg.*)
KURT: Not a very seemly idea.
MARGA: But I want you to.
(*Kurt starts to move on.*)
GRUBBE: We won't let you go.
GRABBE: The lady's wish is law.
PREFECT: Honestly, it's a royal command.
MARGA: But why? They say my legs are very beautiful. How can you possibly not want to? It's not possible.
PREFECT: Kiss it, or else ...
GRABBE: You're acting like some communist swine.
KURT (*Spitting on Marga's leg*): Here! Bitch!
MARGA: Ahh, grab him, grab him. Give me a whip! One! One! One!
(*She beats him.*)
(*Prefect blows his whistle. National militia men run in.*)
PREFECT: Catch him!
MARGA: Louse! Bastard! Idiot!
PREFECT (*pinning Marga's arms*): Sorry, but we'll have to answer for this, he'll remember this.
COUNT: To gaol with him! Thrash him! To the cells!
KURT: Hangman! (*Kurt turns his eyes on Shtumm at the very moment when his arm starts convulsing.*) Impossible!
PREFECT: Get a move on!
(*Kurt is taken away.*)
COUNT: Margaritochka, Margaritochka. (*She is carried away by Grubbe, Grabbe and Pound. To the Prefect*) Thrash that bucket of shit! Have him tortured!
FURTS: But that might provoke questions in the Parliament.

PREFECT: That's true. But don't fret, they won't know.
COUNT (*to the Prefect*): My friend, take all steps necessary to make sure the festival goes off peacefully, first because of the American banks, but also because it's my family's traditional holiday.
PREFECT: I shall discharge my duties, your Excellency.
COUNT: I know how to reward you. (*He goes out.*)
SHTUMM: D'you know who he is?
PREFECT: No.
SHTUMM: He's the secretary of the strike committee.
PREFECT: Aha! So much the worse for him.
SHTUMM: But I'm worried that he recognized me. For God's sake, don't let him out of gaol. For God's sake, or else … (*Worried he takes the Prefect's hand.*)
PREFECT: I understand. (*He goes out.*)
SHTUMM: Well, perhaps he didn't recognize me. To hell with it! (*He goes out, whistling.*)

ACT TWO

Hugo enters, and Dick appears with a sack.

HUGO: What you got there, Dick?
DICK: I've got hold of some potatoes. The kids haven't eaten for two days.
HUGO: It's not much.
DICK: The sack's big, but the spuds ... Those swine are giving us longer hours in the mine again.
HUGO: And the workers?
DICK: Grumbling, but scared.
HUGO: Still scared?
DICK: Sure are. Of losing their jobs, their bread.
FRED (*runs in*): The Socialists are over the moon. They've got a landslide in the elections.
HUGO: Whatever the cost – fraudulent promises and ... the gaols bursting with communists.
DICK: Who voted for them? The bosses and anyone who listened to them. The workers didn't vote.
FRED: Why?
DICK: Gave it up as a bad job. Empty bellies, no fight.
FRED: So there's no hope of waving Moscow's red flag on November the seventh?
DICK: Their backs are still sore from the Fascists' rubber truncheons. They're still digesting the meaning of our burned-out social clubs.
HUBERT (*enters*): Hugo, your brother's been nabbed.
DICK: Kurt?
HUGO: Impossible.
HUBERT: I was with the actors on the stage, and I saw it. He was beaten up.
HUGO (*distraught*): Kurt!

HUBERT: What about Tsorn? Did he get away?

HUGO: Don't know. Elli hasn't arrived yet. One after another, one after another.

DICK: They're clever!

FRED: Maybe someone's ratting on us?

HUGO: What do you mean? Who?

DICK: I've already said that. If you ask me …

HUGO: Stop it! I know. It's impossible. Someone who's been with us for five years, who had his ear cut off when he was in gaol, wouldn't betray us.

SHTUMM (*enters*): Hi, comrades. Is Elli here?

HUGO: No. But Kurt's been arrested.

SHTUMM: What? Really? They'll let him go, probably. Definitely. Did he have his documents with him?

HUGO: That's the problem, he did.

SHTUMM: Where?

HUGO: Concealed in a cigarette, which …

DICK (*interrupting*): Enough blabbing! What about the seventh of November demonstration?

SHTUMM: No-one can come out.

HUBERT: Why not?

SHTUMM: You can see the scaffolding. Evidently on the day they're going to unveil a memorial to the Iron Count, with refreshments handed out to the common people.

DICK: Bloody hell! The devils!

SHTUMM: It'd wreck any demonstration. It's cleverly thought up. Seems to me the idea's hopeless. It'd be better to concentrate on propaganda and come out later – and not with demonstrations but in elections.

HUGO: Not possible. The workers have had enough. They've crushed them, they're going back to being serfs. But the bourgeois bastards are forming special national squads. The Fascists are getting above themselves. But the local districts won't go into action without our say-so. We're the central industrial district. If there's nothing from us, the revolution'll take a long time. We need to make it clear that we're not asleep. Otherwise the workers'll lose faith in communism.

SHTUMM: It still seems hopeless.

DICK: Doesn't matter. If we fail, we fail.
HUGO: It won't work. The militia's too strong. The workers have hardly got any weapons. There aren't enough of them to make any show. We need something else.
SHTUMM: But what else can we think of?
HUGO: Hang on! Hang on! It seems there's only one way. Fred! Hugo! Are there any artists or actors who're with us?
FRED: We can get some.
(*They whisper together. Shtumm edges towards them.*)
HUGO (*turning round quickly*): D'you want something?
SHTUMM: Can I get a light?
DICK: You're already smoking.
SHTUMM: Oh yes! Sorry.
HUGO (*to Fred and Hubert*): Got it? It's risky, but it's our last chance. But be careful. Hubert, the performers have guns, don't they?
HUBERT: In the performance – but they're only stage guns.
HUGO: Swap them, and have them loaded!
FRED: Okay then – at dawn?
(*Elli runs in.*)
HUGO: Elli! What's up?
ELLI: Tsorn – dead. And Kurt.
HUGO: Hugo, hold on! Hugo!
SHTUMM: Bastards! When will this end?
DICK: How did you find out?
ELLI: A *provocateur's* work.
DICK: How did you find out?
ELLI: A *provocateur*, but who is it?
SHTUMM: How do we know they were killed?
ELLI: Comrades, Kurt had time to hand over an envelope with his last note in it. There – the name's in it.
DICK: Who is it? Read it.
ELLI: I can't, it's too hard. Shtumm, you read it.
SHTUMM: Me?
DICK: Quick!
(*Shtumm takes a piece of paper out of the envelope, but doesn't have the strength to open it.*)
SHTUMM: I ca ... ca ... I can't, can't urr ...
ALL: Shtumm!

SHTUMM: Ur ... rrr ...
HUGO: What?
ALL: Death!
HUGO (*makes a sign to Dick who moves behind Shtumm*): Dick.
SHTUMM: No ...
    (*Dick stabs him with a knife. Enter Tsorn and Kurt.*)
FRED: What?
HUGO: I'm going out of my mind!
ELLI: The comrades are alive, saved!
HUGO (*to Kurt*): How come you're here?
KURT: When he escaped from the gaol, there was such a hullaballoo that I didn't stand around to think things over. They only managed to pull out two of my finger nails.
HUGO: Why didn't you say that immediately?
TSORN: We needed to unmask him first.
KURT: I thought it was him, but I wasn't sure.
HUGO: And the note?
ELLI: It was a blank sheet.
DICK: He didn't dare open it.
TSORN: So we go ahead?
HUGO: We do.
KURT: How many people?
FRED: The whole town.
TSORN: Instructions?
HUGO: There'll be hundreds of workers taking the day off. As far as possible, arm them. The rest's taken care of. Let's beat it now, I'll tell you what's what as we go.
DICK (*points at Shtumm's body*): And this?
HUGO: We can't leave him. It'll give us away. Where shall we put him?
ELLI: In that sack.
DICK (*emptying out the potatoes*): Put 'em in your pockets. For the kids, you know. (*Heaving Shtumm's body in.*) In you go, carrion.
HUGO: Kurt! The day after tomorrow's the seventh. Dawn – be here, with Hubert.
FRED: Elli, get it? When this hand shoots ...
ELLI: Shall I make the banner in honour of Moscow?
HUGO: Yes, make it!
    (*Elli goes out.*)

FRED (*coming back*): Hugo!
HUGO: Has something happened?
FRED: No. When you see Dick, tell him I'll need him to help me. I can't manage to carry the portrait by myself.
HUGO: Okay. Let's go. (*They exit.*)

ACT THREE

Daybreak. A few men are busying themselves on the scaffolding. A Guard stands by. Enter Fred and Dick with a long bundle.

GUARD: Password?
FRED: Iron Count.
GUARD: Reply?
FRED: The Ferrous Bank.
GUARD: Who are you?
FRED: One of us. Painter for the scaffolding.
GUARD: What's that?
FRED: Canvas bag – it's got the covering for the monument.
GUARD: It's too heavy for that.
FRED: Don't you believe it – look!
GUARD: Not explosives?
FRED: Have a look.
GUARD (*prods at the bundle with his bayonet*): Proceed!
DICK: Why didn't I grab him by the throat?
FRED: Shh!
DICK: The dog. Dared to touch it with a bayonet, he did.
SECOND GUARD (*entering*): Everything okay?
FIRST GUARD: Yep.
SECOND GUARD: Nothing suspicious going on?
FIRST GUARD: Such as?
SECOND GUARD: The Communists don't sleep. We've got to be ready for any dirty tricks. The Prefect's been out and about for two nights running.
FIRST GUARD: What for?
SECOND GUARD: Communications broke down. Our agent didn't return.

FIRST GUARD: Rubbish. What can they do? Tossers! I must confess I'd really like the Communists to try something. I'd tickle their kissers with my whip. Who's there?
  (*Enter Hubert, Hugo and Kurt with armfuls of rifles and a box of ammunition.*)
HUBERT: Here's our permit.
FIRST GUARD: What've you got there?
HUBERT: Ammunition for the stage muskets.
SECOND GUARD: Who're they for?
FIRST GUARD: Have you got authorisation?
HUBERT: Yes.
FIRST GUARD: Proceed!
  (*They move away.*)
HUBERT: Put down the guns and load them.
  (*Second Guard approaches, watches.*)
SECOND GUARD: They're not real cartridges, are they?
HUGO: Blanks.
SECOND GUARD: Hang on, hang on. Show 'em here.
KURT: So, according to you, blanks can kill someone? Show him what sort of ammo it is! Go on, shoot!
HUGO: Who at?
KURT: Me!
SECOND GUARD: No joking! Come on! (*He reaches for the rifle stock.*)
KURT: Now! (*Hugo fires at Kurt, who clutches himself with his hands to cover the hole in his jacket.*) See? Only, hell, my jacket's got singed.
SECOND GUARD: Okay. You're no sort of coward. Did you smell gunpowder? Eh?
KURT (*weakly*): Smelt nothing.
SECOND GUARD (*looking hard into Kurt's face*): You look pale as a sheet. A shot rabbit.
  (*He goes out.*)
HUGO: Kurt, what have you done?
KURT: Shh! I had to do it. While I'm still conscious, take me away as if I'd been drinking. You can't carry me, they'll pester you and you'll give us away.
FIRST GUARD (*hurries in*): Who was firing?
HUBERT: A cartridge fell out, they gave us rubbish cartridges.

FIRST GUARD: Listen, no kidding, you idiots, buggers. (*He slips on the blood.*) What's that?
HUBERT: Someone spilled the paint.
FIRST GUARD: You could fall smack on your face in this.
HUBERT: He slipped.
FIRST GUARD: Drunk?
HUBERT: What a sin! Drinking on a holiday!
FIRST GUARD: To hell with drunks in this place on a holiday. (*To Kurt*) Oy, you, scum, this isn't a doss-house.
HUBERT (*pretending to be annoyed*): Yes, off you go, lads! Get some sleep! It's disgusting! Do something useful!
HUGO (*pretending to be drunk, and helping Kurt*): Come on, you devil. Eh, Kurt, this is no place, let's beat it, I've still got some tick at the pub.
FIRST GUARD: Get a move on! (*Threatening Kurt with his whip.*)
KURT: It's the whip again.
HUGO (*singing*): Where is honey and beer so tasty?
　　At the table of the Iron Count.
　　Where do young girls weep hot tears?
　　In the bedroom of the Iron Count.
　　Where do roses flower in springtime?
　　In the orchard of the Iron Count.
　　Where does the horsewhip sing on your shoulders?
　　In the stable of the Iron Count.
　　(*Speaks*) Kurt, what have you done?
KURT: Hugo, my belly, ah, my belly! It's over. To Moscow – greetings! (*Hugo lifts Kurt up on his back, and goes out.*)
GRUBBE (*entering to the scaffolding*): Everything ready?
VOICES: All ready!
GRUBBE: Take away the scaffolding! Off with the workers from the square!
FIRST GUARD: Clear the square!
　　(*The workers hurriedly disperse, taking planks and scaffolding poles with them.*)

ACT FOUR

The square prepared for the festival and crowded with ordinary people. At one side, the rostrum for the official party. In the centre, the bas-relief *hidden behind a curtain. A small rostrum for speakers.*

TSORN: Elli, you got the banner?
ELLI: Yes.
TSORN: Where's Hugo?
ELLI: Over there.
TSORN: He looks grey. I didn't recognize him. What about Kurt?
ELLI (*looking away*): Don't say anything to Hugo.
TSORN: Is he dead?
ELLI: Yes. Shh!
GUARD (*to Detective*): Have they found him?
DETECTIVE (*whispering*): Yes.
GUARD: How?
DETECTIVE: The sack of potatoes.
GUARD: He was followed carefully.
VOICES (*from where the spectators are standing*): – They say there'll be handouts.
– Cheese sandwiches.
– Hang on, they just feed us gibble-gabble.
– I've got kids here.
– The Socialists on the town council promised to put up the wages.
– But not necessarily straight away. Everything's difficult.
(*Dick appears.*)
DETECTIVE: That's him.
(*The Guard blows a whistle.*)
HUGO: Scram, Dick!
SECOND GUARD: Remember the sack!

THIRD GUARD: You won't get away.
>   (*They grab Dick.*)

A VOICE (*from the crowd*): Bastards! Dogs!

DETECTIVE: To the gaol!

FIRST GUARD: Take him! Pity – you won't get to see the festival.

SECOND GUARD: I won't? Rubbish, I'll be back again in five minutes. And meanwhile, put in your report, 'While trying to escape ...' (*To Dick*) March!

DICK: Comrades, don't say anything! Be seeing you!

SECOND GUARD (*hitting Dick's back with his rifle butt*): Silence!
>   (*Everyone falls silent, until the tension is broken by a distant shot. A shudder runs through the crowd. Then the orchestra plays a flourish. The procession of dignitaries enters, greeted by the Prefect.*)

PREFECT: Your Excellency, all is in order.

COUNT: Thank you.

GRABBE (*to Marga*): One kiss. You are the Queen of the Festival. Give the signal to begin with this handkerchief.

GRUBBE: Like in a tournament. With this handkerchief you indicate the opening of the festival.

BISHOP: Red?

MARGA: The colour of passion ...

A VOICE (*from the crowd*): Margarita-i-ta-i-ta-i-ta ...

MARGA: What a stench from this riffraff.

VOICES: – Well fed!
>   – They're like fatted calves!
>   – Could make chops for the kids.
>   – Look, that priest's got ... he's kissing her forepaws.
>   – That's it. I'm off to the pub.
>   – You can get pissed, but me ...
>   – They'll probably get pissed on champagne.

POUND (*indicating the* bas-relief): What's that sticking out there?

GRUBBE: The Count's helmet. And to the left, the hilt of his sword.

POUND: Made of plaster?

GRUBBE: You what? It's made of bronze.
>   (*Fanfares.*)

COUNT (*on the platform, to the Bishop*): Will you bless the Festival, your Holiness.

BISHOP: Blessings upon the people and their rulers on this auspicious day.
POUND (*to the Count*): Well then. Here's my present. A copy of my telegram.
COUNT (*reads*): 'New York. Ferrous Bank. I certify that peace reigns here. The Communists have been liquidated. I recommend financial investment. Pound.' (*Pressing Pound's hand.*) This is noble of you!
POUND: They're facts, simple facts.
COUNT: With some emotion, I declare open today's festival as a joyful celebration in honour of my ancestor, the first Count Stal, known as the Iron Count.
FURTS: By reason of this festival, the town council has decided to release from gaol two hundred offenders, petty criminals and lawbreakers.
A VOICE (*from the crowd*): What about the communists?
PREFECT: Who said that?
FIRST GUARD: Arrest him!
SECOND GUARD: Surround that group!
COUNT: Commence the proceedings!

(*Marga wafts the handkerchief. Grabbe appears, clad in the costume of the Iron Count and accompanied by actors – a detachment of soldiers and several priests. Facing them are performers as a group of primitive people with agricultural implements, clubs, hammers, javelins and sickles. As Grabbe declaims his text, these performers act out what he is describing.*)

GRABBE: There's confusion and grouching across the land of the primitives.
They have lived like a herd of wild beasts provocative.
But now there approaches along Time's veranda
What will bring to this land a miracle, a wonder.
'I am come now among you from the one God on High,
I am your Captain and leader hereby.
And I bring with me to you 'neath the sign of the cross
Five preachers of Christ's word to end your cha-os.'

VOICE (*from the crowd*): Anyone getting excited?
MARGA: Oh! Poetical enchantment!
BISHOP: Yes, thoroughly edifying!

(*In the pageant battle, the primitive people, as if by chance, cross a hammer and a sickle.*[76])

VOICES: – The hammer and sickle! Look, the hammer and sickle!
– It's the seventh of November!
– Remember Moscow!

GRABBE: And battle commenced. But God lent a hand,
And the infidel host was utterly unmanned.
A few cut and ran, fled away and decamped,
But the rest bowed their heads in submission to the Count.

VOICES: – Smashed!
– Bastards! Massacred!
– Run, lads, no surrender!
– Hide, while you can!
– Watch out for the lash!

GRABBE: And so the years passed, one after one.
The Count's land bore fruit, ton after ton.
And the hearts of the people, with no more palaver,
Made obeisance to the Count, his truth and his favour.

A VOICE: He takes us for fools!
COUNT: Very good!
FURTS: Bravo, bravo!
VOICES: – Get off your knees, slaves!
– Who are you working for?
– Kids are starving!
– We're starving without jobs.
– We do the work, and the National Militia get to eat.

GRABBE: But the Count was a noble and gracious patrician:
He urged the recalcitrants to come to his bosom.
'Lay down your arms! Come, seize this embrace!
See – your blood brothers await in this place!'

VOICES: – No surrender!
– Stand off!
– No, forward! Smash then!

COUNT: Why are they shouting?
MARGA: They're stopping me hearing.

---

[76] *The hammer and sickle*: the Soviet national emblem, signifying the union of industrial and agricultural workers.

BISHOP: What a mob.
POUND: Extraordinary indiscipline.
VOICES: – Don't hand back the guns!
    – They'll enslave you.
    – Throw you in gaol.
GRABBE: And lo! a miracle came to pass ...
    (*He has to outshout the voices of the crowd. Only some bits of the poem come through.*)
HUGO: Remember Moscow!
GRABBE: ... with weapons shining ...
VOICES: – The hammer and sickle!
    – Down with the traitors!
    – Lackeys, get that uniform off!
    – Oy, you, devil-bastard!
    – Keep a united front!
    (*The group of defeated primitive people in the pageant does not lay down its weapons, but joins the other group, and they all turn to take aim at the Count and the others on the platform.*)
COUNT: Why aren't they laying down their arms?
PREFECT: They're getting muddled.
VOICES: – The united front.
    – Get the Count!
COUNT: Quick, the monument!
GRABBE: ... to the everlasting glory of the Iron ...
    (*Marga waves the red handkerchief. The curtain in front of the bas-relief falls. But in place of a* bas-relief, *there is revealed a colossal portrait of Lenin.*)
BISHOP: Treachery!
    (*He seizes Grubbe by the throat. Furts hopelessly tries to cover the portrait with his arms. The Prefect blows his whistle urgently. The Count shakily takes aim with his revolver at the crowd.*)
COUNT: Shoot!
    (*His bullet hits Marga, seated by the barrier, in the back of the head.*)
THE CROWD (*together*): Lenin! Lenin!
HUGO: Fire! Forward!
    (*Shots are fired.*)
VOICES: – At the Fascists!
    – To the wall with the bourgeois!

– To the palace!
POUND: Hey! I'm a foreigner!
VOICES: – Squash that spider!
>(*Hugo, Tsorn and Elli are on one of the platforms. Elli hitches a red flag to a rifle.*)

HUGO: To the comrades!
VOICES: – Bread!
>– Work!
>– For the commune!

TSORN: To the arsenal!
ELLI: To the gaol!
>(*Flags are handed out, bearing the slogan: 'For a workers and peasants government!'*)

ALL: The Commune! The Commune! Give us the Commune!
HUGO (*to the auditorium*): Moscow! Are you listening, Moscow?!
>(*General answer from the hall:* 'I'm listening!')

Gas Masks
(*Protivogazy*)

(1924)

Melodrama

Translated by Robert Leach

Gas Masks performed
in Kursky Voksal gasworks, February 1924.

Gas Masks

Characters

Director of the Factory
His son, Petya
Secretary
Yegorich, of the factory committee
Dudin, worker correspondent
Engineer
Vaska Dlinny, a worker
Lukach, a worker
Old Woman Worker
Foma, a worker
Stretcher bearers
A Young Man
Komsomol members
Workers
Women workers
Courier

The action takes place inside a factory. Machines, workbenches, a trapdoor to a gas main testing chamber. To one side, the office: a table, an electric bell, a telephone.

First performed by the First Workers Theatre of the Proletkult, Moscow, on 29 February 1924, under the direction of Sergei Eisenstein.

ACT ONE

The Director enters hurriedly, laughing agitatedly. He presses the bell. Enter the secretary.

SECRETARY: At last! They've gone?
DIRECTOR: We've no time. Hurry up. Call the Factory Committee chairman.
SECRETARY (*into the telephone*): Yegor Yegorich – is he there? Can he come to the office? To see the director. Yes. It's urgent.
DIRECTOR: Take this. (*He hands her a piece of paper from those in his brief case.*) It's just come. Just come. In the accounts. Under 'engineer'. File it. And where is the order? Foo, dammit, who says it's too full?
SECRETARY (*looking through his bursting brief case*): Is this it?
DIRECTOR: That? That little rascal is the bill from the restaurant. How's that got here? Ach, you rascal, I'd give a lot to know. I had it in my hand all the time we were in the restaurant. (*He feels in his pockets.*)
SECRETARY (*looking at the bill*): Wow! The total doesn't look bad. They'll get a pat on the back for that.
DIRECTOR: And why not? Ah, you – sublime innocence. I suppose you think I eat like this for pleasure? It's hard for me to manage it, actually. But without a little fellow like this from time to time to buoy me up, I'd be worn out – I'd wear my legs down to stumps going up and down our institution's stairs.
SECRETARY: All the same, if the worker correspondent catches you ...
DIRECTOR: Dudin? In the first place, be so kind as to shred this private document immediately. So he's not tempted. In the second place, so that Dudin ... Do they realize? I am by no means against worker correspondents, but they tend to have a different sense of priorities, a different set of ground rules, and last but not least, the most naive loyalty to the factory. He doesn't give a damn about anything: he

doesn't know the problems, but he calls the tune. And whose head does it sing in? – the director's. Who has to clean up the mess? – the director. And how many heads has the director got? How many heads? How many?

SECRETARY: Er, one – why are you getting so excited?

DIRECTOR: Excited, excited! And where is that order? I ask you – where is that order?

SECRETARY (*takes out some papers*): There. What's that? Our request for the issue of gas masks.

DIRECTOR (*embarrassed*): Well?

SECRETARY: They've forgotten again. We really need that order.

DIRECTOR: Why do you think it's been forgotten?

SECRETARY: Have we had them?

DIRECTOR: How long have you been in charge of the gas masks? What's the problem? What's the problem, I ask you. Do you need a gas mask? Eh? Now? The atmosphere's heavy? Eh?

SECRETARY: Well, it's not light. Shall I file it? (*She tries to take the paper.*)

DIRECTOR: Oi! Leave it here – in the 'completed' file.

SECRETARY: Why? Have you received them? Or not? You can't say that's someone else's responsibility.

DIRECTOR: What's the rush? What is this? – a drama studio? Don't worry. Get a grip …

SECRETARY: But …

DIRECTOR: There's no time to chat. Please be quiet. The gas masks will be here when they're needed. (*The Secretary goes out.*) Two days from now they won't be necessary. It'll all be fixed. Where's that order? (*Yegorich enters.*) Ah, Yegorich!

YEGORICH: Have they gone?

DIRECTOR: Wait a minute! One thing at a time. We've received a little order worth several millions in gold.

YEGORICH: Yes?

DIRECTOR: We've grabbed it with both hands. We've worn out the seats of our pants in meetings and committees. Night never fell …

YEGORICH: Have you written up a report?

DIRECTOR: N-yes, I have.

YEGORICH: That's fine. Our workers' families were getting downhearted, they thought we were going to be laid off, and the factory was going to close down. Can I have a look at it?

DIRECTOR: Of course. I had it just now. It's disappeared. Now the next nice thing is: our clients will be here tomorrow.

YEGORICH: They're a central State Trust?

DIRECTOR: Better than that. They're members of the World Council of People's Managers, including probably the head honcho himself.

YEGORICH: What do you mean, tomorrow? We'll have to clear up before they arrive.

DIRECTOR: Let's get a move on, then. What do we need?

(*They move towards the work area.*)

YEGORICH: We haven't got any gas masks. The workers are furious. There was a meeting. The metal workers get angry when the pipes are twisted or they found the other day the rivets had been put ...

DIRECTOR: The rivets? When there's something wrong with the pipes?

YEGORICH: You know very well. (*He taps on a pipe.*) Listen – it's held up by a wing and a prayer, a child could fracture it. You promised to do something about it three weeks ago. Dudin, our correspondent, has written about it for *Pravda*.[77]

DIRECTOR: Dudin again. All he wants is to have your place on the factory workshop committee. Don't let him get away with it. And you tell the workers that the director will do what he promised.

(*The Courier appears with a large box.*)

YEGORICH: So that's what they send *Pravda* these days.

COURIER: Where shall I put it?

DIRECTOR: Aha, they brought them! (*To Yegorich*) Here you are – the gas masks!

YEGORICH: That's good. Give them to me.

DIRECTOR: No, they'll have to be checked by a chemical worker. (*To the Courier*) Come with me into the office.

YEGORICH: Well, I'll go and settle Dudin's hash. Crafty so-and-so. Schemer.

DIRECTOR: This room needs sweeping and the floor washing. Wipe over the windows. Don't forget to hang up the poster, 'Hygiene comes first at work'. Yes. And see to the cleaning of the club now, as well. Are the portraits of our leaders in place?

---

77   *Pravda*: Communist Party newspaper.

YEGORICH: Well, they're very tatty.
DIRECTOR: Buy some new ones. And buy some red material, too. I think you'd better chuck out the old material – it's all frayed at the edges. And along the edges of the green bunting. Make the letters U.S.S.R. in fairy lights. Take them off the fir tree. Your Komsomols[78] have nothing to do, let them get busy. Near the entrance make an arch of greenery. Invite a symphony orchestra along. But be absolutely certain they've rehearsed the *Internationale*.[79] You do understand, don't you, that this will be the moment of uniting the masses with their leaders ... in this ... but Dudin won't foul it up, will he?
YEGORICH: No, he's in hospital.
DIRECTOR: How's that?
YEGORICH: A fishy business. He wrote about our drinking – Vaska Dlinny, Kosina, Lukach and, er ...
DIRECTOR: And they beat him up?
YEGORICH: Well, someone did. It was one night as he was coming out of the club. They got him from behind, by the furnaces, brought him down, beat him ...
DIRECTOR: Who?
YEGORICH: He said he recognized Vaska by his voice. But Vaskina insists he was at home.
VASKA (*passing through with Lukach and overhearing the conversation*): Is he telling tales?
YEGORICH: Actually it was probably some drunks. They probably began drinking with no evil intentions.
DIRECTOR: Of course with no evil intentions. We're not saints, though. Eh, what? Now, what about the ikons? Haven't they been taken down? Get a ladder quick. Call for help. (*Yegorich fetches a ladder with two workers. Director climbs onto it in the corner.*) This is folly! However do you proletarians manage to do anything in situations like this?
WORKER: He'd make an old woman rebel!

---

78   *The Komsomol*: Communist Party youth organisation, whose members were called 'Komsomols'.

79   *Internationale*: The international anthem of Communism.

DIRECTOR: How can they carry on a conversation? Or take in what's going on in the factory?

(*They make to leave. After a minute, Vaska runs in with one of the ikons that has been taken down, and following him, a crowd of old women.*)

VASKA: She's gone mad. Let go.

WOMAN: You can't get rid of godfearing women. Give back the ikon!

VASKA: Oi, I don't like that tickling.

OLD WOMAN: Give back the ikon! Blasphemer! Drunkard! May lightning strike you! Thief!

(*The Old Woman snatches the ikon and in a fit of temper hits Vaska over the head with it. The ikon breaks in two.*)

WORKER: Oh, the ikon thief has copped one!

OLD WOMAN: Over his topknot like what you'll get in a minute.

VASKA: But who did the lightning actually strike, me or God?

WORKER: Here, take it, take it; stick it together again with oil of holiness.

DIRECTOR: Women, workers, fellow revolutionaries! The duty of the politically conscious proletariat is to have done with prejudice ...

WOMAN: Who's God getting in the way of? Who's upset by it?

WORKER: It's difficult to live without religious gymnastics. Is that it?

(*The Old Woman retreats glowering, looking at the broken board and, in the end, unexpectedly hurling the other ikons into a pile. The other women break off the din they have been making.*)

DIRECTOR ; Bravo, bravo, old woman!

VASKA: So, in a rage, she deserts the house of God.

OLD WOMAN: Yes, I desert it. I don't ask your permission. You can scrabble with your fingers in your own soul. My business is my business, I know what I'm doing.

WOMAN: Granny! What have you done to the ikons?

OLD WOMAN: All in pieces. You can pray yourself to those bits of firewood.

(*Suddenly she turns round and is gone, and the other women behind her.*)

FIRST WORKER (*to the Director*): What tore that to pieces? Has there been a purge? Revisionism, was it?

SECOND WORKER: Such things in a factory – well, at least take the saints away.

FIRST WORKER: Take it, don't take it. We sit here till we get our orders.
YEGORICH: You've had your orders.
DIRECTOR ; The order for five hundred thousand in gold. From the day after tomorrow this factory will be working flat out.
FIRST WORKER: Uh uh!
SECOND WORKER: High time.
DIRECTOR: I think the workers at our factory will show themselves in their true colours.
FIRST WORKER: That's us. We've never shied off work.
     (*The bell rings.*)
YEGORICH: Dinner time.
SECOND WORKER: Come on, mates, let's go and eat.
DIRECTOR: Are all the ikons down now?
YEGORICH: There are the ikons! This pile worries me. They've smashed them into junk.
DIRECTOR: What's junk can soon be thrown away. Don't get so gloomy!
YEGORICH: It's okay for you. You've got the trust eating out of your hand. But for me there's the Dudin lot snooping around.
DIRECTOR: Cheer up, comrade! Smile, Yegorich! We'll have our meeting and the day after tomorrow we'll celebrate my little boy's birthday. Off you go. Ah – the rum! (*Takes out bottle, drinks, offers it to Yegorich*)
YEGORICH: You tempter. Well, what the hell! 'A heavenly serpent.' How old's your little boy?
DIRECTOR: Seventeen.
YEGORICH: Time he was married ...
DIRECTOR: You what? ... Now this is where we'll bring the guests. And make sure we get a photo – 'In the Red Cornfields.' Good publicity.
     (*Three Komsomols appear, vaulting gymnastically over the benches.*)
FIRST KOMSOMOL (*quietly*): The director.
SECOND KOMSOMOL: Petka, you'll cop it from daddy for those gymnastics.
YEGORICH (*getting the Komsomols together*): You'll damage the benches. Have you messed them up? Disgraceful – it's State property! You'd better go now, children, to the forest, and get the greenery to decorate the club.
FIRST KOMSOMOL (*quietly*): It grunted.
     (*Two of the Komsomols go out.*)

DIRECTOR: Er, comrade eldest son.
PETYA: Dad! Our Komsomol needs gymnastic equipment and footballs.
DIRECTOR: How come a weakling like you's interested in gymnastics? You know very well you've got a weak heart. The doctor has forbidden it.
PETYA: It's not for me, it's for the Komsomol.
DIRECTOR: It'll wait, your Komsomol. You'll get a present for your birthday, but that'll be for you.
PETYA: But I've already had my present.
DIRECTOR: Oh. What was it?
PETYA: My Komsomol membership.
DIRECTOR: Hmm. I don't want to say anything ...
PETYA: But what? It's not fair.
YEGORICH: A little daddy-style surprise.
DIRECTOR: No, no, don't say anything! I welcome the suggestion. The initiative of the young people, their Communist education ... But our Komsomol ... Who's the chairman?
PETYA: Dudin.
YEGORICH: Yes, that baleful influence.
PETYA: What? Baleful?

(*Off stage the Komsomol choir can be heard singing: 'Oh you children, oh you Komsomols, Give the factory committee an embrace!'*)

YEGORICH: Did you hear that?
PETYA: So what? What's wrong with it?
DIRECTOR: Well, stop! Don't you worry your head with such things. Let's go home to dinner now. It's nothing to do with me, but is that how your mother talks to you? I don't know.
PETYA: What's mum got to do with it?
DIRECTOR: Well, never mind.
YOUNGSTER (*coming in*): Yegor Yegorich, there's a factory committee meeting now.
YEGORICH: Now? (*To the Director*) Can I have a little glance at that order?
DIRECTOR: Yes. Eh, you, Komsomol, have a look in my coat, in the side pocket, and see if there's an order there. (*Petya goes out.*) What am I? And here's his mother – well, you understand, women's

prejudices. She won't hear a word against the Komsomol. What can I do with her? Don't start breeding, eh?

YEGORICH: Of course, there are different ideas.

DIRECTOR: Yes, and the main one is to do with Dudin's influence. Fathers, of course, they aren't worth a brass farthing, and meanwhile the kids are completely in the pocket of someone else.

PETYA (*coming in*): Er, besides this little *billet-doux*, there's nothing there. (*He tosses it up in the air.*)

DIRECTOR: *Billet-doux*? Give it here! Be careful! Don't tear it!

PETYA: Why? What is it?

DIRECTOR: (*smoothing out the 'billet-doux' without letting Yegorich or his son see it*): Go home. It's time for dinner. I'm coming. I've remembered where the order is. (*He goes to his brief case and shoves into it his smoothed-out 'billet-doux', at the same time concentrating on his exiting son.*) Wait a minute! You're in the choir? You'll have to do something tomorrow. Anything revolutionary. Don't forget. All right, off you go. (*In a shout*) Ah, here's the tormenting thing, hidden under the lining.

YEGORICH: Rather badly crumpled.

DIRECTOR: Look, it's got a bank guarantee. But it's only valid for a month.

YEGORICH: Uh uh uh. Otherwise it's forfeited. If it isn't fulfilled, we'll be bankrupted.

(*The Secretary comes in.*)

DIRECTOR: That's something we'll have to cope with. We demand shock work. To get maximum output. Yes, if we can cope with ...

YEGORICH: Yes, already in the second competition in *Pravda* you're emerging as the top director.

DIRECTOR: That's just vanity and ostentation.

SECRETARY: Unless Dudin spoils things for you again.

DIRECTOR: Dudin again. (*Heatedly*) He's getting a few things wrong! And by the way, that devil doesn't act like a worker. He's always taking time off from the factory. He's a hack who should stick to scribbling – some things are not compatible. That's all.

SECRETARY: I'm just verifying what you've said.

DIRECTOR: You can do a bit less verifying. It's already been completely verified. We've had one dirty trick after another. And it's beginning to get up my nose. I'm not giving anything to him without a struggle.

YEGORICH: Don't torment yourself.

SECRETARY: Calm down. You've been called to dinner.

YEGORICH: Yes, I'm going. (*Under his breath*) Red material, the orchestra, fairy lights ...

DIRECTOR: Take the order.

(*Yegorich goes out. Director looks round.*)

SECRETARY: Don't forget the box.

DIRECTOR: What? Oh yes.

SECRETARY: Are you ready for the visitors?

DIRECTOR: This box? Why should I take this?

SECRETARY: It's for your son. It's his present.

DIRECTOR: My son? No, it's not for him, it's to be kept here, at the factory.

SECRETARY: The factory? Why?

DIRECTOR: They're ... um ... They're gas masks.

SECRETARY: Gas masks? They sent them?

DIRECTOR: They sent them ... Magnificent gas masks. Magnificent people and even more magnificent gas masks.

SECRETARY: Shall I despatch them to the workshop? Now?

DIRECTOR: No, not to the workshop, to my place. And not now, tomorrow.

SECRETARY: The gas masks to your place?! I don't get it.

DIRECTOR: You don't need to get it. You just need to do as you're told.

SECRETARY: Well, you know, from appearances you could run into ...

DIRECTOR: We shan't run into anything here. So much the better. (*The 'Internationale' is whistled outside. In the doorway*) Go on, go and see to the decorating of the club. (*The Secretary goes out past the box.*) Don't kick the gas masks – they're fragile.

ACT TWO

VOICES FROM BELOW: Ahoy! Here, quick!
   (*Two workers run in.*)
FIRST WORKER: I think I heard something. Didn't I?
   (*They listen.*)
VOICE: Quick – qui-i-ick, quick – qui-i-ick!
SECOND WORKER: In the machine room, isn't it?
FIRST WORKER: Not in the pipe? Petka went to inspect the pipe. Shift the hatch.
   (*They move it.*)
VOICE: Com ... com ... comrades ... No air ...
FIRST WORKER: We're here, Petya! What's up?
VOICE: Gas ...
SECOND WORKER: The pipe, is it?
VOICE: Gas ... pipe ... to breathe ... quick ...
FIRST WORKER: The pipe's fractured. Listen – it's hissing. Tie the rope round my waist. Sound the alarm.
   (*He descends. Second Worker sounds the alarm. Workers run in.*)
THIRD WORKER: What's up?
SECOND WORKER (*at the hatch*): Give it here. Is he suffocating? Lie him on the floor.
FOURTH WORKER: Has he broken his leg?
THIRD WORKER: What leg? He's gone dizzy. What's going on there?
FIFTH WORKER: What's that stink? Hey, mates, that's gas.
VOICES: Put out your fags, stop smoking!
   (*There is heard rolling round the factory: 'Put out the lights, put out the lights.'*)
FIRST WORKER: The main pipe line is fractured. There's a hole you could get your fist into. It's not riveted. The sleeve joint isn't on properly. It needs a new one.

THIRD WORKER: Why are you staggering about?
FIRST WORKER: G-a-s – drags you down – take in – poison.
FOURTH WORKER: Carry Petra to the first aid room! Take him!
THIRD WORKER: Get the engineer here quickly, and the director!
A YOUNGSTER: I'll run down now.
FIFTH WORKER: You can't do anything with that pipe without gas masks. Your lungs are eaten by fire in seconds.
FOURTH WORKER: Grishka's knocked out from the gas. Do you remember, last winter?
THIRD WORKER: How many times have we said about gas masks? What's Yegorich looking at?
FOURTH WORKER: The paunch he's growing.
FIFTH WORKER: The factory workshop committee they call themselves.
YEGORICH: Comrades, is it the pipe?
FOURTH WORKER: Yes, the pipe. We need gas masks – to rivet the pipe sleeve. Half an hour of that gas, and you won't remember much.
YOUNG MAN FROM THE CLUB: Yegor Yegorich, you could wrap yourself in the red material and lead us to safety – to the foodstore – or the canteen.
YEGORICH: Go to hell! Me, in the red material?
FIFTH WORKER: Where are the gas masks? Get 'em here, it's life or death.
SECRETARY: The gas masks are in a big case in the office. Run, quick!
ENGINEER (*running in*): What's going on? The pressure gauge has dropped, the place reeks of gas.
SECOND WORKER: The pipe's fractured.
ENGINEER: Where?
SECOND WORKER: The mains pipe.
ENGINEER: Badly?
SECOND WORKER: They say you could put your fist in it.
ENGINEER: Has the light gone?
SECOND WORKER: The generator's buggered. The partition's down, too. They can only grope their way.
ENGINEER: Any casualties?
FIFTH WORKER: No. One. Peter Danilov.
ENGINEER: It's quicker to switch on the portable generator. Is the sleeve joint intact?
FIRST WORKER: Barely. All the joints need rectifying.

ENGINEER: What about the mains safety valve?
FOURTH WORKER: Not working.
FIFTH WORKER: I bet it's the worst you've known.
ENGINEER: Bring a spare joint here. But how can we do it without the gas masks? We can't.
YEGORICH: We've got gas masks, we've got them, we've got them.
THIRD WORKER: They're getting them out.
   (*The box is brought in at the double.*)
ENGINEER: They're in that box? Funny thing to pack 'em in.
FOURTH WORKER: Quicker to undo than a tangle of string.
FIFTH WORKER (*getting the box open*): What the bloody hell?
DIRECTOR (*entering*): What's going on? Don't you dare touch that.
THIRD WORKER: Don't dare what?
FIFTH WORKER (*extracting a bottle*): So this is a gas masks. Oh ho.
DIRECTOR: Who permitted? Who gave it you?
SECRETARY: But you yourself said it was ...
DIRECTOR: What did I say? That you shouldn't poke your nose into what isn't your business.
FOURTH WORKER: This is a gas mask – for Vaskin's snout.
VASKA: Not for me. Best quality alcohol gas!
ENGINEER: Quicker! Quicker! Minutes are expensive. What's behind this muddle?
YEGORICH: Where are the gas masks?
DIRECTOR: Gas masks? What for?
THIRD WORKER: Wake up. Gas is escaping.
FOURTH WORKER: The factory will be halted.
SECRETARY: So where are the gas masks? You said ...
DIRECTOR: It was a mistake.
YEGORICH: What was a mistake?
ENGINEER: Hurry. Where are the gas masks?
DIRECTOR: The box ... it was ... er, not that. You're getting muddled.
FOURTH WORKER: Instead of gas masks – booze? Eh eh!
ENGINEER: So that's it – no gas masks?
DIRECTOR: No.
FIFTH WORKER: No, nothing more to say.
VOICES: – The main pipe's done for.
   – How can we do anything without gas masks?

— We've only one option — to open the gas holder, and let the gas out into the atmosphere.

DIRECTOR: Let the gas out? You can't do that!

YEGORICH: It'd hold up work for at least a week. What about the order then?

DIRECTOR: It's absolutely necessary that that is honoured in full.

THIRD WORKER: Repair it yourself if that's what you want.

YEGORICH: Then it's forfeit.

DIRECTOR: Then it's the end of the factory.

YEGORICH: Then you'll all be thrown out into the street with your wives and children.

FOURTH WORKER: You pay with your days off.

DIRECTOR: There won't be any days off. And with children — you know yourself — there's never any cash.

FIFTH WORKER: And who's responsible for there being no gas masks?

FOURTH WORKER: With gas masks we'd be able to cope properly.

DIRECTOR: What can we do? (*To the Engineer*) But hurry up — the gas is escaping.

ENGINEER: There is a way. I was talking on the telephone to the doctor. (*He whispers in the Director's ear.*) But if you don't agree ...

DIRECTOR: We've got to agree. (*To Yegorich*) Sound the hooter. Get everybody here.

(*Workers run in.*)

VOICES: — Is there a fire?

— Hell, give us a break.

— I had to chuck my dinner away. Cabbage soup, and I'd not taken three spoons.

— Is it a show?

— Shut up, you bastard.

— They're going to give us fresh pineapple. They are! The Central Committee has sent it.

— What's the stink of gas? I'm getting a thick head.

YEGORICH: Is everybody here?

VOICES: Yes.

DIRECTOR: And the Komsomols?

YEGORICH: They're looking for branches of greenery.

DIRECTOR: My Petka is with them?

YEGORICH: I think so.

DIRECTOR (*Quietly*) Oh, Christ. (*To the workers*) Comrades. Your attention. We are in a desperate situation. The pipe is split, and gas is escaping. And with the gas is escaping our opportunity to fulfil the order we received yesterday. You know about it. The gas masks, by an oversight ... by an unhappy ... by an unforeseen chance ...
VOICE: Oh yes ...
DIRECTOR: No. The only way, which is bound to test our proletarian heroism, is a difficult way: the joint must be replaced by workers not wearing gas masks.
VOICES: – Oh ho ho!
– Find some different fools!
DIRECTOR: Yes, without gas masks. Seventy of our workers, each working for three minutes ... I asked the doctor.
VOICES: – And then to the sick bay?
– Three minutes, then sick and off work?
– Repair that, then try and repair yourself.
– Ivan Ushasty'll die in two minutes.
– You'll probably be buried while the orchestra plays.
– All because of this bureaucrat.
YEGORICH: Comrades! This is impossible. The good proletarian, for example, will act on behalf of the collective, and will do what has to be done with no arguing. So, comrades ...
VOICES: – What are you parroting?
– Were you asleep?
– Or having one of your important little chats?
YEGORICH: Comrades! The order's disappearing!
FIFTH WORKER: Better that than brother workers disappearing, don't you think?
THIRD WORKER: Sing for the foreman!
VOICE: His paunch'll swell up in that underworld of the damned.
VASKA: What's all the talk, mates? That's not what we're here for. Let's go home.
(*During the altercation women have gathered.*)
VOICES: – What about our days off?
– Our case rests.
– Bring in the union.
YEGORICH: Comrades. Like heroes of labour, in exemplary fashion, you can write your names in the red roll of honour. Tomorrow

you will be leaders of the proletarian revolution ... Are you going to be able to face it?

VOICES: – Don't worry.
– Here we are, the leaders you were talking about.
– Get that in your head.
– You get to the pipe.
– What's a bit of gas?
– No chance! Come on, mates!
– Open the gas holder, and it's in the bag.
– We'll repair it in three days,

DIRECTOR: You can't open the gas holder.

(*Dudin arrives during the wrangle. He begins to shake his head.*)

DUDIN: You can't open the gas holder.

VOICES: – Dud's arrived.
– Listen to Dud!
– He's dragged himself here – have they patched you up?
– Have you come from the sick bay, Duddo?

(*The workers get ready to go out.*)

DUDIN: Comrades, don't go. A couple of words.

VOICES: – What's he want to say?
– Don't rush us to the slaughter!
– Are you starting to play their lordship's game, Dud?
– Getting in with the bosses?

DUDIN: You're mad. The bosses? What bosses? Who said that? Don't make me laugh! Have you forgotten who the boss is? It's you – you're the bosses. This is nothing to do with the bosses. They're only stewards, rotten little stewards ...

VOICE: Grab hold of them – they're too fat to run away.

DUDIN: No, we've got our work to do now. Who made October? You, and millions of workers like you. Who had nothing to eat at the front? You. Who starved? You. And who's going to give our industries a leg up now? You. Cause who's the boss? You. So be the boss! Not straws in the wind! Cause who's it for? Your children! All the children in the world. Gas is getting out – grab it by the throat! Squash it back. What's a bit of gas? You are the people who founded a workers and peasants republic. So what's saving a factory to you? – nothing! A tinker's curse! You can manage that with one hand tied behind your backs. What's frightening you? A bed in the sick bay? Death? I know you. Stepan! Semyon! Sergei! Nikita! Were you at the front?

VOICES: We were!

DUDIN: Fighting naked, bossless, cold, keeping alive by the skin of your teeth? And didn't you fight in Petrograd, Peter? And weren't you there when the Kremlin was taken in October? And in the kulak areas when bread had to be requisitioned using the threat of machine guns? And when people were dying of typhus all along the Volga? Were you cowards then? No, you didn't hold back. And you haven't got cold feet now. Tomorrow you'll say to these visitors: we saved our bit of the front – of industry. If you're workers and revolutionaries, you won't walk out just cause of a bit of gas. Three minutes each, that's all. Okay! Let's go!

VOICES: – Let's go!
– Right!

WOMEN: – Vanya, don't go!
– Boys, boys, you've got to do it.
– Don't dare turn back!
– Don't go!

DUDIN: They're going mad. Calm down. You're not gentlewomen, you don't have to go off into hysterics.

DIRECTOR: Women, working women, revolutionaries! ...

DUDIN (*to the Director*): What do you want? Get to your place!

WOMEN'S VOICES: – You can't swim against the tide!
– Peter's wife's in the sick bay grieving, he just isn't coming round.
– They're in a whirl, it's torture.

FOMA'S WIFE: Come home! Come home! Petka's ill. So come on!

WOMEN'S VOICES: – Don't go! Finish it – don't go home!

FOURTH WORKER: – You ought to buzz off, woman. Wet your eyes somewhere else.

OLD WOMAN: You should be ashamed of yourself, woman. Didn't you hear that speech? What if the revolution had gone like that at the front? You'd begun to drag him back to the stove. You're not blushing? I've no time for it. Don't get in their way.

DUDIN: Bring the tools! Pulleys! Ropes! Helmet lamps! Get the rope round your waist! Three minutes – take it. (*To the Engineer*) Take charge.

VOICES: – Who's going down?

- Let's draw lots.
- Go down the list.
- What list? Plumbers first.

DUDIN: Shut up! Who's talking about a list? Just get up and go down. Me first.

DUDIN'S WIFE: Go on, get a move on, darling. Cover your mouth with a handkerchief.

DUDIN: I don't need to. Everything's okay. Hook my lamp on.

VASKA (*moving him aside with his elbow*): Don't go down there.

DUDIN: Interfering again? Get behind me.

VASKA: I'm telling you, don't go down. You've got a missus, I haven't. Give me the lamp, I'll take it.

DUDIN: What kind of person are you?

VASKA: What kind? Some kind. No kind. Wait your turn.

VOICES: – He's a young 'un.
– Vaska, you idiot.

VASKA: Here we go!

(*They watch him.*)

DUDIN (*to Third Worker*): Where've you come from, Foma?

FOMA'S WIFE: We're going, come on, we're off.

FOMA (*to his wife*): I can't. Comrades!

FOMA'S WIFE: What have those so-called comrades ever done for you? When you've left the factory, then you can remember your comrades.

FOMA: Not on your life.

FOMA'S WIFE: Petka's calling, the little one. He's feverish, shaking, he's asking for you.

FOMA: Okay, let's go.

DUDIN: Where are you going to?

FOMA: I don't need your permission.

ENGINEER: Next!

DUDIN: You can't leave.

FOMA: Who can't? – my child's dying. Let's go, woman.

DUDIN: And how are you going to look your comrades in the eyes?

FOMA: Doesn't matter how. They'll get tired – I'm leaving the factory now. I'm not a prisoner. I'm not contracted to do this. You're jabbering for nothing.

DUDIN: Get out! Go on, quick! Take your son with you. Don't let him come past this factory, and tell him how his father ran away from the industrial front. His three minutes of gas were added on by his comrades to their sufferings. Going down your burrow, eh? They'll say to him, You're not Foma's son, are you ...
FOMA'S WIFE (*to Dudin*): Be quiet, do you hear, be quiet.
FOMA: Let's go. It's a waste of time talking to this scum.
(*The first stretcher carrying an unconscious body is carried past.*)
VOICE: He's not going now.
DUDIN: He can't go.
FOMA'S WIFE: Foma, you can't go.
FOMA: What?
FOMA'S WIFE: Take your place in the queue. Take it now. Don't stand there – I'll stand behind you.
FOMA (*to Dudin*): Give me a lamp. If anything happens – find my missus.
DUDIN: Okay. Ready?
ENGINEER: Next.
DUDIN: Off you go.
VOICES: – Steady, Dudin!
– I'm next!
(*A stretcher with Vaska is carried past.*)
– Get in the queue, don't sit there.
DUDIN: Someone else out cold.
A VOICE: Get a bit of paper, and write a note for *Pravda* about this. They'd print it if it came from you.
DUDIN: I may do that yet.
ENGINEER: Next.
WORKER'S WIFE (*heart-rendingly*): Koozya, I love you! (*She falls on a worker who is being stretchered away.*)
OLD WOMAN: Hush. He'll soon be in the sick bay. Stay with the stretcher. Touch him. He's there – comfort him.
WORKER'S WIFE (*calming down, holding the stretcher with her husband*): Take care of his head, don't jerk it.
ENGINEER: Next!
DUDIN: The women workers can take a turn with the stretchers.
STRETCHER-BEARER: Don't wriggle.
VOICES: – Listen, you bastard, you're still alive.
– The gas didn't get you.

WORKER ON STRETCHER: Ah, I feel sick. Steady, I said! (*He tumbles off the stretcher.*)
STRETCHER-BEARER: What are you doing?
WORKER: Take me to the director.
STRETCHER-BEARER: What do you need to go to the director for?
WORKER: Do as I say. Take me! I'm telling you.
> (*They take him over; he tumbles off again and, rolling and pitching, he staggers up.*)
ENGINEER: Next!
SECRETARY (*to the Director*): He wants you for something.
WORKER FROM STRETCHER (*to the Director between coughing*): Sir ... sir, Mr Director ... Here ... (*He hits him on the ear.*) That's for the gas masks ... payment. (*He sinks back. To the stretcher-bearers*) Now take me, I'll be easier now.
DUDIN: What was that for?
ENGINEER: Next.
VOICES: – Good luck.
> – He's an ox, that's what.
> – He hit him, gave him one round the lug-hole!
SECRETARY (*to the Director*): You'd better go.
DIRECTOR: My place is here.
SECRETARY: They'll manage without you.
DIRECTOR: Not in this situation.
SECRETARY: What are you still needed for?
DIRECTOR: I'm needed! It's nothing to do with you.
ENGINEER: Next ...

ACT THREE

Workers who have been pulled out from below lie by the hatch, till they are carried away. The queue to it is reduced to about ten or fifteen men. Offstage singing can be heard: 'Oh yes, the young lads, oh yes, the Komsomols, bravo, bravo, the young people.'

ENGINEER: Next.
    (*The singing gets nearer. Then it falls silent. The Komsomols run in excitedly with their greenery.*)
VOICES OF THE KOMSOMOLS: – What's up?
    – An accident?
    – Stretchers?
    – Has it collapsed?
    – An explosion?
DUDIN: What have you got there?
VOICES OF THE KOMSOMOLS: – For tomorrow's festivities.
    – We'll put dill and parsley in the cabbage soup.
DUDIN: I wish you'd cook up a few more stretchers. We haven't got enough of them. Take the ones lying here to the sick bay.
ENGINEER: Next.
DIRECTOR'S SON: What's the matter?
DUDIN: The main pipe's split. We're repairing it without gas masks. A person can be down there for three minutes. Then it's straight from there to the sick bay. The Komsomols could join the queue behind me. Do you understand?
SON: Without gas masks? (*He goes to his father.*)
DIRECTOR: You're here?
SON: How's this happened?
DIRECTOR: What? The pipe?

SON: No. The fact there aren't any gas masks. (*The Director is silent.*) Surely it's not possible. It's an absolute crime.
DIRECTOR: Take it easy, old chap.
SON: No, I simply can't imagine ... (*He staggers.*)
DIRECTOR: What's the matter?
SON: The air's so thick. My head.
DIRECTOR: Is it your heart?
ENGINEER: Next.
SON: Ah, lay off. What do you care?
DIRECTOR: Where are you going?
SON: Over there.
DIRECTOR: You're going out of your mind!
SON: I'm not.
DIRECTOR: You're going out of your mind! You can't. Your heart trouble. You shouldn't joke about it. Come on!
SON: What's the matter?
DIRECTOR: Go home. Your mother wants you. She's been worried.
SON: Mother's on my side. She said so.
DIRECTOR: Fine words. A noble speech.
SON: A noble speech. Who invited who to make a fine speech tomorrow?
DIRECTOR: That's another matter. Steady! I beg you! I entreat you!
SON: That's a shame, dad.
DIRECTOR: What's a shame? What's a shame? Just being here's making you go funny. You can't, you won't dare.
SON: Are you in charge of the work? Are you really? Don't hold me by the arm, let go!
DIRECTOR: No, I won't let go. You must obey your father ...
SON: I've already told you.
DUDIN: Komsomols, into the queue.
SON: I'm going! Let go!
DIRECTOR: But you're my flesh and blood, my dear fellow, my dear boy. Please, be kind to me. Please, run home to mummy. Take her this note. And could you bring me the little notebook that's on my table. It's absolutely essential that I have it.
SON: I haven't time.
DIRECTOR: The queue's not moving very fast. Go on – it'll only take a minute. Besides, you could bring a hood back from the house ...
SON: For a gas mask?

DIRECTOR: Yes. It's important, I agree, to do the work. You are a communist. You don't need to strike a pose, do you? You know, they're sounder than that. Well, go on, run.
SON: Okay. I'll just take the note. (*To Dudin*) Back in a minute, Dudin.
DIRECTOR (*to Secretary*): Quick – to the telephone! Tell them they've got to delay him. I need to go too – he might come back. Let them say ... oh, anything you like ... only he's not to work in the gas – he won't be able to take it. Let them lock him up for half an hour, only half an hour. Phone!
SECRETARY: No.
DIRECTOR: What?
SECRETARY: I'm not obliged to carry out orders outside office hours.
DIRECTOR: You want him to die?
ENGINEER: Next.
SON (*returning*): I won't have time. You take the note.
(*The father seizes him by the arm.*)
KOMSOMOL (*singing*): 'We are the young guards of the workers and peasants.'
VOICE (*in tune*): 'Under their mother's wing they get really comfortable.'
SECRETARY: Go to them. Quick. They're calling.
SON: I'm going.
SECRETARY: Good luck. My own.
DIRECTOR: What's all this?
SON: The baby! Give it a good start. Do what you like, but give it a good start!
VOICES OF THE KOMSOMOLS: – Eh, bugger you, come on!
– Get yourself to Dudin.
SON: Dudin, let me jump the queue.
DUDIN: You're getting out of turn again. Oh well, come on. Hook on your lamp.
OLD WORKER: You're lucky, young fellow-me-lad. You're not a father.
DUDIN: Get plenty of air in your lungs, like this, and don't talk – you'll soon feel dopey.
ENGINEER: Next.
SECRETARY: Go! Go, lad!
DIRECTOR: What? It's no good you moving him to the head of the queue, you just want to hasten his ... What was he saying you've got? What did his tone of voice mean?

SECRETARY: Nothing unusual.
DIRECTOR: It was a tone of command. That he's to be your comrade?
SECRETARY: More than that.
DIRECTOR: What more?
SECRETARY: Husband.
DIRECTOR: What? You've gone out of your mind. Whore! Scum! I'll fire you tomorrow.
SECRETARY: I know.
ENGINEER: Next.
DIRECTOR: They're carrying someone. It's him. Look, sir, he's white! Look out, look out! Sir! Sir! Take him home. Call a doctor ...
WORKERS: His arm's been caught. The women are taking care of it. The doctor should come from the sick bay.
SECRETARY: No, take him to the sick bay, like everyone else.
DIRECTOR: Excuse me, sir. It would be quicker to fetch him here. (*Into the telephone.*) A doctor ... They're busy? It's the director speaking. How is my son? What? Alive? Oh, brilliant, sir! Oh, brilliant of you, sir! (*He sits in exhaustion on the pile thrown down earlier.*) What's up?
SECRETARY: The ikons. They were dumped there.
DIRECTOR: Where? Dumped? No. (*To the telephone*) Doctor! Who's that? ... Where's the doctor? It's the director speaking. Why is nobody going on calling till they get an answer? Why is the receiver off the hook? It's important that he's alive, it's important that he's alive.
ENGINEER: Next. (*To the person crawling out of the shaft*) What's happened?
WORKER (*reeling*): The leak's stopped. The sleeve joint's screwed tight. There's only old gas there. Five minutes from now everything'll be okay.
ENGINEER (*to the Director*): We've finished. It's over now.
DIRECTOR: Glory be to God. You've finished? Hell, I'm trembling. I could do with a drink. (*He takes a bottle out of the gas masks' box. He holds it by the neck, and drinks.*) Everybody did well. (*To the Engineer*) Here's health to the factory! And to you, Petya, little Petya.
A WORKER: Wouldn't gas masks have come in useful?
ANOTHER WORKER: What are you looking at? Let him lap it up. It's marvellous. Hold the joint. (*He drops the pipe.*)

WORKERS: Shit. What a slob! The whole factory's prosperity's disappeared down that hole.

YEGORICH (*to the Director*): Now what? Mmm? We did badly all the same with the gas masks. In the sick bay they're talking about going to court.

DIRECTOR: Rubbish. We'll get out of that. We're not so simple. Are you tired? Take a deep breath.

YEGORICH: What about you?

DIRECTOR: The sooner I get some information from the sick bay the better. How much movement did he have in his arm? (*To the Secretary*) Take this down. 'Telegram. Urgent. To the Board of the Trust. Today at five o'clock in the evening, due to the dilapidation of the factory, the main gas pipe fractured. Despite the harsh conditions for the repair, the red heroes of labour employed at the factory, together with the administration, who developed revolutionary energy, proved to be ...' Have you got that down?

SECRETARY: I'm not even starting.

DIRECTOR: What's the problem? Why not?

SECRETARY: It's lies.

DIRECTOR: If you don't want to, you don't have to. Others can write, too. (*Yegorich comes in and coughs awkwardly.*) From the sick bay? News?

YEGORICH (*in a weak voice*): What news!

DIRECTOR: What? What's the matter? Spit it out.

YEGORICH: Do you really want me to say it here?

DIRECTOR: My son?

YEGORICH: His heart.

DIRECTOR (*muttering*): You don't say ... you don't say ...

SECRETARY: Do you ... still ... want me to write? ...

DIRECTOR: My son ... Yes ... One ... Here ... Write ... (*He dictates in a thick voice*) 'To the District Committee Prosecutor ... During repair work ... a split ... gas ... mains pipe ... the criminal ...negligence ... of the director ... of the factory ...forced ...the workers ... to work ... without gas masks ... with the result that ... seventy workers were poisoned ... '

YEGORICH: Sixty-four.

DIRECTOR: ' ... and were ... in mortal danger. I request ... the institution of proceedings ... against the director ... on criminal ... charges. Until the arrival of the empowered enquiry, the criminal will be found under house arrest.' (*To the Secretary*) Send that without delay. (*As he goes out*) Husband, did you say? Are you going to have a baby?
SECRETARY: I am.
DIRECTOR: What are you going to call it? It'd be good to call it after its father: Petya, little Petya.
SECRETARY: No. The gas mask.
DIRECTOR (*nodding*): Ah! ...
  (*DUDIN enters.*)
ENGINEER: Dudin. Have you been to the sick bay?
DUDIN: I think the others are feeling better. There's no more room there. There's only half a dozen on their feet out of seventy, and they're crying.
ENGINEER: Why?
DUDIN: Over Petya, the Director's son ... They loved him. I'm giving up being correspondent now. Is all the work done?
ENGINEER: Yes.
LUKACH (*entering from the sick bay*): What's going on? Is it all over? Have they saved the factory? The lads from the sick bay wanted to know. They're worried.
DUDIN: Tell them the factory's saved. (*He writes, and reads as he does so.*) 'The unbroken queue of workers went into the toxic gas and in three hours completed the repair work, having had as casualties ...'
LUKACH: Dud!
DUDIN: What's up with you? (*Continuing to read*): 'Out of seventy ...'
LUKACH: Listen. The other night you were in the factory as correspondent. You had your boots right on the edge here. Remember?
DUDIN: Well?
LUKACH: I was here too. Oh no. So long, comrade, I'm feeling sick.
DUDIN: You are? Eh, you're a swine! (*Lukach, poisoned, topples over.*) What's the matter? He's collapsed ... Well, this gas is repulsive. Eh, comrade ... (*Looking around.*) Not a single one of 'em ... Well, hold on, I'll carry you out. (*With difficulty, he lifts him and carries*

him halfway to the exit, swaying, where he sits down.) Oo, it gets my side. Ooh! Here I am, comrade, the guilty one. With my boots on the edge, and I didn't report a thing. Ah, bollocks! (*Fed up, he gets up.*) Now then, Dud, all your strength. One, two ... three! Let's go! With a complete movement! Come on! Oo-oo!

Roar, China!
(*Rychi, Kitai!*)

(1925)

An Incident in Nine Links

Translated by Stephen Holland

With thanks to Anna McGhee for help with the Mandarin language

Roar, China!, the ninth link:
The Boatmen fettered together at the neck.

ROAR, CHINA!
AUTHOR'S INTRODUCTION

The incident depicted in this play took place in June 1924 in the town of Wanxien.[80] Wanxien is deep in the heartlands of China; you need to navigate a good 1,200 miles up the river Yangtse, that broad waterway along which ocean-going ships can sail 600 miles all the way to Hankow.

The gunboats of Europeans patrol this Chinese Volga, maintaining the security of the few whites and Japanese pursuing their trade and missionary work along the length of the river.

In Wanxien there are large American fuel depots. The exporters' offices are located there. They buy up cotton, mustard seed, skins, and most importantly – olive oil.

The American firm Robert Dollar and Associates[81] occupies a prominent place amidst these exporters. Its logo, an 'S' struck through vertically twice, adorns the funnels of steamships, warehouse roofs and the copper signs of offices along the Yangtse's whole length.

Mr. Holey was the Wanxien agent for the firm. Hundreds, perhaps even thousands, of coolies, loaders and boatmen put food in their mouths thanks to his shipments.

Needless to say, relations were far from cordial between this arrogant businessman and the resentful population, always hungry, chasing after every last penny, living, reproducing and dying on their little boats, on

---

80   *Wanxian:* Now the hugely expanded conurbation of Wanzhou District
81   *Robert Dollar:* Though its name provides Tretyakov with a convenient satirical swipe, Robert Dollar and Associates is in fact historically accurate: it was originally a Canadian firm which accrued enormous wealth from its colonial business.

sampans and barges. It is a known fact that a dispute arose between Holey and some of the boatmen, a dispute which escalated into a fight, the outcome of which was the retrieval of Holey's corpse from the Yangtse.

But moored on the river was the English gunboat *Cockchafer*,[82] and the Captain instituted immediate measures to discipline and punish the Chinese, who had dared to raise a hand to one of the 'white gods.' The Captain ordered the town's administration to find the guilty parties without delay and hand them over for execution. If it was not possible to find the culprits, then two members of the boatmen's union, to which coolies involved in the fatal fight belonged, should be executed in their place. On top of this, the Captain also ordered that Holey's body should receive appropriate honours at the funeral and, finally, that his relatives be compensated with a substantial sum of money. As far as we know, the Captain gave a deadline of 48 hours. If the conditions of his ultimatum were not met, the Captain announced that Wanxien would undergo bombardment by the *Cockchafer*'s guns.

In vain did the Chinese administration protest, demanding that the case be referred for scrutiny by the central government and diplomatic bodies, in vain did social organisations send perturbed telegrams – the Captain was unyielding, and in Wanxien, after the lavish funeral of the dead American, two boatmen were executed, sacrificed to the redhaired god of British mercilessness.

This much is fact.

I have barely had to change anything.

More than that: the incident proved exemplary.

The incident with Holey was a tragedy. But Wanxien came to know farce as well. Some months after the '*Cockchafer* incident' (as it became known in Britain), a fight broke out in a dive between the sailors of a French gunboat and some Chinese. One Frenchman got quite a hammering. The commander demanded compensation for the man's broken ribs of some derisory amount (around 100 roubles), threatening once again that failure to pay would incur the comprehensive shelling of the town.

In 1926, Wanxien, which till then had always managed to ransom itself from foreign guns, was razed to the ground after all. As a result of a clash

---

82 *Cockchafer:* The historically accurate name of a British river gunboat of the 'insect' class.

between foreign steamships and a Chinese general, the bombardment of the town began.

This incident prompted some who saw *Roar, China!* on stage to consider the play prophetic.

But any prescience on my part can be attributed simply to its accurate portrayal of the extraordinary similarity and persistence in the methods used by the various colonial powers to pursue their policies, particularly by the English.

THE LINKS

The two principal locations for the action – the imperialist *Cockchafer* and the Chinese river shore – inspired the linked structure of the play, in which the 9 long episodes or "links" are, as it were, attached end to end in one long chain. That said, Holey's drowning is witnessed through binoculars from the gunboat, while in the next link the action (on the river shore) is rewound a considerable amount in order to lead up to that event again.

In order to achieve maximum narrative compactness, I have compressed the Captain's 48- hour ultimatum to 24.

The imperialist gunboat and the Chinese shore represent a juxtaposition of power and resources seen throughout China – between Chinese Peking[83] and its diplomatic quarter, Shanghai and its settlement, Tientsin[84] and its concession, Canton and Xiamen, the latter once the British treaty port of Amoy and, finally, between all of China and its dictators and creditors, the great powers.

Aboard the gunboat all is scrupulously shipshape and Bristol fashion. Dandyish ranks of sailors line up in their peakless caps, adorned over one ear with the short ends of ribbons. The officers' white naval jackets are trimmed with gold braid. They are immaculately shaved. They behave with knightly gallantry towards any women on board. The tables are set with elegant linen and crockery. There is a contemptuous arrogance on this movable piece of Britain.

---

83   *Peking*: Peking was the old colonialist name for Beijing. The city is referred to by both names in the play, depending on whether the speaker is Chinese or colonialist.

84   *Tientsin*: Now known as Tianjin.

Here, when necessary, they slaughter without dirtying their hands, they scoff at their inferiors without raising their voices, and they enforce their bloodthirsty demands by the simple swivelling of the muzzles of their guns. Orders sound out, clipped and distinct. Every movement is regulated. Every action, thought through.

The gravest misfortune of the inhabitants is that they are too numerous. Labour is eternally cheap. The people spend their lives permanently chained to the oar of their boats and sampans or in thrall to a bale. Right there in the sampans their children are born and raised. In their free minutes they smoke, gossiping about their paltry affairs, their troubles and joys. But at a second's notice they are prepared to fly at each other's throats for the sake of a coin flung their way.

They go about their business cheek by jowl with each other, associating together in a way we find remarkable – simple loaders, who own nothing besides a pair of hands each, boatmen, yet also the rich owners of barges and of the sampans which they lease out.

This grey mass of humanity is benighted and illiterate. Many of them persist in the old habit of wearing the Chinese queue, the pigtail abolished by the revolution of 1911 – a sign of their continuing deference to the Manchurian dynasty. They are full of the most naïve superstitions and ready to ascribe their misfortunes to the vagaries of insufficiently appeased gods and spirits. In times of difficulty they are capable of selling a child for a few roubles. They endure the presence of Europeans in their country in the same way as they put up with misery, dirt and poverty. And only occasionally, during particularly dire times, when with some inner intuition they scent an enemy before them, do they rear up and uncurl the terrible claws of revolution.

However, it is not so easy for them to come into direct contact with the Europeans. There is a buffer. This is the comprador. He is the channel through which the European communicates with the crowds of coolies. He is the contractor, through whom payment is disbursed, allowing him to fill his own pockets at the expense of the cheated unskilled labourers.

The slow working Chinese, barefoot, in grey or blue clothing, at first glance apathetic, in the thick of whom are interspersed exalted officials, rustling in their formal black silk jackets, the staid and very corpulent merchants, the young intellectuals in glasses and with European style hats – this is the real China, which in our times we must contrast with false, exotic conceptions of the country, with all those vases, embroidered full length coats, the phoenixes, the princesses, the pagodas with their little bell towers, the refined courtesans, the cruel mandarins, the dancers (of which, incidentally, there are none, as China has no art of the dance) – in a word all the pernicious nonsense with which till now our art has filled the head of the average person.

THE PLACE AND THE PEOPLE

On no account should the Chinese part of the set be decorated with fancifully curved roofs, little umbrellas, dragons, lanterns.

The Chinese wharf is actually a chaos of bales, ladders, boats bobbing on the water or drawn up to dry out, of stalls above whose tables mattings are stretched taut to protect customers and traders from the sun. Portable braziers heat up cauldrons in which porridge bubbles away. Bare chested cooks, their trousers tied tightly round their waists with cloth bands, knead dough and boil up rice. For a copper coin, a coolie can squat by a kitchen and fill his stomach.

The yuan is the Chinese rouble, the jiao – the Chinese 10 kopeck coin, and the cent – the Chinese kopeck. But there is a coin of even smaller value – the dongban. There are ten of them to every cent. They are punched through the middle and carried in bundles on string.

All sorts of people frequent the port. The blind walk in a single chain, clutching sticks. The one in front feels the way, tapping with a cane, and hits a gong. They sit themselves down, play on long, stringed instruments not unlike our Ukrainian banduras and sing songs in a deliberately cultivated, thin and wailing falsetto.

Women and children pass by. They wear either light or dark blue trousers down to their ankles and a tight woman's jacket with a high collar. The jacket is dark blue, often silk, with sleeves to the wrists, close fitting so their breasts are bound in tight and flattened. The jackets finish in semi-circular hems front and back. They fasten at the side.

The girls walk evenly, unsmiling and often bringing up to their nose a handkerchief which they hide up their sleeve under an arm. They have fringes cut just above their eyebrows; neat pigtails, twisted tight on the back of their head, hang down their back. Some of them wear red trousers. This means they are betrothed.

Women in late middle age walk through too. Their hair, pulled back from their foreheads and arranged on top of their heads, is oiled to a sheen and adorned with an artificial flower behind the ear.

Their feet have been bound into little hooves (on stage their gait can be conveyed by actors walking on their heels.) They hold themselves straight and impassively. Their cheekbones, eyelids and part of their temple are rouged. Their faces are powdered white.

The old women are bald. Their yellow heads gleam beneath the tight rim of a black binding. A bare wooden hair stick, to which something may be attached, protrudes at the back.

Many sounds and calls fill the air.

There is the rattling of the corn cutters' small castanets, who unshoe their patients on the spot and dig out their corns with gimlets. The knife grinder circulates, carrying on his shoulders a trestle with a whetstone. He has the longest of trumpets, blaring out a bellicose signal, two notes a fourth apart – the acoustic sign for his trade.

A yoke slung across shoulders with two baskets? That's a hawker. He holds a kind of clapper on a handle – turn the handle and a lead plummet hits a little drum. Sometimes a gong, from which four little weights hang down, wobbles above his back. As he walks, they swing to and fro and sound the gong.

The sellers of fans, of sweets, of feather dusters, each cries their mournful call with long drawn out first and last notes.

A puppeteer puts on his shows. His little dark blue house has a fabric hem behind which this 'director' scurries back and forth. He also beats a gong and, with high pitched shouts, drums up custom for his impressive, costumed puppets, who seem to float effortlessly through the space the opened doors of his little stage reveal.

The river wharf at its leisure is noisy and colourful; but, when ranks of coolies monotonously carry through long lines of bales, that is the wharf immersed in its labour.

Sometimes, though, an ugly mood seizes it, people press together in crowds, their voices begin to clamour hoarsely, and the innocent oar in their hand begins to look more like a cudgel – that is its revolution.

Roar, China!

Characters

The Foreigners

The Captain of the gunboat *Cockchafer*
Lieutenant Copper of the gunboat
Monsieur de Bruchelles, a French business man
Madame de Bruchelles, his wife
Cordelia, their daughter
Holey, Agent of the American Firm, Robert Dollar and Associates
An American journalist
Tourist and his wife
Missionary
Boatswain
Sailors

The Chinese

Comprador[85]
The Mayor of Wanxien
Ship's boy on the *Cockchafer*
Tai Li, a rich merchant
Student, the Mayor's interpreter
Fei, chairman of the Boatmen's Union
Fei's wife
Old Boatman
First Boatman
Second Boatman
Third Boatman
Chi, a boatman
Chi's wife
Chi's daughter
Wife of the Second Boatman

---

85   *Comprador*: a name derived from Portuguese in common usage in colonial times for a native agent.

Their son
Granny, an old woman and procuress
Stoker at the radio station
The Heshang, a Buddhist monk and member of a sect dreaming of the destruction of the Foreigners
Policeman, palanquin bearers, executioners, boatmen and their wives, passers-by, hawkers, cooks, blind people, tradesmen.

First performed at the Meyerhold Theatre, Moscow, on 23 January, 1926, directed by Vasily Federov, with Vsevolod Meyerhold.

FIRST LINK

The location is the river wharf of the Szechuan town of Wanxian. In the middle of the river, hemmed in by mountains, lies the British river gunboat Cockchafer.

On the bank there is the usual crush of a port. Coolies seethe between winches, cranes, gangplanks, upturned boats, stalls and hawkers with yokes slung across their shoulders.

The horizon is intersected by the vertical lines of masts. They belong to large sampans, protected against the sun and the rain by a cover of bast boxes, lined up side by side in several rows, firmly tethered to the bank. On other, smaller skiffs sparrows flurry to and fro; at their sterns each boatman or boatwoman, with a child secured to their back, rocks a single oar in a motion which cuts a perpetual figure of eight in the water. More sampans, loaded down with bales of cotton, barrels of olive oil, rolls of skins, come alongside the edge of the moorings. Planks are flung across the sides of the boats, and the loaders, hoicking enormously heavy bales onto their shoulders, teeter across them from boat to boat on bandy legs.

The coolies are shabbily dressed. Some wear the bare minimum of filthy shorts and a dirty handkerchief covering their heads. Like our stevedores, some of them wear a ripped open sack over their heads and back like the klobuk[86] of our Orthodox priests. Some have a threadbare, sleeveless shirt to cover their torso and straw sandals on their feet.

When they carry their loads, their straw hats, shaped like tapering wash basins, hang down around their chests. When they sit down to rest, they put them back on their heads and light up long thin pipes. Sweat runs down their

---

86   *Klobuk*: headgear worn by Russian Orthodox priests, consisting of a stiff black cylindrical hat (*kamilavka*) to which is attached at the top and front a black veil (*epanokamilavkion*) which is thrown back over the head and down the back.

faces, they fan themselves with simple palm leaf fans shaped rather like tennis rackets.

The older men have retained their pigtails, often gathered up in a bunch against the shaved darkness of their heads. The rest have heads so close shaved they are tinged blue. When they carry their loads, they sing in time, but it is more like a rhythmic exhalation: 'Huya-ho, hai-he! Huya-ho, hai-he!' The Comprador shouts orders to them. He wears a white or light blue Chinese long coat. He holds a fan covered in Chinese characters. A straw boater is perched on his heavily pomaded, combed and parted hair.

The Comprador, having stopped the 'wandering restaurant' of a hawker, on the two ends of whose yoke a whole kitchen is attached complete with brazier, teapots and bowls, is now sipping tea from a little cup without handles. At the slightest sign of unsatisfactory work, he jumps up and rushes into the press of workers, urging them on, criticising, prevailing upon them, trying to ginger them up.

SCENE ONE

A gang of loaders and the Comprador during a moment of rest. The coolies are smoking, the Comprador drinks tea. The merchant Tai Li walks along the wharf at a slow pace. Tai Li wears horn rimmed glasses, he has delicately thin whiskers. A corpulent figure, he has about him an air of conceited composure. He wears a black skull cap with a red ruby above his forehead. When the Comprador spots him, he rushes over in the most respectful way, cups both his hands and raises them to his bowed head, at the same time as he bends one leg and curtsies as though on the point of genuflecting. Tai Li responds in the same way, but he inclines his head less, does not bring his cupped hands all the way to his head, nor does he curtsey.

COMPRADOR (*in the most honeyed, ingratiating tone of voice*): You have been pleased to eat already, most honoured Tai Li?
TAI LI (*dignified and unhurried*): I have eaten.
COMPRADOR: You will not refuse me the honour of drinking tea from my humble pot. (*He moves towards his teapot, but Tai Li stops him with a gesture.*)
TAI LI: The American, your master, will he be here soon?
COMPRADOR: I am expecting him.

TAI LI: Tell him – Tai Li is willing to pay cash for the skins if the deal can be struck before noon today.
COMPRADOR (*simpering servilely*): The bountiful Tai Li will not forget my insignificant commission of a quarter percent?
TAI LI: On the contrary. Tai Li will expect a quarter of your commission from the American.
COMPRADOR: That is hard for me to hear.
TAI LI: Not nearly as hard as no longer hearing at all.
COMPRADOR (*listening*): That sounds like the American coming.
TAI LI (*suddenly in a hurry*): I do not need to meet him here. I will wait for him at my shop till noon.
(*After a repeat of the initial exchange of bows, with their same imbalance, Tai Li exits but with no quickening of his step.*)

SCENE TWO

Holey enters in a cork helmet and tennis outfit with rolled up sleeves. He is a sinewy, well-built young American – he walks jerkily, as though on springs. He is short tempered and peremptory. He has a harsh voice and speaks in a clipped and tense manner.

HOLEY (*quickly taking in the resting coolies but not looking at the Comprador, who is bowing to him strenuously*): That stuff not ready yet?
(*The Comprador launches himself zealously at the sitting coolies. He prods and kicks them, urges them on, harrying them over to the heaps of bales which need to be moved from the wharf to the stores. The exhausted coolies, pitifully paid and poorly fed, move at a pace clearly unsatisfactory to Holey. The Comprador understands. He quickens the tempo of his cries. Huya-ho, hai-he, trying to spur on the workers.*)
COMPRADOR: Hurry, hurry! Hup! Hup! Huya-ho, hai-he!
HOLEY: Unload the rest in 15, tops. And where's that boiler for the radio station?
COMPRADOR (*looking along the embankment*): On its way, sir.
HOLEY: Oh yeah? I don't see it.
COMPRADOR: Very heavy, sir.

HOLEY: So what if it is? We ain't gonna need to hitch the horses, are we? No enda starving mouths in Wanxian to choose from.
COMPRADOR: But, sir ...
HOLEY (*abruptly interrupts the Comprador who is trying to get some words of justification out*): Enough! Go get 20, 30, 50 coolies on that boiler - shift it! Fast!

SCENE THREE

From behind the stage a huge steam boiler is dragged out on rollers by coolies with straps tied over their shoulders, arms hanging loose and almost reaching the ground.

Other workers pull out the freed rollers from behind and, dawdling, replace them in front.

The Stoker from the radio station walks behind holding the end of a rope. He is dressed in dark blue shorts and a dark blue jacket with silver buttons. His head is not shaved.

The Comprador rushes to the crowd dragging the boiler. He mimes the actions of bodies tensed for work requiring real effort and unusual physical strength. He springs back from the front of the boiler to the rear and mimes putting his shoulder to it. Stamping his foot, he starts an encouraging little chant based on a simple scale - la-re – to which the coolies call back extremely slowly and mournfully – mi-re, do-re. The Comprador rushes towards the coolies even more energetically, almost dancing up to them – la-la, re-re – but the coolies don't speed up even by a fraction, replying with a long drawn out chant of mi-re, do-re, a nasal drone with no discernible words.

HOLEY (*watching them work*): To hell with the lot of them – lazy animals! Ten of this scum aren't worth a single American!

SCENE FOUR

The journalist enters, his camera hanging down on his chest.

JOURNALIST: Mr Holey, hallo there.
HOLEY: Hallo.

(*Despite their seemingly non-committal tone, there is a sense that they are on amicable terms.*)

JOURNALIST (*nodding at the bales*): Skins?

HOLEY (*who is writing in a notebook and doesn't look up*): Yeah.

JOURNALIST: Fleecing China, ay?

HOLEY (*fixing the journalist with a surprised stare*): Excuse me?

JOURNALIST: A rather snippy remark from today's leader page. It's that guy, the Mayor's interpreter, flexing his wings, no doubt about it.

HOLEY: A student?

JOURNALIST: From Shanghai.

(*The boiler is now heading down a slope to where both of them are standing.*)

JOURNALIST (*grabbing Holey by the sleeve to pull him to one side*): You'll be crushed!

HOLEY (*not even looking round*): Let them go round.

(*With enormous effort the coolies drag the boiler lopsidedly around the foreigners. Holey notices the Stoker walking behind the boiler, holding a rope.*) Who's that loafer there?

COMPRADOR: He's the stoker at the radio station.

HOLEY: Whaddo I care? (*To the Stoker*) There's a spare rope there. Pull your weight! Cut the useless talk!

STOKER (*winks at the coolies and holds out the end of his rope to Holey*): Here's a rope. Help yourself. Cut the useless talk! (*The coolies laugh and stop unloading.*)

HOLEY (*furious at being laughed at, nevertheless contains himself and turns quietly to the Comprador*): Deduct two of their ten cents – for stopping.

JOURNALIST (*shocked*): Ten cents!

HOLEY: What about it?

JOURNALIST: That's what you pay them?

HOLEY: Yeah ...

JOURNALIST: You know the Chinese exporters have lowered the rate to five cents. So in fact that's ...

HOLEY: Twice as cheap.

JOURNALIST: Yes indeed my man, twice. I've included it in today's bulletin.

HOLEY (*looking at the Comprador, repeats himself, not hearing anything around him, as though in a trance*): Five cents!

JOURNALIST: Well, I gotta go. Oh, I nearly forgot. They wanna see you on the *Cockchafer*.
HOLEY: What for?
JOURNALIST: Something to do with a deal for skins. They say it's urgent. You can use their cutter.
HOLEY (*again walking to one side lost in thought*): 5 cents! ...
JOURNALIST: And the rest, this place reeks of dollars.
HOLEY (*beckons the Comprador*): Come here!
JOURNALIST (*looking round and spotting the Procuress, Granny, some way away*): Hey! Wssht! ...Over here, now! ... pumpkin head! That's it, tippy toe over to me on those little hooves, you bald, cheating bitch!

SCENE FIVE

Enter Granny, an old woman, on bound feet like little hooves, dressed in trousers tied in around her ankles with cloth bindings like a bicyclist. Her pigtail reaches to her hips. Her face is yellow and puckered, and she covers her baldness with a binding over her head.

Granny minces over to the Journalist, bowing as she comes, her hands always held against the seams of her trousers. The Journalist hurries her up.

JOURNALIST: C'mon, c'mon, c'mon! So - what sort of a girl did you send me?
GRANNY: Healthy.
JOURNALIST: What good is healthy when she sits and wails the whole day long?
GRANNY: Attractive.
JOURNALIST: Lying there in bed like a slab of meat, that's attractive now is it?
HOLEY: D'ya pay for a girl every day?
JOURNALIST: No, that's the problem. I pay twenty of their dollars a month and then get the devil knows what. Turns out she was barren, so her husband sold her off as a concubine. Now she just sobs her heart out for him. (*He turns round decisively.*) Now listen!
GRANNY (*nodding firmly*): Shi.
JOURNALIST: You take her off my hands.

GRANNY: Shi.
JOURNALIST: Get me a new one, same type, but healthy, mind.
GRANNY: Shi, shi!
JOURNALIST: Take her round to the doctor at the American hospital. Don't let her turn up without his certificate. *(To Holey.)* These little Chinese girls have a charming concept of the clap. They think if they infect someone they end up half cured themselves. *(After a quick glance at his watch.)* If you want my advice – stick with your skins.
(Exits with Granny.)
HOLEY *(not turning round)*: You there yet? How much we agreed with the loaders?
COMPRADOR *(running up)*: Ten.
HOLEY: Ten what?
COMPRADOR: Ten cents.
HOLEY: Meantime the Chinese are paying 5 cents? *(The Comprador lapses into an embarrassed silence.)* Tell them from today they're on the lower rate. *(The Comprador hesitates.)* Whaddya waiting for?!
(The Comprador quietly explains to the crowd. There is an explosion of discontent.)
THE LOADERS: – Five cent, no!
– Should be tenna cent, one jiao!
– One jiao, tenna cent!
THE BOATMAN CHI *(enraged, thrusting both his splayed-out hands into Holey's face)*: Tenna cent, tenna cent!
HOLEY *(holds up his hand – the shouting abruptly stops)*: So I'm gonna pay more than the Chinese exporters? I'm an American. A democrat. We believe in equal pay. *(The shouting erupts again.)* Cut that out now! *(The crowd roars even louder. Holey turns to the Comprador with a sharp order.)* Pay the bastards off now! How many of 'em? Count up!
COMPRADOR *(disheartened, he pulls out his time board)*: Fifty.
HOLEY: Five cents for each of them – now!
(The Comprador tries to shove the money into each loader's hands. They have formed a tight knit crowd and wave away the money.)
THE LOADERS: No! I don't want it! No good! Bu yao!
HOLEY: Give me the goddam money!

I WANT A BABY AND OTHER PLAYS

(*He seizes the bag of coins from the Comprador, thrusts his hand in and flings handfuls of coins into the crowd. The crowd, which had recoiled back in silence, instantly breaks into a complete mêlée. Chi reaches out for some of the money but is knocked aside, manages to scrabble together some coins but drops them after a blow from another coolie. The coolies are all ready to fly at each other's throats. Holey surveys the frenzied scuffling with a controlling, sardonic gaze.*)

SCENE SIX

Policemen enter and put down the riot striking right and left with their clubs. Two tourists, a man and a woman, enter in palanquins and, pulling back the curtains, climb down into the brawling, snarling crowd. The frenzied loaders are careful not to touch the foreigners.

The palanquin bearers move to one side and survey the fighting. At the end of the scene, two of them will come forward when summoned as 'pushmen'.[87]

MALE TOURIST (*consulting his Baedeker guidebook*): This way to Charity Hill? (*He is emaciated and frail looking. He wears plus fours and prominent glasses. His wife has a camera and is one of those red faced, elderly looking but fleshy Anglo-Saxon women who like to tick off as many of the sights on their list as possible.*)
WIFE: Yes, dear. (*At this moment Chi rushes up to Holey and again thrusts his splayed empty hands up at Holey's face.*)
CHI: Tenna cents give! Jiao give! (*Holey holds out a riding crop and wards him off. The policemen have resorted to wielding the sheaths for their clubs in the thick of the swirling crowd.*)
WIFE: Oh, how interesting! (*She points the camera at Chi as she walks through the crowd.*)
HOLEY (*ignoring the brawl and shouting towards the river bank*): Hey, cutter!

---

87   *Pushmen*: Men who helped to push tourists up a steep hill during their sightseeing.

VOICE FROM THE CUTTER: Coming, sir! (*Holey moves off. Chi takes a step in his direction, his gaze unfocused, and blunders into the Comprador.*)

WIFE (*to Chi*): Don't change your expression. I am just taking a snap. (*Chi spits forcefully in the Comprador's face, who immediately spits back. She is shaken and wipes off where the spit has hit her.*): You dreadful men! (*Then in a tone of rebuke to her husband.*) Wait for me. Where have you got to? (*Meantime a policeman is beating Chi with his sheath.*) Pushmen, pushmen! What are you gawping at? (*Two Chinese who were staring at the scuffle come over and, putting their hands in the small of the tourists' backs, push them up the hill.*)

HUSBAND (*reading from his Baedeker*): The temple is situated at a height of 900 feet and was constructed six hundred years ago.

WIFE: Six hundred years? Oh, how interesting! (*They exit with the pushmen. The policemen continue to beat up and disperse the loaders.*)

SCENE SEVEN

The Stoker appears on the threshold of the radio station. Clenching his fists, he shouts at the fleeing crowd.

STOKER: What have you done, you dogs? Did you really have to....?

POLICEMAN: Got a problem have we?

STOKER (*quickly changing his tone*): I was asking... (*Points with his finger outside the station.*) ... did they really have to shift the boiler like that? They've put a dent in one side ...

(*The Stoker retreats inside the station. The Comprador gives money to one of the policemen. Cries are heard from the river. The Comprador runs to the bank, cups his palms around his ears, listens attentively and begins to repeat whichever words he can catch drifting across to him.*)

COMPRADOR: A car ... at the office ... half past eleven ... Certainly, sir. (*He turns around, notices Chi sitting by his boat and says with vicious deliberation.*) You ... will never ever ... work for me ... again.

SECOND LINK

On board the Cockchafer. *The shelter deck of the gunboat. At a higher elevation the ship's bridge can be seen at the same time.*

Whiteness and polished metal. Awnings stretched against the fierce sun. Electric fans hum. Woven Shanghai chaises longues and chairs are set out for breakfast.

On the shelter deck of the gunboat Cockchafer, the wife of French businessman Monsieur de Bruchelles and his daughter Cordelia are suffering in the intense heat, regardless of which Madame is encumbered in a squeaky corset. She has a dark moustache and an uncommonly stentorian voice. She has the bust of a woman who pours her excess maternal feelings into philanthropic work. Cordelia is a flat chested "young thing", thoroughly pampered and spoilt. It's obvious relations between mother and daughter are somewhat fraught. Cordelia is sulking and keeps looking at her watch.

SCENE ONE

Enter Copper, ship's Lieutenant, in a single breasted white naval jacket with high collar and stripes. His head narrows at the top and has fiery ginger hair. His face is jug shaped and heavily freckled. He's one of those "jolly good fellows", plays football and is a stickler for red tape.

MADAME: Good morning, Mr. Copper. I am so happy, just so happy. I have just participated in the sacrament of baptism.
CORDELIA: Honestly, the place stank to high heaven!
MADAME (*rebuking*): Cordelia!
COPPER: A male child?
CORDELIA (*ever more strident*): A female, but about thirty, with a face like a monkey and a child in her arms.

MADAME: A boatman's wife. She was so pleased with the little cross around her neck. Oh, to think now she'll bring up her little ones in Christian purity.
CORDELIA (*looking pointedly at her mother*): Unlike some who shall be nameless!
MADAME: Cordelia! Aren't you ashamed, in front of the Lieutenant?! All the same, I'm happy.
CORDELIA: And I'm very unhappy. I'm going to miss out on my Chinese suit. I love how tightly they fit! Why has my tiresome father disappeared from sight?
COPPER: He is waiting for Mr. Holey. (*Goes to the rail and looks out over the river through binoculars.*)
CORDELIA: Who's this Holey?
MADAME: He's your suit.
CORDELIA: Oh, so after the moths have been at it then?
MADAME: Your father is trying to fix a deal with him, for those ghastly skins I think, and if it falls through – well then, your suit ...
CORDELIA: But father promised me. And in Tai Li's shop there's one I absolutely adore.
COPPER (*catching only the last words*): Who's that you adore? Lucky man. (*He listens out.*) The cutter has come alongside.

SCENE TWO

Enter Monsieur de Bruchelles, the Captain and Holey. Monsieur is elderly and stout and evidently suffers in the tropical heat. He is wearing a loose jacket and trousers and a woollen cummerbund. His voice is loud and peevish except when he greets someone, when it quavers pathetically and its lower registers turn suddenly into almost a squeal.

When he talks with anyone, Monsieur invariably prods them, slaps them on the shoulder, pats their stomach. He is visibly oppressed by his wife and, like many an elderly father, a little bit in love with his daughter. He is a merchant of the old school, working for himself but getting squeezed out by the agents of the biggest, multi-million dollar American, English, and sometimes even Chinese, firms.

The Captain is a commanding figure amidst all those gathered on the gunboat. Built like a block, square shaped and heavy, in his white naval jacket he resembles nothing so much as a fire-proof safe. Where he treads is holy and inviolable. His self confidence knows no bounds, he doesn't deign to speak to the natives, convinced that a mere glance or flick of his finger is enough to elicit compliance. His collection of Boxer rebellion[88] weapons is both his pride and joy and partly a reflection of his service record. With women he is refined, even sentimental.

Monsieur and Holey pause in the doorway, talking business.

MONSIEUR: I'll come straight to the point. All your skins for 40% cash in advance. The balance payable by letter of credit in Shanghai after delivery. We'll settle the details presently.

HOLEY: We gotta buy up skins from all over the country. We need all the dough up front...Tai Li will pay it.

MONSIEUR (*stunned*): You want to sell to a Chinaman? My dear sir, this is a matter of principle. You surely can't ...

HOLEY: You got 12 minutes, tops.

CAPTAIN: Ample time. Please be seated at the table. (*Introducing Holey to the ladies.*) Madame de Bruchelles. Mademoiselle de Bruchelles. Mr Holey, of Robert Dollar and Associates.

HOLEY (*greeting Cordelia*): Export. (*Madame*) Import. (*Copper*) Steamship navigation.

MADAME: You're American?

CORDELIA (*aside, capriciously*): I hate Americans. (*Seeing the Captain in parade uniform.*) Captain, how smart we are today!

CAPTAIN: I have just been visiting the local Mayor – a most distinguished old man. (*He gestures.*) Shall we breakfast?

COPPER: Boy!

SCENE THREE

A small Chinese boy runs in, wearing a short white jacket and white trousers.

COPPER: Cigars. (*The Boy runs out and returns with a box.*)

---

88   *The Boxer Rebellion:* a violent, anti-foreign, anti-Christian uprising in China, 1899-1901.

CORDELIA (*looking the boy over*): What an exquisite mouth!
HOLEY: You think so?
CORDELIA: And a delightfully shaped head.
COPPER (*feeling the boy's head*): No good for football.
CORDELIA: Ooh! what shape is?
COPPER: Mine.
HOLEY (*peering at him with an expert eye*): You kiddin' me? No way you'd head the ball true.
COPPER (*indignant*): Watch this! (*He jumps into the air and demonstrates how he heads a ball.*) One! (*Flicks his head.*) Two! (*His leg kicks out and catches Holey's shin.*) So sorry!
HOLEY (*unruffled*): No way you're kicking right. You gotta do it like this. (*He stands up and deliberately kicks Copper on the leg.*) Oh, I surely am sorry! (*From now on till the end of Link 2 Copper limps.*)
CAPTAIN (*to Monsieur de B*): I see a man unhappy in his own skin.
MONSIEUR (*roused from his thoughts by the word "skin", to Holey*): These skins.... if I give you half in advance, that should be plenty, shouldn't it?
HOLEY: There's a drought in the region. The cattle are dropping... I gotta keep ahead of the Chinese. Their agents are leaving tonight.
MONSIEUR: What the devil...
CAPTAIN (*taking the Frenchman's side and butting in reproachfully*): So hard hearted, Mr Holey? I'd heard you had a softer side.
HOLEY: Me, be softer? Now that would be sensational!! (*Monsieur and Cordelia exchange meaningful glances.*)
CORDELIA: Mr Holey, do save me! I've gone a week without a foxtrot! Much longer and I shall require rather more thorough rejuvenation!
(*Copper claps his hands. The orchestra strikes up. The pair foxtrot.*)
CAPTAIN (*to Monsieur*): Your daughter is quite an asset in business matters.
MADAME (*observing the pair, to Monsieur*): He'll come round, dear, I'm sure ...
MONSIEUR (*mimicking her sympathetic tone*): He'll come round, dear ... Let's not hold our breath!
MADAM (*wiping her husband's damp brow with a handkerchief*): Poor boy! You've worked yourself into the ground. You're nothing but skin and bones.

MONSIEUR (*to Holey, who has just returned Cordelia to her seat*): You won't be able to trade your skins – Tai Li is pulling the wool over your eyes. He hasn't got that sort of money. Believe me, I've been in this country 25 years now.
HOLEY: Tai Li will deliver.
CORDELIA: You foxtrot divinely, Mr. Holey. You glide along like a swimmer.
HOLEY (*not paying attention to her*): Swim? It's too bad, but I don't swim.
CORDELIA (*spitefully*): So obtuse!
COPPER: I have a feeling that, as we have obviously passed muster here on board, Miss Cordelia will want to stay with us.
MONSIEUR (*to Holey*): 40% in Shanghai and I'll pay you 60 now.
HOLEY: One hundred percent cash on the button.
CAPTAIN (*to Copper.*) Pour him a drink ...
(*Copper sorts through some bottles, chooses one and pours a glass for Holey.*)
MONSIEUR (*raising his glass*): So, 60% cash, can we drink to that?
HOLEY (*raises his glass, which brings his watch in front of his nose. He puts the glass down swiftly and gets up.*): Sorry. My time just ran out.
CAPTAIN: Wait a moment. The cutter will be here in a minute or two.
HOLEY: Don't bother. I'll get a boat.
MONSIEUR (*half whining*): So, we can settle on 60, can't we?
HOLEY: One hundred. I bid you all good day. (*Exits quickly.*)
MONSIEUR (*lets fly at Holey's departing back*): Scoundrel!
HOLEY (*stopping*): You talking to me?
MONSIEUR: No, no. I do beg your pardon. You must have misheard.
HOLEY: Likewise.
MONSIEUR (*chasing after him*): 75%!
HOLEY (*in the doorway*): 100! (*Exits onto the bridge.*)

SCENE FOUR

CAPTAIN: Well?
MADAME de B: What a despicable man!
CORDELIA: And a carthorse! He trod on my feet so much, they're all bruised.

COPPER (*nursing his kicked leg*): He broke the skin on my leg too. They'll have to dress it.
MONSIEUR (*furiously to Copper*): For Heaven's sake, what do I care about your skin, when all mine have just gone up in smoke?
CORDELIA: And my suit!
CAPTAIN (*to Copper*): Arrange a boat for Holey. (*Copper joins the American up on the bridge.*)

SCENE FIVE

Captain's bridge. Copper and Holey.

COPPER (*shouts down to a boatman on the river*): Hoy, you!
  (*The boatman shouts back something. They both listen.*)
HOLEY (*to Copper, puzzled*): What's he saying?
COPPER: I can't tell. (*To the boatman*) Hoy! ... Why are you turning away? (*He shouts down to the shelter deck.*) Boy!

SCENE SIX

The Boy runs up to the bridge at Copper's summons.

BOY (*responding to Copper's call*): Shi! (*He points towards where the boatman must be on the river.*)
COPPER (*to the Boy*): Tell him to come up to the ship's ladder right now!
BOY (*using his hands as a trumpet, he leans out from the bridge and shouts*)
  Ey-hey, hey, hey, hey! Chi! They say you have to bring your boat over now. (*Everyone listens to the reply.*)
COPPER: What's he jabbering on about?
BOY (*mangling the English*): Say, won't come. Say, Merican pay very bad money, beat with stick.
HOLEY: Jeez, have we spoilt these swines, or what.
COPPER: Promise to pay him more.
HOLEY: Absolutely no way! On principle.
COPPER (*to the boy*): Tell that case of yellow fever to bring his boat alongside right now!

BOY: Chi! Chi! The officer is getting so angry! He says you must bring your boat over…right now… (*To Copper*) Say Merican big cheat.

COPPER: What? A cheat? (*He draws his revolver, aims at the boatman and orders the Boatman.*) Get alongside now! I will count to three … One …

BOY (*rushing over to Copper in horror*): No, no!

COPPER (*pushing him off*): Get off me! … Two! …

BOY (*grabbing Copper's hand with the revolver*): Don't do, don't do!

COPPER (*shaking the boy from his hand*): Good God! What the devil has got into you? How dare you? (*He shoves him off and the boy falls into the river.*) Let that be a damn lesson to you! (*He brushes off his sleeve where the boy touched it.*)

SCENE SEVEN

Cordelia rouses herself.

CORDELIA (*ascending languidly to the bridge*): God! This heat!

COPPER (*still beside himself, harshly*): Hot enough to turn the heads of these animals. (*In a chivalrous tone to Cordelia.*) Allow me to escort you under an awning.

(*The Boy, choking, shouts from the water.*)

CORDELIA: What's that? (*Questioningly to the men*) Is someone drowning?

HOLEY (*looking over the side*): Too bad. Tangling his legs like that. He's going all the way to the bottom.

CORDELIA (*runs up to the side*): Man overboard!

HOLEY: Nah, just a Chinese.

CORDELIA: But we must still save him. (*She seizes a life belt with* Cockchafer *written on it.*)

COPPER (*stopping her from tossing the belt*): Miss Cordelia, that is not advisable. The crew are watching.

HOLEY (*still leaning over the side, triumphantly*): Ha! That bastard in the boat is heading our way after all, to save the kid.

SCENE EIGHT

The Captain ascends back up to the bridge.

CAPTAIN: What's going on?
CORDELIA (*still holding on to the lifebelt*): Boy overboard.
CAPTAIN (*sternly*): The lifebelts of a British gunboat cannot be used for the Chinese.
CORDELIA: But Captain, please –
CAPTAIN: That is the disciplinary code of a British warship. Any infringement is punishable by firing squad.
CORDELIA (*coquettishly*): Oh! Including mine, Captain?
CAPTAIN: Yours included. You will face a shot from a champagne bottle. Allow me. (*He offers his arm.*) Shall we continue our breakfast? (*He descends to the shelter deck with Cordelia.*)
HOLEY (*turning around gloatingly*): So our man took the bait. We got him after all. (*Looks over the side again.*) That's it! Get that son of a bitch alongside!
COPPER (*shouts orders down over the side*): Ship's ladder! Hook in the boat! Prepare to embark Mr Holey. (*Listens and repeats words of the crew by the ship's ladder.*) The boy what? ... hurt ... can't make head nor tail ... (*He indicates to Holey that his boat is ready.*)
HOLEY: Thank you. Good day.

SCENE NINE

The Captain and the de Bruchelles family are seated at the breakfast table.

MONSIEUR (*wildly angry*): That man is an imbecile! To turn down a European and sell to a Chinaman!
CAPTAIN: American flirtation.
MONSIEUR (*sardonically*): They smile to our faces, build their universities and hospitals and clubs – and behind our backs they grab our last piece of bread. They are undermining us at every turn!

SCENE TEN

Enter Copper.

COPPER: And here's an example right under our noses: I was forced to draw my gun on the boatman, and our own boy pulled my arm away.
CAPTAIN: He did? Bring him here! (*Copper goes to fetch the boy.*)
CORDELIA: Captain, be gentle with him. He's probably hurt himself quite badly, and besides he has such a lovely mouth.
CAPTAIN (*reproachfully*): Miss Cordelia, we are Christians!

SCENE ELEVEN

The pale Boy enters behind Copper and visibly shrinks under the Captain's stare. His head is bandaged, he has been given a change of clothes. Slowly he kneels down.

MADAME (*breaking the oppressive silence*): Allow me to talk to him. I have experience of these matters.
CAPTAIN: Please do.
MADAME: Boy, you have done wrong.
BOY (*in a wooden voice*): Yes, missis.
MADAME: You have raised your hand against a superior.
BOY: Yes, missis.
MADAME: Recite the Lord's Prayer.
BOY: Ar fazer, chart heaven, howed be name, sy king come, sy wilbdun, give zis day day bread, forgive us tespasses…
CAPTAIN: Stop! (*He taps out the syllables on something.*) Forgive us our trespasses.
BOY: Yes sir.
MADAME: Well then, ask forgiveness of Mr. Copper!
BOY: Me bad servant, Cattin, me behave bandit.
CAPTAIN: Kiss his hand! (*The Boy kisses Copper's hand.*) Be very careful, boy: you won't get a second chance. Get out!
MADAME (*to the boy*): Stay there! (*Enraptured.*) Captain, you are a veritable St. Augustine! … Let's give him a sweet! (*She takes one from a bowl and offers it to the boy.*) There, dear, for you.

CAPTAIN: Don't pet him. (*The Boy exits.*)
MADAME (*to the Captain*): And take some for yourself, put them in your pocket. Here, I'll do it myself. (*She takes the Browning revolver out of the side pocket of the Captain's jacket and puts a handful of sweets underneath.*) Now, when you pass a child, you'll put your hand in your pocket and the sweets will be right there. Such a shame we can't bring out the missionary in you.
MONSIEUR: Ah, but he's chosen to bring out the big guns instead. He's in his element, you can see, and no less worthy a vocation. (*He rises abruptly, pulling the napkin from his chest.*)
CAPTAIN: You're leaving us?
MONSIEUR (*decisively and acidly*): Yes. To upset Mr. Holey's little apple cart. He thinks he can sell his goods to Tai Li. Well, Tai Li is going to find it very difficult to get the money from the bank. He'll be pushed to the wall. Mr. Holey forgot with whom he was playing. (*Exits.*)
CORDELIA (*triumphantly*): I know Daddy. I shall get suits galore.
CAPTAIN (*consulting his watch, to Copper*): What's happening with the cutter? (*Copper goes up to the bridge and looks through binoculars.*)
COPPER (*shouts down to the Captain without taking his binoculars from his eyes*): About half way across, sir ... Yes ... keeping steady ... The American is approaching the shore now.
CAPTAIN (*ascends to the bridge with a glass of whiskey in his hand*): Progress?
COPPER (*continues to look through the binoculars*): Almost there ... he's standing up ... just a minute ... seems to be some sort of argument. (*The steady voice of the Lieutenant changes to an alarmed shout. With eyes glued to the binoculars he gesticulates for help with his free hand.*) Captain, look, Captain!
CAPTAIN (*snatches the binoculars from him, presses them to his eyes. His voice is full of helpless rage*) What is that swine doing? What in God's name is he playing at? (*He flings his glass down onto the deck where it shatters.*)

THIRD LINK

The same river bank by the radio station as in Link One, and towards which Holey will soon travel in Chi's boat. An hour of rest. The boatmen are mending sails and oars amidst the bales and boxes. Some are oiling upturned boats. Old women are darning torn clothing.

SCENE ONE

Three boatmen and the old woman Granny. She is squatting on the bank, looking out at the river.

GRANNY(*rousing herself*): One of you. (*Gesturing out at the river*) That's stubborn Chi's boat isn't it?
FIRST BOATMAN (*peering out*): Where?
GRANNY: Near the foreign boat with the guns.
FIRST BOATMAN: Blimey, mother, you've got good eyes.
SECOND BOATMAN: Yeah, it's him.
GRANNY: He's comin' this way.
FIRST BOATMAN: What d'you want him for?
SECOND BOATMAN: All ready to visit the Captain are we?
  (*The boatmen laugh.*)
FIRST BOATMAN: They've no use for old women. Not with the young 'uns we ferry out.
SECOND BOATMAN: They pay well.
FIRST BOATMAN: A dollar a night – if she's a looker. Silly money. No further rowin' required.
GRANNY (*dolefully*): Not anymore. Our girls'll stand in a queue for a couple of cents. It's hard to make a livin' now.

FIRST BOATMAN (*looking at her carefully and* realising): Hang on! It's you bargainin' for Chi's daughter, isn't it?
GRANNY: But I can't pay ten dollars for the girl.
SECOND BOATMAN: How much then?
GRANNY: Three.
FIRST BOATMAN (*outraged*): Three dollars! She's ten. That wouldn't even cover the milk she's got through!
SECOND BOATMAN: They pay three dollars for a fortnight.
GRANNY: Before, yes. And I'd part with ten for her back then. But now there's the drought, and no one's got a cent to spare. They give their girls away for a song.
FIRST BOATMAN: Well, go and take her then, even if you'll lose out ... Why are you pesterin' Chi anyway?
GRANNY (*with real feeling*): His little girl has a good voice. She'll hold a tune, I can tell.
SECOND BOATMAN: And Chi knows too. He won't let her go, he's stubborn as they come.
GRANNY: He's strugglin' to feed his family though ...
FIRST BOATMAN: Aren't we all?

SCENE TWO

The Journalist comes down the steps from the radio station, sagging from the heat. The boatmen, as though wrenched from their spots, rush towards the foreigner, offering their services.

FIRST and SECOND BOATMEN: Cattin, Cattin! Wan boat. Ride ten cents. Need ride – Cattin! Cattin!
(*The Journalist stops, focuses his camera on them, changes his mind, yawns and goes on.*)
FIRST BOATMAN: (*shouts after him, nastily*): Ginger devil!
SECOND BOATMAN: Pockets full of dollars, but no – he has to walk. Couldn't give a toss about our livin'.
FIRST BOATMAN: Chop his legs off. He'd need a boat then!
(*The Stoker enters with a sack of coal on his back on his way to the radio station. He catches the last remark and responds in kind.*)
STOKER: Chop his head off.

FIRST BOATMAN: He'd sprout another!

STOKER: Take that off too then.

SECOND BOATMAN (*jabbing his oar out at the gunboat*): See those guns? It'll be your heads for the chop! ... You say you seen the gingers lose their heads?

STOKER: I have.

FIRST BOATMAN: Where?

STOKER (*motions with his chin as his hands are supporting the sack*): That way.

SECOND BOATMAN: Beijing?

STOKER: Further.

FIRST BOATMAN: I don't know no further.

STOKER: There is a country, believe me.

FIRST BOATMAN (*drawing nearer to the Stoker secretively and disbelievingly*): They cut off English heads?

STOKER: No exceptions.

GRANNY (*ironically*): A man gets a drink inside him, he grows a very long tongue.

STOKER: That's rich coming from you, woman, who trades in child meat! You hold your own tongue!

SCENE THREE

The Heshang, a Buddhist monk, passes by, tinkling little bowls together. His head is so closely shaved it has a bluish tinge. His face is deeply furrowed, accentuating his cheekbones, his skin is scorched by the sun, his eyes gleam malevolently and fanatically. He is wearing a brown or blue monk's robe with very wide sleeves, wrapped around him differently from the robes of ordinary Chinese with their high collars and full-length side fastenings which start from under the arm. His dirty, sunburnt chest pokes out prominently above his stomach. In one hand he holds a rosary. When he tells it, he mumbles a prayer. In the other hand he has two little copper bowls, one inside the other. He makes them chime, trying to attract the attention of his god.

THE HESHANG (*chanting*): Hail, Amida Buddha! Na-mu A-mi to Fo! (*He exits, his chanting dying away.*)

FIRST BOATMAN: Alright. So you can cut off a head. But so's they can't shoot you, you need to get a piece o' yella cloth with a prayer on it, from the likes of him, the heshang from the monastery. You pin it on your chest, then a bullet can't get you.
SECOND BOATMAN: That's what them rich peasants said twenty years ago.
STOKER: Nothing like rich peasantry for total stupidity. A scrap of cloth won't stop a bullet.
FIRST BOATMAN: It won't? (*With certainty.*) Well then, can't be no such place as you say.
SECOND BOATMAN: That's right.
STOKER: There is, I tell you.
FIRST BOATMAN: No need for a piece o' cloth?
STOKER: No, just a rifle instead.
FIRST BOATMAN: You bin there? You a soldier?
STOKER (*his voice more measured*): Me, no, I'm just a coolie. I stoke the stoves in the telegraph office over there. Foof! You wouldn't believe how hot it gets!
SECOND BOATMAN (*suspiciously*): Do you read newspapers?
GRANNY: You're a wrong 'un. The police'll have you.
STOKER (*throws his sack down, grabs Granny's shoulders and shakes her violently*): Want to go in the water?
GRANNY (*reeling in his grasp, suddenly points at the river*): Mister Chi!
FIRST BOATMAN: Where'd he pick up the white man? Lucky devil!
SECOND BOATMAN (*shrilly and gleefully*): Unlucky, more like. He's picked up the American. He'll get a couple of cents if he's lucky.
GRANNY (*grasping the situation*): Ah-hah! (*She gets up and, swaying on the little hooves of her deformed feet, totters to the mooring point.*)
FIRST BOATMAN: But Chi's wilful. He'll call him all sorts.
STOKER: Is that all? What about a crack over the head with his oar?
FIRST BOATMAN: What are the courts for? What do policemen carry clubs for? You're a right Confucius, aren't you? (*Facing the river, in an alarmed voice.*) Wo! Wait a minute!

SCENE FOUR

Holey and Chi in the boat on the river. Holey is in the bow, Chi rows desultorily in the stern.

HOLEY: Faster! Jeez!
CHI (*slowing down, sullenly*): Money pay! Two cent.
HOLEY (*quietly*): When I'm ashore, you'll get what you deserve.
CHI (*more insistently*): Money! Two cent.
HOLEY: I said, when I'm on the bank, you'll get it. (*Chi stops rowing. Holey sits quietly a second, trying to stare Chi into submission. Then he shouts loudly.*) OK? You wanna play it like that? (*He shouts to the boatmen on the bank.*) Boatman!
(*The Second Boatman dashes forward ready for business but the Stoker restrains him.*)
STOKER (*sternly*): No! Chi's in the right.
HOLEY (*shouts to the bank*): Five cents, that's right, five cents to get me to the bank.
FIRST BOATMAN (*rushes forward, warbling with delight*): Five cents! I don't believe it!
STOKER (*holding him back*): No, you mustn't!
HOLEY (*shouts caustically*): Oh, so we got a new strike on now, do we?
CHI: Take trip steamboat. Money pay.
HOLEY (*losing his temper*): Get me to the goddam bank, right now, or I'll call the police.
CHI (*sullenly*): Your plice, call. My money give.
HOLEY: Jesus Christ! I have had it! Here's yer goddam money! (*He flings coins into the boat.*)
CHI (*picking them up and then agitatedly*): Five cash? Half cent? Take! Pah! (*He pokes the coins in front of Holey's face.*) Two cent give!
HOLEY (*stepping back from Chi's gesticulating hand*): Goddam Bolshie!
CHI: No go shore! Five cash, pah! (*He flings the coins at Holey's feet.*)
HOLEY: See how ya like this then! (*He gets up and takes a step towards the stern.*)
CHI (*defending himself with an oar*): You no can. You no dare. You – cheat!
(*The American lands a punch on the bridge of Chi's nose. Chi squats down not letting go of his oar. Holey raises his arm for a second*

blow. Chi dodges it and rolls to one side of the boat. As the boat tips over, Holey lands his punch on air and falls out.)
HOLEY (*floundering in the water*): Help, aa-aah-aahhh!
(*Laughter from the bank. Chi brings his boat in to moor with vicious swipes of his oar.*)

SCENE FIVE

The boatmen, Granny and Chi on the bank.

FIRST BOATMAN (*gloating*): One wet and arsey American!
SECOND BOATMAN: Oooh, what's this? Fish in me pockets?
    (*Laughter.*)
CHI (*fussing round his boat*): Bugger's broken my oar, not paid his money. Ginger beast! (*He flings away the stump of the oar and shakes his fist at the river.*) He should pay for the bloody oar too!
    (*The river grows quiet enough to make the boatmen turn round. A frightened, tense silence descends on them.*)
FIRST BOATMAN: Oh no ...
    (*Silence.*)
GRANNY: He can't swim.
SECOND BOATMAN (*to Chi*): You've got it comin' to you now.
STOKER: You'd better scarper – fast.
CHI (*distractedly*): Where to? Without my boat?
FIRST BOATMAN (*looking along the bank*): There's people nearly here, they're runnin'.
CHI (*frozen with terror*): I can't leave. My son'll die of hunger. I'll die of hunger. The whole family. Where would I go?
GRANNY (*insinuatingly*): Mister Chi? Remember our little chat?
CHI (*letting out his fright in anger*): You again! I told you already!
GRANNY (*like a siren*): Six dollars. See here. (*She jingles the coins in her hand.*)
CHI: Get away from me!
GRANNY (*holding her hand with the silver under Chi's nose*): Six dollars. A mouth less to feed. They'll go a long way.
CHI: Ten.
STOKER: The police – run!
GRANNY: Six.

FIRST BOATMAN (*shaking Chi*): Run!
STOKER: Get away. Hide yourself. Don't answer anyone who shouts for you. Not even your own son.
   (*Chi prepares to run. Granny grabs his arm.*)
GRANNY (*avidly and demandingly*): Give me the girl, in front of witnesses, or they'll say I stole her.
CHI: Alright, alright. Take her!
   (*Granny pulls the girl out of Chi's boat. She tries to cling to her father. Chi prises her fingers from his clothes.*)
FIRST BOATMAN (*watching Granny take away the girl*): Sell her to an American, and she'll have a right little earner there.

SCENE SIX

Chi's wife enters and rushes towards Granny.

CHI'S WIFE: Where are you takin' my daughter?
CHI (*stops his wife*): Quiet! I've sold her!
CHI'S WIFE: Sold? How much?
CHI: Six.
CHI's WIFE (*counting up the coins*): Too cheap. (*Shouts at Granny as the latter leaves.*): You've cheated us, old woman! (*She notices the general agitation.*) What's the matter with you all?
   (*The First Boatman takes her aside. Chi looks round and in one huge bound leaps away from the police running in and disappears into the crowd. His wife sits down and stays there, rocking to and fro. The coins drop out of her hands. She searches for them and closes a hand around them again.*)

SCENE SEVEN

A more senior policeman enters at the head of three watchmen. He is wearing a grey cap with a flattened, disc shaped crown. There is a patterned badge on his white cap band. His jacket, a little like a katsaveika[89], with copper buttons,

---

89   Katsaveika: a type of short, fur-trimmed, Russian jacket.

fits tightly over his stomach. His sleeves are very wide and short at the wrist. His baggy trousers are caught in around the ankles with white puttees. He is wearing soft shoes. His sabre clanks in its metal scabbard and gets tangled between his legs. His subordinates wear only simple skull caps and carry zebra striped bamboo sticks.

POLICEMAN (*swooping down on the boatmen*): Where is he?
SECOND BOATMAN (*pointing to the river*): There!
POLICEMAN: Who d'you mean?
SECOND BOATMAN: The American.
POLICEMAN: Which boat was he in?
SECOND BOATMAN (*pointing to Chi's boat*): That one.
POLICEMAN: What about the boatman?
SECOND BOATMAN: Dunno.

SCENE EIGHT

The Boatswain and two sailors from the Cockchafer land and climb up onto the wharf. The ribbons on their naval hats are cropped short and fall over their right ears.

BOATSWAIN (*running in*): Where's the boatman?
SECOND BOATMAN: Me no know.
POLICEMAN (*runs up to the Boatswain obligingly and points to the river*): Here place here.
BOATSWAIN (*snarls at the Second Boatman*): Devil take you, you yella bastard. You'll be lucky to keep your teeth. What 'ave you got eyes for? Right lads, look sharp and get in the water. (*He shouts at the boatmen.*) An' you pigs, out on the river and start searching!
(*The sailors fling off their shirts, bell bottomed trousers and hats and dive into the river in their shorts. The boatmen rush towards their boats.*)

SCENE NINE

Enter the Journalist.

JOURNALIST (*runs in and issues commands to the sailors and to the boatmen bustling up and down the bank*): More to the left! More to the left! Dive deeper! Further downstream! Further ... Look in that still patch there. In that still patch! ...
GENERAL EXCLAMATION: ... Aaaah!
    (*The sailors carry up Holey's soaking body.*)
JOURNALIST (*fussing*): Carefully, carefully now! Put him into the boat. Here!
    (*They pull off the American's clothes, put a cushion underneath him and start artificial resuscitation. The Chinese press round in a tight circle.*)
SAILOR (*moving Holey's arms about. Out of breath*): Won't do no good, sir, 'ee was layin' on the bottom.
BOATSWAIN: Maybe 'ee's just unconscious?
SAILOR (*looking over at the* Cockchafer): They want to know what's going on, sir.
BOATSWAIN: Right. (*Turning to the second Sailor*) Send a signal.
SECOND SAILOR: No flags sir!
JOURNALIST (*nodding at the Chinese*): There's your solution.
    (*A sailor wrenches a jacket off one of the Chinese, tears it into strips, which he ties to some of the policemen's bamboo sticks. He asks the Boatswain.*)
SAILOR: What's the message sir?
BOATSWAIN (*raising Holey's hand and letting it fall once more*): Dead.
    (*The 2nd Sailor signals.*)
FIRST SAILOR (*to the Boatswain who is looking at the* corpse): One more try sir?
    (*The Boatswain applies pressure to the corpse, then gestures hopelessly. Over the water comes the clatter of the* Cockchafer's *anchor chain being drawn up.*)

BOATSWAIN (*abruptly*): He's gone.
CHI'S WIFE (*looks towards the horizon and, as if defending herself against a ghost, cries out hysterically*): It's moving.
SECOND SAILOR: She's coming across, sir.
 (*The boatmen run helter-skelter.*)
FIRST SAILOR (*trying to grab some of them by the sleeve*): Oi, stop. You boatmen, you get over 'ere now!
BOATSWAIN (*grabbing the sailor and calming him down*): Sod 'em. They won't get far.

FOURTH LINK

SCENE ONE

The Captain and Copper back on the Cockchafer's *bridge as in the second Link. The shards of the broken whiskey glass have not yet been picked up. The Captain is in a fury.*

CAPTAIN (*spluttering and pacing up and down by the handrail*): A guest of mine! A white man! They forget who they are dealing with.
COPPER (*echoing the Captain shrilly*): Yellow swine! Monkeys! Dirty dogs! They want the bowsprit run up their arses.
CAPTAIN (*turning round abruptly*): Lieutenant Copper!
COPPER: Captain, sir! (*He comes stiffly to attention.*)
CAPTAIN: Bring the ship around!
COPPER: Bringing the ship around, sir!
CAPTAIN: Prepare a squad!
COPPER: A squad, yes, sir!
CAPTAIN: Convey the deceased to the chapel!
COPPER: To the chapel, yes, sir!
CAPTAIN: Form a guard of honour!
COPPER: Guard of honour, yes, sir! (*Copper salutes and exits.*)

SCENE TWO

CAPTAIN (*shouts to one side*): Boy! Bring me some grog. (*The Boy runs in with grog. The Captain drinks it down in one go and stares into the Boy's face.*) Little shit!

(*He throws the dregs in the Boy's face. The Captain exits. The Boy picks up the pieces of the previous glass. The shelter deck. Enter Monsieur de Bruchelles and Copper. Monsieur is holding a soda water siphon in one hand, a glass in the other.*)

MONSIEUR: Confound it! My nerves are in shreds.

COPPER: Mine too.

MONSIEUR: And all because of that American.

COPPER: Exactly.

MONSIEUR: He slipped through my fingers, the nasty piece of work. I hope he comes to grief.

COPPER: He has.

MONSIEUR: What?

COPPER: The man's dead.

MONSIEUR: What? Was he killed? Was it a fight? When? (*In his agitation he presses the siphon and sprays a jet of water over Copper and lets out a shriek.*)

COPPER (*moves out of range of Monsieur*): For God's sake, cease fire! (*Jumping out of the way, he blunders into Madame and Cordelia as they enter.*)

MADAME (*to her husband*): Now what on earth has got into you?

MONSIEUR: A dreadful misfortune! Mr. Holey's been killed!

CORDELIA: Gracious! I've danced with a deceased.

MADAME: Who killed him?

COPPER: A boatman.

MADAME (*shaken*): My goddaughter this morning – what if she's his wife?

MONSIEUR (*beside himself*): Mark my words! Today – Holey. Tomorrow – me. The day after – it'll be your turn.

MADAME: There, there! Don't upset yourself like that.

MONSIEUR: They've grown insolent. They stab the missionaries to death. They run rings round the agents. They boycott the Japanese. Imagine! In Shanghai a Chinaman struck a European with a stick. In Peking a European was hit in the face – by a soldier.

CORDELIA (*naïvely*): What for?

MONSIEUR: Because the yellow degenerates weren't allowed in the European park. Lousy syphilitics – of course they weren't!

MADAME (*shocked by his language, moves Cordelia away*): In front of the child! For God's sake!

MONSIEUR: Twenty-five years ago I came to China. All that time I've struggled like a fish out of water, I've ended up with rheumatism and fever in this den of thieves, all just itching to help themselves from my pockets or stick a knife between my ribs. And for what? So the next damn ruffian can crack my skull open without a second thought!

MADAME (*trying to stroke her husband*): Calm down, dear, calm down. I do understand, I do.

MONSIEUR (*petulantly*): Leave me alone! No mollycoddling! (*It's not immediately clear if he is referring to himself or to the political situation.*) An end, I say, to the mollycoddling!

CORDELIA: But the murderer will be tried, won't he?

MONSIEUR: A trial? (*With a bitter smile.*) Already given a damn good flogging, I don't doubt. (*Getting agitated, he walks up and down squirting the siphon.*) We can't take this lying down. Otherwise there will be carnage!

CORDELIA (*looking out over the river*): Look at all those boats coming over from the town!

MADAME (*in a voice stricken with horror and clutching her husband's hand who is equally terrified.*) Chinese?

CORDELIA: Europeans!

(*Copper goes to the ship's ladder to greet the arrivals.*)

SCENE THREE

Copper's voice is heard giving directions to the boats. During the scenes that follow, he moves between the ship's ladder, where the fleeing Europeans are arriving, and the shelter deck, for his lines with the other characters.

Enter the Missionary. He wears a black frock coat and a full white collar. His grey hair is thinning. He is shrivelled with age.

MISSIONARY (*his voice trembling*): Lieutenant, you must excuse me. I consider it far from safe to stay in town.

MONSIEUR: Too true.

MISSIONARY (*sinking carefully into a wicker chair*): What an appalling act! That poor Mr. Holey. They say he was tortured for a long time, taunted, then drowned. This can't go unpunished, can it?

MADAME (*to the missionary, in the tone of Mary Magdalene addressing Christ*): And to think they might have laid hands on you. (*A silence falls as they all contemplate the horror that might have happened.*)
MISSIONARY: Dear God! Yes, yes.
(*Boxes, suitcases and trunks fly onto the stage.*)

SCENE FOUR

Enter the Tourist and his Wife. She can't bear to part with her hatboxes and parcels which hang from her arms like a bunch of balloons.

TOURIST (*embarrassed*): Do put them down, dear.
WIFE (*peevishly*): Get off! Those are my hats. I can't leave them to the mercy of bestial murderers.
TOURIST (*half whispering*): But my dear ...
WIFE (*at the top of her voice*): The Captain will forgive me. He's our only protection.
TOURIST (*to Copper*): Officer, can it really be true? Three Americans – in broad daylight?
WIFE (*interrupting*): I was told at least seven and two women.
TOURIST: Dragged into a boat and stabbed to death.
WIFE (*looking at Madame*): Horrible! Horrible! Horrible!
MADAME (*looking at the Wife, simultaneously, in her deep bass*): Horrible! Horrible! Horrible! (*They embrace.*)
MONSIEUR: This is only the starting gun, you'll see.
WIFE (*to Copper, hysterically*): You won't turn us away? You won't let us be torn to pieces! (*Spitefully to her husband*) I told you what would happen if we went to China. But you dug your heels in like a turkey.
TOURIST: How was I to know?
WIFE (*walks up to him*): What if they had got hold of me?
TOURIST (*with a pitiful sigh*): Oh, oh ...
WIFE: They would have gagged me.
TOURIST (*dolefully*): Ooh, ooh ...
WIFE: And raped me.
TOURIST (*despairingly*): Oooh ... Ooooh.

WIFE: I took a snap of that boatman this morning. Do you remember the way he looked at me? To think I've got him on the same reel as you. I can't bear it!
(*She takes out her camera, pulls out the reel of film and flings it away.*)

SCENE FIVE

Enter the Journalist catching the film reel in mid run.

JOURNALIST: What are you doing? You can't throw away something that sensational! (*To Monsieur, in an affable way*) That Holey, helluva fool, yeah? Starting a punch up in a boat when he can't swim.
MONSIEUR (*reining him in with an icy stare. He replies tersely and with distaste*): I am aghast at such an unseemly remark.
MADAME: To think of how they tortured him.
JOURNALIST (*at a loss*): Tortured?
WIFE: They say his eyes were put out.
TOURIST: The soles of his feet set light.
MISSIONARY: His body defiled.
JOURNALIST (*confused*): Excuse me? Hold on there.
MONSIEUR (*beside himself*): I will not excuse you!
MADAME (*beside herself*): To mock the dead body of a martyr. We will not excuse it.
MONSIEUR: We must have a reckoning. We must not let the reputation of the great powers be trampled into the mud.
JOURNALIST (*going along with them uncertainly*): Uh-huh ... Uh-huh ... (*It dawns on him.*) Okay! Now I get it! I get it!
MONSIEUR (*tersely*): How gratifying.
JOURNALIST (*snatching out a pen and writing on his cuff*): So – bringing pressure to bear in Peking and Washington – formal diplomatic complaints – indignation.
MONSIEUR: Peking! Washington! To hell with shilly-shallying!
MISSIONARY: Any delay is unthinkable.
WIFE (*shrieks, on the brink of losing complete control of herself*): Apologies! Declarations! Mediators! Captain!

MONSIEUR (*outraged*): What are you suggesting? Drag the matter through the embassies? Captain!

SCENE SIX

The Captain appears as if summoned by their conjurations. He is transformed. In full dress uniform. His chevrons give him the appearance of a gilded idol. A pause precedes his pronouncements.

CAPTAIN: We shan't involve the embassies.
JOURNALIST: So ...
CAPTAIN (*with deliberation*): The thing is, what I am considering ...
MONSIEUR: Did you stop to consider, Captain, when you put down the Boxers?
CAPTAIN (*ignoring him*): What I am wondering is, how many Chinese one murdered white man is worth?
MADAME: Ten at the very least.
CAPTAIN: And our drowned man?
WIFE: Would be how many?
CAPTAIN (*putting an end to the bewilderment*): Two should be adequate. We must not go to extremes. Understood?
MONSIEUR: Spoken like a true soldier and gentleman.
(*Copper comes up to the Captain.*)
COPPER: The Mayor has arrived, sir.

SCENE SEVEN

Enter the Mayor and his student interpreter. The Mayor is a heavily built, elderly Chinese man. His eyes peer out from above puffy bags. He is wearing a grey long coat on top of which is a black silk jacket, a Ma-gua, which reaches to his hips. On his head he has a black, gleaming skull cap. His demeanour is slow and very distinguished. The student wears a grey long coat, under which can be seen European trousers and short boots. He has horn rimmed glasses and a felt hat. His abruptness contrasts with the unthreatening calm of the Mayor.

The Boy also creeps in and, unnoticed, pressing himself back against a bulwark, behind the chairs on the deck, listens to everything. The Chinese and the Captain exchange bows without offering their hands. A murmur of "Murderers!" escapes the crowd of newly arrived Europeans.

CAPTAIN: Please leave us alone. Mr. Copper. Escort our guests to their quarters.
(*They all exit except the Journalist and the Boy who continues to hide.*)
STUDENT: His Honour the Mayor of Wanxian has come to express his deepest condolences upon the death ...
CAPTAIN (*interrupts*): You mean the murder.
(*In what follows, the Captain takes up the Student so quickly that their lines become one continuous block of speech.*)
STUDENT: As far as we were informed –
CAPTAIN: Very badly informed –
STUDENT: But Mr. Holey attacked –
CAPTAIN: Mr. Holey is a gentleman. What's more, he is dead. I'll thank you not to insult him.
STUDENT: Of course. There should be no question of insult.
CAPTAIN: And yet the whole affair is one blatant insult – to our flag.
STUDENT: Mr. Holey was an American.
CAPTAIN: But still one of us!
(*The Student and the Mayor confer quietly in Chinese.*)
STUDENT: You insist that a crime has been committed?
CAPTAIN: Categorically.
STUDENT: Accept our assurances that an investigation will...
CAPTAIN: I will not.
STUDENT: His Honour the Mayor emphasises his extreme regret...
CAPTAIN: Devil take his regrets. Do you think an attack on the European settlement can go unpunished? No sir! This is no laughing matter. We must have amends for this piracy.
STUDENT: Amends! What amends?
CAPTAIN: You want to know? (*Counts on his fingers, bending each one back.*) One – the body to be accompanied to the grave by the highest authorities of the town. Two - the town to place a cross on the grave. Three – compensation to be paid to the family of the murdered man.
STUDENT: As far as we know, he had no family.
CAPTAIN: We'll find whoever there is. And you will pay.

STUDENT (*exchanging whispers with the Mayor*): The Mayor instructs me to say that, though he considers these terms ... an insult to the town's honour, to avoid aggravating matters, he will agree.
CAPTAIN (*still holding up two fingers.*): You are not getting off as lightly as that.
STUDENT: You demand more?!
CAPTAIN: Punishment for the murder.
STUDENT: The investigation will take place as soon as possible.
CAPTAIN: Tomorrow morning at nine o'clock the murderer must be put to death.
STUDENT: Without a trial?
CAPTAIN: That is your business. Try him if you want.
STUDENT: And if we can't find him?
CAPTAIN (*deliberately*): Then ... you will execute two other men from the Boatmen's Union.
STUDENT (*flaring up*): Even a British captain should know some limit.
CAPTAIN (*enraged*): Impudent whelp! You dare to answer back? Which university taught you that? You study at our expense and then what? You murder us!
STUDENT: That money is not yours. It is ours – from the Boxer indemnity.
CAPTAIN: Enough, I say!
STUDENT: We will not consent to your terms.
CAPTAIN: Out of the question.
STUDENT: We will lodge a protest.
CAPTAIN: After the execution.
STUDENT: Your Prime Minister MacDonald, a man of the people himself, should be informed immediately of your craven behaviour.
CAPTAIN: I don't know of any Prime Minister MacDonald, 'man of the people'. I do know of His Majesty's Prime Minister Sir Ramsay MacDonald.
STUDENT: Feeling a little uneasy, no doubt, Captain? We citizens of the Chinese Republic cannot have meaningful talks with you on these matters.
CAPTAIN: So be it. I will have my guns talk to your town instead.
STUDENT (*shuddering*): Savagery!
CAPTAIN (*coldly.*): I will overlook your gentlemanly expression. The

order of the bombardment will be as follows. *(He motions along the horizon.)* First, the factory and warehouses over there will be blown up. Then Tai Li's buildings. Next, the Mayor's residence and offices. We will then target the boatmen's hovels and the market. After that, the rest of the town will be shelled by grid square.

STUDENT: Have you forgotten, Captain?! This is not Africa!

CAPTAIN: If I am not mistaken, this is China – I have forgotten nothing.

STUDENT: We will not agree to murder innocent men.

CAPTAIN: And I will not discuss this further. Tomorrow morning, by nine o'clock. Bring the requisite men to the shore.

STUDENT: No. *(He exits with the Mayor. He turns around and throws his last remark back at the Captain.)* This very day the whole civilised world will know of your arbitrary justice.

SCENE EIGHT

Copper and the Journalist enter

CAPTAIN: Lieutenant Copper!

COPPER: Captain, sir!

CAPTAIN: Signals.

COPPER: Signals, yes, sir!

(A signalman appears on the mast and awaits instructions.)

CAPTAIN: Occupy the telegraph office and the rest of the radio station.

COPPER: Telegraph office and radio station, sir!

(The signalman waves his flags.)

JOURNALIST *(tears a leaf from a notebook and extends it towards the Captain)*: Can I get you to correct this, sir?

CAPTAIN: Very well.

JOURNALIST *(skim reading)*: 'Merican brutally murdered ... trigger for general massacre ...*(With emphasis)* Captain shows resourcefulness and resolution typical of the BritishNavy ... 24-hour ultimatum.' I wanna wire this immediately, if you'd let me use the cutter?

CAPTAIN *(collecting his thoughts)*: Yes, take it. Here. *(Takes the Journalist's pen and writes on a card.)* You won't get in without this. *(The Journalist exits.)*

CAPTAIN: So! It's war. Boy! Whiskey!

(*At this summons, the Boy bolts out of his hiding place, knocking over one of the chairs he hid behind. The Captain and Copper rush to the rails. Backing away from the Captain, the Boy sees that Copper has spotted him and rushes off.*)
COPPER (*conspiratorially and ominously.*): A spy.
CAPTAIN: Put him under close watch.

FIFTH LINK

SCENE ONE

The wharf as before in Link One. A blind man passes by, his unseeing face looking upwards, beating a drum hanging from his arm. The boatmen bustle on the shore and in their boats. As a line of British sailors files through the wharf, it grows hushed. They march to the radio station and take up position inside. A boat pulls in with the Mayor and the Student. A policeman and boatmen rush up to the boat. The Mayor and the Student come up the steps from the river and begin a conversation. They are surrounded by onlookers.

THE MAYOR (*in a flat, colourless voice*): In whose boat was the American?
POLICEMAN: Chi's.
MAYOR: Find him.
POLICEMAN: We have searched.
MAYOR: Arrest his wife and children. Force them to reveal where he is.
POLICEMAN: Yes, sir.

SCENE TWO

Fei, the Chairman of the Boatmen's Union, steps forward from the crowd. He is solidly built, of high rank and well dressed. He carries a cane. The boatmen treat him with respect.

FEI: They don't know.
MAYOR (*hardly paying him attention, continues to the policeman*): Take them through the town, make them call him to come out. (*Raising his voice*) I cannot allow the whole town ...

FEI (*alarmed*): What about the town?
STUDENT: He wouldn't dare. He was just drunk.
MAYOR: He would. He dared 23 years ago, and he will dare now.
STUDENT: But that was a different China. We can protest now, loud and clear.
MAYOR: No one will listen.
STUDENT: We have so little time. I'll send a telegram to Beijing immediately. We shall get a reply before evening. Do you have your seal?
(*The Student begins to dash off a telegram there and then, resting on one knee.*)
MAYOR: Yes. (*He takes out a small case with the seal and inks*): Write quickly. (*Thoughtfully*) Tomorrow is the American's funeral. We shall follow the coffin.
THIRD BOATMAN (*astonished*): Follow the man's coffin when he nearly killed Chi? When he struck him in the face?
MAYOR: We shall lay a cross on his grave.
SECOND BOATMAN: But he broke Chi's oar and only gave him five cash! Half a cent!
MAYOR (*still very quietly*): He should have accepted five cash! He should have accepted nothing at all.
SECOND BOATMAN: And how would that feed us?
MAYOR: Better for one to go hungry than for thousands to flee the town.
FIRST BOATMAN: What d'you mean, flee? (*The Boatmen look at each other, alarmed and bewildered.*)
STUDENT: It's ready. (*He jumps up and gives the paper to the Mayor.*)
MAYOR (*reads it through*): Good.
(*He places his stamp on it. The Student runs towards the stairs of the radio station. Towards him comes the Stoker, slipping down, driven out by the sailors' rifle butts. The Stoker has dropped a small white bundle, which he picks up under a rain of blows.*)

SCENE THREE

All previous characters, the Stoker and two sailors.

STOKER (*at the top of his voice*): I'm the Stoker. You can't do this! (*The sailors try to snatch his bundle.*) You can have my head before I part with that. (*He wrenches the bundle back and tumbles down the steps. The sailors position themselves at the top of the steps by the entrance to the station and cross their rifles against the Student running up towards them.*)

STUDENT (*showing the telegram to the sailors*): An official telegram. With the seal of the Mayor.

FIRST SAILOR (*blocking him*): No communications allowed.

STUDENT: How dare you? This is our telegraph station.

SECOND SAILOR: Get lost!

STUDENT: Let me through now. (*He grasps a bayonet, wanting to push it to one side.*)

FIRST SAILOR: I said - clear off! Now! (*He pushes the Student back with his rifle butt. The Student's body hits every last step as he bounces down.*)

STUDENT (*lying at the bottom of the steps*): Animals! (*He has dropped his telegram which is lying on one of the top steps. The Second Sailor picks it up.*)

SECOND SAILOR: That'll 'ave to go to the Captain. (*He puts the paper away in his pocket.*)

STUDENT (*furiously to the sailors*): Give it back!

FIRST SAILOR (*leading him away unceremoniously*): Shift your arse now! (*The sailors remount their guard at the door.*)

SCENE FOUR

The Journalist elbows his way through the crowd.

JOURNALIST (*pushing his way forward*): Gimme some space here!

SECOND SAILOR: Oy! Stay where you are!

JOURNALIST (*runs up the stairs and reaches out his card*): Captain's permit. Urgent wire.

FIRST SAILOR: Very good.
   (*The rifles part before him.*)
STUDENT (*from amongst the crowd*): So, *he* gets through? Why does *he* get through? (*He is consumed with fury and hate, prepared to rush at the bayonets again with his bare hands.*)
STOKER: He's allowed. He's an American.
STUDENT (*to the Mayor*): What are we to do?
MAYOR: Order a cross.
STUDENT: Anything else?
MAYOR: Is the Chairman of the Boatmen's Union here?
FEI: Yes, here. *(He bows.)*
MAYOR: Please come with me. *(To the policeman)* Continue the search for Chi. (*The Mayor and Fei, surrounded by the crowd, move away slowly. The Stoker shouts exultantly after them.*)
STOKER: You will never find him!

SIXTH LINK

SCENE ONE

The eating house of the Boatmen's Union.
   Makeshift benches line long tables. A hearth under an awning. On sieves, placed over cauldrons of boiling water, rice is steaming. A cook, naked to the waist, wearing a coarse apron, is kneading dough for the little steamed buns called mantou. *First one, then another boatman approaches the hearth, receives a big bowl of broth, sits down and begins to pick out the meat with 'kuaizi', chopsticks, and then, holding the bowl to his lips, slurps down the liquid.*
   An old boatman stands out from the crowd. His thin grey pigtail hangs down his back. Around his eyes and mouth is a thick growth of coarse, wiry hair. He squats, his gaze lost in the glowing coals of the fire, smoking a pipe. He speaks in a calm, unruffled tone, while the Second Boatman, nervy and clearly agitated, frets and raises his voice.
   The old man belongs to that breed of fatalistic Chinese, who, having no fear of death, would hire themselves out as substitutes for execution. He is a Buddhist and believes steadfastly in retribution and reincarnation in the next life. What holds real terror for him is the mutilation of the body in this life, which has grave consequences for the fate of the soul. It is considered a cruel punishment to cut off the head and place it between the legs of a corpse, because the soul will then linger on, headless, in the world.
   The boatmen's talk is subdued. A sense of dread has already descended on the town.
   The Stoker is also present but does not speak until Scene Two.

OLD BOATMAN: Trouble's comin'.
FIRST BOATMAN: Wanxian's in for it.

SECOND BOATMAN (*agitated, as described* above): First the drought. Then the floods. Nothing to put in our mouths. More beggars than full stomachs.

THIRD BOATMAN: We cost less than a handful of rice.

OLD BOATMAN: Chi still lying low!

SECOND BOATMAN: The coppers marched his son round town, forced him to shout 'Dad, come out, or they'll kill me.'

FIRST BOATMAN: I think he went off with the Honghuzi.[90] He'll make a good bandit.

THIRD BOATMAN: Fei went off with the Mayor, and he's still not back.

SECOND BOATMAN: He showed his face once. They say he was pale as a ghost.

THIRD BOATMAN: All the whites went over to the ship. With their suitcases!

OLD BOATMAN: We're in big trouble.

SECOND BOATMAN: But I don't get it, they've not laid a hand on a single boat yet. You know that shrivelled up woman, the one who goes round wailin' her prayers? She caught sight of me, let out a scream like I'd stabbed her or somethin', and I got a whack from one of the sailors.

THIRD BOATMAN: Suddenly we're killers, are we? When we'll turn our oars for a few measly coins?

SECOND BOATMAN: Why did all the whites go across to the ship?

SCENE TWO

Fei enters slowly and sits on a bench, silently staring down. All the boatmen start a hubbub - 'Fei's arrived'.

OLD BOATMAN: Come on then!

FIRST BOATMAN: Spit it out!

SECOND BOATMAN: It's really bad, isn't it?

FEI: Alright! (*He notices the Stoker.*) What are you doing here? You're not a boatman.

---

90   *Honghuzi*: Chinese for 'red beards', the Honghuzi were armed bandits in the eastern Russia-China borderlands.

STOKER: Just a coolie from the radio station. The sailors drove me out with their rifle butts.
THIRD BOATMAN: He's sound. Come on, Fei.
FEI: No point in talking. Get ready to die.
SECOND BOATMAN: You what? Who's goin' to die?
FEI: Us.
OLD BOATMAN: How come?
FEI: Instead of our comrade.
FIRST BOATMAN: You're makin' no sense!
FEI: The ginger Captain says Chi killed the American.
SECOND BOATMAN (*exploding with rage*): Liar!
FEI (*continues quietly*): That's what he says ... so we have to execute ...
THIRD BOATMAN: Execute?!
FEI: Two of us. (*There is a stunned silence.*)
OLD BOATMAN: Did the Mayor agree?
FEI: He did.
THIRD BOATMAN (*furiously*): So he should be for it, not us!
SECOND BOATMAN (*warily*): Shouldn't it be Chi? He's the guilty one.
STOKER: He's not to blame.
SECOND BOATMAN (*leaps right up to the Stoker*): It was him who wouldn't take his money, his boat the American fell off!
FIRST BOATMAN: They should kill Chi's son, his wife. They wouldn't dare lay a finger on us.
THIRD BOATMAN: We've killed no one. They can't touch us.
SECOND BOATMAN (*to Fei*): Did you tell the Mayor the same?
FEI: No.
ALL THE BOATMEN: Why not?
FEI: If we don't hand over two of us for execution, then tomorrow morning the guns of that ship are going to set fire to our town.
FIRST BOATMAN: The ship's guns?
FEI: Yes. And they won't stop till they've burnt it to the ground and killed the lot of us.
STOKER (*to anyone who will listen, in a piercing, vicious voice*): The English! I've seen what they can do. They think nothing of razing a whole town.
SECOND BOATMAN: Then we need to run for it. (*He grabs his meagre bits and bobs.*) We're not guilty. (*He fusses around frantically.*) Grab

our families and run now. There's still time. We can hide outside town – plenty of places. (*He runs towards the door.*)

FEI: Comrades, we're surrounded.

THIRD BOATMAN: You've done a deal with the Mayor! You've sold us down the river! (*The Boatmen press around Fei. He is surrounded by a ring of threatening hands.*)

FEI (*jumping up on a bench*): I'm here, aren't I? Facing this nightmare just like the rest of you. (*The tension amongst the boatmen evaporates.*)

FIRST BOATMAN: Alright then. Let the Mayor take his choice of us.

FEI: The Mayor says – choose yourselves.

SECOND BOATMAN (*sitting on the floor and clutching his head*): It's not right. I haven't killed anyone. It's not right.

FIRST BOATMAN: You're our leader. You should die.

FEI: I'm just one of you.

SECOND BOATMAN (*in torment, banging his head against a box*): Lose my head, for someone else? Am I a murderer now?

STOKER (*comes up to him, puts a hand on his hand*): Chi is a worker. You are a worker. In their eyes you will do just as well.

FIRST BOATMAN: You know what you said before? Where on earth have you seen people dyin' for others?

STOKER: Believe me, I have.

OLD BOATMAN: No such place.

STOKER: There is. Out there. (*He gestures into space in the same way as in the Third Link.*) Poor coolies just like us drove out their masters.

FIRST BOATMAN: Even the English?

STOKER: The English, and the French, and their own. It wasn't easy. More English arrived to avenge their dead. The coolies held firm. They fought back. When the masters won, they didn't bother to weed out the fighters, they killed every tenth person, every fifth, sometimes just everyone.

SECOND BOATMAN: Why?

STOKER: Because they were coolies. Because the likes of them had driven out their masters. Because the likes of them had turned rich merchants and mayors into simple coolies.

(*A silence falls. The Boatmen cannot absorb what has been said.*)

THIRD BOATMAN (*sarcastically*): They just fought for themselves. So's they could take the clothes of the masters, their food, their houses.

STOKER: No! They went hungry. They only had the rags they stood up in. They weren't just fighting for what they could get.
FIRST BOATMAN: Who were they fightin' for then?
STOKER: For you.
FIRST BOATMAN (*astounded by what sounds like a tall story*): For me?
STOKER: Yes. They want coolies to be masters everywhere in the world. They starved and died for you - you coolies here in Wanxian. Learn from them. Learn to die for all the boatmen in all the towns trampled down by the English.
SECOND BOATMAN: Then why don't they come and help us here?
STOKER: They're exhausted. They need time to get strong again.
SECOND BOATMAN: You're making this up, just stringing us along!
FEI: And meantime, we're expected to die.

SCENE THREE

The Heshang has entered during the conversation with the Stoker, and he suddenly springs up in the middle of the crowd, which parts for him. His sentences are abrupt and commanding, with stress laid on the last words of each sentence.

HESHANG: We need not die! We must fight! We must conquer!
STOKER (*jeering*): Against guns! You and whose army?
HESHANG: Let them fire. Let them scorch us. In the end we will all be dung. The strong will escape.
FIRST BOATMAN: The rich will escape. The ones with carts will escape. What about us – the beggars? Run from the guns and starve instead?
HESHANG: In the end we will all be dung. The strongest will survive. They will raise others. Until they are many. They will come down upon the whites. They will drive them out.
STOKER: Oh yes? With bayonets at their throats?
HESHANG: Fear not. Here. (*He takes out a yellow, triangular piece of cloth with characters written on it.*) Wear it on your chest. A holy prayer. Zidan bu hui cichuan. Shi jian pianzhuan. 'The bullet will not pierce. The sword will be deflected.'
OLD BOATMAN (*with a dismissive wave of his hand*): We will all be dung, ay? But you're already full of shit!

HESHANG (*shaking his cloth*): Holy clothing. Blessed clothing.
STOKER: Only idiots wear something like that. It won't win you a battle.
FIRST BOATMAN: Show me anythin' on this earth a man could wear to win his battles.
STOKER (*his voice taking on the fanatical stridency of the Heshang*): I can. I will.
FIRST BOATMAN: You expect us to believe that?
(*The Boatmen turn away from the Stoker to the Heshang. The Stoker is left alone.*)
STOKER: It's the truth! Here! (*He snatches a coolie's jacket and trousers from the hands of the Second Boatman. Watched mistrustfully by the boatmen, he turns to the Heshang.*) You hate the whites, don't you?
HESHANG: I do.
STOKER: Are you brave?
HESHANG: I am.
STOKER: And are you with us?
HESHANG: I am.
STOKER: Will you help us?
HESHANG: I will.
STOKER: Take these. (*Offers him the clothes.*) Put them on. You'll become a boatman. And tomorrow you can lay your head beneath the axe.
HESHANG (*not understanding*): Beneath the axe?
(*The attitude of the boatmen towards him sours rapidly. Their voices begin to jeer. Someone jostles him from behind.*)
FIRST BOATMAN: Bottlin' it now are we? The old man's right, you are full of it.
HESHANG (*mechanically*): We need not die! We must conquer!
THIRD BOATMAN: Brave, my arse! (*Several boatmen strike the Heshang. Suddenly, with a powerful lunge, he pushes them all aside, backs away, making to go, shaking his yellow cloth.*)
HESHANG: Blind men! Cowards!
OLD BOATMAN: But we're not the ones doin' a runner, are we?
(*The Heshang exits.*)
FEI (*quietly*): When a boatman dies, we look after his family. When they cut our wages, we down oars and demand more. We are brothers. A slur on one is a slur on us all. If one of us is guilty, then all of us are. If one of us dies, then they die for all of us.

OLD BOATMAN: I'm not afraid to die. I'm afraid to lose my head. No peace for my soul after that.

SECOND BOATMAN (*blurting out his words unevenly*): I don't want to die! I have a son! When I hold him in my arms, he laughs. (*He stops suddenly and listens in terror.*) Who's that comin'? Do we kill him?

SCENE FOUR

The Student comes in.

FEI (*to the Student*): Already?

STUDENT: Can you hear? That's their music. They dance to it.
   (*In the silence that has fallen, the sound of an orchestra playing a foxtrot carries across faintly from the river.*)

FIRST BOATMAN: Like tigers! They smell blood.

STUDENT: Perhaps their music has made them gentler.

STOKER (*sardonically*): The likes of them!

STUDENT: The Mayor is going across to them again. We will beg for mercy. Come with us, Fei.

FIRST BOATMAN (*passionately*): Tell them my arms are strong. I'll ferry them safely and take no money from them.

SECOND BOATMAN: Tell them I have a son.

OLD BOATMAN: They mustn't cut off our heads. Let them strangle us. A soul cannot be without its head.

THIRD BOATMAN: Kiss their feet. Beg for mercy.

SECOND BOATMAN: Why? Why are we going to die? (*He lies down on the floor, shuddering.*)

STOKER (*stopping the Student and pointing at the Second Boatman*): Student. Explain to him. A coolie will always die for another coolie.

SEVENTH LINK

On the Cockchafer. *The evening of the same day. A searchlight shines from the mast and probes the far shore of the river. Green and red lights on the shelter deck where a banquet is being held. The whole of Wanxian's European colony is on board. This link begins with the final chords of the British national anthem. The men are dressed in white dinner jackets with black trousers and white summer tailcoats, which end in shortened, funny little wedge-shaped tails at the back. The women are very décolleté and bejewelled. Everyone is holding a glass.*

SCENE ONE

MONSIEUR de BRUCHELLES (*in the middle of a pompous speech*): The Captain's health! We bring industry to these savages. They should crawl up on their bellies and lick our hands. They were paid a cent – now we give them ten.

MISSIONARY (*taking him up*): They were mired in superstition - we brought them our faith.

TOURIST'S WIFE: They were infested with vermin and lived in squalor - we built them shelter.

TOURIST: Their science was still in the Middle Ages. We gave them universities.

MADAME de B: When a pupil raises their hand in such savage anger against their teacher, then we must be merciless ...

MISSIONARY: ... In the name of our Lord Jesus Christ.

MONSIEUR: Dollar for dollar. Blood for blood. That's how it will be. It's written on the banner of ... err ... (*Loses his thread.*) On the banner of ... dammit ...

CORDELIA (*prompts helpfully*): Of old Europe.

MISSIONARY: And of young America.

CAPTAIN (*firing his words off like a volley of shots*): Correct. Factories. Schools. Churches And ... (*Raises his glass.*) Our Navies. We were sent here at the behest of our states and we will not leave. Rule of law. Duty. Service.

JOURNALIST (*floridly and fluently*): I know for sure right here, right now that the hearts of all Aryan races are joined with us. In their ministries and embassies, in their banks and offices, on board the steamships plying the oceans and in every compartment of every train, speeding nobly even now to its vital destination. I raise my glass to our white race, Empress of the earth. I raise my glass to our Captain, to his iron hand and golden heart, who has so generously granted us shelter on board his fortress where...

TOURIST'S WIFE (*interrupting*): In a moment of mortal danger for us all. (*They all draw near to clink glasses with the Captain.*)

CAPTAIN: I thank you all. (*There is a pause with a sense of finality. The change of watch sounds.*) Time to repair to our cabins. We should all try to get a little sleep.

MADAME (*to the Missionary*): What enthusiasm! What spiritual unity! Your Reverence, I imagine the very saints in Heaven at the throne of the Almighty must feel like this, just like this.

MISSIONARY: You are infinitely right.

SCENE TWO

The Boy enters with a bowl of fruit. They all step back from him. He is very pale.

CORDELIA (*capriciously.*): Ooh yes, I'll have some, here, over here! (*The boy comes right up to her. She holds his chin and turns to Copper who is standing next to her.*) Why is he looking so pale? I'm not so taken with this mouth of his after all. Ugly!

COPPER: He was caught trying to make his getaway from the ship. (*Scornfully to the Boy.*) And did you succeed, Boy?

CORDELIA (*with idle curiosity*): What will happen to him now?

COPPER (*ominously*): Oh, he knows alright.

(*The Boy flinches and drops the bowl of fruit. The fruit rolls all over the deck.*)

CAPTAIN (*with disgust in his voice*): Get out of our sight!
(*The Boy scrabbles around picking up the fruit. Copper listens out in the silence that has fallen.*)
COPPER: Excuse me one moment. (*He exits, followed by the dejected Boy.*)
CORDELIA (*petulantly*): Honestly! Nothing's gone the way I wanted it to!
MADAME: Come to bed, dear, come to bed. Daddy's gone already!
(*Madame and the remainder of the guests exit. Cordelia stays behind with the Captain.*)

SCENE THREE

Copper enters again. The Captain looks at him questioningly.

COPPER: It's the Chinese again, sir.
CAPTAIN: See the beggars off, Lieutenant! (*Copper exits.*)
CORDELIA (*flirting, draws closer to the Captain*): Good night Captain! You really are so impressive! Till now I'd only read about men like you in novels.
CAPTAIN (*in a disarmed and paternal tone*): Sweet child! In the British fleet there are hundreds of captains just like me. (*Cordelia exits.*)

SCENE FOUR

Copper enters again.

COPPER: They implore you to see them, sir. They say it is vital.
CAPTAIN: Why don't they just crawl back under their stone? (*A pause. He relents.*) Very well! Let's get this over with quickly! I'll give them five minutes.
(*Copper exits and comes back in a moment with the Mayor, the Student, Fei, and Tai Li who is carrying a woman's suit made of silk in his outstretched arms. Fei holds back and remains hidden in the shadows, unseen by the Captain until Scene Six.*)

SCENE FIVE

CAPTAIN: Well sir?
STUDENT: The Mayor takes the liberty of disturbing you a second time at such an unfortunate hour to ...
CAPTAIN (*abruptly*): To confirm he accepts my ultimatum. (*To Copper.*) Is the grave ready?
COPPER: Within the hour, sir.
STUDENT: The Mayor begs the Captain most humbly...
CAPTAIN: How gratifying to hear the change in your tone. I take it the Mayor has satisfied himself a crime was committed.
STUDENT: He implores you most humbly for one thing ... not to put to death citizens of his town.
CAPTAIN (*as though he is softening*): I see. I see!
STUDENT: He agrees to whatever compensation you think fit. He will give any guarantee that an incident like yesterday's will not be repeated.
CAPTAIN (*completely sincerely*): Well now. Very good.
STUDENT: He hopes your compassion will allow you to spare innocent men. They have families, little children. And Tai Li asks if he may offer the gift of this suit for the young lady on board.

SCENE SIX

Monsieur de Bruchelles enters in a dressing gown and creeps up to the group. Tai Li sees him and hands over the suit, which Monsieur begins to examine minutely.

STUDENT: Tai Li also offers any compensation for business lost ...
MONSIEUR (*confidentially to the Captain*): I'd say that's worth discussing because ...
CAPTAIN (*cuts him off brutally*): I do not bargain over my orders!
(*Monsieur leaves insulted, taking the suit with him, his slippers shuffling over the deck as he goes.*)
STUDENT: The Mayor is willing to entreat your forgiveness in the most lowly way he knows.
(*The Mayor and, behind him, Tai Li kneel before the Captain. The*

Student remains standing. Fei, still unseen in the shadows, remains standing.)

CAPTAIN (*a little more conciliatory*): Very well. Very well! (*To the Student.*) And what about you, young man? (*The Student kneels. The Captain takes a piece of paper from his pocket and waves it in the direction of the Student.*) Your telegram, I believe?

STUDENT (*casting his eyes down*): Yes.

CAPTAIN: Do you admit that it is a lie and a despicable slander against a British captain?

STUDENT (*gritting his teeth*): I do.

CAPTAIN: And would you not concur that, as punishment for such an outrage, I would be well within my rights to demand from your authorities a thorough beating on your feet with bamboo canes? In the town square? Well?

STUDENT: I agree.

CAPTAIN (*almost kindly*): Well now. Way past our bed times. It can't be easy on your knees down there.

STUDENT (*gets up joyously*): So the boatmen are...

CAPTAIN (*graciously*): You need not behead them. (*The way the petitioners move indicates their relief.*) Merely throttle them instead.

STUDENT (*shouting*): So this is your ...your....

FEI (*shouting and shaking his fist*): *Wangbadan*!

CAPTAIN (*noticing him for the first time, shouts*): And who in God's name is this?

STUDENT: A boatman.

CAPTAIN: What is he saying?

STUDENT: That you are the son of a whore. He is proud not to have licked the boot of a murderer.

CAPTAIN: You appalling, insolent dogs! Get out of my sight, get off my ship, back to your filthy kennels now! Now!

(*The Chinese leave. In a fury the Captain paces up and down the bridge.*)

COPPER: Captain, are you retiring to your cabin, sir?

CAPTAIN: No! I am not!!

(*They both exit.*)

SCENE SEVEN

The Boy appears on the empty stage. Humming a sorrowful tune, he strings a noose above the Captain's door. He continues his wordless, melancholy song for a long time. When he has finished, he groans and catches hold with agitated fingers of the swaying rope noose. The lights go out. The mournful sound of a distant factory siren cuts through the silence. Lights. The body of the Boy is hanging from the captain's door.

VOICE OF MADAME DE BRUCHELLES (*offstage*): Cordelia, you should be in bed.
VOICE OF CORDELIA: In a minute.

SCENE EIGHT

Cordelia enters in her new suit. The Boy's body is lit up in front of her by the searchlight.

CORDELIA: Oh!! (*Grasping the rail, in a choked whisper*): Quickly - Mr. Copper – quickly – get me ...
COPPER (*runs in. He is stunned by what he sees*): What in God's name?
CORDELIA (*her gaze fixating on the Boy, she reaches a hand back to Copper*): Can you get me ... as quick as you can ... (*Copper seizes a tumbler from a table and pours out some water for her.*)
CORDELIA (*irritatedly*): No, no! Not that! My kodak and magnesium. You can't deny it, can you? Extraordinarily striking.
(*The Captain runs in.*)

SCENE NINE

The Captain is left reeling. He leans with his back against the railing, his breathing laboured. He raises his hand as if to strike the dead Boy.

CORDELIA (*in a whisper to Copper*): Oh dear. Has he lost his temper, do you think?

COPPER (*his voice resonating with fear*): The Boy's hanged himself on the Captain's door. It's how their subjects revenge themselves on the mandarins here, when they've been driven beyond desperation.
CORDELIA: So what do the mandarins do then?
COPPER: They are supposed to leave.
CORDELIA: Leave? Well, I never! Is the Captain superstitious?
COPPER: The Captain is a sailor.
   (*Cordelia tiptoes away.*)
CAPTAIN (*still staring mesmerised at the dangling Boy*): No! I will not leave! (*Hoarsely.*) Copper! Whiskey!

EIGHTH LINK

The Eating House as in the Sixth Link. It is not yet dawn. The people are stiff and weary from waiting through a sleepless night. From time to time one of them goes to the door and listens attentively, then sits down again where they were.

SCENE ONE

The Boatmen and the Stoker.

FIRST BOATMAN: They're comin'.
THIRD BOATMAN (*listening out*): No. All quiet.
SECOND BOATMAN: Surely goodness an' mercy'll find a way through that thick skin of 'is? Look. The sun's comin' up. The river's peaceful. My little boy is sleepin' in my boat. When he sleeps he makes these sweet little sounds with his mouth. (*He imitates the way his son gently smacks his lips together.*) The Captain probly 'as a little boy too.
OLD BOATMAN: Give it twenty years and 'is son'll be firin' on yours.
STOKER: Wrong. In twenty years his son (*points at the Second Boatman*) will have his boot on the neck of the English boy.
THIRD BOATMAN: They're comin'.

SCENE TWO

Enter Fei and two women. Fei is incensed. His wife, dressed in smart silk clothes with a handkerchief in her hand, follows fearfully behind him. The Second Boatman's wife is in rough, homespun clothing. In her arms she holds a child with little pigtails and hair sticks.

FIRST BOATMAN (*to Fei*): Well?

FEI (*choking with anger*): That man is pure viciousness inside an armoured shell.

THIRD BOATMAN: Meanin' what?

FEI: They're going to execute two of us.

>   (*The women sit, wailing quietly and rocking to and fro. Fei's wife uses her handkerchief. The Second Boatman's wife wipes her tears away with her hand.*)

FIRST BOATMAN: Who?

FEI: Whoever we choose.

THIRD BOATMAN (*infuriated*): They'll have to come and get us then. We're not goin' to send our comrades to their death.

FEI (*halts him with a gesture*): Yes we will. We will choose them. And then remember. (*Prophetically*) The day *will* come when we can say to those murderers: do you remember the Wanxian boatmen?

OLD BOATMAN (*knocks out his pipe, blows out the ash, shoves it in his belt, spits and goes up to Fei*): Send me.

SECOND BOATMAN (*in a low voice*): Who else?

>   (*There is silence except for the wailing women.*)

FEI (*pulls himself together*): I will go.

FEI'S WIFE (*shrilly*): Why? Why you? Have you killed anyone?

FEI (*leading her away. To the Old Boatman*): Come on, father. Together we will save the town.

FEI's WIFE (*hysterically rushing between them, mortal fear in her voice*): No! No! You mustn't! Lose your head? Why? For what? For what?

FIRST BOATMAN (*reproachfully to Fei and the Old Boatman*): No! We can't let it happen this way. We're all in the same boat.

>   (*The Old Boatman moves away and squats again with his back to them.*)

FEI: Who then?

FIRST BOATMAN: We'll draw lots. (*He takes a bundle of chopsticks from the cook and snaps two of them.*)

SECOND BOATMAN (*to his wife and trying not to look at the chopsticks being broken*): Let me hold my son. (*He looks him over closely.*) What's this blood on his leg? Has a dog bitten him?

SECOND BOATMAN'S WIFE: He crawled into Chi's boat and scratched it on a broken nail.

FEI (*to First Boatman*): Ready?

FIRST BOATMAN (*holding up a bundle of chopsticks*): There's two short ones.
THIRD BOATMAN (*ironically*): Beheaded already.
FEI (*pointing to the Stoker*): He can hold them. (*First Boatman gives them to the Stoker.*)
FIRST BOATMAN: Come on.
>(*There is a long pause while they stand mesmerised, staring at the chopsticks. The Old Boatman, who sat down again with his back to them, suddenly starts to hum in a high, thin voice, gets up and goes to the Stoker. Slowly he draws a stick and contemplates it.*)

OLD BOATMAN: Short – I knew.
FIRST BOATMAN (*draws*): A – a long one. (*Almost breathless with joy, he is about to show it to the Old Boatman but brings himself up short.*)
FEI (*draws, looks at it and throws it away*): Not me.
>(*Two more boatmen draw long ones in silence and the suspense intensifies.*)

SECOND BOATMAN (*shaking, clutching his son closely to him*): I can't move! (*The Stoker comes up to him. The Second Boatman jerks his hand back from the bundle, as though he has been burnt.*) Aaahhh! (*He holds his son under the shoulders and thrusts him out to the Stoker.*) Let him choose, my good luck boy. (*The son pulls out a chopstick and shows it to his father. The Second Boatman inspects it, enfolds his son in his arms and collapses silently on the floor.*)
THE STOKER (*picking up the dropped chopstick*): Short.
>(*Offstage a bugle sounds a military signal.*)

SCENE THREE

Enter a Policeman and 2 watchmen.

POLICEMAN: Ready?
FEI (*turning his back on him*): Ready.
POLICEMAN: Which of you then?
>(*The Boatmen stand aside to reveal the two condemned men. The Old Boatman embraces the Second Boatman and claps him on the back encouragingly. The Policeman grabs the Old Boatman by the sleeve.*)

OLD BOATMAN: I'm comin'. I'm comin'.
>   (*The Second Boatman, suddenly truly taking in what is happening, wrenches himself free and rushes away.*)

SECOND BOATMAN: No! No! You can't take me! I need to live. My son …
>   (*The Policeman and the two assistants pinion him. He struggles, howls, and they almost have to carry him out, screaming and struggling. Fei and the women follow them out.*)

FIRST BOATMAN (*in a frenzy*): When are they comin' then? When?

THE STOKER: Who?

FIRST BOATMAN: The ones out there, who drive out their masters.

THE STOKER: They are here already.

FIRST BOATMAN: Show me even one of 'em!

THE STOKER (*pointing to the Boatmen*): Him. And him. And you. No need to wait. Do it for yourselves. Pick up a gun. In all your towns. Rise up. As one. Have you heard of Canton? Have you heard of Sun Yat-Sen?[91] You know the words written across the chests of the Canton workers: 'Die for the people.'

---

91   *Sun Yat-Sen*: Sun Yat-Sen, writer, philosopher and revolutionary, led the revolution of 1911, and is considered the founding father of the Republic of China, which existed from 1912 to 1949.

NINTH LINK

SCENE ONE

The Wharf as before. On the left, two posts, taller than a man, have been erected for the strangling. On the right is Holey's grave. Near it – a temporary pulpit. The grave is encircled by a line of sailors, all in white. The rhythmic beating of big drums sounds nearer, and a procession, headed by the condemned men, enters.

The Old Boatman and the Second Boatman are fettered together at the neck in one iron stock. There are policemen in front and behind them. Two fierce looking executioners in turbans enter with them. They have ropes and bags attached to their belts. More boatmen, some with their oars, follow on after them with their wives.

SECOND BOATMAN (*staggering as he walks and calling dully*): Give me more baijiu. More baijiu! (*Out of the crowd someone passes him a cup of this Chinese vodka.*) I worked – and now they murder me. I starved – and now they murder me. I have a son – and now they murder me. Why are they killing me? Why are they killing me?
STUDENT: Because you are Chinese.
(*The procession stops in front of the posts. The policemen push the crowd back from the empty space in which the two condemned men have now sat down.*)
MISSIONARY (*from the pulpit above Holey's grave*): Ashes to ashes. Dust to dust. Martyr, rest in peace. The hand of a foul evil doer has cut the bright thread of your life. God is great. We cannot escape his judgment. Most terrible it is to be delivered into the hands of our living God. He will wipe the wicked from the face of the earth. He will brand them with a red-hot iron. He will cast our tormentors

into Hell's scorching fires. Hearken! The last trump of judgment day sounds out already ... (*Offstage a military bugle sounds.*) Peace be upon you, spotless lambs of Christ's flock. (*He blesses the whites. Some coolies carry in a cross. Behind it come Tai Li and the Mayor. They erect the cross on the grave. It bears the inscription: 'Thou shalt not kill.'*) This cross is given by the grief-stricken citizens of the town.

TOURIST'S WIFE (*in a dissatisfied tone*): Why is it only a wooden one? (*Tai Li confers with the Missionary in a low voice.*)

MISSIONARY: The Chairman of the Merchants' Guilds asks me to say that this cross is only temporary and will be replaced by a stone one as soon as possible.

CORDELIA (*admiring the cross*): Ooh, it will look lovely from the river!

MISSIONARY (*moved by the ceremony, offers his hand to Tai Li*): We, the friends of the deceased, thank you for your heartfelt participation in our mourning. (*Tai Li recoils in horror from the Missionary's hand.*)

CAPTAIN (*watching this interaction*): The old fool's gone soft on us! (*The wreaths are brought forward and placed on the grave. Their ribbons are straightened and the inscriptions read out.*)

TOURIST: 'Blessed are the pure of heart.' From Robert Dollar and the Company.

COPPER: 'To a martyr.' From the crew of the gunboat *Cockchafer*.

MADAME de BRUCHELLES: 'We shall meet in Paradise.' From the de Bruchelles family.

(*The wife of the Second Boatman bursts through the line of sailors to the Europeans.*)

SECOND BOATMAN'S WIFE: Let me through! Let me through!

MADAME (*peering down at the woman kneeling before her, sympathetically*): Goodness gracious! This is actually my godchild. What does she want? I can't understand her.

STUDENT: She says she has a little son.

MADAME: Oh, does he need a place in the orphanage?

STUDENT: No! She begs for mercy for his father. He is about to be executed.

MADAME (*sharply*): That is not my concern. I am powerless to help. (*Turning to the Woman*) You poor creature! Prayer will be your only comfort. The Lord God will lend his succour. (*She makes the sign of the cross over the woman and turns to the Student.*) Please tell her what I said.

STUDENT: I shall not.

SECOND BOATMAN'S WIFE (*still kneeling, cries after Madame as she walks away.*): You baptised me. Say your God is kind. Your God – is an animal. He is the gun. He is the rope for a neck. He chops heads. (*She tears the little cross from her neck and flings it at Madame.*) See! Not my God!

MADAME: Such blasphemy!

(*The sailors manhandle the screaming woman over to the policemen, who drag her away into the crowd.*)

CAPTAIN: Are we finished?

MISSIONARY: Yes.

CAPTAIN (*as a formal command*): All Europeans – return to the *Cockchafer*. (*They all go except the sailors, Copper, the Journalist, Madame and Cordelia. The Journalist carries a huge camera hung around his neck and has already taken a photograph of the ceremony.*)

CORDELIA (*to the Captain*): You will let me stay, won't you?

CAPTAIN (*formally, as if not noticing her*): All Europeans – return to the *Cockchafer* now.

CORDELIA (*offended and tartly*): This is blatant disregard for the request of a lady!

CAPTAIN: Mademoiselle, I am on official duty now.

MADAME: Have you lost your senses! This is no sight for a child. Daddy's already gone. He's so sensitive. Who do you get this from? Come away this minute – people are looking at you.

(*Cordelia goes up to the condemned men, inspects them through her lorgnette, then, throwing a contemptuous glance back at the Captain, exits with her mother.*)

CAPTAIN: Are the guns trained?

COPPER: Ready, sir!

(*The Student approaches the Captain.*)

CAPTAIN: What do you want?

STUDENT: Your religion teaches the forgiveness of your enemies.

CAPTAIN: There is no such paragraph in the Naval Regulations.

STUDENT: Your religion...

CAPTAIN: Enough! How dare you presume! (*Looks at his watch.*) A further ten minutes only remain at your disposal.

SECOND BOATMAN: Give me baijiu. Give me more baijiu! (*The policemen unyoke the condemned men.*)
OLD BOATMAN (*aside, to the Captain*): Kill me! Let the young 'un go.
STUDENT (*sardonically*): Save what breath remains to you, old man. He's never learned a single word of our language.
SECOND BOATMAN (*noticing the Captain, in a fury*): Is that him? Let me get my hands ...(*He throws himself at the sailors who bristle their bayonets in defence. He seizes the bayonets, then, losing his balance, falls to the ground face down.*)
CAPTAIN (*checking his watch*): Two minutes remain to carry out the sentence. (*To Copper.*) When I wave my handkerchief, open fire on the town.
COPPER: Yes sir! (*He walks towards the radio station.*)
(*The executioners place the Old Boatman and the Second Boatman up against the posts and loop their necks to the posts with rope. Then they insert a stick as a handle at the back of each loop.*)
OLD BOATMAN: My people, am I a criminal?
THE CROWD: No! (*A pause, then more loudly.*) No! No!
OLD BOATMAN: My people. You won't forget me then?
THE CROWD: No!
(*An executioner puts a sack over his head and slowly turns the stick, forcing the Old Boatman's throat back against the post. The crowd groans.*)
SECOND BOATMAN (*struggles against the bag being placed over his head*): No! No! I won't ... No! Let me speak! Let me speak!
STUDENT: Let him speak.
SECOND BOATMAN (*shouting to his wife over the heads of the crowd*): Show me my son! (*She lifts the child up above her head. He stares at the boy, then turns abruptly to the executioner.*) Finish me then! (*His head is covered with a sack and he is strangled in the same way.*)
THE HESHANG: (*giving the wife of the Second Boatman a piece of yellow cloth*): Give this to your son. No bullet will pierce. He will grow to be a man and destroy the whites.
VOICE OF THE STOKER FROM WITHIN THE CROWD: They cannot conquer us like this.
(*The Journalist rushes towards the posts, focusing his lens.*)
CAPTAIN: Where are you going?
JOURNALIST: Gotta get a shot o' these bodies. It'll be one helluva

sensation ... One second. (*He walks forward, not looking at anybody, staring through the lens of his camera and kicking aside any Chinese in his way.*)

VOICES FROM THE CROWD: – Why is he photographing our sorrow?
– Don't let him.
– Stop him!
– Shield our comrades!

(*They form a wall between the bodies and the Journalist.*)

JOURNALIST (*waves his camera around trying to line up a photo of the executed men*): Alright, take it easy! Outta the way!

STOKER (*from behind the backs of the Chinese*): Heshang! Come to Canton! We will teach you how to fight the gingers.

JOURNALIST (*still glued to his camera*): You're in my way, all o' ya. Goddammit!

(*The crowd parts before the movements of his hand and right in front of him stands the Stoker. He wears the uniform of the Canton workers' militia – dark blue shorts and shirt with turn down collar and a red ribbon across his shoulder. The Journalist looks up abruptly from his lens, faces the Stoker fearfully and shrinks back from him.*)

JOURNALIST: He's Canton militia!
CAPTAIN: What's wrong?
JOURNALIST: He's a Canton militia man. One of their agitators.
CAPTAIN: Where?
JOURNALIST: Over there!

(*But the crowd has already closed around the Stoker.*)

CAPTAIN (*puzzled*): They're just boatmen.

(*The Stoker appears in another spot.*)

JOURNALIST: Look, there's another.
CAPTAIN: Where?
JOURNALIST: They're everywhere.

(*The Captain begins to think the Journalist may be playing a joke on him.*)

CAPTAIN: Get a grip sir! You're hallucinating. (*But he strides aggressively towards the crowd.*) What's all this?

STUDENT (*barring his way*): Not had your fill yet, Captain?
CAPTAIN (*threateningly*): Be very careful, now! Very careful!
STUDENT: Your object lesson is over. (*The Stoker walks away from him*

but remains present in the crowd until he speaks again at the end of Scene Two.)

CAPTAIN: We will decide when the lessons are over. (*To the boatmen.*) A boat to the *Cockchafer*! Now! One dollar! (*The boatmen take a step forward, leaning on their oars.*) So that's how it is, is it?
(*The boatmen brandish their oars and beat them against the ground. In response to their threat the Captain swiftly draws the revolver from his pocket. The gun strews the sweets, placed there by Madame de Bruchelles, on the ground. Holding the crowd back at muzzle point, the Captain takes a step back. The son of the Second Boatman crawls towards a sweet.*)

CAPTAIN (*at the top of his voice*): Two not enough for you! Shall I make it ten? A thousand?! (*The pent-up crowd takes a step forwards, closer to the Captain. The little son has grabbed hold of the sweet and stood up. He wobbles and, to steady himself, clutches the Captain's leg. The Captain does not immediately take in who has grabbed him and jumps back with a cry, gasping as though he is about to be lynched.*) Aaahh ... What!
(*He angles the revolver down at the child. The Second Boatman's wife rushes up, seizes her son and snatches the sweet away from him.*)

SECOND BOATMAN'S WIFE: Leave it! Throw it away! Poison! Give it back! Not one morsel from this ginger race. Not one drop. (*She flings the sweet at the Captain's feet.*) There! There! (*She wipes clean the child's hands and mouth.*)

CAPTAIN (*turning his revolver away, disconcerted*): Idiot woman! We don't fight children.

SECOND BOATMAN'S WIFE (*goes up to the Captain with the child in her arms. Gasping, she shouts at the child, forcing him to look the Captain straight in the eye*): Look into his face! Remember him! Never ever forget him! See! The steely eyes. The blood red cheeks. The gold in his teeth. He murdered your father. If he begs for food – keep it from him. If he gasps for water – deny him. Whatever he demands – refuse him. Grow up quickly! Kill him! Kill him and his children! (*To the Captain.*) Go away, you bloodthirsty dog! Get out of our sight! Out!

CAPTAIN (*not letting go of his revolver*): I am here! And no power on this earth can force me to leave.

SCENE TWO

Copper runs down the steps of the radio station and across to the Captain.

COPPER: Captain, sir! An urgent message, from Shanghai. (*Gives him the dispatch.*)

CAPTAIN (*reading it and becoming annoyed*): Abominable timing! (*He crumples the dispatch and flings it to the ground.*)

JOURNALIST (*suddenly spotting the Stoker again, cries out*): There's the militia man! Arrest him!

CAPTAIN (*brushing him aside*): No time for that now. (*Shouts to the river.*) Cutter! (*To the sailors.*) Cover the crowd and the radio station steps. (*They all retreat, covering the crowd with their rifles. The Chinese surge towards them. Raising his revolver*) Get back! We haven't left yet!

STOKER: (*retrieves the dispatch and reads it with the Student, then shouts after the Captain*): But you are, you are leaving right now. (*To the Chinese.*) They can't stay here. Their guns are needed somewhere else. The foreigners are gathering their gunboats. Shanghai is rising. Now he's running too. (*He snatches a rifle from a policeman, jumps onto a box and shouts towards the cutter.*) Run! Run!

THE CROWD (*clustering around him*): Run! Run!

STOKER (*brandishing the rifle towards the departing cutter*): I swear by this rifle – you shall not come back! Count the hours. Your end is near. China roars. (*In an almost amused voice.*) Ah! Have you seen me now? Shoot! I may fall, but ten will rise in my place!

THE HESHANG (*jumps up onto the box beside the Stoker and covers his own chest with a yellow rag*): Bullets hold no fear. Bu pa zidan. (*A shot rings out from the river. The Heshang is hit and tumbles into the outstretched arms of the crowd.*)

STUDENT (*incensed*): Roar China! Roar in the ears of all the world. Let these crimes be known across the earth. Roar! Now! Out, out of our China!

ALL: Out! Out! Out!

CURTAIN

I Want a Baby
(*Khochu Rebënka*)

(First version)

(1926)

Translated by Stephen Holland

Note: Stephen Holland's earlier translation of this play was published in 1995 by the Department of Drama and Theatre Arts, University of Birmingham, to whom acknowledgement is made.

I Want a Baby: El Lissitzky
at work on his stage design for the play.

I Want a Baby

Characters

Saxoulsky, amateur drama producer
Superintendent of the flat block
Undertaker
Filirinov, a self-styled poet
Dr Softer
Barbara, work colleague of Milda
Angelica, a tenant
Bob, leader of the Voluntary Organisers
Milda Grignau, a cultural-educational worker
Grinko, a building worker
Yakov Plumer, a building worker
Club Secretary
Kitty, a would-be actress
Senya, Saxoulsky's assistant
Gripe, a tenant
Stoneturner, an inventor
'Aunty', a tenant
Childless female singer
Andryusha, a tenant
Ksenichka, his girl friend
Detective
Arshkin, a worker
Olympiada (Lipa), Yakov's girl friend
Block Caretaker
Little Old Man (Temporary Corpse)
Man in a Tolstoy Blouse
Drunken Typesetter
Engineer
First, second, third, fourth and fifth fathers
Landlady
Loosha, a cleaning lady
Skivvy, Clerk, Flower Seller,
Women workers who support Milda's nursery project
Other women and wives who turn against Milda's revolutionary behaviour

Workers on the building site,
Old Woman
Female students in the drama group, drama group "guard of honour", more fathers, Voluntary Organisers, visitors to the flat block, more tenants including the very nosey ones, hooligans, vigilantes, policemen, two bourgeois lady and gentlemen dancing couples, more "bohemian" dancers, a working man, a horrible woman, a little girl, other voices both on and off, gamblers, fashionable women.

The action is set in and around an overcrowded flat block in Moscow in spring, 1926. The final scene takes place four years in the future, i.e. in 1930, or perhaps in Milda's dream.

SCENE ONE: THE FALL

A shout upstairs: 'What are you doing? Aii!' The sound of a heavy body falling down. More shouts: 'An accident! – He's fallen! – To his death!' – a crowd comes running in and surrounds the fallen object.

ENGINEER: Eh, something's up on the scaffolding! Quick!
WORKER: What?
ENGINEER: Who's fallen off?
WORKER: We're all okay.
ENGINEER: Fuf! Too close for comfort.
WOMAN'S VOICE: Valya! My little girl!
YOUNG GIRL AT THE WINDOW: Mama, I'm here. It's not me that fell.
OLD WOMAN: There's so many packed into this building, they're sleeping on the window-sills.
SAXOULSKY: Didn't someone come out of the club? Where's the block superintendent? Comrade block superintendent!
SUPERINTENDENT: The club's shut. Eh! Who is it there? A man or a woman?
VOICE: You can't see. It's a man's hat.
WOMAN'S VOICE: It's the typesetter – he's keeled over, drunk. The typesetter who lives in the half-basement.
  – Smashed to bits, I reckon.
  – Caretaker, bring us a sprinkle of sand for the priest to bless.
UNDERTAKER: 'Oo is a relative of the deceased? Are there relatives of the deceased?
VOICE: Leave it out.
UNDERTAKER: The best hundertakers are 'After Grave Bliss'. 'Earses, and burial wreaths made in-parlour.
VOICE: It's enough to drive anyone to the crematorium

UNDERTAKER: Hi'll thank you for leavin' the crematorium out of this!
VOICE: Let the doctor through.
VOICE IN THE CROWD: He's stirring!
> (*The crowd parts. Filirinov is sitting there. Dr Softer comes to him.*)

SOFTER: Filirinov. You!
FILIRINOV: Me, doctor.
SOFTER: All right?
FILIRINOV: All right. Why?
SOFTER: From the sixth floor?
FILIRINOV: Well?
SOFTER: Was it you?
FILIRINOV: No. Him. (*He drags out from under him a tailor's dummy. The crowd spits expressively and disperses.*)
WOMAN'S VOICE: And I thought it was a person what'd fell. But it's just a dummy. That's akshually not exactly earth-shatterin'.
SOFTER: So what happened?
FILIRINOV: I was agitated. I was waving my arms about. I flung myself over to the window to read this monstrous bit of paper. I don't know. If it's serious, then romance in this world's finished.
SOFTER: What bit of paper?
FILIRINOV: Here. Where is it? Oh, hell. Don't say I've lost it. Oh, hang on, it's on the window-sill. Barbara! Barbara!
BARBARA (*from above*): What? (*A piece of paper, disturbed by the movement, flutters off and flies down.*)
FILIRINOV: Nothing. (*He catches the paper.*) Right, here we are. 'I request the allocation of three days leave in order that I may engineer a successful conception.' Well?
SOFTER: Handwritten. I recognize the writing. Give it here.
ANGELICA: What's all the noise? What's that piece of paper?
SOFTER: The last lines of the poet Filirinov.
FILIRINOV: Filirinov – that's me.
ANGELICA: But poetry's not a patch on this weather. Look what a spring we're having.
BOB: Comrade Block Superintendent, I must continue to insist that a corner of the club be made available for the Daily Life Organisers Brigade.
BLOCK SUPERINTENDENT: Stop pestering me. I don't know anything about any brigade. Sort it out with the club director.

BOB: But you gave permission to comrade Milda and her women.
BLOCK SUPERINTENDENT: Who's this Milda? Oh, that was last week. Such a horse of a woman.
ANGELICA: You're being unjust to Milda.
BLOCK SUPERINTENDENT: What's brought you here? (*Indicating Bob*) This dummy? One look at your Milda is enough to put you off for good.
ANGELICA: You're wrong there. Very wrong. Just you think about it.
BLOCK SUPERINTENDENT: I prefer you.
ANGELICA: I feel sorry for you.
BLOCK SUPERINTENDENT: How do you mean? Come on.
ANGELICA: You've no chance.
BLOCK SUPERINTENDENT: Because?
ANGELICA: None of your business.
SAXOULSKY (*to Block Superintendent*): They're about to knock down the salon. Its committee is offering a substantial amount of money for alternative premises.
BLOCK SUPERINTENDENT: There aren't any.
SAXOULSY: Yes there are.
BLOCK SUPERINTENDENT: Where then?
SAXOULSKY: The club. It's only half used by the drama group in any case.
BLOCK SUPERINTENDENT: But the club may be needed for other functions.
SAXOULSKY: Think it over. Just make sure you think it over. (*He exits.*)
BOB: Comrade Block Superintendent!
BLOCK SUPERINTENDENT: What kind of daily life organiser are you, when all you do the whole time is disorganise me?
BOB: Disorganise the disorganisers – that's a good slogan!
BLOCK SUPERINTENDENT: I'm getting on with my work.
BOB: I'm right behind you. (*He exits.*)
UNDERTAKER (*to Filirinov*): I gather you're hundertaking the journey to poetry, citizen?
FILIRINOV: Journey?! I've arrived!
UNDERTAKER: Since I've lorst out on you this time, I wonder if I might ask for an halternative recompense?
FILIRINOV: What?

UNDERTAKER: Write some deeply-felt verses to advertise our hundertaking hestablishment and make it clear 'ow much better we are than the crematorium.

FILIRINOV: I'm a lyric poet, citizen, not some kind of copywriter.

UNDERTAKER: Hexcuse me, I'm sure.

FILIRINOV: How much per line?

SOFTER: You write lyrics? Where've you been published?

FILIRINOV: I am a lyric poet. Deep in my soul I'm one. But I can't dig down to the poems. I write reviews, stage adaptations, agit rhymes about fire safety, slogans for co-operatives. But for my lyrics, for the stuff that's torn from my soul, I never have time ... And there's no market for my poems. (*He sniffs cocaine.*)

SOFTER: Ah ha.

BARBARA: Where's the dummy?

FILIRINOV: Coming. (*He picks the dummy up.*)

SOFTER (*looking at the piece of paper again*): I see. Spring – the happiest time.

UNDERTAKER: Hexactly. Spring – the 'appiest time: lorts of deaths.

SCENE TWO: THE CLUB

Milda, in men's clothes, enters with her back to the audience. She is trying to catch a cat.

MILDA: Pss-pss-pss-pss prr pss.
    (*Grinko and Yakov come in through the window.*)
GRINKO: Get your leg over.
YAKOV: Let me wipe my feet.
GRINKO (*looking about him*): They've covered the chapel with posters. Look at the state of it. (*Seeing Milda*) It's ... Hey, it's Frolka! He said he had to join his regiment, but here he is in the club. And he's stroking kitties instead of women. Okay. Hold on, Frol.
    (*He grabs Milda from behind under her arms, and whirls her round.*)
YAKOV: You'll smash the statue.
GRINKO (*at once, letting go*): It's not a man, it's a woman.
MILDA (*gasping*): Explain yourself, comrade!
GRINKO: Only a joke. Hell! A woman in trousers, and just like Frolka.
YAKOV: Anyway, is this the place the wiring's got to be done? They ask for yer, and then nobody shows. I dunno, eh, Grin? (*Three women enter.*) Cor! Now that's more like it!
FIRST WORKING WOMAN: Comrade Milda!
    (*Milda is silent.*)
SECOND WORKING WOMAN: There's something fishy here.
THIRD WORKING WOMAN: Perhaps he's been bothering her.
SECOND WORKING WOMAN: Perhaps he's her husband?
FIRST WORKING WOMAN: She hasn't got a husband.
MILDA: He pounced on me. Grabbed my breast.
THIRD WORKING WOMAN: Oh, I know him. A metal worker from the building site. Yesterday he was poking around up our water pipes. What are you hanging around for, you hooligan?

GRINKO: Anna, sweetie.
THIRD WORKING WOMAN: Watch it, watch it! Don't touch me! I'm on maternity leave. Can't you see?
GRINKO: Oh, the hell with it!
THIRD WORKING WOMAN: Why are you staring at him?
MILDA: He's going red. He's making eyes at me.
GRINKO: And we're Miss Picture Perfect, are we?
YAKOV: Grin! You devil! Come here.
(*Saxoulsky enters.*)
SAXOULSKY: Have you come to rehearse? I couldn't get here earlier. What do you want?
YAKOV: We're workers off the building site, got called over 'ere to the club. Hurry up, sir.
SAXOULSY: Not 'sir', call me 'citizen'. I run the drama group. I'm Saxoulsky. Haven't you heard of me? You're not here about the scenery?
YAKOV: I dunno. They just called us in.
SAXOULSKY: Wait. Just a tick. I'll fetch the club secretary here now.
(*He goes out.*)
SECOND WORKING WOMAN: The work they're doing to the block. The people from the top floors have been moved into the lower ones. They're smashing the ceiling. They say they're building on five extra storeys.
(*Enter Saxoulsky and the Club Secretary,*)
GRINKO: Are you the club secretary, citizen?
CLUB SECRETARY: Not 'citizen', call me 'comrade'. Yes, I am. I asked the foreman to send a couple of sensible workers here to do a trifling bit of work on the scenery.
YAKOV: What?
SAXOULSKY: It's the scenery for the plastic symphony of the emancipation of women. This is the dream grotto from where the bewitching sounds will emanate.
YAKOV: You lost me after 'plastic', citizen.
SAXOULSKY: At the same time as the sounds change, the colour of the flowers alters to red. So, it's a question of wiring up the lamps in the various colours of these flowers.
GRINKO: And is this a funnel?

SAXOULSKY: No, it's not a funnel. It's the flower of emancipation. The first violin will draw it from its orifice at her apotheosis, and she'll freeze with it in a Bacchic pose.
(*The workers consult one another.*)
YAKOV: What about the wiring there – we'll have to make it triple.
GRINKO: There'll be the cuff to solder.
YAKOV: And we've no rheostat. That's a big job there, mate.
GRINKO: 'Bout three hours work.
YAKOV: Tell you what, citizens, this really isn't one for us. We don't want to be messing about for ages.
CLUB SECRETARY: So what if it is a long job? It's still got to be done.
YAKOV: Anyway, there's no point to it. We'll be getting our hands dirty for nothing.
CLUB SECRETARY: You'll allow us to decide whether it's worth it or not.
GRINKO: Keep yer hair on.
YAKOV: Let's be off.
(*They go out. On the way, Grinko glances round at Milda again.*)
SECOND WORKING WOMAN: Eh, eh. Don't start getting ideas.
CLUB SECRETARY: So obstructive! And for the simplest of jobs compared to the rigours of art! (*He notices the women.*) Have you come for the rehearsal?
SAXOULSKY: Absolutely not.
MILDA: About the organisation of the day nursery for the block.
CLUB SECRETARY: Who's allowed you to meet in the club?
MILDA: The block superintendent was informed.
CLUB SECRETARY: A written authorisation, of course.
MILDA: Comrade, let's be a bit less bureaucratic.
CLUB SECRETARY: We're preparing for Women's Day. And you will be getting in the way.
SECOND WORKING WOMAN: Comrade, comrade! My husband arrived home drunk three days on the trot, and beat little Nikita. I got the police on 'im.
FIRST WORKING WOMAN: Hang on a minute! We're talking about the nursery here.
SECOND WORKING WOMAN: That's what I'm on about.
THIRD WORKING WOMAN: Hold your horses, not everybody's here yet.
(*A group of women drama students enter.*)

SAXOULSKY: Mesdames.
CLUB SECRETARY: You're late, citizens. You're late. This is a Soviet country – above all here we believe in the economical and rational utilisation of time.
MEMBERS OF THE GROUP: – I had to do overtime.
– Look, a lorry splashed me. (*Points to her leg.*)
SAXOULSKY: The driver was jealous. Get changed now. (*He goes out with the Club Secretary.*)
A GROUP MEMBER (*to Milda*): Would you go away please, comrade. We're uncomfortable changing with you here.
MILDA: Why?
GROUP MEMBER: You're a woman?
THIRD WORKING WOMAN: They don't mind undressing for men, but they won't do it in front of women. Might have known. They'll only have themselves to blame, shameless hussies!
SECOND GROUP MEMBER: Do you have a problem? I'm not aware your opinion was asked for.
FIRST GROUP MEMBER: Don't waste your breathe. Talk about effrontery.
SECOND WORKING WOMAN: Oooh, listen to her. Miss La-di-dah! We can talk our way too. Listen to this, princess, then see what you have to say. Ofokafay.
THIRD WORKING WOMAN: Ooh, yes, go on!
SECOND WORKING WOMAN: Whafat kifind ofof foofools arfare thefese?
FIRST GROUP MEMBER: They're calling us fools.
THIRD WORKING WOMAN: Thefey neefeed thefir lefegs breafakifing.
MILDA: Stop squabbling.
FIRST WORKING WOMAN: I keep asking my hubby. He won't agree to five roubles a month.
(*Saxoulsky and the Club Secretary return, along with Senya, Saxoulsky's assistant.*)
SAXOULSKY: Okay, away we go. Form up. Let's rehearse all three parts. First – women in chains; second – breaking the chains; and third – the apotheosis by the dream grotto.
(*In the ensuing dance Saxoulsky now and then interrupts with approving exclamations. The dancers press in on Milda's group – they are forced to back away in order not to interrupt their conversation.*)

FIRST WORKING WOMAN: My little Fenka has got a bad stomach again, and Pyetyunka almost tipped the samovar over her.
MILDA: Didn't you get some medicine from the out patients' department?
FIRST WORKING WOMAN: What do you mean, out patients? It was the middle of the night when he got the cramps. I had to spend my own money.
MILDA: Reckon it all up – both the medicines and the fact that you can't get away from the child – and it's obvious it's at least five roubles.
CLUB SECRETARY: Charming! Every gesture! Every movement of Katerina Sergeyevna is fit to be cast in bronze.
THIRD WORKING WOMAN: Perhaps we can get hold of the room on the cheap?
MILDA: What are you thinking? It's not just a club, you know, amateur arts groups workshop here as well – and they give the block administration its income. If we can collect the same amount, then we can demand that they allocate us our own spot without another group on top of us.
SECOND WORKING WOMAN: But where will we get the money from?
MILDA: From your husband.
FIRST WORKING WOMAN: He's already given you what you're getting.
THIRD WORKING WOMAN: Yeah, a smack round your chops. You know what, I'm going to have another abortion.
MILDA: Why?
THIRD WORKING WOMAN: There's a fat chance of getting this nursery. But without it either you ditch your kid or you drown yourself. If you work on the trams like me, and you're absent for three days, you get your marching orders.
MILDA: What about your husband?
THIRD WORKING WOMAN: Forget him. Dirty swine, it was him wot got me up the duff. And now he's gone and died on me. He was repairing a high voltage wire. The current did for him.
CLUB SECRETARY: Art – the sweetest fruit of spiritual culture.
THIRD WORKING WOMAN: The only thing left for me to do is to hang me and my baby round somebody else's neck.
SECOND WORKING WOMAN: Get married again?
THIRD WORKING WOMAN: But where do you find a decent

husband? They're not lined up ready in the tram park. You've got to go out and look for one. But I can't – tram and home, from my conductor's bag to my primus stove – that's all I do.

FIRST WORKING WOMAN: They're all swine. Dogs. I'd corner another one for myself on purpose, just to make them pay – too bad if it's his kid or not. Feed it, pay for it, raise it.

SECOND WORKING WOMAN: They just crawl up under your skirt. It's okay if it's just a hand – you don't get babies from that.

FIRST WORKING WOMAN (*at the dancers*): Bugger this lot. They've kicked us to death here. Let's hide behind Ilych.[92]

MILDA: Let's go into the corridor for a while.

(*They go. Milda meets Bob.*)

BOB: Comrade Milda, have they driven you out?

MILDA: It's difficult to work ...

BOB: That's absolutely obvious. Either we have a nursery here or this ballet. One or the other.

MILDA: No need to get hot under the collar, Bob. We can have both the nursery and the ballet.

BOB: Both-and – or either-or?

MILDA: Both – both.

BOB: Since when did you start to love ballet?

MILDA: I didn't and I don't.

BOB: So?

MILDA: Am I the only person to be considered? For goodness sake, make yourself scarce. Or I won't be responsible for my actions. You carry on the struggle against hooligans, but I get the feeling you sometimes behave like a hooligan yourself. (*They go out.*)

CLUB SECRETARY: I've looked through a couple of these. There's nothing of interest here for the drama circle. They're crude agitprop.

SAXOULSKY: Oh! The masses don't want crude agitprop.

MEMBERS OF THE GROUP: We won't allow crude agitprop.

SAXOULSKY: One second. Senya, you remember the end of that foreign play?

---

92   'Ilyich': familiar name for Lenin. In the play at this point, it refers to a statue of the Soviet leader which is probably in the place where a statue of the Virgin Mary would be expected. 'The Club' was a chapel before the revolution.

(*Saxoulsky lies down on the bench. He plays a general, Senya his son.*)

GENERAL: It's stifling ... unbearable ... The incessant sounds of Paris beyond these walls. Who's there?

SON: It's me, your son.

GENERAL: No Bolshevik's a son of mine. There are no commissars in the Polyudov family. In my veins flows the blood of Catherine's court. There's no place for traitors in our family. ... For ten years I have been in the front rank of the émigrés, and I will go to my grave a dyed-in-the-wool old émigré. Others come to take my place, not you.

SON: Forgive me, father.

GENERAL: There's no forgiveness. He who raised his hand against his brothers will be crushed by the people.

SON: Understand – I had no other choice. Strike me, father.

GENERAL: Strike you? I wouldn't dirty my hands. But if I press this button they'll come and throw you out. Go back and rot in your Bolshevik camp. There's no place for you under the tricolour.

SON: Don't say such things, father. (*The general's hand falls on his face.*) He's growing cold. Dead. (*He sobs over the body.*)

CLUB SECRETARY: Would you believe it? Get that curtain down. This is ideological claptrap.

SAXOULSKY: Of course, I don't suggest it should be like that. Senya, let's do it again. I'll be an old Bolshevik. Senya's a White Guard officer. It's stifling ... unbearable ... The incessant sounds of Moscow beyond these walls. Who's there?

SON: It's me, your son.

SAXOULSKY: No White Guard's a son of mine. There are no tsarist cavalry captains in the Polyudov family. In my veins flows the blood of Pugachov's fighters ... There's no place for traitors in our family. For ten years I was in the front rank of the revolutionaries, and I'll go to my grave a dyed-in-the-wool old Bolshevik. Others come to take my place, not you.

SON: Forgive me, father.

SAXOULSKY: There's no forgiveness. He who raised his hand against his brothers will be crushed by the people.

SON: Understand – I had no other choice. Strike me, father.

SAXOULSKY: I wouldn't dirty my hands. But if I press this button, they'll come and throw you out. Go back, and rot in your émigré camp. There's no place for you under the red flag.

SON: Don't say such things, father ... He's growing cold. Dead. (*He sobs.*)
(*A guard of honour enters, saying: 'If you are not one of us, go now!'*)

CLUB SECRETARY: Now that's artistically valuable and ideologically consistent.
(*Kitty enters.*)

KITTY (*timidly*): Is Citizen Saxoulsky here?

SAXOULSKY: That's me. Are you Kitty? Have you brought a piece? Good. Let's go over into the corner, shall we?

KITTY: 'I have so many tender and melodious words for you. It is I alone who could have thought of them for you – loving you as I do.'

SAXOULSKY: Cut straight to the emotional ending.

KITTY: 'I have a shimmering sea of kisses for you ... If you desire – in that sea, I will drown you.' (*Saxoulsky is picking his teeth.*) How was I?

SAXOULSKY: Hell, I've been eating sprats. I've got a bone stuck in my teeth.

KITTY: Will you recommend me to the theatre? Mm?

SAXOULSKY: Do you live by yourself?

KITTY: No, with my aunt.

SAXOULSKY: How perfectly foul.

KITTY: Why?

SAXOULSKY: It's impossible at mine. There's my wife and all the others.

KITTY: What do you mean?

SAXOULSKY: Where could we meet this evening?

KITTY: What for?

SAXOULSKY: So we can sleep together.

KITTY: How dare you?!

SAXOULSKY: You want to get into the theatre for nothing? Without any hanky-panky?

KITTY: But you said I had talent.

SAXOULSKY: Talents like yours, they're two a penny down at the Art Workers Agency. What's the matter? I say, what innocence! But this is theatre, your debut, success, flowers, a car. Well?

KITTY: And you won't cheat me?

SAXOULSKY: What a question. Don't go away. There's a room next door. There's something on in there now, but that's where they store the drums. When they break up, we can sneak in there.

KITTY: I don't know.

SAXOULSKY: Come come, kitten. What don't you know? Here, look. I'm writing a note to the administrator and I'll give it to you. Understand? You come along tomorrow evening. I'll introduce you to all the people you need to know.

KITTY: Now?

SAXOULSKY: Here's the note. (*The note lies in his hand. Kitty stretches out and takes it. Saxoulsky squeezes Kitty's hand in his own.*) The drama students can go now.

(*The members of the group go out. Milda and the three women return. Saxoulsky and Kitty go into the room. Barbara stands in the doorway.*)

THIRD WORKING WOMAN: There she is.

MILDA: Barbara!

BARBARA: Hello.

THIRD WORKING WOMAN: You don't want us, I'll bet. You're after the men.

MILDA: It's been two whole days, hasn't it?

BARBARA (*looking round*): He's not here?

THIRD WORKING WOMAN: Someone's on heat – those stockings ... how much, d'you reckon?

BARBARA: Has anyone been asking for me?

MILDA: Where are all your reports and notes?

BARBARA: At home.

THIRD WORKING WOMAN: Honestly, look at those heels, look at those heels!

MILDA: Barbara, I must have a little talk with you.

BARBARA: I don't want to. I'm fed up with these little talks.

MILDA: Let me finish.

BARBARA: You know what you can do with your little talks. If anyone asks for me, I've gone to the Olympic cinema.

MILDA: Barbara, I must clear something up with you.

BARBARA: Just stop it! Mind you don't get blisters on your backside with all your meetings. (*She goes out.*)

MILDA: Wait! (*She rushes after Barbara. First Working Woman holds her back.*)

FIRST WORKING WOMAN: Stop! You're rushing off too. Write it down for me first, then away you go.

I WANT A BABY AND OTHER PLAYS

CLUB SECRETARY: It's time for me to go. Comrade, when you leave, lock the club and give the key to the caretaker.

MILDA: Very well..

(The three working women go out. Enter Fourth Working Woman.)

FOURTH WORKING WOMAN: Are you in a hurry?

MILDA: Don't worry about that. Explain yourself. Why haven't I seen you at any of the meetings? And you weren't at the conference. What's the matter with you? Are you ill?

FOURTH WORKING WOMAN: No.

MILDA: Is money tight?

FOURTH WORKING WOMAN: No.

MILDA: What then?

FOURTH WORKING WOMAN: I'm not going to work any more.

MILDA: What do you mean, not going to?

FOURTH WORKING WOMAN: Just that – not going to. I've left the Party.

MILDA: Left the Party?

FOURTH WORKING WOMAN: I'm tired out. It's my husband, he's nagged me to death. He comes home from work hungry, in a bad temper, bawling: 'Other blokes' wives get things ready, the way it's supposed to be, but our place is a pigsty.' It's impossible to leave my little boy, Lenka, without someone to keep an eye on him.

MILDA: I've seen him. His hand's in a bandage.

FOURTH WORKING WOMAN: He burned it on a primus stove. I can't stand any more. I've got to choose: either I chuck the family or the Party.

MILDA: Isn't there room for both?

FOURTH WORKING WOMAN: I could solve the problem with my son, if there was a day nursery. One way or the other, I could hold down my job. But with my husband ... Anyway, I've been sacked.

MILDA: Why?

FOURTH WORKING WOMAN: My husband earns enough.

MILDA: So you're now a housewife?

FOURTH WORKING WOMAN: Yes, a housewife.

MILDA: But don't you feel just awful leaving the Party?

FOURTH WORKING WOMAN: Don't give me any more grief about it, alright? It doesn't matter. It can't come too soon for me. That's all there is to it. Don't blame me, but I'm not reporting in any more. It's late. My husband'll start growling.
(*Milda has walked up to the door, and now she rattles the keys. In the next room, somebody knocks over a drum.*)
MILDA: Is anybody there? I'm locking up the club.
SAXOULSKY (*leaping out, dishevelled*): What's the matter? We're just going through some work.
MILDA: Going through the motions, more like.
SAXOULSKY: Give me the key. I'll lock up myself.
MILDA: The key has to be handed to the caretaker.
SAXOULSKY: I'm in charge of the drama studio.
MILDA: But you're not the caretaker.
SAXOULSKY: It's a pity there's no policeman nearby.
KITTY: I simply don't understand. (*In readjusting her clothes, she drops the piece of paper.*)
MILDA: You've dropped something, citizen. (*Saxoulsky picks it up.*)
KITTY: Give it back.
SAXOULSKY: I'm keeping it.
KITTY: But you yourself said ...
SAXOULSKY: Don't make a fuss now. (*He goes out.*)
MILDA (*looking over the club*): There's room for sixty cots here!

SCENE THREE: FATHERS

Softer comes in, ahead of Milda who is lagging behind.

MILDA: Where are you hurrying to?
SOFTER: The cinema. To give a lecture.
FLOWER SELLER: Buy my flowers.
SOFTER (*buys a bunch*): Do you like flowers?
MILDA: No. They're the plant's sex organs.
SOFTER: You're horribly rational. You're a blue stocking.
MILDA: That's better than a flesh-coloured one.
SOFTER: You don't like nature, then? Mountains, waterfalls, wild places?
MILDA: I love it when there's a turbine on the waterfall, mines in the mountains and sawmills in the wild woods, and regular plantations.
SOFTER: But surely the idea of solidarity grows out of people's deep rooted affinity for one another. You have to think about yourself just a little bit, don't you?
MILDA: There's no such thing as human solidarity. There are well-equipped factories. A correctly laid-out day. A network of military posts. A precise railway timetable and a truly charted course to socialism.
SOFTER: And what about the soul? The tenderest, most intimate things in the human soul?
MILDA: Aren't you ashamed of yourself, a biologist, to come out with such rose-tinted rubbish about the soul?
SOFTER: It's hard without it.
MILDA: Yes, well, we don't live in easy times.
SOFTER: I must run. I'm late for my lecture.
MILDA: Go well, comrade!
    (*Softer exits. Twenty fathers come rolling out, carrying their babies. The children are howling.*)

GRIPE (*at a window*): Is this a life? Or not? They've started a concert under my window. Is this a children's home? Or not? People are living here. (*Mimicking a child's crying. The children get louder.*) Ah-ha! Ah-ha! Because of this racket – sit in my own tobacco fug. (*He slams the window.*)

MILDA: Listen. They're crying. And it seems to me like a man kissing me on the lips.

FIRST FATHER: His nappy's soaking. I'll have to change it. (*To one of the other fathers.*) Take him a minute.

SECOND FATHER: Okay, hand him over.

MILDA: Let me hold him.

FIRST FATHER: Thanks. (*Changing the nappy.*) Look, it's yellow and all week it's been green.

MILDA: How many months old is he?

FIRST FATHER: Four.

MILDA: Is it a boy?

FIRST FATHER: Girl.

SECOND FATHER: Comrade father, do you use any sort of powder?

FIRST FATHER: Just lycopodium.

MILDA: Perhaps she's crying because she's hungry?

FIRST FATHER: No, her mother's only just fed her, and she's getting her own breakfast now. You haven't got one of these?

MILDA: No.

FIRST FATHER: Why not?

MILDA: I haven't started yet.

FIRST FATHER: You'd produce something pretty good. Pelvis – a hundred and twenty centimetres, and you'd give plenty of milk.

MILDA: Are you a doctor?

FIRST FATHER: No, I'm a political instructor. I'm comparing you with my wife. This little girl has a brother, who popped out at Perekop.[93] We shoved him into a felt boot and carted him about. He survived, but he's delicate.

MILDA: Why?

---

93   *Perekop*: the battle of Perekop, 1920, was a turning-point in the Russian Civil War, when the Red Army achieved a decisive breakthrough.

FIRST FATHER: He was created in a hurry somewhere on the march. They were hungry times. We were undernourished, me and the wife. Then there were the battles – our nerves took a thrashing.

MILDA: Is that important?

FIRST FATHER: Oho! This one's a NEP[94] child. A lovely little plump one, well-fed and chubby. Look how round she is. That's because when we got down to making her, both her daddy and her mummy had plenty to eat, we were at peace with the world and in love. You don't mind me talking as openly as this?

MILDA: On the contrary. Is it very expensive to keep a baby?

FIRST FATHER: How shall I put it? So far it's not too bad. When she begins to wear out pairs of boots, I'll feel it. For now, it's about ten roubles a month.

SECOND FATHER: It can be cheaper in the first year.

THIRD FATHER: Here's my problem. You can feed 'em for kopecks, but when they're ill – it's roubles.

SECOND FATHER: Was yours born sickly?

THIRD FATHER: A weakling from birth. First it's scrofula, then it's ...

FIRST FATHER: Is Mom healthy?

THIRD FATHER: Mom's down with consumption, she attends the health clinic.

FIRST FATHER: See that man with the bandage? His kid's an imbecile – it's his third and it's an imbecile.

SECOND FATHER: If you marry your cousin, you're bound to have either an imbecile or a kid that's deaf and dumb.

(*The children cry. Above someone bangs a window bad-temperedly. Girls in stockings pass by. The fathers stare at their legs.*)

GIRLS:

FIRST: Where are you going this evening?

SECOND: I'll be at home.

FIRST: I'll come round to yours.

SECOND: No, please don't.

SOFTER: Not bad – fine flanks, but not for production. (*To the young father*) Watch out, you're dropping your son. Hey, lathe operator! Never seen women's legs before?

---

94   *NEP*: the New Economic Policy, introduced by Lenin in March 1923, which restored a limited level of capitalism.

FOURTH FATHER (*disconcerted*): It's the stockings – they're very attractive.
SECOND FATHER: We know all about stockings. (*Indicating baby.*) You've manufactured one, now you're lining yourself up for another.
(*Hooligans appear. First Hooligan spits.*)
SOFTER: Don't spit. Can't you see there are children here?
FIRST HOOLIGAN: Yeah. Don't need no lectures from you. (*He spits.*)
MILDA: Wipe that up!
FIRST HOOLIGAN: What kind of birdy's this?
SECOND HOOLIGAN: Birdy – bighead. Tss-tss.
FIRST HOOLIGAN: Take a cloth, lady muck, and wipe it up yourself. (*He spits again.*)
(*A Father, looking like a peasant woman with a bandaged gumboil, melancholy and indifferent, puts his child on the bench and goes over to the hooligans.*)
MILDA: Where's a policeman?
FIFTH FATHER: He's not needed. (*To the hooligans*) Fancy a three month stretch, citizens?
FIRST HOOLIGAN: How d'yer make that out, then?
FIFTH FATHER: It was you that spat, wasn't it? Wipe it up, please.
FIRST HOOLIGAN: Back off. I'll send the last of yer teeth flying.
FIFTH FATHER: Really? And how are you going to do that?
FIRST HOOLIGAN: Keep your hands off. Want the knife? (*He pulls out a Finnish knife.*)
FIFTH FATHER: Eh, young people!
FIRST HOOLIGAN: Ha! (*He lunges with the knife. The father pulls the knife from him in a bored way. He knocks him down, drags him by his leg, and, grabbing him by the scruff of his neck, wipes his face in the spittle.*)
FIFTH FATHER: Let go of my hand, young man, and wipe up that spit with your little nose. Let go of my hand, otherwise I'll be dragging you around till evening, which'll be very trying.
(*Both hooligans run off.*)
FIRST FATHER: You sorted him out all right.
FIFTH FATHER: I worked as a circus artist, but now I suffer with my teeth. It was nothing special, citizens. (*He picks up a rattle and comforts his son.*)

FIRST FATHER: It's getting dark. And a bit chilly. We'll have to go home.
  (*They go out slowly, in a line.*)
SOFTER: Milda, why don't you come round to my place sometime?
MILDA: I don't go anywhere unless I have to.
SOFTER: Milda, there's this person I know. Spring makes her go all funny. And there's a man that she knows.
MILDA: A member of the intelligentsia?
SOFTER: Yes. And a well-educated, very quiet and tactful person. He'd be easy to live with, he'd make a splendid husband.
MILDA: But what sort of a father?
SOFTER: According to eugenics, the intelligentsia are a select group of the people, and a better posterity can be obtained only from them.
MILDA: Softer, does this young man have a beard?
SOFTER: Yes.
MILDA: He'd better shave it off. It doesn't suit him. Where can I find you?
SOFTER: During the day, at the Dispensary on the building site.
MILDA: Goodbye.
SOFTER: Goodbye.
  (*They part.*)

SCENE FOUR: AT HOME

'Aunty' is washing children behind one of a number of partitions. Stoneturner is cramming from a book, occasionally turning his head towards the woman.

STONETURNER: Bath time, then!
'AUNTY': What? (*To the children*) Hey, you, stop scratching your sister. Stop it, or you'll get a good slap. Don't rub your eyes like that, don't rub them.
STONETURNER: Is it soaping up?
'AUNTY': What?
STONETURNER: So the soap – is it soaping up just so?
'AUNTY': What's he on about ... soaping up? (*To the children*) Don't splash – wiping the floor after you does my back in. You were sent to torment me, you little tyrants.
CHILD'S VOICE: Ah ah ah, in my eye-yi-yi ... soap ... yow-ow-ow-ow ...
'AUNTY': Oh, you ... damn and double damn ... I wish the floor would open up and swallow you ... I'm sick of it, curse you. Stoneturner, help, move the bucket out of the way.
STONETURNER: Is the soap working?
CHILD'S VOICE: My eye-yi-yi ...
STONETURNER: And not smelling?
'AUNTY': What's it going to smell of? Soap is soap.
STONETURNER: No, not quite. I boiled it up myself, actually.
'AUNTY': Oh yes, Stoneturner? So now we're studying at the university of soap boiling up, are we?
STONETURNER: I'm a chemist.
'AUNTY': A chemist? ... Shut up, you wretches ... Look at them, they're chemists, too.
MALE VISITOR: How do I get to Prudnikov's?

STONETURNER: Third on the left. Where they're making such a racket.

SCREEN 2

GRIPE (*from behind a ledger*): Have your cats stopped lapping up the milk? Or not? Is it getting on my nerves, or not?
VOICE: Pussy, he's a wicked man. A nasty man. Spit on him.

SCREEN 3: THE BOOZE-UP

HE: Have you heard about Prokhorenko?
FEMALE SINGER: Has he spent all his money?
MALE VISITOR: No, some hooligans mugged him on the street.
HOUSEWIFE: They weren't hooligans, they were engineers.
VOICE (*from behind another screen*): Hey, give the engineers a break, will you?
HOUSEWIFE: There's an engineer who's a tenant here. I went and forgot.
HE: Nonsense. It's nothing to do with you. They're not talking about present company.
ENGINEER: But when you said it, I wasn't present.
MALE VISITOR: Then you couldn't have heard anything.
ENGINEER: Yes, I could.
MALE VISITOR: Well then, you were eavesdropping.
HE: Okay. Have you got your guitar?
ENGINEER: Yes.
HE: Come round to our place, then. We'll have a sing-song.
  (*The Engineer joins them. They all know each other. The Engineer sings a romantic song. Something starts jabbing into their side screen from 'next door', Screen 4. The visitor tries to touch the foot doing the prodding.*)
SHE (*splitting her sides with laughter*): What are you doing? They're ... They're newly-weds ...
ALL: Oy-oy-oy.
HE: She used to live here with her epileptic father. Today they went to the registry office. She had nowhere to live. So they moved her father to her husband's room, and themselves ...

VOICE FROM THE FIFTH SCREEN: It's stupid to play a low card against that lead. You haven't got a clue. Stop messing things up. Play your queen.

VOICES FROM THE SIXTH SCREEN:

MALE: The laws of deflection. The laws of deflection of light state that a beam ... that a beam ... the laws of deflection ...

FEMALE: Listen, why does Zoshchenko write so little?

VOICES FROM THE SEVENTH SCREEN:

– Petyenka, which do you prefer? A green or a pink lampshade?

– Mmm.

– Petyenka, really, this little rug makes things cosier, don't you think?

– Mmm.

– Kiss me, Petyenka, darling.

THIRD SCREEN (*a sharp groan, a blow, and from Screen 4 through the side curtain onto the table of Screen 3 a naked leg protrudes in long johns*):

MALE VISITOR: One. Is that all?

HE: Oi, you, mind what you're doing!"

MALE VISITOR: Tickle it! (*They tickle it with a fork, but the foot does not move.*) Well? Try again! (*The foot does not react. The Visitor pulls back the front curtain of screen 4.*) It's their father.

SHE: A dead body in the house.

FEMALE SINGER: I feel sick. I'm going back to my place. (*She goes behind screen 7.*)

ENGINEER: We'll have to call out the authorities.

HE: You'll have to get rid of him. We can't have a deceased in the house.

STONETURNER: There was a human being, and now – nothing.

'AUNTY': May he rest in heaven.

STONETURNER: And there's little use to be had of him now. Maybe as a skeleton for a school. But there's not enough fat for even half a pound of soap.

'AUNTY': Show some respect! What are you trying to tell me – that you make soap out of human fat?

STONETURNER: What do you think that's made out of? (*He points to the soap.*) And you washed the kids with it.

'AUNTY': From human beings? (*She flings the soap away.*) You filth! You'll poison the children. Get out of the room. Take your books with you. And take your scabby odds and ends, too. You sacrileger!

STONETURNER (*going out into the corridor*): So here, where even the dead have somewhere to lie down, am I, a living intellectual, with nowhere to go.
MILDA: Stoneturner? You? In the corridor?
STONETURNER: I haven't got a room any more.
MILDA: You've quarrelled with your landlady?
STONETURNER: Driven out, like all inventors. No prophet in his own ...
MILDA: Is Barbara here?
STONETURNER: No. Barbara has, I would say, slipped the lead ... tss. (*He tuts.*)
FEMALE SINGER (*from behind screen 7*): – My dear friends, so, so dear to me ... You mustn't think I'm drunk. It's just things are so hard for me.
FEMALE SINGER (*comes out to Milda and Stoneturner*): Listen, do you know this song? I'm a performer. I can sing.
    LULLABY (to a son who is not yet born)
Night comes creeping, creeping softly,
On furry paws comes creeping nigh,
Baby boy was made for weeping,
Mama to croon her lullaby.

Let me banish all his nightmares,
Drive out dreams which make him sad,
Let him sleep, my little baby,
Let him sleep, my little lad.

Let my little lad grow stronger,
Boldly say: 'I'm stepping out!'
Tight round his neck his Pioneers' tie.[95]
Stand prepared without a doubt.

Yet for now one step's beyond him,
Wobbling forth on chubby legs.
Dream, my little grey-eyed baby,
Dream, my little grey-eyed speck.

---

95   *The 'Pioneers'*: Communist Party organisation for young adolescents, not dissimilar to the Scouts.

Now the fate that's fashioned for him
Her young man shoulders like his kit,
A Komsomol[96] with soft grey eyes,
No more than down upon his lip.

Letters marked with distant postmarks,
Unknown stamps stuck on askew,
My son will send a simple letter,
I will get a present, too.

Boats don't tarry in their home port,
Soon they sail away, away.
Boys are made to grow to sailors,
Mothers wait through night and day.

Now her hair has turned to snow
As the years whirled on their way.
She hears her heart speak, 'I am weary,
In this world it's hard to stay.'

Just then, as she accepts for ever
This is her fate, and dries her tears,
Words come rushing over rivers,
Over towns straight to his ears.

Pallid, white, as printer's paper,
Dark and smudged around his eyes,
Now the son weeps bitterly
For mama, watching as she dies.

But for now, for now at least,
None of this has yet come true.
Baby boy sleeps on in peace,
And mama's singing just for you.

---

96   *The Komsomol*: Communist Party youth organisation, to which a Pioneer would graduate.

STONETURNER: Comrade, calm yourself.
FEMALE SINGER: I can't calm myself. I want a little son. And what have I had? Fifteen abortions. So now the doctor said I can't give birth. I prostrated myself before him – doctor, I want a son, I can't go on without a son. I'm not frightened of giving birth. Even if I am delicate, even if my hips are narrow. Let me have a son. In nine months, my son will say to my bones: make way! And I will lie down and scream. (*She screams.*)
STONETURNER: There there, calm down.
FEMALE SINGER: I'm not in pain. It's not pain. I'm not screaming with pain. I'm screaming with joy. My belly. It's here. A son is coming. A son is coming.
MILDA (*to the lodgers of the third screen*): Give her some water.
LODGERS: Excuse us, citizen. She's got a primus, let her boil some herself.
(*Stoneturner takes the hysterical woman back behind the seventh screen. Barbara enters. She is radiant. Seeing Milda, she stops short and goes quickly behind a screen. During the conversation, she gets undressed and changes her footwear.*)
MILDA: I was coming to talk to you, Barbara.
BARBARA (*spitefully*): Surprise surprise!
MILDA: Barbara.
BARBARA: Stop that – 'Barbara'. It makes me sick. We're not all mother superiors, like you. You can sit out the years without a man, but I can't. That's all there is to it.
STONETURNER: When you're angry, Barbara, count. One, two, three. It's the best restraint. One shouldn't just let it out.
BARBARA: You don't need to say anything. I know. 'You ought to be ashamed. You're neglecting your work. You're running after a bloke. Why have you put on those yellow stockings? Why's your hair permed? Why've you got lipstick on? Why are you made up? Why do you have boots with high heels?'
STONETURNER: And why do you have those boots with high heels? Watch.
BARBARA: They're more attractive. Why else?
STONETURNER: No, watch. (*He walks round with the boots on.*)
MILDA: It's to make you seem taller.

STONETURNER: No. Can you really not see? The shape of the body? No? ... These heels give your backside a nicer shape, and your bust sticks out more. You get the idea?
BARBARA: Clear off, you idiot!
STONETURNER: Are you convinced?
MILDA: Stoneturner, go away. I have to talk privately to Barbara. (*Stoneturner withdraws.*)
BARBARA: Well, get on with it. Are you thinking of nagging me for long?
MILDA: I don't intend to give you a moral lecture. I've come to you ... for a very special reason.
BARBARA: What's that?
MILDA: Well ... You know lots of ... tender words.
BARBARA: To sympathise with you?
MILDA: When you talk to a man you love, you say endearing words to him, don't you, and he starts getting very tender. Could you tell me these words?
BARBARA: Are you crazy? Don't you know anything yourself?
MILDA: I only partly know Russian – I'm just a Latvian farm girl. But actually I've hardly heard any tender words in Latvian either. Nobody ever spoke lovingly to me.
BARBARA: But you churn out resolutions like a factory. What do you need these for?
MILDA: I just need them. Tell me. (*She takes out a notebook.*)
BARBARA: Eh-eh-eh, I don't know.
MILDA: Well, when you kiss a man, what do you say to him?
BARBARA: Eh? Well, I'd say something like: 'You little piggy,' or 'you poison pudding.'
MILDA: Tell me seriously.
BARBARA: I am being serious. Um, 'little piggy features', 'silly little piggy', 'little toadstool', 'scarecrow'. 'Sweetie-weetie', 'itsy-bitsy', 'umpsy-wumpsy'.
MILDA: So you can just take an adjective or noun and add –itsy or –umpsy
BARBARA: Or –let like in 'piglet', –est like in 'dearest', or like I said, just add a 'y' and a 'w' like in 'piggy wiggy'. Now will that be all?
MILDA: Er, no. You haven't got a dress?
BARBARA: Why?
MILDA: To wear.
BARBARA: You?

MILDA: Yes. I won't ruin it.
BARBARA: Marvellous. Anything else?
MILDA: Have you got the file with my papers?
BARBARA: Here it is.
MILDA (*rummaging in it*): There was a little note with them. Where is it? Damn! Where can it be? Listen, has someone been going through these? Tell me, I'm only asking.
BARBARA: Filirinov.
MILDA: Ah, that's who you're with now ... Be careful, Barbara.
BARBARA: Of what?
MILDA: He's a drug addict. A degenerate.
    (*Near the second screen:*)
UNDERTAKER (*enquiring at the third screen*): Who's in 'ere? You rang me? Where's our dear deceased? Here 'e his, all by himself! Well, never mind, we'll find the relatives. (*He goes to 'Aunty'.*)
'AUNTY': What do you want?
UNDERTAKER: You couldn't find a little bucket of water, my beauty?
'AUNTY': Where's a cheerful Charlie like you appeared from?
UNDERTAKER: We are from the Bureau of Hundertaking Processes. We were notified of a dear deceased 'ere ...
'AUNTY': Here's a bucket for you – I was washing the kids, only –
UNDERTAKER: We're not borrowing it for nothing. Please accept this little fifty kopeck piece. Please do. There. Now we'll make a start. (*He disappears.*)
LITTLE OLD MAN (*the 'corpse', now gets up*): There wouldn't be a little drinky anywhere ... I'm faint. But everywhere's shut. They spilled my vodka all over me. My daughter isn't at home. I've got a weak heart. (*The shocked lodgers scatter and exit.*)
STONETURNER: Here's some water. Get that down you, great-grandad. (*The Little Old Man drinks.*)
UNDERTAKER (*bustling in*): Now then, where's the deceased? The deceased – where is he?
STONETURNER: I reckon a whole bucket of water's too much for a dead person.
UNDERTAKER: To wash it with?
STONETURNER: No, to drink.
UNDERTAKER: To drink? This is our hactual deceased? How on earth can that be? Gracious me! Grandad!

OLD MAN: Thanks, thanks a lot. I'll remember you gave me that water till the day they carry me out in my coffin.
UNDERTAKER: What coffin? Listen, aunty, I don't need the bucket now. The little old man's resurrected 'imself. So you'd better let me have my fifty kopecks back.
'AUNTY' (*flirtatiously*): No chance. The fellow hasn't been born who can get fifty kopecks out of me.
UNDERTAKER: Don't you believe it, aunty. Still, today I'm feeling rather hard done by and you're bein' very hobstreporous. I'll come back for my fifty kopecks another time.
STONETURNER: Is business bad?
UNDERTAKER: I'm sittin' hon coffins.
STONETURNER: Dearie me. Too bad. Your stock's decaying, I suppose. Are the ones made of zinc okay?
UNDERTAKER: Hi think so.
STONETURNER: Are they pure zinc?
UNDERTAKER: Yes.
STONETURNER: I suppose they're heavy?
UNDERTAKER: 180 pounds of pure zinc each.
STONETURNER: And expensive?
UNDERTAKER: About three hundred roubles each.
STONETURNER: You know what, you could sell me half a pound of coffin. For electrical elements.
(*The Undertaker runs out.*)
MILDA: Barbara, thanks. Go well. Do apply yourself and come to the meeting. Stoneturner, come on.
(*They exit. A detachment of voluntary organisers enters the house.*)
'AUNTY': What do you want?
VOL ORG: We've come to reconstruct the flat. Where are the lodgers?
'AUNTY': They legged it when the corpse woke up.
VOL ORG: Where shall we start from?
(*The 'reconstruction' begins. Lodgers run in.*)
LODGER: Why is it being taken to bits?
FEMALE LODGER: Are they plumbers?
LODGER: Why have they taken up the carpets?
FEMALE LODGER: The rubber plant! Mind the rubber plant!
LODGER: Whose grubby aunt?
FEMALE LODGER: Get the caretaker.

VOL ORG: This corner'll be for work, that one over there – the communal sleeping quarters, here – the dining area ...
CARETAKER: What's all the hoo-ha about?
FEMALE LODGER: They've turned everything upside down. Hooligans!
CARETAKER: And who might you be?
VOL ORG: We're a detachment of daily life organisers. We were sent for.
CARETAKER: Here?
VOL ORG: Here's our schedule of duties.
CARETAKER: Flat 5, but this is number 3. You'll have to clear off.
VOL ORG: Citizens, it really is much better like this.
LODGER: Get out! Get out!
FEMALE LODGER: That's my cosy cuddly!
CARETAKER: Maybe it is better, but you'd better make yourselves scarce. If you wouldn't mind, citizens.
(*Vol Orgs go out.*)
VOL ORG (*coming back*): I've squashed a bedbug here. So allow me to return your bedbug to prevent you making a claim.
FEMALE LODGER: It's not my bedbug, it's my neighbour's.
LODGER: She's a liar, dirty thing.
FEMALE LODGER: God, it's so depressing when there are so many idiots around.
LODGERS (*from behind the screens*): You're the idiot!

SCENE FIVE: HOOLIGANS

Gates into the park leading to the club. Music is coming out of the club. Two hooligans.

FIRST: Not at the ball, Cinderella?
SECOND: They won't let me in. Bastards. They've recruited a bunch of vigilantes. I'd like to smash their legs to pulp with a brick.
FIRST: Don't be daft. Best do it on the quiet. On the sly. Just lob it in.
SECOND: They'll recognise me. My mugshot's pinned up. There's some nosey parker on the door.
FIRST: But the girls are there. And it's warm there. And there's music there.
SECOND: Leave off.
FIRST: Stop pussyfooting around. The bloke on the door won't go away. I'll try to worm my way in. Let's get a gang together and we'll beat hell out of their brigade, and then we can all get some beer down our necks. Stay there!
(He runs off. Andryusha and Ksenichka enter.)
ANDRYUSHA: Don't go, Ksenichka.
KSENICHKA: I must, Andryusha. My sister'll tell me off otherwise.
ANDRYUSHA: Ksenichka. I've brought you this far. Now you can see me to where the fence ends.
KSENICHKA: Andryusha, it's so late.
ANDRYUSHA: Ksenichka, soon I'll have a motorbike in the garage for us – I'll drive it myself.
KSENICHKA: And you'll take me for a drive?
ANDRYUSHA: Course I will, Ksenichka.
KSENICHKA: Andryusha, you are nice.
ANDRYUSHA: And in the hostel, I'm partitioning off my own corner with plywood. You'll come to me, Ksenichka?
KSENICHKA: Andryusha, what are you saying?

(*They go out.*)
VOICES FROM THE CLUB: – Eh eh!
– Give it to him!
– Piss off, you swine. Piece of shit!
– Comrade, stop shouting.
(*A mass of bodies comes rolling out, as the vigilantes eject the hooligans.*)
VIGILANTE: Pack it in, comrade, stop going for me.
SECOND HOOLIGAN: What do you think you're doing? Hooligan.
SECOND VIGILANTE: You're the bloody hooligan.
THIRD HOOLIGAN: You've grabbed the wrong bloke.
FIRST VIGILANTE: Never mind 'wrong bloke'. Stop trying to trip me.
ARSHKIN: I'm a worker.
FIRST VIGILANTE: A hooligan is what you are.
ARSHKIN: You can't kick a worker out of the workers' club.
SECOND VIGILANTE: You shouldn't smash the crockery, should you?
ARSHKIN (*raises a brick*): Never mind the crockery. I'll rearrange your face, you shit.
VIGILANTE: That's enough! We won't let you in. Get back!
SECOND HOOLIGAN: My cap's still in there.
FIRST VIGILANTE: Whistle up a policeman.
SECOND VIGILANTE: It's not worth it. We can cope with this.
FIRST VIGILANTE (*to Arshkin*): Move off!
ARSHKIN (*nipping in from the side*): Stitch that, swine.
SECOND VIGILANTE: Hurt your head? Has he drawn blood?
FIRST VIGILANTE: Doesn't matter. I'll be okay, I can still walk. Don't let them get in.
(*The vigilantes step back. The hooligans start following them. One hooligan standing by the wall, hisses to a second to come over. They whisper together. Ksenichka and Andryushe re-enter*)
KSENICHKA: ... And I said to him: 'No, don't you dare speak to me in such an impertinent tone.'
ANDRYUSHA: In the corridor?
KSENICHKA: Well yes, and in broad daylight.
ANDRYUSHA: I'm sorry I wasn't there to help you.
HOOLIGAN: Comrade.
ANDRYUSHA: Me?
HOOLIGAN: Give me a light.

(*Andryusha gives him a light.*)

KSENICHKA: Andryusha, let's say goodnight, then.

ANDRYUSHA: Ksenichka, just one more time.

KSENICHKA: I really can't, Andryusha. My sister will shout at me, she'll say I'm too free and easy.

ANDRYUSHA: She wouldn't dare, Ksenichka. Please, just come as far as that telegraph pole. Don't dig your heels in.

KSENICHKA: Oh, Andryusha, you're so persistent. Well, perhaps it's all right just to there.

ANDRYUSHA: Ksenichka. I'll hang a rug on the partition wall and on the rug I'll put two daggers made of silver chocolate wrapping paper.

KSENICHKA: Andryusha, here's our telegraph pole. I can't come any further.

ANDRYUSHA: Well, I'll still walk you just two little poles further. Ksenichka, look, if he starts talking in the corridor again ...

KSENICHKA: I won't even listen.

ANDRYUSHA: You watch out, Ksenichka.

KSENICHKA: Andryusha, how can you not believe me?

ANDRYUSHA: Ksenichka.

KSENICHKA: Well, here's where we say byebye.

ANDRYUSHA: Just another five paces.

KSENICHKA: Oh, Andryusha. Don't force me. Here we are, that's five paces.

ANDRYUSHA: And now I'll take five paces with you. One, two, three, four, five. Ksenichka, I haven't got the rug yet. But if you'd like to come back with me?

KSENICHKA: What are you saying?

ANDRYUSHA: What about tomorrow?

KSENICHKA: I don't know.

ANDRYUSHA: Ksenichka, come here. It's dark here. Let me just whisper in your ear.

(*Hooligan coughs. Ksenichka starts away.*)

KSENICHKA: Someone's watching. I feel ashamed. Don't keep following me. What if my sister comes out and sees me, she'll give me such an earful. Off you go.

(*Andryusha goes out. Ksenichka moves back. The noise of the gang can be heard from the garden.*)

VOICES: – Smash his face in.
– Didn't you try round the back?
– The brigade was everywhere.
(*Ksenichka goes past. First Hooligan stands in her way.*)
FIRST HOOLIGAN: Young lady.
KSENICHKA: I'm not giving ... Oh, let me past.
FIRST HOOLIGAN: Would you mind giving me a light?
KSENICHKA: What are you saying? (*She flings herself to one side. In her way is the Second Hooligan. She turns back.*)
SECOND HOOLIGAN: Young lady, have you got – ?
KSENICHKA: I don't smoke. Andryusha!
(*He shuts her mouth, grabs her. He starts to drag her. Third and Fourth Hooligans run in.*)
THIRD HOOLIGAN: Get in the queue!
FIRST HOOLIGAN: I'm first.
FOURTH HOOLIGAN: You'll go last.
FIRST HOOLIGAN: Why?
FOURTH HOOLIGAN: You've got the clap. Everyone'll get it from you.
FIRST HOOLIGAN: I don't give a monkey's.
FOURTH HOOLIGAN: You go last.
FIRST HOOLIGAN: Get in line quick. Be quiet.
ARSHKIN: What are we in line for?
THIRD HOOLIGAN: Don't jump the queue.
ARSHKIN: But what are we lining up for?
FOURTH HOOLIGAN: I'm third.
ARSHKIN: But what about me? I'm about eighth, I suppose.
FIRST HOOLIGAN: Shut up ... You'll get us all nicked.
ANDRYUSHA (*running in*): Where is she?
ARSHKIN: What are you shoving for?
FIRST HOOLIGAN: Want the one you were with?
ANDRYUSHA: Well, yes –
FIRST HOOLIGAN: She went off. That way.
ANDRYUSHA: I thought someone was calling me.
(*Andryusha runs off.*)
THIRD HOOLIGAN: Shut her mouth. Shove a handkerchief in.
ANDRYUSHA (*running in*): No, it's as if she was shouting from here.
ARSHKIN: What are you worrying about, mate? Get in the queue.
ANDRYUSHA: What queue?

FOURTH HOOLIGAN (*stopping Arshkin's mouth*): For the bus.
ARSHKIN: Fo-fo-for the bus.
ANDRYUSHA: Where's it going?
ARSHKIN: I'm from the building-site. And that's where I'm going – to the building-site. I'm a plasterer. I'm eighth, and you'll be fourteenth.
ANDRYUSHA: Oh my God! I did hear her scream.
FIRST HOOLIGAN: There's a cop on the way. (*To Second Hooligan*) Go and keep him busy.
SECOND HOOLIGAN: What do you mean, keep him busy?
FIRST HOOLIGAN: Make it look as if you're picking a fight with Lenka. You can square it with him later. (*They go out.*)
VOICES: – They've thrown the copper off the scent.
– They made a good job of that fight.
– He's come to separate them.
– Quick. Quick there.
(*Policemen and two hooligans.*)
POLICEMAN: Citizen, don't try to get away.
SECOND HOOLIGAN : Just lay a finger on me ... Lemme go!
POLICEMAN: Citizen, calm down.
SECOND HOOLIGAN (*trying to get away with the third*): I'll teach you to tear my sleeve.
POLICEMAN: Stand still, citizen. Stand still, I say. (*The hooligan tears himself away and starts to run. The policeman puts his whistle to his lips. The hooligan knocks it out of his mouth.*) Oh, you would, would you? Stand still, or I'll shoot. (*He whistles. Where the queue was, the last person has taken to his heels.*) You don't fool with a bullet.
ANDRYUSHA (*running past*): My God! She's not at her sister's.
SECOND POLICEMAN: The citizen in the leather jerkin, come over here.
ANDRYUSHA: Why? What do you want? I'm busy.
SECOND POLICEMAN: Give me a hand with this one –
FIRST HOOLIGAN: I had a light from you, and now you're turning me over to the cops.
FIRST POLICEMAN: Well, citizen, do you hear me?
ANDRYUSHA: I haven't time. (*A groan, and Ksenichka crawls out.*) Who's that?

FIRST POLICEMAN (*to the hooligans*): Stay where you are! Put the knife away. You can't kill all of us. If you killed me, another policeman would step into my place.

KSENICHKA: Andryusha ... It hurts ... They did it ... a lot of them ...

ANDRYUSHA: Ksenichka! Ksenichka ... You're hurt! Who's done this?

KSENICHKA: A lot of them ... in the queue ...

ANDRYUSHA: They raped you ... Ksenichka ... Bastards ... The queue ... for the bus ... Ksenichka ... Who was it?

KSENICHKA: There. (*At the hooligans.*)

ANDRYUSHA: Policeman! Comrade ... My ... this ... my ... She had promised me. They defiled her ... completely ... Left their mess ... and just now they ... around the corner ... Policeman ... comrade ... slit them open till the blood runs dry, the scum. Give it me (*snatching a revolver*), give it me, let me shoot them all. I can't stand it, can't bear it!

POLICEMAN: Hands off the revolver.

ANDRYUSHA: Give it to me. It's too much. I'll kill them with my own hands ... They ... My ... Vermin ... They should be shot.

POLICEMAN: If necessary – Soviet power will shoot them. Don't take things into your own hands.

ANDRYUSHA: Ksenichka ... how could ... And what about the rug?

SCENE SIX: I WANT A BABY

Milda's room. Milda enters with a briefcase, Stoneturner with his little bundle.

STONETURNER: Can I bed down in this corner again like I usually do?
MILDA: Of course. Why ask?
STONETURNER: I thought perhaps you'd got new rules now, or perhaps you'd taken to pacing up and down the room.
MILDA: Nothing of the sort. Do you want some tea?
STONETURNER: Tea's bad for you before bed. It's the alkaloid tannin – it overstimulates you.
MILDA: Are you going to bed now?
STONETURNER: 'Yis', as Chamberlain would say. In the first place, I have work to do in the morning, and in the second I can see you have work this evening.
MILDA: Fine, settle yourself down. I won't look.
STONETURNER: You can look if you want. I'm not shy with you. Milda, you're a good chap. I don't think of you as a woman. There's only one thing wrong with your place – not enough Turkish divans. You see, inventor though I may be ...
MILDA: Take the sheepskin. (*She throws him a long overcoat.*)
STONETURNER (*getting undressed*): Working on your resolutions again?
MILDA: Yes, for the conference of cultural-educational workers.
STONETURNER: Boring people.
MILDA: What do you mean, boring? So you've joined the reactionary tendency?
STONETURNER: Aren't you fed up with cultural-educational workers?
MILDA: What I'm fed up with is you and your rumbles, Stoneturner.
STONETURNER: Ah, Milda, you're so slow Russianizing yourself. You live in the Russian Soviet Federative Socialist Republic, yet you don't know that you can't say 'rumbles' like that in Russian.
MILDA: Well, your rumbling gets on my nerves.

STONETURNER: 'Rambling', Milda. Or you could say my 'rambles'.

MILDA: Alright, but you know what I mean.

STONETURNER: I understand, of course, that to quarrel with one landlady may be considered a misfortune, but with two, in one evening – sheer recklessness! (*He lies down, fidgets.*) Milda!

MILDA: ... agreement among district organisations. (*Keeping her finger in her place on the page.*) What?

STONETURNER: Have you seen *The Mandate*[97] at the Meyerhold Theatre?

MILDA: Yes, I've seen it. It's a good play.

STONETURNER: I'm not asking you about the play. You're not Blyum.[98] Do you remember how the servant sat down on the pistol?

MILDA: I do.

STONETURNER: With me the position is exactly identical. I can feel a pistol, but I can't get at it. Remove this artillery piece!

(*Milda pulls out a revolver from the overcoat.*)

MILDA: How can you sleep in your boots, Stoneturner?

STONETURNER: Well, what if there's a fire in the night, how will I make my getaway?

MILDA: So unhygienic.

STONETURNER: I could take them off. (*He takes off his trousers and puts them on a chair. Some flash cards fall out of his pocket.*)

MILDA: What are these? Cloakroom tickets?

STONETURNER: No, Milda, this is one of my best inventions. I invented it yesterday, because there's so much bad language about these days. People expend such a lot of energy on bad language. So what I've done is simplified it. Each abusive word has its own number. For example, number two means 'silly ass', number three means 'fool', four is 'idiot', number eight means 'bastard'. So now, calmly, without raising my voice, I just hold up a number. Simple. A definitive solution for the foul-mouthed. 195 – that's a fantastically bad word, incredibly filthy! (*He is picking his toes.*)

---

97   *The Mandate*: play by Nikolai Erdman which opened at the Meyerhold Theatre on 20 April 1925. It was extremely popular and remained in the theatre's repertoire for many years.

98   *Blyum*: Vladimir Blyum, influential theatre critic of the 1920s who argued that *I Want a Baby* should not be banned. See Introduction.

MILDA: Listen, Stoneturner. You're filthy – like 'vien tsu-uks.'
STONETURNER: Kindly translate.
MILDA: That's Latvian for 'You stink like a pig.'
STONETURNER: Hmm ... Not translating was also an option.
MILDA: It's probably a year since you went anywhere near a bathhouse.
STONETURNER: Milda, that's stupid. How can I go to the bathhouse? All sorts of riffraff go there, the devil knows who. It's rife with disease and a completely uncivilised way of getting washed, corresponding to the low level of productive forces in a peasant economy. As a consistent socialist, I believe that in every citizen's house there should be a bath, as in all the best hotels. And on every bath, taps – one hot, one cold. That's when I'll sink into a bath, turn on the taps, and put the old hooves under ...
MILDA: You mean, until we've got socialism, you won't wash your feet.
STONETURNER: 'Agreement among district organisations.'
MILDA: What agreement?
STONETURNER: That's where you stopped in your resolution. Carry on. Good night. (*Fidgets.*) Ah! (*He holds up a gadget.*)
MILDA: What now?
STONETURNER: My electrical element. Made out of a coffin lid. (*Milda takes it and puts it on her desk. Music comes from behind the partitions.*)
MILDA: That music again. It's hard to work with that going on.
STONETURNER: But it puts me to sleep.
(*Milda whispers, turning over the pages of her book and making notes in the margin. There is a tap on the door.*)
MILDA: Yes.
(*The Block Superintendent comes in.*)
MILDA (*glancing round*): Uh-uh? Comrade superintendent. Have you come about the central heating? Something's cracked over there. (*She points to a central heating pipe.*)
SUPERINTENDENT: What do you mean, the heating?
MILDA: The central heating. (*She is checking back and forth in her book, making her replies preoccupiedly.*)
SUPERINTENDENT: I didn't come about that. I've finished work for today. May I sit down?
MILDA: Yes ... Sit down.

(*He turns the key in the door, then approaches the table. His next lines are hesitant and awkward. She breaks them up with phrases such as 'Aha' ... 'Yes' ... 'I see'.*)

SUPERINTENDENT: You know comrade Angelica? She was talking to me about you. A lot of interesting things.

MILDA: Fame at last ...

SUPERINTENDENT: You're all bound up with work. Do you ever relax? Do you ever take a break?

MILDA: When I sleep.

SUPERINTENDENT: Do you drink beer?

MILDA: Hardly ever.

SUPERINTENDENT: Do you go to the theatre?

MILDA: I don't like it.

SUPERINTENDENT: What about music?

MILDA: Can't stomach it.

SUPERINTENDENT: I work like a packhorse, too. Eight hours a day. But I know how to relax, as well. Without a bit of fun, there's no relaxation. And my nerves'd be shot to hell. I'd lose the knack of laughing. I'd just grin through clenched teeth... But with a good stiff drink ... Do you drink? Have a drink, maybe? I'll go and get us a drink.

MILDA: No.

SUPERINTENDENT: You're not listening to me. You see, comrade ... what I said probably seemed to you, well, a bit cold ... but I know you as someone who's absolutely without prejudices ... That's not just a compliment ... It's a fact ... Are you listening? Well, you see, my wife went off to stay with her father a week ago ... I'm all by myself ... A sufficient period for me to develop an irresistible physical urge for a woman ... I won't go to prostitutes, I'm sure you understand ... I've been observing you for a long time, I know you're a healthy, robust person, you're on your own ... you're an excellent comrade. You really wouldn't deny a comrade such an understandable request ... would you? I mean, will that be all right?

MILDA (*dragging her eyes away from the book*): Sorry, comrade, I wasn't listening properly. Could you repeat that?

SUPERINTENDENT: Devil knows what ... in two words ... Look, my hands are shaking, I'm in a complete state: my wife's gone away – I need a woman –

MILDA: What's that got to do with me?
SUPERINTENDENT: It's you I'm asking ... You're a living human being ... you can't do without a man, can you? ... it's only for half an hour ... like comrades ...
MILDA: Comrade ...
SUPERINTENDENT: I know, I've gone a bit off the rails here. (*He takes her by the hand.*) I'm an absolutely normal male, absolu –
MILDA: Comrade.
SUPERINTENDENT: What's the matter? If you see someone who's ill, you give him medicine. If you see someone who's hungry, you give him bread.
MILDA: If someone was ill, I'd get him first aid, and if someone was hungry, I'd direct him to a feeding point. But as for you, comrade ...
SUPERINTENDENT: What are you afraid of? Getting pregnant? Don't worry, I know all about contraception. I've got one with me ... How blinkered. Is that what you're frightened of?
MILDA: What am I frightened of? I'm frightened of gonorrhoea ... Go out on the streets, or –
SUPERINTENDENT: Or?
MILDA: Or go and resolve the question by yourself in your own room.
SUPERINTENDENT: Huh. That's your considered opinion, is it? You're sure?
MILDA: Masturbation at your age and in your position, in my opinion, can do nothing but good.
SUPERINTENDENT: That's none of your business. So you don't want to?
MILDA: I don't want to.
SUPERINTENDENT: What idiotic narrow-mindedness. Such an obtuse, banal attitude.
MILDA: Have you finished?
SUPERINTENDENT (*puts his hand over her mouth and drags her down onto the bed*): To hell with it ... lie down ... lie down ...
(*Milda gropes with her free hand for the revolver, doesn't find it, puts her hand on a book, knocks the superintendent sideways with the book, and pushes him away.*)
MILDA: Get out of here!
(*The superintendent jumps away, and treads on Stoneturner.*)
STONETURNER: Watch out! What a shit! Milda!
SUPERINTENDENT: Ah-ha-ha! I get it now ... Excuse me ...

STONETURNER: Get what?
SUPERINTENDENT: None of your business. I'm talking to her.
MILDA: Stoneturner! Show him the door.
SUPERINTENDENT: Get off! Don't you dare let that bouncer get his hands on me!
STONETURNER: Me, a bouncer? You son of a bitch.
SUPERINTENDENT: Keep your voice down!
STONETURNER: Clear out, you turd.
SUPERINTENDENT: I'll thank you to keep your voice down, sir! This isn't a brothel, there are people asleep here.
STONETURNER: Swine! Scum! I will rearrange –
MILDA: Stoneturner, stop it ...
STONETURNER: ... your ugly mug ...
MILDA: Stoneturner, use your numbers!
STONETURNER: I will make mincemeat out of you!
MILDA: Listen to me now! Use ... the ... numbers!
STONETURNER: I'll disfigure you, burn you away with vitriol.
MILDA: Stoneturner!
STONETURNER: Come here, you ...
MILDA (*getting between them*): Numbers!
STONETURNER (*pitifully*): Two ... three ... four ... (*He wants to throw out the Superintendent, who is sitting on the floor, but the door is locked.*) Milda, have you got the key?
MILDA: The door's open.
STONETURNER: It's locked.
MILDA: You had it all set up, eh? Unlock it! (*The superintendent's hands are shaking.*) Stoneturner, you do it. (*Stoneturner's hands are shaking.*) Give it to me. (*She opens the door.*)
SUPERINTENDENT: I'm having nothing more to do with this sordid business.
MILDA: Absolutely correct, comrade superintendent.
VOICES IN THE CORRIDOR: – What's up?
– A bust-up?
– Who's making the racket?
GRIPE'S VOICE: Is one able to work? Or not? Stop that! It's disgraceful!
SUPERINTENDENT: There are unauthorised citizens strewn around the rooms.
MILDA: Is that what you came here for?

SUPERINTENDENT: Shsh! After ten o'clock talking in the corridor is prohibited. I would ask you to respect the rules. Goodbye. Please observe the rules, goodbye.

MILDA: There were snakes in the civil war, and they're here again now.

STONETURNER: Milda! Shall I lock the door?

MILDA: No need. He won't come back now.

STONETURNER: Socked him with volume five, eh? (*He picks up the book.*)

MILDA: That little book came in handy. Did he hurt you when he trod on you? Go back to sleep. (*Silence. Milda is studying.*) The coordination of schools ... schools ... coordination of schools with polit ... Ugly little prock (*mispronouncing 'prick'*) ... he just waltzed in on the off-chance ... contraceptives ... coordination of schools ...

STONETURNER: You were wrong to make me count.

MILDA (*after a pause*): Disgusting man, he's put me off my work. Better go to bed. (*She lies down. It's dark. She calls out.*) Stoneturner.

STONETURNER: Mm?

MILDA: Not sleeping?

STONETURNER: No.

MILDA: That fellow ... came barging in – his nerves, you could see, all unstrung. He wanted it, but I find it so revolting.

STONETURNER: Dysfunction ... sexual neurosis ... Nowadays we all suffer from it.

MILDA: No. Listen. I'm all muddled up. What do you think, is it possible for a woman to want a healthy baby but not a husband?

STONETURNER: What do you mean, 'possible'? She must want one. And indeed without a husband. What have we got these days? Chaos, everything happening by chance. People fling themselves into intercourse on the spot where they meet: on the train – on the train; in the office – in the office; at the hostel – at the hostel. Milda, there are native tribes in which a newly-wed couple is forbidden to drink at the wedding, in order not to damage their posterity. But in our country people choose maximum inebriation on purpose. Is it any wonder when the kids of drug addicts, syphilitics, alcoholics, turn out to be cretins, epileptics or scrofulous, or neurotic. Syphilis is a swine. It keeps its head down and jumps out four generations later, and devours a person. Look what strains of wheat, what heads of cabbage, what amazing horses and dogs you get with selective breeding.

MILDA: Steady on, Stoneturner.

STONETURNER: No, Milda. To hell with husbands! They only make problems! What do you say to the syringe? That the State gives the most productive women workers the best sperm. The State encourages this method of selection. It takes responsibility for the upbringing of these children, and develops a strain of new people.

MILDA: I'm not asking you about that, Stoneturner.

STONETURNER: In this way scientific control of the human being can be exercised not only during the child's formative years, and not only at birth, but also at its conception.

MILDA: Will you just stop rattling on for one moment? Without a husband – what I mean is, I want a baby, but I don't want a husband, and I've no wish for a family. But suppose I said to a man: Give me a baby!

STONETURNER: You? You mean, you?

MILDA: Stoneturner, you fool, do you really not understand? Are you having fun with me?

STONETURNER: Me?

MILDA: In your opinion, am I a woman, or not? (*Stoneturner is dumbfounded. He rushes over to his clothes, throws his trousers on, and runs out.*) I want a baby. A little baby for me. I can't bear it. I've completely lost track of my work. I want a baby.

SCENE SEVEN: THE SHIMMY

Enter Saxoulsky, two male and female dancing pairs, some of the female dancing students, Kitty and Filirinov.

SAXOULSKY: Citizens, hurry up.
FIRST DANCING PARTNER: Hurry up.
FIRST LADY: Hurry up, darling, hurry up.
SECOND PARTNER: Rup-rup-rup!
SECOND LADY: How empty it is, not very cosy.
FIRST PARTNER: Cosiness – we'll make our own cosiness.
FEMALE DRAMA STUDENT: Is this your little salon? Why is it so empty? The builders were about to knock it down, but for some reason they didn't have time. How very pleasant.
FIRST PARTNER: So, from tomorrow morning our little salon will cease to exist, will it?
SAXOULSY: There's every chance we'll be able to transfer to the club room.
SECOND PARTNER: What's the hold-up?
SAXOULSKY: Money is not the problem. A group of mothers has formed some kind of co-operative here. They want to stick the club in nappies.
FIRST PARTNER: So there's a risk mothers might take over the club?
SAXOULSKY: We are taking measures, citizens, taking measures.
KITTY: I saw those mothers today.
SECOND PARTNER (*to Saxoulsky*): Mum's the word, then.
KITTY: Awful bores.
SAXOULSKY: Right, enough chattering. Time to strike up!
SECOND LADY: We have no concert grand.
FILIRINOV: They swung the piano over the pavement today, like a varnished victim hanging from the gallows, and the passing trams were reflected in its top.

SAXOULSKY: We don't need a grand piano. We ourselves will be the piano. The whole orchestra.
(*They form a mouth orchestra, and begin to play a shimmy. They dance and hum at the same time. Through the window, Grinko, Yakov and a technician appear on a cradle.*)
GRINKO: Look what's going on here! Crikey! Paunch to paunch! And she's got the fatty's ear in her teeth. Our girls couldn't do that. No, they'd have no idea.
SAXOULSKY (*to Kitty*): Are you enjoying yourself?
KITTY: Very much!
SAXOULSKY: They're delightful company, aren't they? They're the most Bohemian people imaginable!
KITTY: Am I Bohemian too, now?
SAXOULSY: Yes.
YAKOV: Calm down. You'll rock the cradle. Look at that red neck, like a piece of ham hanging over his collar. Yuk, what I wouldn't give to get my hands round it! Bourgeois!
SAXOULSKY: That one over there in the black dress is Yartseva.
KITTY: Ah, and who are they?
SAXOULSKY: Well, that thin one's Svistelsky.
KITTY: Is he really?
SAXOULSKY: And those three are Smursky, Snarsky and Lersky.
KITTY: They're fantastic.
GRINKO: What a bunch of bourgeois. He's an accounts clerk, and there's another one over there. Look at them, silk stockings, legs like bloody tinsel. She's as good as glued to him. It's like a four-legged person with two arses dragging itself round the room. What a bloody circus!
YAKOV: Has this foxtrot been forbidden on Soviet soil or not? Give us a brick. I'll sort that lot out.
GRINKO: Stop it!
YAKOV: What do you mean, stop? Get out of my way!
GRINKO: Put the brick down. Don't be a hooligan.
YAKOV: Are you protecting bourgeois and NEPmen? You swine!
GRINKO: Cut the crap. They're not doing any harm. They pay their rent. Put the brick down. (*He grabs Yakov's hand which is holding the brick.*)
YAKOV: You watch your step or I'll drop one on you.

GRINKO (*gets Yakov in an arm lock and shouts over his shoulder*): Comrade foreman.
FOREMAN: What?
GRINKO: Can we get stuck into the old club?
FOREMAN: Tomorrow morning we start.
GRINKO: And if there happen to be some extra bodies around, could we start now?
FOREMAN: Okay.
GRINKO: Do you want to knock down the ceiling?
YAKOV: I want to beat up the NEPmen.
GRINKO: You can't beat up the NEPmen. You can knock down the plaster. Are you going to come and knock down the ceiling?
YAKOV: Beat up the bourgeois with the plaster?
GRINKO: There you go again, one-track mind! Nobody's beating up anybody. What we're going to do is get on with the next stage of the construction work in flat number 23A, see what I mean?
YAKOV: Aaahh ... you're a sly one, you are, brother.
(*Just when the shimmy is in full swing, the cradle descends into the club under the ceiling. Plaster pours down.*)
GRINKO: Excuse us, citizens. It's urgent work. You see, it's got to be done in three shifts. We've got to speed up the reconstruction of the block. Sorry for any inconvenience.
CRIES FROM THE CROWD: – Absolutely shocking!
– Really insulting!
– So humiliating!
YAKOV (*chiselling at the ceiling*): Eh, brother. This wood's a bastard. Bloody plaster. This wood's a real bastard.
GRINKO: Knock it out! Bang it out. Ba-ba-ba-bang it. Give it some stick. Da-da-da-da-da!
(*The couples run out. The room becomes deserted.*)
YAKOV (*shining a lamp into the corners*): It's crawling with rats here. It's either the mildew or we're feeding you.
GRINKO: And if you'd thrown that brick, think: if you'd torn one of their dresses, ten roubles gone; if you'd dirtied a dicky-bow, docked another seven silver ones; for the insults, fined a five rouble note. What a loss to the workers' state that would have been.
YAKOV: Ten, plus seven, plus five – twenty-two roubles.

GRINKO: Spot on!
BOTH: Da da-da da-da-da-da.

SCENE EIGHT: SELECTING THE FATHER

The building site.

MILDA: Comrade Softer?
SOFTER: Comrade Milda, hello. You want me?
MILDA: Yes, you.
SOFTER: You're pale. You're looking edgy. It's probably the din in your ears. Mm? Or insomnia? Mm? Your nerves? Mm?
MILDA: I don't have any nerves at all, doctor. I've got nerves – like these cables. I'm strong as a horse.
SOFTER: Well, well, why such exaggerations?
MILDA: You see, doctor –
SOFTER: Mm, I'm listening. Tell me all about it.
MILDA: I, you see, it's not anything for myself, but there is something a girl-friend of mine wants to know.
   (*A disturbance below. A detachment of militia forms a chain around the building site.*)
DETECTIVE: Perhaps he's not from here. You made a mistake.
ANDRYUSHA: I'd know his face. Is he called Arshkin?
DETECTIVE: Arshkin.
ANDRYUSHA: Emelian?
DETECTIVE: Emelian.
ANDRYUSHA: He's here on the building-site.
FIRST WORKER: What's going on over there?
SECOND WORKER: The place is swarming with cops.
FIRST WORKER (*to Arshkin*): You're sure they haven't come for you? Your lovely mug fits the bill.
SECOND WORKER: Tell us, was it you smashed the windows in yesterday? Or did you lay somebody out in the club?
FIRST WORKER: Why are you going pale? Need a hair of the dog?

DETECTIVE: Are you Arshkin?
ARSHKIN: What's going on, comrade? What do you want?
DETECTIVE: Are you Arshkin?
ARSHKIN: Well, yes.
DETECTIVE: Come with me.
ARSHKIN: Why, what is all this?
FIRST WORKER: Why are you pulling that lad away from his designated work?
SECOND WORKER: What are you accusing him of?
DETECTIVE: Have you forgotten about that young girl yesterday?
GRINKO: Why are they dragging him off?
SECOND WORKER: Been fooling around with a girl, have we?
  (*They bring Arshkin down. He comes face to face with Andryusha.*)
ARSHKIN: What do you want?
ANDRYUSHA (*dashes forward, the detective restrains him*): Comrade.
ARSHKIN: I'm asking you, what do you want?
ANDRYUSHA: Forgotten, have you?
ARSHKIN: I was drunk.
ANDRYUSHA: How you took that girl behind the wall, and there was a queue standing over her, and you were eighth. You even boasted about that.
ARSHKIN: And what business is it of yours? Who are you in all this?
ANDRYUSHA: Who am I?
ARSHKIN: Yeah, who are you?
ANDRYUSHA: I'm the fiancé of the girl. Do you know what you did with her? You know what you'll get for it? The death penalty. Yes you will.
ARSHKIN: Listen to you then, who do you think you are? (*Two workers approach with a stretcher. Arshkin thinks it is the body of Ksenichka on the stretcher.*) What's that? (*The workers put the stretcher down.*) No, don't do it! Take it away! Please, don't! I don't want to see! (*The militia take him by the arms.*) What are you bringing bodies here for? Take it away! (*The workers remove the bast covering to reveal tubs of paint. They begin to paint.*)
DETECTIVE (*to Arshkin*): Were you alone?
ANDRYUSHA: No, it was him and his mates.
DETECTIVE: Right, let's get to the bottom of this. (*He starts to grill Arshkin.*)

ARSHKIN: Okay, okay. We all had a go, we should all cop it. You think I'm gonna be the fall guy? So get the rest of them as well. They were all in the queue.
(*Detective is making notes.*)
FIRST WORKER: It's that scum off the estate! They must have egged him on.
GRINKO: That's what you get for chasing tail.
YAKOV: That's rubbish. It's wrong. He did get his paws on the girl. But it's the girls who're to blame, the mean bitches.
GRINKO: What are you yelling about?
YAKOV: I'm not yelling about anything. But it's their own fault. What can a bloke do? He has a drink, can't see straight, and climbs on top of a woman. But look how these women carry on! They walk round the streets like it was their bedroom. Pink stockings on their legs, all smoothed round. They stick their arses out. And their lips are bruised red from kissing. They really get me going with that. But will they ever come and sleep with me? They'll only go to bed with you if you've got plenty of money. I get so hungry for a woman – but she goes off down the street, wiggling her bum. She reeks of perfume, made up to the eyeballs. She'll be prick-teasing like that all day wherever she is – in the office, or the canteen, anywhere at work. Stuff it! If she got caught, she shouldn't point the finger.
SOFTER: Hear that?
MILDA: They're hooligans.
SOFTER: Why hooligans? They're strong, fit fellows, I'd say. You'd be hard put to find someone as red-blooded as this Yakov – they're rare birds, those two.
MILDA: Are they healthy lads?
SOFTER: No consumption, they're not neurotic, no VD – perfect specimens. The cream of our sports team. Well, we're getting off the point. Carry on. What about your friend?
MILDA: My friend?
SOFTER: Well, yes. She asked you to find out something from me.
MILDA: It went clean out of my head. I'll remember in a minute.
SOFTER: You do that, then.
(*Milda goes to the two workmen.*)

YAKOV: When you've got a bloke going like that, he's bound to go the whole way.
GRINKO: Do me a favour. There was ten of them fucked that girl.
FIRST WORKER (*to the fiancé*): Did she die?
ANDRYUSHA: Of course not. What kind of fiancée would that be? Only I won't let it go like that. I'll find them. I want them shot.
MILDA: Comrade.
GRINKO: You after me?
MILDA: Yes, and your comrade. Over there.
GRINKO: Frolka! Fancy seeing you here!
YAKOV: Grin. Bring the crane half a metre to yer left.
GRINKO: Hang on a minute.
YAKOV: What's up?
GRINKO: Remember this comrade in the club? I started to swing him round, but he turned out to be a woman.
YAKOV: So what's it got to do with me?
MILDA (*to Yakov*): Good day, comrade. Can I ask you to come down here for a minute?
YAKOV: Not really. Anyway, I didn't see him grab hold of you.
MILDA: I haven't come about that.
YAKOV: Okay, I'm listening.
MILDA: Tell me, were your father and grandfather from peasant stock or were they workers?
GRINKO (*mockingly*): And what were you doing before the revolution, and if not, why not?
YAKOV: Is this a questionnaire you're filling in?
MILDA: No, I need it for myself.
GRINKO: For a lecture?
MILDA: Yes, sort of.
GRINKO: Our womenfolk told us you were always giving them lectures. Very strict, they said. About inefficiency. And time-wasting. And wasting energy. They're all vices.
MILDA: Why did they say that?
GRINKO: They're teasing you for being too strict – just like a man, they say.
YAKOV: Are you the one who's getting the nursery going?
MILDA: Yes. Why?

YAKOV: Nothing special – it's a good thing. I saw the plans the engineer had. When the building's finished, it won't just be a nursery here, it'll be a palace for mothers and children, where the old club was. And the club – they'll shove that in the basement.

MILDA: Excuse me, but we've got off the subject.

GRINKO: You were on about grandfathers. My grandfather was a peasant, but my father was a reader in church. But him – he's your aristocracy through and through. Dad and granddad were steelworkers at the Putilov works.

MILDA: One more question – were there any drunks in your family?

GRINKO: My people were all Old Believers.[99]

LIPA: Oi, watch out there! (*She rushes down in a trolley on rails.*)

GRINKO: Careful! (*He grabs Milda and pulls her back. Yakov jumps over the rails.*)

YAKOV: Lipa, you idiot. You could have run us over. Have you gone round the bend, or what?

LIPA: Don't snarl. And don't gawp. Else I'll give you something to think about after work.

GRINKO: Go on, smack him one. Hell, he was abusing your sisters just now –

MILDA: Don't go for a minute – I'll be right back. (*She goes back to the doctor.*)

LIPA: Who's she?

GRINKO: Some kind of soldier-girl. Dead serious type. And she's interested in us.

LIPA: Watch out, Yashka.

YAKOV: I am watching out.

SOFTER: Have you remembered what your friend wanted to ask about?

MILDA: Yes, I have. She put the question this way: who would make the better father – a cautious man or a daring one?

SOFTER: Well, you'd need to consider the mother's character. Is this woman a hot-tempered one, a bit of a spitfire, or not?

MILDA: No, she's rather reserved, calculating, pedantic ...

SOFTER: Then she should take the man who jumped over the rails ... My mistake, I meant to say the daring one.

MILDA: Thank you, doctor.

---

99   *Old Believers*: followers of the traditional, unreformed Russian Orthodox Church.

SOFTER: Don't mention it, comrade Milda. Didn't your friend ask anything else about what to do?

MILDA: No. All –

SOFTER: Comrade Milda. If your friend hasn't had a baby for a long time, tell her it's very important for a sound conception that the mother's womb is washed carefully with a solution of sodium bicarbonate. Do you want me to give you a prescription?

MILDA: All right. (*She takes the prescription.*) Thanks. Wait, you've written the prescription in my name. Can you amend it? My friend's name is ...

SOFTER: I won't bother to amend it. All the best!

GRINKO: You're holding us up, comrade.

MILDA: I just wanted to get something cleared up.

GRINKO: About my grandad?

MILDA (*to Yakov*): It's you, comrade, who particularly interests me.

GRINKO: I never have any luck. Missed out 'cos of a church reader.

MILDA (*to Yakov*): I gather you're one hundred per cent proletarian?

YAKOV: Well, not quite one hundred per cent. He was winding you up. He's a bit of a joker.

MILDA: How do you mean, not one hundred per cent?

YAKOV: Well, my father was a railway guard, he didn't work at the Putilov factory.

MILDA: But he wasn't an intellectual?

YAKOV: No, course he wasn't.

MILDA: Comrade, I'd like to ask you a favour. It's awkward talking about it here, and you've got your work to do anyway. I wonder whether you could call on me tonight?

YAKOV: I'm not the world's best talker. Or do you want to give me some kind of job?

MILDA: Yes, that's it. So will you come? Could you make it around nine o'clock, or ten?

YAKOV: Ten o'clock? That's a bit late. I'm off out to work at six.

MILDA: Well, let's say nine, then.

YAKOV: Okay. Where shall I come?

MILDA: That's my address. That's all, comrade.

GRINKO: Comrade!

MILDA: Yes?

GRINKO: You know my great grandfather was a bandit.

MILDA: Ah, very interesting.
GRINKO: But not very relevant?
MILDA: No. (*She goes out.*)
GRINKO (*throwing down his cap*): Eh! Our boring old grannies! That girder needs to be half a metre to the left. Oi, plasterer, bastard! Why aren't you in your place?
YAKOV: First you called me down, now you're telling me to get up. (*He runs up.*)
LIPA: Yakov, see you tonight in the park?
YAKOV: I don't know. I can't say. If I'm free, I'll come.
(*Arshkin and two others are escorted out.*)
DETECTIVE: Let's go.
ARSHKIN: See ya then, lads.
TWO WORKERS (*sullenly*): Right then.
(*The flat block superintendent approaches the detective. Saxoulsky and he have been watching the procession.*)
SUPERINTENDENT: So you've caught the little darlings. Now things will be easier.
SAXOULSKY: It's been impossible for our wives to walk down the street because of them. These weeds have got to be pulled up.
SUPERINTENDENT: They should shoot a few of these young thugs, that would keep the others quiet.
MILDA: They'd be quiet on the streets, but what about in private?
SAXOULSKY: What do you mean?
MILDA: You're fine ones to talk. (*She goes out.*)
SAXOULSKY: That's the nursery woman, isn't it
SUPERINTENDENT: Yes – an extraordinarily dangerous creature.

SCENE NINE: THE CONCEPTION

The house. Illuminated windows. Filirinov and Softer.
VOICES: – Turn the red one on.
    – No, don't.
    – Open the piano. (*Music.*)
FILIRINOV: And after dusk there's a certain hour, when with our work each one of us finishes. Then the houses bill and coo like amorous hippopotamuses.
SOFTER: Have we lived without art? Without poetry, without music, without amorousness? The houses groan with exhaustion.
(*Some poeticizing begins in the house.*
It was where the waves were rolling.
Oh again, oh again, and no returning.
Burst into the squares.
Below, in the gateway, the figures of a hooligan and a woman.)
HOOLIGAN: You coming to the boozer?
WOMAN: I'll come. Let go of me.
HOOLIGAN: Yeah, all right.
(*Just on the highest note of its declaiming, the choir chimes in with the ecstatic sound of two cats on the roof.*)
FILIRINOV: The more I groan, the more aroused I become.
SOFTER: Sexual neurosis. Sexual psychopathy.
FILIRINOV: Stop it, they won't hear you.
MAN'S VOICE: Closer.
WOMAN'S VOICE: No, don't.
MAN'S VOICE: Close …
WOMAN'S VOICE: You've bruised my lips. Let me go. Go away! The sun, the sun …
(*From somewhere or other the singing of marching troops coincides with the last word:*)

The sun at midday,
Unbearable heat,
Budyonny's cavalry
Scattered on the steppe.
(*Howls, and whistles.*)

FILIRINOV (*in a narcotic stupor*): My city, my giant. Steel, concrete, glass. In my name trains rush, trams clank, buses snarl, and horse cabs gallop. I am the master.

POLICEMAN: Move on, citizen. You'll get yourself run over.

SOFTER: You've sniffed yourself stupid again. Until you've done an outline of the health education play, I won't give you a kopeck of the advance.

FILIRINOV: The outline. I wish to depict syphilis as the king of Assaragon.

SOFTER: Rein in your Muse.

FILIRINOV: I could always depict syphilis as a petty trader in a long belted blouse?

SOFTER: Why?

FILIRINOV: Couldn't I ...

SOFTER: Absolute piffle.

(*Milda enters her room. She throws down a package.*)

MILDA: Ten to nine. Oh dear! Oh dear!

(*Angelica bursts in.*)

ANGELICA: Milda.

MILDA: Yes, it's me.

ANGELICA: Don't get changed.

MILDA: Why?

ANGELICA: Let's go. I'll tell you on the way.

MILDA: Where?

ANGELICA: To the club. It's bedlam there. Without you it'll come to blows.

MILDA: What on earth?

ANGELICA: It's about the nursery. It all started with an unscheduled meeting of the women workers, and then the wives stuck their noses in. Then after the wives, the drama students started to kick up a stink. It's a free-for-all there. And now the Young Communist women organisers have waded in as well.

MILDA: But why didn't you calm them down?

ANGELICA: In the first place, I wasn't sure what was going on, and in any case, with my voice, I couldn't get a word in edgeways. (*Undoing the parcel.*) I thought this was something to eat, but it's actually –

MILDA: There's something to eat on the table. But comrade Angelica, I must beg your pardon. I'm afraid I have no time for that now.

ANGELICA: You're ordering me to piss off?

MILDA: Why be so rude? I'm not ordering you at all. But I'm busy. I'm expecting guests.

ANGELICA: I can stay there, behind the screen.

MILDA: No, Angelica, it's not convenient.

ANGELICA: Not convenient? I don't understand.

(*A knock at the door.*)

MILDA: Come in.

(*Enter Yakov.*)

YAKOV: Hello. I've made it. I'm not late?

MILDA: No, you're on time. Introduce yourselves.

(*They do so.*)

YAKOV: I came straight here from the building-site. I haven't even washed my hands.

MILDA: There's the washstand. Carry on, comrade.

ANGELICA: You don't work on that big building-site, do you?

YAKOV: The very one.

ANGELICA: You didn't hear whether the shouting in the club was still going on?

YAKOV: That women's racket? Yes, it was still going on.

MILDA: Comrade Angelica, it will be very remiss of you if you don't go back there.

ANGELICA (*as if she hasn't heard*): Comrade, why do you speak so scornfully – "women's racket"?

YAKOV: Scornfully? I'm just a simple bloke. They're screaming away, and you can hear them four blocks from there. So it's a racket, there's no other word for it. It ain't puppies squealing, I'll tell you that for nothing.

ANGELICA: You're harsh towards women, comrade. Really rather harsh.

YAKOV: Why be tender with them?

ANGELICA: So you don't think you need to be tender? Absolutely never? You've really never needed to be tender yourself? What if you like a woman, then …

YAKOV: You're talking about love now?
ANGELICA: You can call it love, if you like. Wouldn't you be tender even then?
MILDA: Comrade Angelica, you promised me you'd go back to the meeting.
ANGELICA: Nothing of the sort.
MILDA: Well, I'm asking you now once more.
ANGELICA: But it's much more interesting to stay here and get to the end of the argument with this comrade.
MILDA: Comrade Angelica –
ANGELICA: You told me you were busy. Please, finish your business with this comrade quickly, then I'll leave with him and we can finish our argument on the way. Alright?
YAKOV: Suits me. And you? (*To Milda*) Did you want me to answer some questions for you?
MILDA: I'll detain you a little longer, comrade.
ANGELICA: Carry on, I'm not in a rush. (*To Yakov*) So you think you have to glower at women? Like a bull?
MILDA (*to Angelica*): You think it should be the other way round?
ANGELICA: Actually, I can't understand why people have to create so many problems, make things so earnest and awkward in a relationship. They should be lighter, less serious, more casual.
MILDA: Lighter, less serious, more casual. That's your principle, is it? It's a fine principle, only the after-effects aren't always so fine.
ANGELICA: Comrade Milda, what are you on about?
MILDA: Your gonorrhoea didn't start from one of these casual affairs, then?
ANGELICA: You're out of your mind! I got rid of it! What's got into you? In front of this comrade ...
MILDA: What's so bad about that? What have you got to hide? Lighter. Less serious. More casual.
ANGELICA: You're jealous! That's all. This is stupid. You could have just told me straight.
MILDA: I've been telling you straight for the last half hour.
ANGELICA: Huh ... Prig. Down with romance, down with romance, but you're tickling your carp on the sly. Gonorrhoea ... Bitch! (*She goes out.*)
MILDA: You shouldn't swear, Angelica.

YAKOV: Your friend got you angry all right.

MILDA: She didn't, I just couldn't find the formula to get through to her. Are you in a hurry?

YAKOV: No, I've got half an hour.

MILDA: No longer?

YAKOV: It's just that I promised ... er ... someone I'd meet them in the park.

MILDA: And you want to go? For a drink?

YAKOV: No, I don't drink. I like listening to music, or going to the cinema. Actually, you were asking me about my grandfather. I was thinking back and I remembered some more about him: my grandfather was a strongman, used to throw all the wrestlers in the circus, and then he went off his rocker.

MILDA: Went off his rocker?

YAKOV: He became violent.

MILDA: Was he ill?

YAKOV: How can I put it? It wasn't because he was ill, exactly – more because he was so healthy. His wife was, well, not very faithful. In a fit of rage he throttled her, and she was ill for a long time, and they put him in a straitjacket. I remember that jacket – the sleeves went down to his feet. And you, comrade, you're a writer, are you?

MILDA: No.

YAKOV: It's just that's everything I can remember for you about granddad. Are you getting all this together for some sort of lecture?

MILDA: I can explain it to you now, comrade. Will you listen carefully? I'm not very good at explaining, and this matter is very difficult anyway.

A VOICE: Citizen, there's someone for you at the front door.

MILDA: Please would you be so kind as to open the door, and say I'm not in. (*To Yakov*) Of course you know that here everything's being newly constructed. They're setting up co-operatives, hospitals, schools, in a word, everything to improve people's lives.

VOICE: They don't believe you. They say some woman friend of yours has sent them here.

MILDA: Close the outer door. They'll ring, then go away. All the same, I'll lock this door.

(*She locks the door.*)

YAKOV: Things getting on top of you?

MILDA: Yes. Now, where did I get to? Yes, but I'm not putting this the right way. You see, comrade, how can I explain this more simply for you? You know, we have production. That is what we get when the factories or the soil produce things, and then we have reproduction – that is, when mankind renews itself, or, to put it more simply – people have babies.

YAKOV: Right, I get you.

MILDA: But when production isn't properly planned, you get a poor quality product. And when you don't properly plan human reproduction, you get poor quality people: from infected parents you get infected children, from alcoholic parents you get feebleminded children, and from the mentally abnormal – you get suicidal children.

YAKOV: Right, I get you.

MILDA: And then you drag marriage into it, and the family, which brings up the children all wrong, in their own image and to be like them –

VOICE: Citizen, were any letters for number forty-two delivered to you, by any chance?

MILDA: Please don't keep disturbing me. I don't know anything about a letter.

VOICE: When it's go to the door, it's "be so kind", but if it's my letter – "don't disturb me."

MILDA: Well, I'm sorry if I was sharp, but I'm in the middle of something here. (*Silence. Somewhere a child begins to cry.*) Listen, it's crying. It's probably got a tummy ache.

YAKOV: More likely it's asking for some titty, it's starving. You interested in babies, then?

MILDA Yes. You're very close, comrade. I, comrade, want to have a baby, but I want to have a sound baby, one whose father is a healthy fellow, and a working man. There.

YAKOV: There you go. Not a bad idea.

MILDA: So, you agree to be the father?

YAKOV: Me? The father?

MILDA: Yes, you. The father.

YAKOV: Are you bonkers, comrade?

MILDA: I'm absolutely in my right mind.

YAKOV: In the first place, comrade, I already have, er, how shall I put it, a woman. And I'll probably go to the Registry Office with her. It's what I want. You want a bit of a fling, but I'd be the one to pay.

MILDA: Comrade! One minute. Let's consider it point by point. What can happen to a woman is that something seems to take her by the throat, so strongly that even the work she's supposed to be doing starts to go by the board. I don't want a husband. I want a baby. It's not you personally I need, it's your sperm. As for me, I'm absolutely healthy – I've got a note from the doctor here, dated yesterday. So you won't be taking any risks. And I'm not going to interfere with your relationship with another woman. There will be no obligation on you, if you're afraid of paying maintenance – I've taken care of all that. I've got a document here, legally attested, stating that I waive any right to make claims of any kind on you. And so, just to recap. You will come and sleep with me until such time as my pregnancy is confirmed, after which we will part, having no claims on each other whatsoever.

YAKOV: Comrade, I understand you. But why me? Are there so few blokes in the world?

MILDA: Comrade, I've been looking around for a long time. I needed a man who was not only healthy and strong in himself, but whose father and grandfather were too.

YAKOV: Oh, so that's why you were asking about my grandfather?

MILDA: Well, yes. Besides, I want the father of my baby to be one hundred per cent proletarian.

YAKOV: You could have taken Grinko. I mean, he took a shine to you.

MILDA: But he's more cautious than you. And I'm cautious too. And cautiousness multiplied by cautiousness might produce a dolt.

YAKOV: So I've got to be the father, you reckon.

MILDA: Yes, you.

YAKOV: Blimey! I've never heard anything like it! Never! (*He laughs.*)

MILDA: Comrade, do you think this is a joke?

YAKOV: Not bad for a laugh. A caper like that, seriously? Come on, you're having me on.

MILDA: Comrade, I'm quite serious. I'm not going to repeat myself. I think you understand it all perfectly well.

YAKOV: I understand it okay ...

MILDA: So – what?

YAKOV: What d'you mean, what?

MILDA: Do you agree?

YAKOV: Oh God, I don't know. It's all a bit of a rigmarole.

MILDA: It's not a rigmarole. You're going to stay here tonight.

YAKOV: Tonight?

MILDA: Why not?

YAKOV: I don't get it. How can you just set about making babies on purpose?

MILDA: Why are you digging your heels in?

YAKOV: I don't know how to tell you, comrade.

MILDA: I know, I'm not very beautiful.

YAKOV: What do you mean, not very beautiful? A girl's a girl.

MILDA: I'm not a girl, I'm a woman.

YAKOV: Well, it's all the same, a wench is a wench.

MILDA: So what's the problem?

YAKOV: Sorry, comrade, but I just don't seem to, how can I say, I just don't fancy you.

MILDA: I understand.

YAKOV: You know how it is, people can't keep their hands off each other when they get up to mischief – when they're getting excited that way. Then you've got everything that goes with it – a laugh and a giggle, music, one thing and the other. But this – it's like a court appearance.

MILDA: I know. I foresaw that. Wait here, comrade, just a minute. (*She goes behind the screen. Yakov frets. From behind the screen*) What's your name, by the way?

YAKOV: Yakov. Yakov Plumer. What's yours?

MILDA: Milda.

YAKOV: That's not a Russian name.

MILDA: I'm Latvian.

YAKOV: Ah, they're good snipers, Latvians. Good workers, too. They stick at their work. (*Walking up and down.*) Comrade!

MILDA: Yes?

YAKOV: Comrade, look, you know what I think. It's not right, this, what you've dreamt up. I'm being a swine to Olympia – that's the first thing, and the second is, I don't know, what do you take me for? A stallion, a stud, or something? What ever were you thinking of? I'm not really up for this!

MILDA: Comrade, just a minute.

YAKOV: Why should I wait? We're not going to agree. I'm going, comrade. Sorry. Oh, the door's locked. Have you got the key, comrade?

MILDA: Wait!

YAKOV: I don't want to wait. Give me the key. I'm out of here. I'm quite clear. It's not going to happen. No way!

MILDA: Stay there!

(*A knock on the door. Milda dashes to it, knocking over the screen as she does so. She has waved her hair, she is made up, and powdered, and she has a low-necked dress.*)

MILDA: Who do you want?

LIPA (*behind the door*): Is Plumer there? Yakov Plumer?

(*Yakov signs to Milda to deny it.*)

MILDA: No, no.

LIPA: You're not telling the truth. He is there.

MILDA: He's not.

LIPA: Open up.

MILDA: I can't.

LIPA: Yakov, I heard your voice. Answer me! You promised you'd come. I've been waiting an hour. Yasha, Yakov! Are you keeping something from me?

MILDA: Comrade, there's no-one here.

LIPA: I don't believe you. Please, Yakov! ... Right, then! Stay there if you want. See if I care!

YAKOV: What the hell is going on? ... It's like a different person. (*Looking at Milda*)

MILDA: You mean her?

YAKOV: No, you. How'd you get yourself looking like that?

MILDA: Same way as every other woman. At the perfume shop, at the hairdresser's ... Yakov.

YAKOV: Y-yes.

MILDA: Come here. (*She leads him to the bed.*) Don't think of anything else. Listen, you're strong, you've got nice eyes. We're bound to have a good baby between us.

YAKOV: You're a cracker. You've got such round, strong hands.

MILDA: In these hands I shall rock our likkle wumpsy, goldeny woldeny, dearest, delightfullest droplet.

YAKOV: You're a funny woman. You don't know how to use make-up. Your lips are blood red.

MILDA: This mouth will sing lullabies for our baby babbler, our kitteny creature.
YAKOV: You've got good round breasts, firm.
MILDA They'll ripen with sweet milk for the itsy-bitsy, squealy-wealy, eentsy-teentsy-weentsy one.
YAKOV: And your hips are big and wide.
MILDA: They'll help me bring forth, Yasha, our cutesie, crawly-wawly, bright-eyed bud. Yakov, give me a fine baby.
YAKOV: Closer. Move up closer.
MILDA: Turn off the light.
(*He puts out the light.*)
(*They are overheard.*)

A

MAN (*in braces, with his ear to the wall*): Bah, you'd think butter wouldn't melt in her mouth. It's a scandal for this corridor. She's locked in with a stranger. Hell, I can hardly hear anything. (*A baby starts to cry.*) Shh, you rascal, he doesn't even sleep in the evening.

B

A horrible woman and a little girl. The horrible woman pulls the girl by the ear.

HORRIBLE WOMAN: How dare you not keep an eye on the milk? It's disappeared. How dare you?
GIRL (*squirming*): Let go!
HORRIBLE WOMAN: Don't you dare shout! You mustn't make a noise after ten o'clock. I'm telling you! I'm telling you!
GIRL: Can you hear?
HORRIBLE WOMAN: What?
GIRL: The bed creaking.
HORRIBLE WOMAN: Where?
GIRL: At our neighbours. (*She runs to the wall.*)
HORRIBLE WOMAN: Look through the crack.
GIRL: It's dark.
HORRIBLE WOMAN: The light's out. Godforsakenness.
GIRL: They're whispering. There's two of them.
HORRIBLE WOMAN: Two? Give us a look. Where? (*The girl helps her*

to look.) Nothing. It's quiet. (*To the girl*) Get away from that crack. Are we going to let little monkeys watch every bit of filth? Give me that ear again! Why didn't you look after the milk? Why? Don't you dare yell! You're not allowed to yell after ten o'clock. Why didn't you look after it?

C

BASS: My advice is – don't open the portals till you're definitely engaged.
DRUNKS: Bravo, bravo ... Brrr ... (*Hiccups.*)

D

OLD WOMAN (*enters*): If it's the last thing I do, I'm not going to kick the bucket till I've seen how those disgusting so-and-sos fornicate. Number 32. Along the corridor, they said. She's wheedling all the cooks into taking the Party card, and the club – she'll turn it into a maternity unit at this rate. And what goes on in her own room ... If it's the last thing I do, if I have to drag myself there, I shan't peg it till I've seen how these Bolsheviks fornicate.
WORKER ON THE BUILDING SITE: Watch out! What d'you want, granny?
OLD WOMAN: Where are these good-for-nothings fornic –
WORKER: There are no good-for-nothings 'ere. This is a building site ... You better watch out.
OLD WOMAN: But they said my neighbour was ...
WORKER: Let's take the sledge-hammer to her ... old twat ... Get off our site!

SCENE TEN: VITRIOL

Yakov, with nails in his mouth, is hanging curtains in Milda's room, and singing quietly.

YAKOV: Our women in the health resorts
    Get larger round the girth,
    When they come back, you'll find out why,
    They'll all be giving birth.
    (*Lipa has come into the doorway quietly. Her hand is in her pocket. Thinking she is Milda, Yakov carries on without turning round.*)
    You see how nice it's going to be. These are expensive curtains. They were a snip at Smolensky market. I mean, your room was more like a garage with a bed parked in it. I've welded the bedstead. And I've made the table legs level so it won't wobble any more. So I've made you a bit more comfortable, comrade Mildie, eh? See?
LIPA: I see.
YAKOV (*jumping down*): There we go. (*Startled.*) Olympiada!
LIPA: Well?
YAKOV: Bloody hell! What are you doing here?
LIPA: Nothing to do with you. The citizen who lives here, is she in?
YAKOV: Why?
LIPA: I've brought her a summons.
YAKOV: Put it on the table. She'll be here in a minute.
LIPA: She has to sign for it.
YAKOV: I can do that.
LIPA: I don't accept the signatures of liars and cheats.
YAKOV: Listen, Lipa –
LIPA: No, citizen, I won't 'listen', and I'm not 'Lipa' to you, either. Just carry on with the good work. Those are very fine curtains, very fine! And wherever did you buy these sweet bedsheets? They say

the pillow cases from Smolensky market are sooo lovely. And have you still not got the chamber pot mended? Oh, and by the way, do keep your eye on the little door key – you never know, one night, the door may open ...

YAKOV: Lipa, stop playing the fool.

LIPA: Who's playing the fool? Who said, 'Come at ten o'clock', and then hid behind the door? And then who scarpered the next two nights as well?

YAKOV: All this is neither here nor there.

LIPA: Well, now we know which side he thinks his bread is buttered – if it's a choice between no room and his nibs in hostel number 5, or a room that just needs some nice little curtains!

YAKOV: Lipa, will you keep your hooves to yourself. (*He tries to take her hand which is in her pocket.*)

LIPA: Get your hands off! Do you hear? Get your hands off! I'll scream! Get away!

YAKOV: Why are you being like this? Have I changed so much for you?

LIPA: You're like a postmarked stamp now. Only it's not my postmark. So go shove yourself in the right letterbox.
(*Enter Milda.*)

YAKOV: Olympiada ... (*Noticing Milda.*) Comrade ...
(*Milda pushes him aside.*)

MILDA: What?

LIPA: Citizen, please accept ... this summons, and sign for it.

MILDA: Yes. Is that all?

LIPA: As for him ...

MILDA: What?

LIPA: You can have him without a signature.

MILDA: Excuse me, comrade. Didn't I see you on the construction site?

LIPA: Who cares what you saw on the construction site?

MILDA: Do you think he's going to be my husband?

YAKOV: Oh, right – I'm your nephew, or is it your grandfather?

MILDA: He'll never be my husband.

LIPA: Well, lover.

MILDA: And not my lover.

LIPA: He's the painter and decorator, the floor polisher ...

MILDA: He's going to be the father of my baby.

LIPA: And that's not the same as a husband?

MILDA: Certainly not. We made an agreement of a purely temporary nature. A few more days, then he'll go.
LIPA: Sent away with his tail between his legs, eh?
YAKOV: That's it. Kick a bloke when he's down. Go on, go on!
LIPA: I'm not a horse. Shut up! I've cried my eyes out, for all you care. Why are you goading me?
MILDA: Comrade, this is just laughable.
LIPA: Laughable! Taking someone else's bloke to bed with you – that's laughable, eh? Shoving me out the door – that's laughable?
MILDA: Comrade, this is blind jealousy, an unworthy feeling.
LIPA: Blind ... No, I'm not blind. You'll be blind.
MILDA: Calm down, comrade.
LIPA: Laughable, eh? And I'm blind! Just one big joke, eh? Go to hell! You cunning little louse. (*The hand in her pocket is quivering. From the bottom of her jacket vitriol is dripping.*)
YAKOV: Olympiada! Something's dripping!
LIPA: You cheating dog, keep away! I'll get you, you evil bitch, I'll leave my mark on your eyes. (*She takes her hand out.*)
YAKOV: Lipa!
LIPA: There!
(*She splashes vitriol. Yakov manages to break her throw. The vitriol flies onto the curtain. A drop or two lands on Milda.*)
YAKOV: Wipe it with a piece of cloth. Don't smear it!
LIPA (*in a frenzy*): All right! Don't arrest me! I'll go myself! (*She tries to take the top off the little bottle.*) I don't want to live any more!
MILDA: She's going to poison herself!
LIPA: Go away! Don't touch me! Don't you dare! Don't you dare! (*Milda intercepts the hand with the bottle in it.*) I missed ... what the hell. You're still an ugly cow, face like a witch! I ought to shove this in your gob ... there. (*She spits.*) I don't want to be here. Don't you dare touch me. I've got to get out! Let me go! Let me go, go ... go ...
(*She becomes hysterical.*)
VOICES (*in the doorway*): – They've had a right bust-up!
– Whose throat's been slit?
– It stinks of vitriol.
– Get the police on 'em.

VOICES (*from the little ventilation windows*): Couldn't you find another time to start hysterics? Pack it in! Stop that raving. There's no reasoning with them. A complete rabble.

YAKOV: Give her some valerian drops.

MILDA: I haven't got any.

VOICES: – There's first aid in the communal room.
– Take her there.
– Stop this performance!
– You've gone a step too far this time.
(*Milda and Yakov take Lipa out. The sound of her hysterics dies away in the distance. A crowd of people jostles into Milda's room. They rummage through everything.*)

VOICES: – Her briefcase. Is she a Party member?
– She's got *The Works of Lenin*.
– Eug ... eugenics.
– A sausage. Would you look at that? Smoked, as well.
– To treat her fancy fellow.
– A revolver. Watch out, it's a revolver.
– Probably unauthorised.
– It creaks. (*About the bed.*)
– The blanket's full of holes. Feather pillows.
– Most likely not washed the sheets all week.
– They're probably filthy from yesterday's screw.
– What's in the bag?
– Dirty linen. Wait! Her brassiere!
– Yes yes. And powder. A box of powder with a powder puff.
– And perfume – 'Violets'. Hee hee hee.
– Tell me about 'Violets', please. Is that lipstick, too?
– Soldiers' trousers.

A CLERK: But no plasterer's trousers?

A VOICE: Look at this, look at this! We've caught her! We've got her! An electric gadget, for boiling water. On the communal meter.

VOICES: – She's been stealing electricity from everybody in the house.
– Pinching it! Got to make them a drink of tea after bed, hasn't she?
– Here's her nightie.

MILDA: Citizens, did I invite you in? (*She points the revolver at them.*) Stand back from the door! Put everything back! You forgot the nightie! Tidy the bed. What's that you've taken, put it down!

CLERK: I'm not going to. Don't even try! It's against the rules of the block administration. You've no right. It's not your meter.
MILDA: And now, get out. One, two, three! (*They all run out.*) Why haven't you gone with her?
YAKOV: They wouldn't let me anywhere near her, they were calling me all sorts. All the women came rushing in, wanting to know every fart and comma. All bawling at once. And the block superintendent trying to shush her up. To hell with her!
MILDA: Yakov, you mustn't be like that. She's really ill, unhinged. Look what she did – vitriol in your face.
YAKOV: Yeah, I caught a few drops.
MILDA: She needs looking after.
(*Pause.*)
YAKOV: What are you counting?
MILDA: I'm working out my budget. My salary is ninety-six roubles. My outgoings, rent for my room and everything – twelve roubles, my meals – thirty-three, papers – a rouble fifty, laundry – four roubles. I have to send twenty roubles to my mother, which leaves twenty for me, but actually it's less than that, about fifteen roubles. And I've got to get nappies ready for the little one.
YAKOV: What little one?
MILDA: My baby. Or have you forgotten? The reason for all the scenes round here.
YAKOV: So what do you reckon? Are you going to be short?
MILDA: Well, I need to stretch those fifteen roubles to find something to treat Lipa.
YAKOV: Says who?
MILDA: It's our fault she's running around hysterical. I should have seen it coming.
YAKOV: She wouldn't take it.
MILDA: No, but you will. Buy whatever she needs. Take her to the doctor's. She won't know where it came from.
YAKOV: I've got my own money for that. Up yours, Miss Accounts Department!
MILDA: I think we'd better sleep apart tonight. Go home. These upsets aren't exactly wonderful for the nerves.
YAKOV: Well, see you then ...
MILDA: Come again ... (*She consults a little book.*) ... two days from now.

(*Yakov goes out. Hysterics are heard a long way away, getting closer. Milda runs to lock the door. The key is not there. She casts about for it. Stoneturner enters with a small spinning gadget.*)

STONETURNER: Sound convincing?

MILDA: What's that? Is it Lipa?

STONETURNER: No, no! Actually it's more of a twister.

MILDA: Is that you, Stoneturner?

STONETURNER: Watch. Simple, isn't it? (*Twists the gadget. It screeches.*) But you absolutely can't tell the difference.

MILDA: Have you finally taken leave of your senses?

STONETURNER: I made a bet with Saxoulsky. He says genuine hysteria only occurs when the person is taken over, it's the result of great and genuine nervous tension, and it's impossible to reproduce it mechanically. But I say you can. Who's right? You just listen.

MILDA: Stoneturner! Who on earth cobbled you together?

STONETURNER: My background's very mixed, actually, Milda. Five nations in varying degrees took part in assembling yours truly: 50 per cent of my blood is Jewish – that's where I get my musicality from; 25 per cent Russian – that's where my Tartar obstinacy comes from; 12 and a half per cent Tartar – that's where my Russian broadmindedness comes from; 6 and a quarter per cent German – that's where my perseverance comes from; one and one forty-ninth per cent gypsy – that's where my inventiveness comes from.

MILDA: Stoneturner, you know what? Instead of this screechy thing, invent a device that chuckles like a two-month-old when you say 'Goo-goo' to it. Can you do that?

STONETURNER: You bet.

SCENE ELEVEN: PRIMUSES

The communal kitchen. Primus stoves are blazing and hissing. On a washing-line two shirts are drying. Women from the block stand behind the primus stoves. First Wife is humming a scale.

GRIPE: Are you unable to stop, madam? Or not?
FIRST WIFE (*humming*): It's allowed till ten o'clock at night.
GRIPE: Vexation! Enervation! Certification!
CHILD'S VOICE: Mummy-y-y! Mummy-y-y!
SECOND WIFE: I'm coming!
MAN'S VOICE: Where's the joint?
FIRST WIFE: I'm bringing i-i-it!
CHILD'S VOICE: Mu-ummy-y!
SECOND WIFE: I'm comi-i-ing!
THIRD WIFE: They're at it again in thirty-two.
  (*Everybody falls silent and listens.*)
FIRST WIFE: They really are shockers!
FOURTH WIFE: What do you reckon, Loosha, do you trust her?
LOOSHA: No way I trust her.
FOURTH WIFE: I'm not against the Soviets, not at all. But I ask you, what's going on – every night it's a different bloke.
THIRD WIFE: She takes 'er pick from the workers, likes 'em on the young side.
FIRST WIFE: 'Ardly surprisin' the fiancées are getting their knickers in a twist.
SECOND WOMAN: I'd be furious too, so I would. (*She goes out momentarily, and then returns.*)
THIRD WOMAN (*after she has gone*): To hear her talk, you'd think she was a blushing bride!

FOURTH WOMAN: Well, you be the judge, Loosha. Do we 'ave debauchery in the block, or not?
SECOND WOMAN: She'll have your hubby off ya next, so she will.
FIRST WOMAN: And give all yer whole family syphilis.
FIRST WORKING MAN: So what was she creating about the nursery for?
FOURTH WOMAN: That's 'er gettin' 'er oar in with the authorities.
FIRST WOMAN: She en't up to much if that's all she's got up her sleeve.
(*Saxoulsky has entered, together with a Man in a Tolstoy blouse, Milda and the Second Wife.*)
MAN IN BLOUSE (*to Milda*): Nonsense. You've been bribed by the skivvy. Money was paid to you.
MILDA: That's your considered opinion, is it?
SECOND WOMAN: None of your business.
FOURTH WOMAN: What have you got to say for yourself?
(*Enter the Block Superintendent.*)
SUPERINTENDENT: What's all the noise?
LOOSHA: You need to sort out that bloody woman.
MILDA: This citizen ... (*But noticing the derisive glance of the superintendent*) ... It's obvious I'm not going to get a fair hearing from you. (*To the Superintendent*) You're in league with these toads. I shall have to act through a general meeting of the residents.
SUPERINTENDENT (*chewing an apple*): The general meeting's next week. I shall certainly ask you to be present.
(*Milda goes out.*)
FIRST WOMAN: Stoopid rules. The likes of 'er should be out on their arse so fast their feet can't touch the floor.
SECOND WOMAN: Toad ... So we're toads now, are we?
MAN IN BLOUSE: When I was in England, persons of reprehensible behaviour were simply ejected with the help of a policeman.
FOURTH WOMAN: Why expect manners from a slut?
SAXOULSKY: Which Eve presented you with this apple?
SUPERINTENDENT: It's a Cox's pippin. Do you want one?
SAXOULSKY: I'd like something else. (*Takes him aside*) I feel this is a most opportune moment to safeguard the club premises from the encroachments of our ladies of the nursery.
SUPERINTENDENT: Mmmm ...

SAXOULSKY: In so far as you will most probably need to settle the matter with the residents, and of course you'll be doing it over a cup of tea, I have therefore been authorised to hand over to you this for your indispensable expenses.

SUPERINTENDENT (*negatively*): Mmm ...

SAXOULSKY: Nonsense! It's not for you personally, is it? It'll be spent on the residents – in one way or another ... jam ... buns ... and Cox's pippins.

SUPERINTENDENT (*returning the envelope*): Most thoughtful, but it really won't be necessary. We'll get rid of her on two counts. The general consensus is on our side.

MAN IN BLOUSE: Has she got a room?

SUPERINTENDENT: Yes!

MAN IN BLOUSE: I ask you to bear me in mind regarding the occupation of her living space, otherwise I shall be hanging round my sister's neck. I've not long arrived from England.

SUPERINTENDENT: Yes, indeed, most trying. Why not? It's perfectly possible.

(*Saxoulsky, Man in Blouse and Superintendent go out.*)

FIRST WOMAN: Toads?

SECOND WOMAN: Toads.

FOURTH WOMAN: We're toads?

SECOND WOMAN: She's the toad, so she is.

FOURTH WOMAN: She's a slut compared!

FIRST WOMAN: To 'ear 'er cheek.

SECOND WOMAN (*going past, she gets tangled in one of the blouses*): Now just who has hung this up all in the way?

SKIVVY: It's thirty-two's.

SECOND WOMAN: Picked her spot, so she did.

(*She pulls the blouse down. The other gossips kick the blouse about with their feet.*)

FOURTH WOMAN: Bend down for that then!

FIRST WOMAN: Smell her washing!

SKIVVY: Watch out, it's getting filthy dirty!

FIRST WOMAN: Well, she shouldn't 'ave 'ung it up in the way.

SECOND WOMAN: You don't know how we do things round here.

FOURTH WOMAN: Rules are there to be obeyed, not treated any old how.

SECOND WOMAN: So get rid of this rubbish.
FIRST WOMAN: I've found a nit.
FOURTH WOMAN: Yeugh!
SECOND WOMAN: Squash the wee thing with your fingernail, why don't ya?
FIRST WOMAN: Give it a good crack.
FOURTH WOMAN: So we won't smell it.
  (*Milda enters, goes to the shirt that's hanging up and takes it down.*)
WOMEN (*together*): Just a moment, please –
MILDA: What's the matter?
FOURTH WIFE: Is that yours?
MILDA: Yes.
SECOND WOMAN: What about this – ? (*Straightening out the blouse they were kicking and hanging it up.*)
MAN IN BLOUSE (*comes back*): Is my blouse ready?
SKIVVY (*without looking*): It's on the line.

SCENE TWELVE: GENERAL MEETING

The whole block. The superintendent chairs the meeting. The clerk is his secretary. People are entering all the time.

CLERK: We need more benches. Grab those benches.
VOICES: – Squeeze up, please.
    – Too kind.
FIRST WORKER: Why are they fannyin' around? It's time we got started.
VOICES: – Come on, come on.
    – Hold on!
    – Where is she?
SUPERINTENDENT (*to the secretary*): Go and have a look. Can't we hurry her up?
ANGELICA: She'll do a runner.
SUPERINTENDENT: If she doesn't turn up, we'll resolve it in her absence.
    (*Clerk goes out.*)
FIRST WORKER: Superintendent! Comrade superintendent!
VOICES: Shh ... !
FIRST WORKER: What d'yer mean 'shh'? No point wearing out the chairs for nothing. Our problem is this – what's going on with the bog on corridor three is indescribable. The last time they cleaned it, they took out half a brick and a long female riding-boot, and now it's blocked up again so badly that ...
SUPERINTENDENT: Citizen –
FIRST WORKER: We need a motion – that the Block Management Committee ought to pay for a lock on the bog, and personally give out keys to everyone who uses it.
VOICE: How would that help?

FIRST WORKER: What do you mean, how? Number one, it'd be a regular process, and number two, it wouldn't get so crappy, 'cos we'd be keeping an eye on it all, for goodness' sake.

SUPERINTENDENT: The matter is in hand, comrade.

FIRST WORKER: In hand! More hot air! Same every time!

CLERK: She's coming!

(*General buzz and movement. Enter Milda.*)

CLERK: She hasn't got a chair.

SUPERINTENDENT: Can't one be found?

(*Silence. Chief Clerk puts his own chair out.*)

CLERK: There we are.

A VOICE: Crawler!

SUPERINTENDENT: And what are you going to sit on?

(*Clerk takes his chair back.*)

MILDA: Never mind. We'll manage.

A CHARACTER: You don't say.

MILDA: I'm going to ask you not to keep me for long. I've got work to do.

CHARACTER: Not 'alf!

SUPERINTENDENT: As you wish. As you wish. It was precisely because we took your work into consideration that we didn't begin the meeting.

MILDA: Let's get down to business, then.

SUPERINTENDENT (*to the Clerk*): Be so kind as to read it out. The resolution of the Block Management Committee.

CLERK: Right away. (*Mumbling, and fumbling with his papers.*) One moment, the claims of the residents.

(*From a distance, there drifts in a song from* La Traviata.)

LOOSHA (*the cleaning lady*): Fill full the goblets.
And let us drink to happiness, wine and love.

(*She is carrying a chamber pot. She stumbles into the meeting by chance, stops short, covers the pot with her apron and moves backwards under the reproachful stare of the superintendent.*)

FEMALE VOICES: Loosha, chuck, keep an eye on the primus stoves, will you?

(*Sound of the same song fading away.*)

CLERK: The Block Management Committee wishes to put to the general meeting the question of the illegal and immoral behaviour of the following resident in number 32 –

MILDA: Can't you make it shorter?
CLERK: The aforesaid behaviour, namely –
FIRST WORKER: Stop witterin'.
VOICES: – We know all this.
— Men spend the night with her.
— She goes about in men's clothes.
— She 'as night-time orgies.
— She swears with VD words.
— Families and children have to listen to that filth.
— She 'as the workers off the building-site.
— She calls the workers' fiancées all sorts.
— She drives people to hysterics.
— To suicide.
— There's shouting and fights in the corridor.
GRIPE: Is there any kind of life to be had, or not? Can we work, or not?
VOICE: It's a brothel.
MILDA: Citizens, there's been a misunderstanding here –
VOICES: – Misunderstanding? Pull the other one! It's crystal clear.
— Shh!
— 'Oo are you shushing?
— Shh!
MILDA: I repeat, there's been a misunderstanding. I wouldn't be speaking to you otherwise.
VOICE: She wouldn't be speaking to us otherwise.
MILDA: If somebody hadn't put these foul ideas into the heads of working mothers –
WORKER: Don't try to wriggle out of it.
WOMAN: We weren't born yesterday.
VOICE: We've all had a little bite of the cherry, you know.
MILDA: The matter is very simple.
VOICE: Too right – you just fall into bed.
MILDA: At the moment, we're getting a good harvest of children. After the wave of abortions, a wave of births is upon us. We have to make good the losses of the wars and the revolution.
VOICE: That's not a matter for the likes of you.
MILDA: Everyone who can afford a child is having one. But ...
WORKER'S VOICE: Get to the point.

MILDA: Everyone and his cousin has jumped on the production line – drunks, sick people, those with terrible heredity, consumptives. Such children aren't children, they're rubbish.
VOICE: You're the rubbish.
(*Laughter.*)
MILDA: Conception must be organised.
VOICE: They've been popping out all right up to now, thank you very much.
(*The drunken typesetter enters. Behind him, his wife.*)
TYPESETTER: Lea' me 'lone. I'll be quiet. (*Sits down with a growl.*)
MILDA: Having a husband isn't important. What's important is who produces the baby.
VOICE: It's your clients who're important.
MILDA: The professors say, use the sperm of the intelligentsia.
VOICE: You think you're going to get an intellectual?
MILDA: I want the father of my baby to be healthy, and besides that, to be one hundred per cent proletarian. So the baby acquires the stamp of his class.
VOICE: Allow me to propose myself. I can satisfy all your requirements.
MILDA: I shall only need him –
VOICE: That's enough yattering.
MILDA: Until it is certain that –
VOICE: Spare us the bullshit.
MILDA: I'm pregnant. This will be a child –
VOICE: Get rid of the slut!
MAN IN BLOUSE: I've been in England. In England they deal with individuals like this quite simply.
VOICE: She's a prostitute.
ANGELICA: I demand that she be examined.
(*She puts her hand up as if to vote.*)
MILDA: Have me examined? To see if I'm a prostitute? Is this the demand of the Block Committee?
CLERK: Of course not. What are you saying? The Block Management Committee put on the agenda the fact that persons with no permit have been staying overnight in your room, and because of the presence in your room of unauthorised electrical heating devices. (*He holds up Stoneturner's zinc device, taken from Milda's room by*

the lodgers in Scene 10.) But your private life is of no interest to the Block Management Committee. That's none of our business.

SECOND WORKER: We're from the other corridor. How do they know she's some kind of tart? Maybe she really is doing it for a baby. Who's seen her at it?

SUPERINTENDENT: I saw a man in her room one night in his underpants, and then the next day it was somebody else.

VOICE: Everybody's seen it.

ANGELICA: Let's have a show of hands. (*She waves her hand.*)

STONETURNER: He's seen it? He's seen it? (*He crosses the room towards Bob. To the superintendent.*) Have you seen it? (*The superintendent is embarrassed.*) One ... two ... three ... four ... five ... six ... (*suddenly loudly*) one hundred and ninety-five! (*He whispers to Bob.*)

A ROAR: Prostitute!

SAXOULSKY: Get her out of her room, and don't let her come into the club. She'll infect the whole place.

MILDA: Let's have all the women examined. Beginning with her (*Indicates Angelica.*)

ANGELICA ; What gives you the right?

MILDA: And let the results of the examination be put up on the block noticeboard.

ANGELICA: How vindictive can you get?

MILDA: The men will find it very useful – let them find out who they can sleep with. When shall we have the examination? Today? Please vote!

(*Giggling in the rows of women workers. Some of them go up to Milda.*)

TYPESETTER: You're too big for your boots. That's what I say. Lady of the manor! Bossin' ev'rybody 'round.

MILDA: Comrade!

VOICE: Let him speak. Don't you dare interrupt.

TYPESETTER: You need the proletariat in bed! Yeah? Hundred per cent. Whas wrong wi' me? I'm a proletarian. Hereditary. Why don' you ask me?

TYPESETTER'S WIFE: You've gone clean off your head, you idiot. Shut up.

TYPESETTER: I won' shut up. You won' ask me? Need a young 'un, nice an' 'andsome? Well, is it my fault the consumption's left me wiv no lungs? Twenty-eight years I've bin a typesetter, got lead in me blood. Fair 'nuff, I won' do ... I don't 'ave the right to make kiddies. Off you go, Mother Mary. Find yourself a stud. Go and get a bun in your oven.

VOICE: It's a crying shame.

MILDA: You're talking nonsense.

VOICES: – How dare you! You listen to him, that's the authentic voice of yer genuine proletariat.

– Have your say, comrade.

TYPESETTER: No, I won' say no more. Lady of the manor. She's making a little master. Why play Happy Families when there's Doctors and Nurses? Take me, I've produced half a dozen, and they're all good-for-nothings. Piss off, Mother Mary.

VOICES: – But why do they keep throwing vitriol at her?

– She's taking money off the young men, when they should be out courting.

MILDA: You're lying.

VOICES: It's true, it's true.

TYPESETTER: No way I'm lying.

VOICES: – Finish your say, comrade. We'll support you.

– Have your say, comrade.

TYPESETTER (*taking in the crowd of NEP people and office employees with a dull, drunken gaze*): Comrade? Whose comrade? Am I your comrade? Where's all this comrade stuff come from? Think 'cos you've moved in, you've bought my conscience? Nine years ago, with my rifle, I made October. Which stove were you stretched out behind, snug and warm? What you smirkin' at? Comrade ...

VOICE: Pissed as a newt.

TYPESETTER: Don't butt in. 'Snothin' to do with you. Me 'n' her'll sort it out 'tween ourselves. Back off, you son-of-a-bitch.

VOICE: Pack it in! You just try it!

TYPESETTER: Back off! I'll shoot.

SUPERINTENDENT: Hooligan!

TYPESETTER: You shut it, you crook. You're talkin' to the boss here.

(*He tries to wave a chair around. Collapses in the crowd. We see him vomit over someone's clothes.*)

VOICES: – See him off!

– Dirty pig.

(*Milda bounds over to him.*)

MILDA: You dare lay a finger on him. Just you dare. Get your hands off him.

LOOSHA (*from some distance*): What's goin' on 'ere? The primuses 'ave gone out.

(*All the wives rush over in that direction.*)

SUPERINTENDENT: I'll call the police.

MILDA: Help me bend over. Help me, now.

STONETURNER: Milda, what's the matter with you?

MILDA: I feel ill ... My head ... I feel sick ...

WOMEN WORKERS: – What's up with Milda?
– They've done the poor girl in!

BOB (*stubbornly*): Call the police.

SUPERINTENDENT: What's the matter?

BOB: Call them. The worker's faction will put two matters into their hands: first – there's the hate campaign directed against Milda.

STONETURNER: What's the point, he's in on it, too.

BOB: Are you prepared to answer?

SUPERINTENDENT: No.

BOB: You can answer to the people's court.

MILDA: I feel really bad ...

STONETURNER: I can see that ... (*He exits. The women workers surround Milda.*)

FIRST WOMAN WORKER: Milda ...

MILDA: What?

SECOND WOMAN WORKER: Listen carefully.

MILDA: Leave me be!

FIRST WOMAN WORKER: Mifilifidafa, wefee arefor sofo soforry.

SECOND WOMAN WORKER: Don't start that daft talk now.

THIRD WOMAN WORKER: Those cows (*indicating the wives*) have really brought her down.

MILDA: They're not cows. They're sheep. The primus stoves have turned them nasty and stupid.

(*Enter Stoneturner with Dr Softer.*)

STONETURNER: Here she is. She held out through the battle. Went white as a sheet. Now she's feeling sick.

SOFTER: And you don't realize what's the matter with her?

STONETURNER: No.

SOFTER: Comrade Milda, let me be the first to congratulate you!
MILDA: On the outcome of the meeting?
SOFTER: No, on something quite different. (*He takes Milda aside.*)
FIRST WORKER: So does this mean that bog's going to stay all filthy?
BOB: What do I care? The worker's faction is meeting now.
SECOND WORKER: You've worn your bums out meeting.
LOOSHA: Oi, clear off, whoever you are. You've turned the place into a pigsty.
BOB: There's supposed to be a meeting here now.
LOOSHA: I've had it up to here. All you ever do is bloody meet. Pity your arses. I can never finish my cleaning with you lot. (*She hitches up her skirt. The man in the blouse comes back.*) What are you staring at? Never seen a woman's legs before? You clapped-out old nag!
MAN IN BLOUSE: Would it be possible not to shout in the presence of these people?
LOOSHA: 'Would it be possible not to ...' Get out while you're still alive, or I'll splash some of this on yer trousers. You leery bugger, gawping at my legs. Want to see right up to my navel, do yer? You're no better than a randy dog!
BOB: What are you swearing at, Loosh?
LOOSHA: Just clear orf, clear orf. You're all dogs.
BOB: Come on, now, it's me. Look ...
LOOSHA: You're a dog, too. And look out there (*indicating the auditorium*), all those dogs, sitting staring. What I wouldn't give to smack 'em with this toilet brush. Get out! Clear orf – the lot o' ya! Git, git, git!

SCENE THIRTEEN: A FATHER IS UNNECESSARY

Milda sits in her room, very tired. There are phials on the table. Yakov runs in with a pram.

YAKOV: Comrade Milda, are you hurt?
MILDA: Yakov! How many times have I told you – they can't hurt me?
YAKOV: Don't give me that! They told me all about it. They grabbed hold of you, kept on at you, messed up your clothes. And you tell me, if you please – 'they can't hurt me'!
MILDA: In the country where my class is sovereign, and I control the newspapers, the public prosecutor and the chief of police – who can hurt me? If they'd hurt me, I would have gone to a People's Court, don't you worry about that. But I've come to my room instead.
YAKOV: Your face is white as chalk, and I can smell these valerian drops. You're putting on a brave face, aren't you? Tell me.
MILDA: It's the baby, Yakov.
YAKOV: What's the baby?
MILDA: The baby is here.
YAKOV: You never? Well, I … well?! Have you known for long? When?
MIKLDA: I just found out.
YAKOV: It's as if I guessed. (*Showing her the pram.*) Look. I was going past Sukharyovka – it was just standing there. It's as solid as a bus. The wheels'll last fifteen years. The wickerwork's brand new, all it cost me was my loose change. So it's a baby, right?
MILDA: A baby.
YAKOV: Crackin'! Just imagine! (*Fantasizing*) We take him, and settle him in the pram. Are you comfortable, your Honour? Please, comrade baby, get your toes out of your mouth. Look, comrade baby, a jackdaw on the telephone wire. Let's go. Keep to the pavement.

Er, excuse me, citizen, move aside. Careful now, we're crossing a new little citizen here. Old woman, save yourself, any way you can. A citizen is on the move. Stand aside! Cars, give way! Don't cry, comrade son, we'll get across the road. Policeman, clear a way through. Hold up your truncheon! Bus, stop! Motorbike, stop! My little citizen, we're on our way! (*He seizes Milda in his arms.*) Milda!

MILDA: Yakov, let go!

YAKOV: Oh-ho-ho! We're commissars now! Oh-ho-ho! Now we'll show 'em!

MILDA: Yakov, don't you dare lift me up.

YAKOV: I'm not lifting you. I'm lifting the little one. What are you? You're just the wrapping. Wrapping-paper! Wrapping-paper! Wrappappa-boom-de-ay! Hold tight! She's only gone and done it!

MILDA: Put me down, for heaven's sake! How dare you touch me!

YAKOV: Mildie! I could eat you up – (*He puts her down.*)

MILDA: Well, thank you very much.

YAKOV: What do you mean, 'thank you very much'?

MILDA: We've made a good job of it, haven't we?

YAKOV: Well, there you go ... Me too ... Anybody'd think we'd just put up a house.

MILDA: Do you think it's that simple? I'm exhausted with worry.

YAKOV: What d'you mean, worry?

MILDA: Because you sit there and it's just as though you were listening to your own belly: will I come on or won't I? Will I or won't I? Now I know. So, once again, thank you, Yakov. Now you can go.

YAKOV: What do you mean, 'go'? How can I go? Till this evening, do you mean?

MILDA: No, there's no need. There's absolutely no need for you to come back at all.

YAKOV: What do you mean, no need at all? I don't get you.

MILDA: It's very simple. Didn't we make an agreement?

YAKOV: What agreement?

MILDA: That you'd come to me till it was clear there was a baby, and then the relationship would end, with no claims on either side.

YAKOV: What do you mean, none?

MILDA: Just that, none.

YAKOV: Am I his father or not?

MILDA: You are the father.

YAKOV: Then I have rights.

MILDA: None whatsoever. When the baby's born, I'll show it to you, but you don't have any other rights.

YAKOV: How do you make that out – none? Anyway who's going to bring him up?

MILDA: I am to begin with, then the children's home, then the nursery, then –

YAKOV: And who's going to maintain him?

MILDA: Me. You've forgotten. Remember the paper I gave you that night? Saying I renounced all claims.

YAKOV: What paper? I chucked your damned paper away.

MILDA: No. I slipped it into your pocket. (*Yakov searches for it.*) Not in that shirt – that's your Sunday best, you were wearing one for work then.

YAKOV: Your idea's barmy. If you were to die, who'd pay for him?

MILDA: I thought of that. I've insured my life in the name of the child. Go now, Yakov. Don't make a fuss.

YAKOV: Ah, so that's it – I've served my purpose now. Finish. Just like a stud horse. We have a few fucks, and then it's cheerio. Yeah?

MILDA: Yakov, don't make a scene.

OFF STAGE: – They've kicked off again.

– Let her into the room, let her in.

YAKOV: You do my head in.

MILDA: Yakov, you've got Lipa. Yakov, go to Lipa.

LIPA (*on the threshold*): Aha! Is Yasha being shown the door? She said she would. Well, off you go. We'll see, maybe I will take you back.

MILDA: Comrade Lipa, don't taunt him, he's not quite himself at the moment.

LIPA: Not quite himself at the moment? So what are you saying, you asking me to take this parcel away?

MILDA: Comrade Yakov!

(*Yakov flies into a rage.*)

LIPA: We don't need a little signature this time, do we? Come on, then, darling. (*Someone in the crowd laughs. Lipa goes up to them.*) Did I just hear a horse?

VOICE: Show some manners in somebody else's house.

LIPA: You should be grateful there was no charge for the show.

(*Yakov grabs the pram, lifts it over his head, as if about to smash it to bits. Milda intercepts him.*)

MILDA: Comrade, control yourself. That's an item of value. Don't let yourself down.

YAKOV: Not seen the last of me. (*He goes quickly. At the door he takes Lipa's hand.*) Come on, Lipa. (*To the crowd*) Scum. Worse than bloody animals. Shoo!! Lipa, keep hold of my hand. (*The crowd scatters. Milda is left alone. She walks about the room. Then she parks the pram in the corner. She opens her notebook, and reads: 'Nutrition for Pregnant Woman. Estimates.' A knock at the door.*)

MILDA: Come in.

BARBARA: Hello, Milda.

MILDA: Ah, Barbara. The parcel's behind the screen.

BARBARA: What parcel?

MILDA: With the dress I borrowed from you, remember? It's been washed.

BARBARA: You might still need it, you can hang onto it.

MILDA: No, I don't need it now, and I won't need it again. Did you come about something? I'm rather busy.

BARBARA: I did want something.

(*During Stoneturner's interruption, Barbara moves out of sight.*)

STONETURNER (*sneaking up*): You say – nothing can shock me, nothing can shock me, nothing can shock me. But listen to this, Milda. It's been decided in the block that the nursery won't be built.

MILDA: Impossible!

STONETURNER: Did you get a shock?

MILDA: Well, of course.

STONETURNER: So we've finally dispelled the myth of your unshockability.

MILDA: Stoneturner! You idiot! You're lying.

STONETURNER: I am. And you – are you getting agitated?

MILDA: Well, of course. That's not nice.

STONETURNER: The place'd be a help to you.

MILDA: Not for me, for the baby.

STONETURNER: The baby? Holy Moses! Milda – our Iron Maiden. A baby! Ye Gods!

MILDA: What are you holding?

STONETURNER: Oh, I invented this device for getting the mould off pickled mushrooms. But it's of no consequence now. A baby, indeed. Yes, yes, and here's the pram.

MILDA: Stoneturner, look at the state of your hands. You've got it all grubby.

STONETURNER: It's not grubs, it's not grease. I was on the building-site. I saw where the nursery's going to be. (*Showing his hands.*) These are colour samples. They're going to paint the walls in this. (*He looks for something to wipe his hands on.*)

MILDA: Hands off. That's a pair of trousers.

STONETURNER: You won't need those any more.

MILDA: Enough of that. You get some soap, a towel, a loofah, and fifty kopecks – and get off to the bathhouse double quick.
(*She throws him out. On the threshold Stoneturner bumps into Bob.*)

BOB: I'd like a word.

MILDA (*to Stoneturner*): Off to the bathhouse. (*She chases him out.*) What do you want, Bob?

BOB: After what you said today, the block support group has elected you to the Volunteer Organising Group. They've made you an honorary Volorg.

MILDA: 'Volorg' – sounds like a dog. Don't move. Let me take a good look at you. Congratulations. You've really surpassed yourself this time.

BOB: What've I done?

MILDA: Perhaps you'll be nailing up a sign on the house? Oh! But have I got a little spot ready for the plaque? Next thing you'll be commissioning a portrait by Brodsky![100]

BOB: I don't understand you, comrade.

MILDA: What is there to understand? But when I grow old, I hope the Commission for the Protection of Old Monuments will assign a few kopecks for my upkeep, made possible by the benevolent assistance of your support group. (*She drops a curtsey.*)

BOB: Bah!

MILDA: A volunteer organiser, but he spits. You couldn't just make me an ordinary volunteer, could you? I had to be honorary. (*Barbara appears back in the doorway.*) Barbara, come in. What's the matter?

---

100   *Brodsky*: Isaak Izrailovich Brodsky (1884-1939), famous portrait painter, especially of Soviet leaders.

BARBARA: I thought you were on your own now.
MILDA: No, I was just saying to this comrade –
BOB: I'm going. I won't get in the way. I'm going. (*Exit Bob.*)
BARBARA: Milda, what's the matter with you? There's something about you today.
MILDA: You can congratulate me on carrying out my programme.
BARBARA: Have you arranged the mother's co-operative?
MILDA: No, I've arranged a baby.
BARBARA: Milda, is it true? So you're actually going to have a baby? Will you nurse it yourself? Milda, that's the very reason I came to see you ... Me too.
MILDA: You're pregnant?
BARBARA: Yes, yes. Milda, I'm so happy. I'm going to work like a devil. I'll put some money aside and I'll nurse him myself.
MILDA: Whose is it?
BARBARA: Whose is what?
MILDA: Your baby.
BARBARA: You know.
MILDA: I don't.
BARBARA: Filirinov's. But that's not important. You said yourself a husband's a burden. It's true. I said so to his face. He gave a whistle, then he hopped it.
MILDA: You'll have to earn extra money.
BARBARA: For the baby?
MILDA: No, for the abortion.
BARBARA: Milda! Why an abortion? I want a baby.
MILDA: The baby will be shoddy goods. Its father is a drug addict.
BARBARA: Milda!
MILDA: Barbara, I'll give you this note for Dr Softer, he'll help you to arrange it. (*She starts to write.*)
BARBARA (*weeping*): I feel wretched ... Milda ... Have I really got to, then?
MILDA: Here you are.
BARBARA: I don't want to. What if it does turn out a bit of a shrimp? How come you're allowed to have one, and I'm not?
MILDA: Do you remember our agreement? A harvest of sound children.
BARBARA: I remember. (*She takes the note, and sobbing, goes out.*)

MILDA (*alone*): To work. To work. Where are my files? My papers? My reference books? Right then. I need to call together the heads of the literacy centres. I'll order a new set of teaching materials ...

YAKOV (*bursts in, drunk*): Aha!

MILDA: Yakov!

YAKOV: Who's that who just left you?

MILDA: Barbara. What do you want?

YAKOV: What I want is – I'm not leaving you. I'm the father – and that's that.

MILDA: Yakov, please go.

YAKOV: Mildie, don't play hard to get. I'm the daddy.

MILDA: Yakov, stop.

YAKOV: You don' wan' me? I'll have my way, all the same. I know why you kicked me out. You've got yerself another bloke. I don' wan' another bloke mucking up my son.

MILDA: You're drunk.

YAKOV: So what if I am drunk? Wasn't your money. Take yer note back. Come here. I'm going to sleep here tonight.

MILDA: You'll do no such thing.

YAKOV: It's my baby. I'm the boss. Give me back my baby. I'll cut you up!

MILDA: Yakov, you'll regret it.

YAKOV: I'll kill you.

MILDA: Yakov, get back!

YAKOV: Bitch! (*He tries to kick her in the stomach.*)

MILDA: Yakov. (*She hits him over the head with her revolver.*)

LIPA (*appears in the doorway*): You've murdered him!

MILDA: I've just knocked him cold. Help me get him onto the bed. Hold the smelling salts to his nose ... He'll have to be bandaged. Tear up a shirt. Here.

(*They bandage him up.*)

YAKOV (*tossing about*): My head ... Mildie ... Lipa ... My head ...

LIPA: Did you have to hit him so hard?

MILDA: He'll be alright soon enough. Apply some water. Don't leave him till he starts making sense again. Take him away. I'm going to sit and work.

LIPA: Wait! (*Milda holds out her hand. Lipa does not take it.*) I'm not on about making up. What are you going to call him?

MILDA: Call who?

LIPA: You had a knock on the head too? Harvest our children, you say, produce a healthy generation, you say, but you yourself –

MILDA: I don't understand.

LIPA: You can't see further than your own stomach.

MILDA: What can't I see?

LIPA: I'm going to have Yakov's children too. There now, I've said it, so I will. They'll grow up. And then, suppose yours and mine meet. What then? Brother and sister are going to marry, are they?

MILDA: Brother and sister?

LIPA: It'd be incest. So, as I say, what are you going to call yours?

MILDA: True, absolutely true. So, what shall I call him? I hadn't really given a thought to names. For the patronymic – Mildovich or Mildovna, and surname – Grignau.

LIPA: Here's what we do. Write down my address. When it's born, write to me straightaway, and I'll do the same for mine. And we'll din it into their heads where their brothers and sisters are.

MILDA: Listen, you're being stupid, Lipa! –

LIPA: I'm being stupid?

MILDA: Don't interrupt. Let me have my say.

STONETURNER (*enters, sees Yakov*): A hospital case, and harsh words!

MILDA: Give it a few years. They'll finish building the block. The days of primus stoves and poky little rooms will be long gone. Unemployment will be eradicated. The concept of the housewife will be outmoded. People won't be on edge all the time. There'll be a nursery. Not just a little one, though – a properly appointed one for the whole block. Sister, we will both take our little ones there. And we will be friends.

LIPA: That'll never happen.

MILDA: You mark my words. Do you want a bet?

LIPA: Not for anything!

MILDA: I say we will! (*They shake hands.*) Stoneturner, come and break it.

LIPA: But I'm not taking your hand in friendship, only for the bet.

MILDA: All right. (*She counts on her fingers.*) April, May, June, July, August, September, October, November, December, January. Right, insurance, be ready to pay Milda's leave in December.

STONETURNER: When a person's had a bath, he's a better human being.

SCENE FOURTEEN: THE CHILDREN ON SHOW

(*Milda's dream.*)
The building has been completed. In front, a nursery with people milling about. Voluntary Organisers form a chain to cordon off the mothers' area. Posters: 'Healthy parents – healthy output', 'From the cradle onwards – our children's collective', 'State nurseries free the woman worker', 'A healthy conception – a healthy pregnancy', 'An easy birth needs healthy nourishment', 'A harvest of children'.

The Superintendent is selling apples from a tray. The Club Secretary is selling various publications. Saxoulsky is a crooked bookmaker.

CLUB SECRETARY: Come and buy, citizens! Interesting books! Sexual problems solved for thirty kopecks! (*Policemen step forward.*) *Resurrection* – novel by Tolstoy. State Publishing House calendar for 1930.
SUPERINTENDENT: Cox's pippins!
POLICEMAN: Oi, you, hawking that stuff!
(*Superintendent stays still.*)
ANGELICA: What's going on?
SAXOULSKY: It's the Kids on Show.
ANGELICA: Kid goats?
SAXOULSKY: No, children. Humans.
MAN IN BLOUSE: When I was in England, this sort of thing was commonplace.
ANGELICA: Putting the kids on show? Why do it?
MAN IN BLOUSE (*disregarding her*): You feel you really understand where the smells of milk and muck come from.
(*Mothers step back and crowd in front of the doors.*)
BOB: Attention! The medical committee is now considering who is to get the prize for the one-year-old infants.

VOICES OF GAMBLERS:
FIRST GAMBLER: Who's that mother there?
SAXOULSKY: Grignau.
FIRST GAMBLER: The one who got first prize last year?
SAXOULSKY: The same.
FIRST GAMBLER: I'll put three roubles on her.
SECOND GAMBLER: I'll lay five roubles on that one with the big hips. She is taking part?
SAXOULSKY: She is. Don't crowd me. Move over to the fence.
   (*They move away.*)
BOB: Don't crowd like that.
ANGELICA: Don't you fancy getting in among the fillies!
   (*Laughter of fashionable women.*)
THE WOMAN WITHOUT A BABY (*who was the female singer in scene 4*): Let me through! I'm an important comrade! Can I join you? I can't have a baby. I'm going to work as a state child minder. (*Laughter.*) Go away, damn you. You've got it cushy! You're nobodies! How dare you laugh at me?
BOB: Come here, comrade.
THIRD GAMBLER: I'll lay another three roubles on Grignau.
SECOND GAMBLER: Are these doctors going to show up soon?
MILDA (*to the back of a woman with a baby*): You're new here, comrade?
LIPA: Yes.
MILDA: Lipa?
LIPA: Milda!
MILDA: Your little boy?
LIPA: Girl. My first is a boy, but this is my second, a daughter, Lipa. What's yours called?
MILDA: The boy's called Yasnich, and this one – Yuna. Do you remember, Lipa?
LIPA: Remember what?
MILDA: Our bet.
LIPA: Well?
MILDA: I lost.
LIPA: Let's change over. (*They exchange babies.*)
YAKOV: Now then, comrade, let me through.
VOL ORG: Over there?
YAKOV: I've got business.

VOL ORG: Are you an orderly?
YAKOV: More senior than that.
VOL ORG: A cook?
YAKOV: More than that. Keep going.
VOL ORG: A doctor?
YAKOV: Even more than that. I'm the most important person. I'm the father.
VOL ORG: Let the fathers through.
YAKOV: There's my offspring without her dummy.
VOICE: Well I never ... what an expert he's become!
YAKOV: Aha!
WOMAN: A-a-ah. Hush. Look, there's daddykins. See? Give daddy a little waveykins. Say: daddy, here we are, daddykins, here we are. (*Stoneturner enters and walks towards them.*) Here's daddykins. (*Stoneturner is in front of her.*) Citizen, move to the side. You're blocking the child's view of its father. Come on, daddy. We've missed you. See, he nodded his little head, daddy, there, he sniffle-snuffled, and lifted up his lickle handy.
(*Enter the undertaker, with 'Aunty' and their child.*)
UNDERTAKER: Hang on, he's not cryin'. He was supposed to cry.
STONETURNER: I remember you. We met about four years ago. You're the undertaker, aren't you?
UNDERTAKER: Hi beg your pardon. I'm a hofficial of the Moscow crematorium. But you're welcome.
STONETURNER: What's this then? All because of a fifty kopeck piece? Quite a bargain.
UNDERTAKER: Certainly was. This little lad won the third prize last year. But 'e got through 'alf a bottle of milk a day all year, cost me nearly fifty roubles. Quite a hundertaking.
STONETURNER: My congratulations upon your success.
MILDA: Will any prospective fathers or mothers come here now, please? It's from this point that we will all be going into the club for the lecture.
YAKOV (*to Lipa*): That's never mine.
LIPA: Not yours? He is! Who do you think this is?
MILDA: Hello, Yakov. Here's yours and Lipa's.
YAKOV: Heh-heh! I've bumped into both of them at once ...
MILDA: You haven't made this one's acquaintance yet –

YAKOV: How d'you manage with work and children?
MILDA: I breast feed them myself, then I hand them over. To the Children's Home.
YAKOV: Can't be easy to tear yourself away.
MILDA: It's always difficult to part from people. Do you think it was easy for me back then to give you the brush-off?
BOB: Quiet! The doctors are coming!
YAKOV: Here we go, fellas. They're going to hand the prizes out now.
SOFTER: Having examined the thirty-nine one-year-old infant competitors who were entered, their physical and nervous health, also the quality of their parents, the judges of the Exhibition of Children have decided to present the first prize –
VOICES: – Don't crush us!
– I can't hear.
– Raise you another three roubles!
SOFTER: To give it to ... numbers four and seven jointly.
SAXOULSKY: To two of them? Damnation!
SOFTER: Number four – the child of Milda Grignau, and number seven – the child of Olympiada Plumer. The father of both children is Yakov Plumer.
VOICES: Mothers, form a queue.
FIRST GAMBLER: Citizens, the bookmaker's done a runner. Grab him!
(*Policeman whistles. Some people run out.*)
SOFTER: Out of three second prizes, the first is awarded to child number sixteen.
BARBARA: That's me.
MILDA: Barbara, you? Who's the father?
SOFTER: May we know who the father is?
BARBARA: No, I'm not saying.
(*Saxoulsky is brought in by a policeman.*)
VOICE: Show us the winners!
(*The children are raised aloft.*)
VOICES: Bravo! Bravo, Yakov!
MAN IN BLOUSE: When I was in England, I never saw anything like this.
STONETURNER: Excuse me. I shan't beat about the bush. I've come here to present as a donation to the Children's Home my latest inventions. A centralised electrical self-comforter. Press this

button – and in every cradle a rattle is activated. A self-rocking cradle triggered by the infant cry. There's nothing to laugh at. A modest observation, if I may. More than half the world's geniuses have been childless.

YAKOV: Hooray for the heroes of our age!

(Music from all the children's instruments. Procession of mothers and fathers.)

I Want a Baby
(*Khochu Rebënka*)

(Second version)

(1927)

Translated by Robert Leach

I Want a Baby

Characters

A Peasant Lad
Ivan Baran, a peasant
A Latvian peasant
Milda Grignau, an agronomist from Latvia
Old Man
Woman Teacher
Likhar, a balladeer
Stripes, a traveller
Four Fathers with babies
Angelica, a work colleague of Milda
Doctor at the Fertility Clinic
A Mother
Hysterical Woman
Other women at the Fertility Clinic
Vadim Sergevich Softer, a doctor
Stoneturner, a research worker
Dynda, a male work colleague of Milda
Foreman on the building site
Grinko, a building worker
Yakov Nikitich Kichkin, a building worker
Four Cavalerios
Four Ladies
Lipa, a postal worker
Old Woman
Milda's neighbours
A young couple
An arguing couple
Nurse
Doctor at the children's home
Parents, onlookers, etc

SCENE ONE: AGRICULTURAL CENTRE

A queue. A lad, Ivan Baran, and Latvian.

LAD: I think the specialist's in the beet field. She's probably just chatting away. I'm sick of waiting.
IVAN BARAN: Well, what are you waiting for? What have you got to ask her about?
LAD: I've got something quite important.
IVAN BARAN: You can come back tomorrow.
LAD: Come back tomorrow yourself. I'm waiting for her. So don't try pushing me out.
(*Milda appears with an old man and a teacher.*)
OLD MAN: The soil's lousy here.
MILDA: That doesn't excuse you for such a bad cabbage crop.
TEACHER (*offers her a bough of apple blossom*): Look, this is covered in blossom.
OLD MAN: Well, this year we've had a very good spring – all the fruit trees are in blossom now. It's a real beauty.
MILDA: It's not a beauty at all. There'll be very small fruits on the trees.
TEACHER: But just smell this – it has a beautiful fragrance. (*Milda smells it.*) Well?
MILDA: What's beautiful about it?
OLD MAN: You take a deep breath, and close your eyes. Then you get it.
MILDA: Ah, yes.
TEACHER: Isn't it wonderful?
MILDA: Wonderful? Well, it smells of creodine. Did you spray creodine on your apple trees as an insecticide? Have I guessed it?
IVAN BARAN: Comrade agronomist –
LAD: Hang on, I'm first.

IVAN BARAN: Who says? You snotty-nosed runt, don't try pushing in in front of your elders and betters.

LAD: Stay there. Wait your turn.

OLD MAN: You shouldn't talk like that at your age.

MILDA: What's the matter, comrades?

IVAN BARAN: Well, I've got something ...

LAD: I'm first. You're jumping the queue.

IVAN BARAN: I've brought this young ...

MILDA: Just a minute. Let this citizen speak.

IVAN BARAN } (*at the same*   Citizen!

LAD   }   *time*)   See. Don't push in.

IVAN BARAN: He's no citizen. Damn you.

LAD: Don't swear. You want to behave yourself.

MILDA: I'm listening.

IVAN BARAN: But he's got nothing worth talking about. He's come with some bloody rabbits. Bloody hell! I've got much more important business – about the oats, they didn't germinate.

MILDA: But they were high grade seeds.

IVAN BARAN: High grade seeds! All they grew into was beet!

LAD: Comrade, do you mind? Don't jump the queue. Listen, he's lying to you. He sold all the high grade seeds and only planted beet.

IVAN BARAN: Lies. I never sold them. I put in what I had.

LAD (*bringing out his rabbits*): Here. Look. I'm unlucky, you know. I've got two rabbits, a doe and a buck, both white, and look – after two months, she littered, and half the babies were all white, but the rest were black spotted. Those pelts don't fetch anything like what the white ones do. My granny says to me that because the doe jumped through some charcoal, that's why some of the litter are covered in black patches. But I don't believe that.

IVAN BARAN: She's right, it did jump through some charcoal.

MILDA: Rubbish. It means that one of the rabbits is a pure white, its parents had pure white genes –

LAD: Genes?

MILDA: And the other one has one gene which is white and the other gene is black. That's why you have the phenomena of black patches in a litter from all white parents. (*She notices that the Latvian is meddling with the plough.*) Hey, comrade, please, leave it alone.

LAD: He doesn't understand. He's not Russian. (*Something squeaks on the plough.*)
MILDA: Leave it alone. Vy yu ni boos meera.
LATVIAN: Latvesh. No Riga.
MILDA: Ney no mullaga. Paguid bizhkit.
LATVIAN: Larb, larb.
LAD: So you're Latvian as well. You're compatriots. (*He indicates the rabbits again.*) But what shall I do now? Which of the litter has these mixed genes? (*To Ivan Baran*) Be careful. Treat animals properly. You'll suffocate them.
MILDA: My advice is to go on breeding, but take a white pair and only allow them to mate. Don't let any of the spotted ones in to them. That way you'll be selecting the pelts you want.
IVAN BARAN: Nothing of the sort will happen. You can't allow incest, you can't mate a mother with one of her own sons, or brothers and sisters.
MILDA: Not at all. In fact the purest pedigrees are worked out in precisely that way. It's probably not a good idea for incest to occur among specimens which have degenerate characteristics, but with the best ones you can certainly do it.

(*Likhar, with an accordion, appears, singing a chastushka.*[101])

LIKHAR: Oats, oats, will you tell,
            When all your pods begin to swell,
            When you are like to taste so fair,
            Must you grow such shaggy hair?
MILDA: Go away, you're disturbing us.
LIKHAR: What's that?
OLD MAN: This isn't some kind of party.
MILDA (*to Lad*): Go and try, and come and see me in town some time. I'll explain it to you in more detail then. Here's my address. You'll see a large building overlooking three streets. It's got three storeys and part of it is being altered. I live on the second floor, along the corridor ...
LIKHAR (*grabs one of the rabbits and throws it up in the air*): Ai, ha ha! Jump, little one, enjoy life, before you're shot.
LAD: You bastard! Get out of here! Don't touch them!

---

101   *Chastushka*: traditional humorous Russian folk song.

LIKHAR: One more word out of you, sonny, and I'll give you such a belting you won't forget it for a long time.
LAD: Give me? And I'll do you so –
MILDA (*interrupts*): Don't fight.
LAD: He's vile. He'd better watch out.
MILDA: Take him to court.
LAD: Court's not what he wants.
MILDA: Then write to the papers.
LAD: No newspaper would touch it.
MILDA: You'll have to go through the Party organisation.
LAD: I'm not a Party member.
MILDA: Well, you'd better apply. It's no good using hooligan tactics against a hooligan.
LIKHAR: You called me a hooligan.
IVAN BARAN: Who did?
LIKHAR: I'm not talking to you. (*To Milda*) I'm a hooligan, am I?
MILDA: Citizen, please calm down.
OLD MAN: He is, though.
LAD: She's not the kind you could grab hold of.
IVAN BARAN: Just buzz off!
MILDA (*to Likhar as he comes closer to her*): Citizen, please keep your hands to yourself.
LAD: You'll see. She'll deal with him. She'll give him one to remember. She's as strong as a horse. Just touch her and she'll lay into you so you won't be able to sit on your arse for a week. Look, watch, watch, watch.
LIKHAR (*embraces Milda*): How do you like that? (*He lets her go.*) Hit me, go on, try it.
LAD: She'll give it him now. Watch. (*Milda sits down, breathing heavily.*) He's offended her. Comrade agronomist.
MILDA: You're a nasty bit of work, filth.
LIKHAR: But I know how to rouse a woman. (*She tries to hit him with her pocket book, but he runs away.*)
LAD: You should have hit him, Baran.
IVAN BARAN: I have something for you, comrade. Turnips, from last year.
MILDA (*takes turnip, looks at it, but is still agitated by her encounter with Likhar*): Yes, turnips. So what? Just a second. What are you talking

about? (*She gets up sharply.*) I'm sorry, citizen, I'm unwell, I can't concentrate.

LAD (*to Ivan Baran*): You'll have to come back tomorrow.

MILDA: What? Tomorrow. Yes. And the day after that the other agronomist will be returning from leave. (*She leaves.*)

IVAN BARAN: What a bastard that guy was. Did you see how he felt her up?

OLD MAN: What would he have done if somebody had done it to him?

SCENE TWO: FATHERS

Street. Milda enters with her briefcase. She stands, and looks about her. There are several fathers looking after their babies. Some of the children are crying.

STRIPES (*at a small open window*): When I was in England, there was nothing like this. Turn off that noise. This is not a kindergarten, people are living here. (*He pulls a face at the children, who cry even louder. He slams down the window.*)
MILDA: Listen to them. Just listen. They're crying. It gives me the feeling of a man kissing me passionately on the mouth.
FIRST FATHER: This nappy's soaking. (*To another Father*) Could you hold it?
MILDA: Give it to me. I'll hold it.
FIRST FATHER: Thank you. (*He clicks his tongue.*) Oh well, at least it's not dirty. Its bad tummy's better. Now it's yellow when it's dirty, but for ages it was green all the time.
MILDA: How old is he?
FIRST FATHER: Four months.
MILDA: Is he a boy?
FIRST FATHER: No, actually, she's my daughter.
SECOND FATHER (*to First*): Do you use any talc?
FIRST FATHER: Just Likopody.[102]
SECOND FATHER: I use talc.
MILDA: Perhaps she's crying from hunger.
FIRST FATHER: No, her mother just fed her, and now she's eating okay. Have you got a child?
MILDA: No.
FIRST FATHER: Why not?

---

102   *Likopody*: soothing herbal medication, applied in the form of powder.

MILDA: I haven't got round to it.
FIRST FATHER: You'd produce something pretty good. Your hips are the right size, and you look like you'd have plenty of milk.
MILDA: Are you a doctor?
FIRST FATHER: No, I'm a political worker. I carry out ideological work among the people. I only commented about you as a comparison with my wife. This is my second child. I have a son as well. He was conceived near Perekop, the famous civil war battlefield. And because the time was so hard, and so cold and wet as well, he's not very healthy.
MILDA: Why not?
FIRST FATHER: When you're in a hurry on that sort of thing, and the time is not really suitable ... It was a time of starvation, I wasn't eating enough, nor was my wife, we were both exhausted, the battle was so hard, you know how it was at Perekop.
MILDA: What difference does that make?
FIRST FATHER: Oh well, this one's completely different. Look how healthy she is. All plump and happy looking! When you think of conceiving a child, I mean, when you're ready to procreate, it's quite important that you both are well-fed, calm and full of life. And that you're both in love. Do you mind me talking so openly like this?
MILDA: Not at all. Is it very expensive to keep a baby?
FIRST FATHER: So far it's not too bad. About ten roubles.
SECOND FATHER: Or even cheaper.
THIRD FATHER: Oh, I'd have problems. What he eats doesn't cost much, but the doctor's bills are certainly high.
MILDA: Why not put him in a State Children's Home?
THIRD FATHER: No, I don't believe in those institutions.
FIRST FATHER: And you – would you give your child away?
MILDA: Of course I would.
FIRST FATHER: Ah, you can talk like that now. But when you've got a baby sucking at your breast, you'll change your mind. You'll be attached to it then. Well, it's getting cold now, I'll have to go.
(*Most of the Fathers go, leaving only First and Fourth (the youngest). Angelica enters. She is dressed to kill.*)
MILDA: Hello, comrade Angelica.
ANGELICA: Hello.

MILDA: I haven't seen you for ages.
ANGELICA: What do you mean?
MILDA (*inspects her dress*): Oh – er.
ANGELICA (*defensively*): What does that mean, oh – er?
MILDA: Nothing. I was just admiring your dress. Have you been to a dance? Or some kind of party?
ANGELICA: No, I've been at the office all day. I know you prefer thick boots to shoes.
MILDA: What sort of message are you sending to the Institute Club? Do you want them to know that our Agricultural Department consultant, Angelica, hasn't got time to read her paper on farm price codification to them?
(*Angelica, offended, walks away.*)
FIRST FATHER: Look at you. You've got such a good body, you're so well built, but you haven't produced anything yet. (*To Fourth Father, who is gazing after Angelica.*) Hey, don't forget you're holding your baby. What's the matter? Haven't you seen female legs before?
FOURTH FATHER: But have you seen her stockings? Aren't they beautiful? "Victoria."
FIRST FATHER: We know about these "Victorias."

SCENE THREE: THE CONSULTATION

Fertility clinic. On one side, a desk and chair. On the other side, a waiting area, where there are women waiting. Doctor and Milda enter.

DOCTOR: Well, that's that. Gynaecologically, everything's fine. Let me look into your eyes. Okay. If you like, if you're still worried, you can have further tests done – here's the address of the laboratory.
MILDA: Okay. But, er, can I –
DOCTOR: Yes. But some problems you can't treat with pills or medicine, you know. There's only one way of doing that – having a baby, I mean. But you're perfectly healthy, you could carry triplets, if you conceived them. You should have an easy birth, too. You'd better talk to your husband.
MILDA: Husband? I haven't got a husband.
DOCTOR: Oh, I'm sorry. You're so unpredictable.
MILDA: Me? Unpredictable?
DOCTOR: Sorry, don't take everything so seriously. I didn't mean 'husband', I meant your – what do you call him? Your partner? – who you live with.
MILDA: I don't live with anyone.
DOCTOR: Oh, no-one. Well, if you feel the urge to have a baby, but you haven't got anybody to go with, why don't you put on some nice stockings, you know, "Victoria"...
MILDA: But it's so filthy.
DOCTOR: What do you mean, filthy?
MILDA: The women who wear those stockings.
DOCTOR: They're not filth. It's the men who're filthy. Don't you understand the disadvantaged position women are in, economically? Okay, it's all right for you, you're independent. But others have to look for a husband, and use whatever means

they can. There are many fewer men than women, don't forget. And anyway, if you searched out all the men who are available, you'd find many of them were not suitable ... And besides, there's a very strange phenomenon these days – you'd be surprised how many men in present society are suffering from impotence. That's why we have such a high demand for semen, far greater than ever before. So of course, hunting for decent specimens of the human male, women have to use whatever means they can, and this often involves putting something on which will stimulate the men's sexual desire. So they wear skirts that are a bit shorter, or they put on silk stockings. And do you know why we have so many abortions nowadays? Because our contraceptives don't work properly. And why don't our contraceptives work properly? Because the men have such a low potency, they can't perform when they're wearing them. As studs, they're hopeless.

MILDA: Well, I've got no chance then. To find a healthy, suitable stud is going to be almost impossible.

DOCTOR: I didn't say that. I was only talking generally about the sexual market which is available today for a woman. I mean the availability of good male studs. Are you looking for a good stud to father a baby for you?

MILDA: Yes, I am.

DOCTOR: Someone pretty exclusive. You know what I'd suggest? Just hold on a moment.

(*He goes to where the other women are waiting.*)

WOMEN: – Doctor, I think I'm pregnant again.
         – My kid won't suck properly.
         – It's my ovaries again, Doctor.

DOCTOR: Who's not taking the breast? Give him to me. You, little comrade, you know what you've got to do? Who's your mum?

MOTHER: Me.

DOCTOR: I don't think it's baby's fault, I think it's yours. Will you step into the cubicle, please?

A HYSTERICAL WOMAN: Doctor, I've been to the polyclinic. Here are the papers.

DOCTOR (*glances over them*): Yes. It's exactly what I said.

HYSTERICAL WOMAN: They told me I can't have children. I can't have any.

DOCTOR: You should be pleased with that. Having children for a woman of your build could be dangerous.
HYSTERICAL WOMAN: It's not dangerous, it's not dangerous. I don't agree. I may have narrow hips, I might have a difficult labour, but I still want a baby.
DOCTOR: Please, calm down. Try to be a bit more detached. We may still be able to do something for you. We'll have another go at a scrape.
ANOTHER WOMAN: Doctor, I think I'm pregnant
DOCTOR (*to Milda*): I'll refer you to my colleague. He's a doctor. He has good health, he's got an even temper, plenty of stamina, and the main thing is, he's a man with a highly impressive heredity. There couldn't be a better stud. You realize these factors are what count, scientifically, and he's exceptional. You have a very sound peasant heredity yourself, so that ought to make a very interesting combination. Yes. He has a clinic in the building on the main road.
MILDA: Oh, that's where I live.
DOCTOR: Well, that's even better. You know the health centre in that building? He works there. Just a second. (*To Dr Softer who is passing*) Vadim Sergevich, can I have you for a second? Can I introduce you to my patient? This comrade will come to you, she has some unusual business for you.
SOFTER: That's fine.
MILDA: You work in the building on the main road?
SOFTER: Yes.
MILDA: When are you there?
SOFTER: I work there evenings.

SCENE FOUR: IN SEARCH OF CARESSES

Sitting in Angelica's room, Milda and Stoneturner with a bundle.

MILDA: Stoneturner.
STONETURNER: Yes.
MILDA: I don't think Angelica will be here for a bit yet. Are you going to wait?
STONETURNER: I might as well.
MILDA: Aren't you busy?
STONETURNER: No, I'll just sit here. I haven't got anywhere else to go. I need to see her.
MILDA: What for?
STONETURNER: I've invented something.
MILDA: Something filthy, I suppose.
STONETURNER: On the contrary, it's a beautiful toilet soap. The recipe and the technology are entirely mine. The main ingredient comes from human body fat. The principle involves the utilization of dead bodies. By the way, could I stay at yours?
MILDA: Yes – but without your soap!
STONETURNER: Thanks. (*Silence.*) Milda!
MILDA: Mm?
STONETURNER: Angelica won't be happy about you being in her room, you know. You've offended her somehow. I heard her recently saying some pretty uncomplimentary things about you – in fact, they were so uncomplimentary that I told her to count – one, two, three, etcetera, etcetera – so her anger would subside. That's the best remedy, you know, counting.
MILDA: Did it work?
STONETURNER: She just turned on me and started abusing me.

(*Angelica enters, sees Milda, pretends she hasn't. She goes to the back of the room and during the next lines changes her clothes.*)

MILDA: Ah! I want to see you.

ANGELICA (*irritated*): Getting a bit familiar, aren't you? Charming!

MILDA (*meekly*): Sorry. Comrade Angelica.

ANGELICA: Stop it. We're not all solipsists like you. Okay, you've proved it's possible to spend years without a man. But I can't. That's all there is to it.

STONETURNER: One, two, three ...

ANGELICA: One more number from you and you'll be out the door. (*He is quiet. Milda makes to speak, but Angelica notices, and speaks herself.*) You can say what you like. I know what's being said by some people – that I'm skiving my job because I'm having an affair. That I put on these yellow stockings. I've had my hair permed, I put on lipstick, I use powder. I even wear expensive boots with high heels.

STONETURNER: And why do you have those high heels? Eh? To make yourself taller? No.
(*He goes and puts on a pair of high-heeled boots and struts before them.*)

MILDA: Of course to make yourself taller.

STONETURNER: No way. Look – can't you see the shape of my body? No? What happens when you wear high heels, your backside has a nicer shape, and your bust sticks out more. That's the whole idea of high heels.

ANGELICA: Out, fool!

STONETURNER (*to Milda*): Look – can't you see?

MILDA: Please, Stoneturner, go away. I have to talk privately to Angelica.
(*Stoneturner goes out.*)

ANGELICA: Right. Fire away. You want to go on nagging, I suppose.

MILDA: Don't worry, I'm not going to give you some moral lecture. No, I've come about something ... it's very private, personal ...

ANGELICA: Oh, it's about my lecture.

MILDA: No. But you know lots of ... caressing words.

ANGELICA: To calm you down?

MILDA: No. You've been with plenty of men. What do you say to them? Mm? When you talk to a man you're in love with, don't you say some caressing words to him? So that after them, he's much more tender, and loving. Could you give me a list of words?

ANGELICA (*taken aback*): Are you mad? Don't you know anything yourself?

MILDA: I do know Russian, but I wasn't brought up speaking it. But actually, I don't know the caressing words in my own language. Nobody ever talked sweetly to me, or tenderly.

ANGELICA: You write pretty well at work. Why do you need these words?

MILDA: I just do. Tell me. (*She takes out a notebook.*)

ANGELICA: I don't know what to say. You're crazy.

MILDA: Well, when you kiss a man, what do you say to him?

ANGELICA: Eh? You're mad. Well, I say – 'You little sweetie' ... or, 'you little yumyum' ...

MILDA: Please, I'm being serious.

ANGELICA: I am being serious. And then I say, 'You little toadstool' ... or, 'my little scarecrow' ...

MILDA: Mm. But tenderer.

ANGELICA: Er, 'lickle one, lickle pussy-cat, sweetie-heartie, umpsy-wumpsy, itsy-bitsy ...'

MILDA: So all you do is take ordinary words and give them diminutives?

ANGELICA: That's it. There's plenty of others – you can use the names of animals – 'my little lambkin, little mousie, buzzy bee,' anything. (*Milda writes.*) Easy, isn't it?

MILDA: Er, yes. I'd like to ask you about your dress, too.

ANGELICA: My dress?

MILDA: Could I borrow it for a couple of days?

ANGELICA: You?

MILDA: Yes. I won't damage it.

ANGELICA: I'm sure of that. (*Getting the dress for her.*) And what else do you want?

MILDA: Show me how you put your lipstick on.

ANGELICA: Like this. (*She puts her lipstick on.*)

MILDA (*shouts*): You can come back now!

STONETURNER (*enters*): What was all that about?

ANGELICA: Well ...

STONETURNER: Yes?

ANGELICA: You see, it's to do with the dress.

STONETURNER: I suppose she's going to act in a show.

ANGELICA: Yes, Milda's in a show.

STONETURNER: Why not? She could be in one of those agit shows with a pompous title like 'How the Middle Peasant, Semyon, Sold His High Grade Seeds.'
ANGELICA: Yes, and she's compiled a whole list of nice words as well.
STONETURNER: Fine. They'll make good names for cows.

SCENE FIVE: I WANT A BABY

Milda's room. Milda enters, carrying a brief case, and Stoneturner with his bundle.

STONETURNER: Can I bed down in this corner again?
MILDA: Why ask? Of course.
STONETURNER: I thought perhaps you had new rules now, or perhaps you've taken to pacing up and down, thinking.
MILDA: Nothing of the sort. Do you want a cup of tea?
STAONETURNER: I can't take tea before going to bed. It's the alkaloids – they stimulate me.
MILDA: Are you going to bed now?
STONETURNER: 'Yis', as Chamberlain said at Locarno. First of all, I have to go to bed now because I have to get up early in the morning, but there's a problem: you have to work now, I suppose –
MILDA: Don't worry, I can manage, I'm not mollycoddling you.
STONETURNER: You can mollycoddle me. I'm not shy of you. Besides, Milda, you're a good chap, I don't think of you as a woman. The only thing wrong with you is you don't have enough sofas in your room.
MILDA: You'll have to make do with this. (*She throws him a thick, shabby fur coat.*)
STONETURNER (*getting undressed*): You're working on your thesis again?
MILDA: No, I'm reading a German book about fertilizers.
STONETURNER: Do you read German?
MILDA: Only with a dictionary.
STONETURNER: Don't you ever get tired of working?
MILDA: Listen, all I get tired of is you and your rambles.
STONETURNER: You can't say 'rambles' like that in Russian.

MILDA: Oh, ramble.

STONETURNER: 'Rambling', Milda. You'd have to say 'I was rambling'.

MILDA: Oh, drop it. Don't go on.

STONETURNER: I'm not going on. I'm happy, I'm warm. I'm in your room, Milda.

MILDA (*reading, under her breath*): Dadadada. (*She puts her finger on the page.*) There.

STONETURNER: I'm lying on something hard here. It feels like some kind of gun. (*Milda takes a revolver out of the pocket of the coat.*)

MILDA: How can you sleep in your clothes and with your shoes on?

STONETURNER: If there's a fire, I can make a quick getaway.

MILDA: It's unhygienic.

STONETURNER: I could take them off. (*He takes off his trousers and puts them on a chair. Some flash cards fall out of his pocket.*)

MILDA: What are these? Cloakroom tickets?

STONETURNER: No, Milda, this is one of my best inventions. I invented it yesterday, because there's so much bad language about these days. People spend ever such a lot of energy on foul language. So what I've done is simplified it. Each abusive word has its own number. For example: the number two means 'silly ass', number three means 'fool', four is 'idiot', number eight means 'bastard'. So now, calmly, without raising my voice, I just hold up a number. That's all. So I never have to use abusive language. 195 – that's a fantastically filthy word, incredibly foul! (*He is picking his toes.*)

MILDA: Listen, you – ka visi pu uko.

STONETURNER: I do what?

MILDA: That's Latvian for – You stink like a swine.

STONETURNER: No need to translate.

MILDA: You don't look like you've seen a bath for a whole year.

STONETURNER: Milda, that's stupid. How can I visit bathhouses? Do you know who uses bathhouses now? All kinds of riffraff, God knows who. No, they're full of diseases, it's the most uncivilized way of having a bath, going to the communal bathhouse. Only the lowest, least socially aware classes do it nowadays, peasants and worse. As a consistent socialist, I believe that taking a bath should be something you do at your leisure, in your own private house. You sit there, in the bath, looking at the two taps, one hot, one cold. You turn on the taps, the water runs and fills it up ...

MILDA: Are you trying to say that until we've built a socialist society, you're not going to wash your feet?

STONETURNER: Shall I tell you a joke? Listen. It's in the classroom. The teacher picks on a kid who's miles away. 'You. Tell me who wrote *Eugene Onegin*, the most famous Russian poem ever written.' And the boy, who hasn't been listening, says, 'It wasn't me, sir!'

MILDA: Oh yes. Where was this?

STONETURNER: Where? What's that matter? Er - in Moscow.

MILDA: Well, why didn't you inform the Moscow Education Department about it?

STONETURNER (*annoyed*): Milda, do you have a sense of humour?

MILDA: Yes.

STRONETURNER: Prove it.

MILDA: Well, if you want to know what I find funny, I think little gherkins are funny. Aren't they?

STONETURNER: Milda, I'm worried about you. There are geniuses of the revolution. There are geniuses of stabilization. You are the genius of one hundred stabilizations. You're running on a set of rails which are fixed for a hundred years straight ahead of you, being driven by a hundred tons of inertia.

MILDA: What kind of idealistic nonsense is that?

STONETURNER: And even if your father was tied to the rails, you'd just carry straight on over him. Actually, did you have a father, Milda?

MILDA: Yes, I did. He was a labourer on Goldstein's farm. (*She reads.*) Da dada dada dada. (*Loud music is heard.*) That music again. I can't work with that going on.

STONETURNER: It helps me to go to sleep, though. (*Milda returns to her book. She makes notes. There is a knock at the door.*)

MILDA: Yes? (*Dynda enters.*) Comrade Dynda, you've come for my article for the journal? I haven't finished it. But have a look at what I've done. (*She gives him a pile of papers, then turns back to her book.*)

DYNDA: I didn't come about your article. I've finished work for today. Can I sit down?

MILDA: Yes ... sit down. (*She carries on reading, while he turns the key in the lock and approaches the table. His speech is hesitant and awkward, punctuated with 'ah ... um ... er.'*)

DYNDA: You know Comrade Angelica? She mentioned you to me, said some quite interesting things about you.

MILDA: Uhuh.
DYNDA: That you're very bound up with your work, for instance. But do you ever get a chance to relax? Have a break?
MILDA: When I sleep.
DYNDA: What about going to a film?
MILDA: Hardly ever.
DYNDA: Or the theatre?
MILDA: I don't like it.
DYNDA: Music?
MILDA: I can't stand it.
DYNDA: I work like a slave, too. Eighteen hours a day. But I still need to relax. Or my nerves'd be wrecked. I'm so tired, I don't laugh any more, I just grin through my teeth. Sometimes I have a drink. Do you drink?
MILDA (*still reading*): Yes ... I do ... Oh, no, of course I don't.
DYNDA: Do you want a drink now? I'll fetch some.
MILDA: No.
DYNDA: You're not listening to me, Milda. You see, comrade ... er, I came to you about a problem ... but please, don't look at me as though I'm a stranger. I've known you for a long time as a comrade who has absolutely no prejudices. I'm not just complimenting you, it's the truth. Listen. You see, I have this problem. My wife went away a week ago, to visit her father, and at the moment I'm facing this terrible problem – I have this irresistible physical need for a woman. I mean, I can't go and see a prostitute, I'm sure you'd agree. Um, but we are neighbours, and we've known each other quite a long time now. I mean, you're pretty strong and healthy, and you're probably lonely as well ... er, you're a fantastic comrade ... reliable. I know you won't refuse a comrade when he's got a problem which is so understandable like that.
MILDA (*still with her eyes in the book*): Sorry, comrade, I wasn't listening properly. Could you repeat all that?
DYNDA: Bloody hell. How can I say it ... in two words ... Look at my hands, they're trembling, I'm going crazy. Look, my wife's gone away, I need a woman ...
MILDA: How does that affect me?
DYNDA: It's you I'm asking ... you're a human being ... can you be without a male? ... it'll only be half an hour ... like comrades.

MILDA: Comrade?

DYNDA: I know, I know. (*He takes her by the hand.*) I'm an absolutely normal male, absolute –

MILDA: Comrade.

DYNDA: If you see someone who's ill, you give them medicine. If you see someone who's hungry, you give him bread.

MILDA: No, if someone was ill, I'd call an ambulance. And someone who was hungry I'd send to the canteen. But as for you, comrade –

DYNDA: What are you afraid of? A baby? Don't be, I know all about contraception, I've got one with me. Don't be stupid. What are you frightened of?

MILDA: What am I frightened of? I'm frightened of diseases, of syphilis. I'm frightened of conceiving a child who'd have a neurotic for a father, probably an alcoholic ... All I can say to you is – go into the street and pick somebody up. Or ...

DYNDA: Or – ?

MILDA: Or go and solve your problem by yourself without a woman present.

DYNDA: Huh. That's your idea, is it? You're sure?

MILDA: Masturbation even at your age is perfectly understandable. And I'm afraid it's the only solution I can see.

DYNDA: That's got nothing to do with it. So you refuse?

MILDA: I don't want you.

DYNDA: You're a prude. You don't know anything.

MILDA: Have you finished now?

DYNDA (*puts his hand over her mouth and drags her down onto the bed*): To hell with it ... just lie down ... (*Milda grabs up the book and whacks it down on his head, then pushes him away.*)

MILDA: Get out! (*Dynda jumps away, and falls over Stoneturner where he's lying.*)

STONETURNER: Watch out! Bloody shit! Milda!

DYNDA: Oh, I get it now ... Oh, sorry ...

MILDA: Get what?

DYNDA: Of course. How can one woman serve two men? In a single night, or at the same time?

STONETURNER: What's the matter?

DYNDA: None of your business. I'm talking to her.

MILDA: Stoneturner, open him the door.

DYNDA: Get off! Bouncer, eh? Don't touch me!
STONETURNER: I'm no bouncer! Bastard, I'll get you!
DYNDA: Belt up, this isn't a public bar. Everyone's asleep, it's a decent place here.
STONETURNER: Bastard! Sewer rat! I'll get you!
MILDA: No, stop it!
STONETURNER: I'll make mincemeat of you ...
MILDA: No, count!
STONETURNER: I'll splatter you!
MILDA: Please, you said you'd count.
STONETURNER: I'll spread you all over this place.
MILDA: No!
STONETURNER: I'll do you – (*Milda gets between them.*)
MILDA: Count!
STONETURNER (*pitifully*): One ... two ... three ... four ... 195. (*Tries to open the door.*) Milda, the key!
MILDA: The door's open.
STONETURNER: It isn't.
MILDA: You had it all set up, eh? Open the door. (*Dynda's hands shake so that he cannot open the door.*) Stoneturner, you do it. (*But his hands are shaking too much, too.*) Give it here. (*She opens the door.*)
DYNDA: I'm finished with this shit.
MILDA: Quite right.
VOICE IN THE CORRIDOR: What's up? A scandal? Who's having a go? Stop the row!
DYNDA: There's someone here who hasn't got a Residence Permit.
MILDA: Is that what you came here for?
DYNDA: Eh? (*Clicks his tongue*) After ten o'clock any kind of conversation in the corridor is not allowed, so you're breaking the regulations.
MILDA: There were scum ready to betray us in the civil war, and there are still some around, I see.
STONETURNER: Milda, shut the door.
MILDA: No need to lock it. He won't come back.
STONETURNER: We'll see. (*He picks up the book.*)
MILDA: The book came in handy. The State Publishing House is producing really useful stuff these days! Did he hurt you when he fell over? Never mind, go to sleep. (*Silence. Milda sits down with the book again. She mutters words from it.*) Chilean guano ... Chilean

guano ... hard wood ... hm hm ... leaves turned up ... Chilean ... contraceptive ... guano ...

STONETURNER: I wish I hadn't counted.

MILDA (*after a pause*): I can't concentrate any more. I'd better go to sleep. (*She turns out the light and lies down. After a little while*) Hey!

STONETURNER: Mm?

MILDA: Are you asleep?

STONETURNER: No.

MILDA: That fellow ... came here, disturbed me, talked about his problems, you know. He wanted to have sex, and I felt so squeamish.

STONETURNER: Try and understand ... he's a sexual neurotic.

MILDA: No, listen. I'm confused. What do you think? Is it normal for a woman to want a healthy baby?

STONETURNER: What do you mean, 'normal'? It ought to be normal. But today you can't tell. I mean, take what's happening now, in our life. It's complete chaos. People can't stop fornicating – they do it at any old time with any old partner, whenever they meet. You see it in the train, in the office, in the dormitory, wherever. But on the other hand, Milda, there are some native tribes in which newly-weds are not allowed to drink on the day of the wedding in case their children are abnormal. But in our country, it's just the opposite – on the day of the wedding, everybody gets filthy drunk. But then people are surprised that children of drug addicts, syphilitics, alcoholics, have less intelligence or are epileptic or suffer from all kinds of neuroses and allergies. I mean, take a large grain of wheat, or a huge cabbage – how do we get them? Look at the work we do on the pedigree of horses or dogs. We have to artificially inseminate the best specimens of the species.

MILDA: But is it normal to want a baby without wanting a husband?

STONETURNER: To hell with the husband! They only make problems! What would you say to this idea: that the State should give the best female specimens in the country the best sperm from a sperm bank, that it should encourage this kind of selective conception. Then when the children are born, the State takes them away and cares for them, so in the end it's engineered a new kind of human bloodstock.

MILDA: I'm not sure about that –

STONETURNER: It means the scientific control of the human being not only during its immaturity in school, not only during its birth, but even in its conception.

MILDA: Hang on a minute! Without a husband, you see, I want to have a baby – I don't want a husband or a family. But suppose I found a man and said to him: Give me a baby ... ?

STONETURNER: Fine. Go on.

MILDA: Would he refuse?

STONETURNER: Why the hell should he?

MILDA: That's what I'm asking.

STONETURNER: You tell me. I agree with you.

MILDA: Fool! I see, you're just mocking me.

STONETURNER: Me?

MILDA: Am I a woman or not?

STONETURNER: I never thought of it like that. (*He looks at her with new eyes. Suddenly he gets up, grabs his trousers, puts them on hastily and rushes from the room.*)

MILDA (*left alone, gets up anxiously, paces up and down tensely*) I want a baby! I want a baby! I want a baby!

SCENE SIX: SELECTING THE FATHER

Courtyard, with a large building at the back. At the bottom, what was formerly a night club is being worked on by builders, so it resembles a building site. There is also a small health centre. Foreman and two workers are on stage.

FOREMAN: Is everything out?
FIRST WORKER: Yes.
FOREMAN: And all the scaffolding's down?
FIRST WORKER: Yes.
FOREMAN: So it's all ready for demolition?
SECOND WORKER: Today?
FOREMAN: No, tomorrow.
FIRST WORKER What are they going to put up here?
FOREMAN: A Children's Home.
SECOND WORKER: What used to be here?
FOREMAN: A sort of whore house, dancing and that.
    (*They go out. Four cavalieros and their ladies enter.*)
FIRST CAV: Ladies and gentlemen, make haste.
SECOND CAV: Hurry up!
FIRST LADY: Come on, come on!
SECOND CAV: Rup-rup-rup!
SECOND LADY: How empty it is here now, how unwelcoming.
FIRST CAV: Welcoming – that's inside yourself.
FIRST LADY: Our poor little rendezvous.
FIRST CAV: This is a wake for our poor little rendezvous. From tomorrow
    it will cease to exist.
FIRST LADY: For ever.
FIRST CAV: Measures have been taken to eradicate such places.
FIRST LADY: What will they put in its place?
SECOND CAV: They're going to erect a State Children's Home here.

FIRST CAV: Or a so-called Mother's Co-operative.
FIRST LADY: A burial chamber!
SECOND LADY: Did they have to do this just for a Children's Home?
FIRST CAV: Okay, cut the cackle. Bring on the instruments.
SECOND LADY: We have no concert grand.
THIRD CAV: I watched them swinging the concert grand out of the window on a crane. It looked like a shiny victim hanging from a gallows. Its black top was so highly polished, you could see the trams running in the streets below in it.
FIRST CAV: We don't need a grand piano. We are grand enough ourselves. We're a whole orchestra. There are no lights. But there is cognac. And there are glasses. Here's good luck. Here's to the light!
(*They form an orchestra, and 'play' with their lips – 'Tootootootoo ...' They start dancing, and singing. On a workman's cradle above the window, Grinko and Yakov appear.*)
GRINKO: Look what's going on here. My God! Look at them. That tart's holding the guy's ear in her teeth. How can she? How can she?
YAKOV: Careful, you'll fall out. Keep still. Look at his fat red neck bulging over his collar. I'd love to give him a good slap. Bourgeois bastard!
GRINKO: Yes, the bourgeoisie! Intellectuals! This one's an accountant, that one over there's an actor. I've seen him in the club. And what about the tart? She's got stockings, silk stockings, on her legs. And can you see how she's clinging to him? They look like a four-legged animal with two arses. It's like the circus.
YAKOV: The foxtrot is prohibited in the Soviet Union. Isn't it? Give me a hand down, and I'll stop them.
GRINKO: Stay where you are. Don't be a hooligan.
YAKOV: Are you protecting bourgeois elements? You scum!
GRINKO: Don't get involved in a fight. They're not doing any harm. They pay their rent. Put the brick down. (*He raps Yakov's knuckles and tries to make him drop the brick.*)
YAKOV: Don't touch me, or – (*Grinko twists Yakov's arm, which is still holding the brick.*)
GRINKO (*over his shoulder*): Comrade foreman.
FOREMAN: What?
GRINKO: When can we demolish this sin shop?
FOREMAN: Tomorrow morning.
GRINKO: And if we work overtime – I've got a volunteer – can we start now?

FOREMAN: Yes.
GRINKO: Starting with the ceiling.
YAKOV: Blast the ceiling. I want to get the bourgeois.
GRINKO: There's no need for that. You can start demolishing the building now, though, if you want to. Begin with the ceiling.
YAKOV: I want to get the bourgeois.
GRINKO: Shut up. You've got much more important work to do. Okay?
YAKOV: You're cunning, you are, brother.
> (*He shouts to the cradle operator. They clamber out of the cradle through the window into the room. At the height of the cavalieros' and ladies' shimmy, the men start demolishing the ceiling. The plaster begins to fall. Yakov eyes the chandelier. The dancing couples scatter in a panic.*)

GRINKO: Sorry, citizens, it's urgent. This is reconstruction work, to be done as quick as possible. Sorry to disturb you.
> (*The dancers shout their protests. Yakov carries on demolishing the ceiling.*)

YAKOV: Hey, brother, this is good wood, and good stucco work.
GRINKO: Use this lantern, direct the light into the corner. Ugh, there are rats here. (*Imitating a drill.*) Dadadada. (*The couples flee.*)
YAKOV (*shining the lamp in the corner*): They've had enough. Too draughty, or too greedy.
GRINKO: And what'd have happened if you'd thrown the brick? If you'd spoiled one of their dresses, it'd have cost you about twenty-five roubles. One of their shirts would have been about ten. For your disorderly behaviour you'd probably have been fined five roubles. What a loss that would've been to the workers' state.
YAKOV: Yes – twenty-five plus ten plus five equals forty.
GRINKO: Right.
BOTH (*drilling*): Dadadada.
> (*Milda enters and walks towards the health centre.*)

MILDA: Doctor.
SOFTER: Yes.
MILDA: Do you recognize me?
SOFTER: Yes.
MILDA: I came to see you.
SOFTER: Yes, the doctor you saw told me about you.
MILDA: So you know I'm looking for a father for my baby.

SOFTER: I do know.
MILDA: And can you help me?
SOFTER: I will. Er, we can talk about it.
MILDA: Okay.
SOFTER: When? And where?
MILDA: Well, can you help me find a strong worker?
SOFTER: A worker?
MILDA: I don't want an intellectual for the father of my baby.
SOFTER: Oh. As you wish.

(*Milda and Dr Softer make for where the building workers are.*)

GRINKO: Did you see how those couples ran?
YAKOV: Yes, the men skedaddled first, and left their whores to follow them! Scum!
GRINKO: Don't shout like that.
YAKOV: I'm not. But don't you see how I feel about it? When you walk down the street, it's like walking down a big bedroom with all these women with their tight skirts so you can see their arses. And they have those fucking pink silk stockings on. And have you seen their lips? All smeared with kissing. You know what gets me about all this, too? None of them'll ever go with me. Not one of them. They'll only go to bed with you if you've got plenty of money. And I get to feel so damned sexed off, especially when one's walking in front wiggling her hips. And you get a sniff of that beautiful perfume, and you know they've got powder on. Yes, if I ever got hold of one like that she'd never get away from me, I can tell you.
MILDA: Not a hooligan, mind.
SOFTER: No no, I'm only taking you to the kind of person you're looking for.
MILDA: Which one?
SOFTER: Either would probably make a good stud.
MILDA: Comrade.
GRINKO: Me?
MILDA: Yes, you and your comrade.
GRINKO: Yakov.
YAKOV: Grin, you can have a go at this now.
GRINKO: Hang on a minute.
YAKOV: What's up?
GRINKO: Come down here.

MILDA: Hello, comrades. Can I speak to you for a minute?

YAKOV: It's not a very good moment, but go on.

MILDA: Your parents, are they peasants or workers?

GRINKO (*mockingly*): And what did they do before 1917? And if you didn't participate in the revolution, why not?

YAKOV: Is it some kind of questionnaire?

MILDA: No, I need it for myself.

GRINKO: For one of the papers.

MILDA: No.

GRINKO: For some kind of report?

MILDA: Well, something like that.

GRINKO: My grandfather was a peasant, my father was a low grade priest. But this guy – his father and grandfather were workers at the Putilov steel works.

MILDA: Just one other question: is there anybody in your family who suffers from alcoholism?

YAKOV: I think my granddad used to drink a bit.

GRINKO: My people were all Old Believers.

MILDA: Er, any of them have syphilis?

GRINKO: In my family! (*He waves his hands to indicate that the very question is a joke.*)

(*Enter a post van driven by Lipa.*)

LIPA: Oi, watch out there!

GRINKO: Careful! (*He pulls Milda out of the way, while Yakov jumps clear.*)

YAKOV: Lipa, you idiot! You could have killed us. Have you gone mad?

LIPA: Be ready, and watch out. If you're like that at work, what good are you going to be later?

GRINKO: He deserved it. You should have heard him running down women just a minute ago.

YAKOV: Have you got any more questions?

MILDA: Could you just hang on another moment? (*She goes to Dr Softer.*)

LIPA: Who's she?

GRINKO: Some kind of commissar woman. She's pretty serious. She's interested in us.

LIPA: Watch out, Yakov.

YAKOV: Okay.

MILDA: Doctor, which do you think would be more suitable, the cautious one or the one who couldn't care less?
SOFTER: Depends what the mother's like.
MILDA: She's pretty level-headed, pedantic even.
SOFTER: If the mother wants the child to be even more level-headed and pedantic, then –
MILDA: No no, she doesn't.
SOFTER: Then you'd better choose the one who jumped over the rails.
MILDA: Thank you, Doctor. (*Milda goes to Yakov.*)
GRINKO: I'm out of luck here. Let down by my priestly ancestor.
MILDA (*to Yakov*): You're one hundred per cent proletarian?
YAKOV: Well, I'm not really. That's not quite true.
MILDA: What do you mean?
YAKOV: Well, my father was a gang leader, not just a worker.
MILDA: But at least he wasn't an intellectual?
YAKOV: No, he certainly wasn't that.
MILDA: Comrade, I'd like to ask you a favour. We can't talk it over here. Anyway, you've got work to do. I wonder whether you could call on me tonight?
YAKOV: I'm no good at talking. You have some kind of job in mind for me, do you?
MILDA: Could you make it between ten and eleven?
YAKOV: Okay, I'll try.
MILDA: It's just here, in this block, room 32. See you, comrades.
GRINKO: Comrade.
MILDA: Yes?
GRINKO: You know who my great great grandfather was? A robber.
MILDA: Ah. Very interesting.
GRINKO: But not very relevant for you?
MILDA: No.
GRINKO (*goes back to his work*): Eh well, our grannies were very interesting. (*To Yakov*) Shift the girder a bit to the left, will you? Hey, give us a hand. What are you doing?
YAKOV: You told me to come down, and now you're telling me off cause I'm not up there.
(*He climbs up again.*)
LIPA (*returns*): Yakov, see you tonight in the park?
YAKOV: I don't know, don't ask me. I'll come when I can.

SCENE SEVEN: THE CONCEPTION

Milda's room. Milda enters with a parcel.

MILDA: Ten to nine already. Uh uh.
    (*Angelica enters.*)
ANGELICA: Milda.
MILDA: Mm?
ANGELICA: Don't get changed.
MILDA: Why?
ANGELICA: You've got to go out. Come on, I'll tell you about it on the way.
MILDA: Where?
ANGELICA: You've got to go out. I have to bring you dead or alive. An unexpected American visitor is giving a paper.
MILDA: Really?
ANGELICA: Yes. We had no notice.
MILDA: I'm not coming. (*She starts to wash her face.*)
ANGELICA: Milda, you're mad.
MILDA: I'm not coming.
ANGELICA: It's not as though it's far away.
MILDA: Well, I haven't received any notification.
ANGELICA: You're a real bureaucrat.
MILDA: I'm busy.
ANGELICA: You've only just come in. Okay, come twenty minutes late.
MILDA (*referring to her own business*): I'm late already, I can't afford to be any later.
ANGELICA: Please, Milda, come on.
MILDA: Sorry, I can't. You go instead of me. As a favour.
ANGELICA: No. I've been at work since first light. I'm tired. I'm not going anywhere on my own.

MILDA: Comrade Angelica, I beg you. I'll explain everything you have to do there.
ANGELICA: No, I'm exhausted. Besides, I want to eat. Oh, you've got some nosh here. Can I? Is it sausage? Cheese? (*She sniffs the packet.*) Smells of the chemist. Milda?
MILDA: Leave it alone! Do you hear? Leave it alone!
ANGELICA: What is it? Why are you shouting?
MILDA: I'm not shouting, I'm just asking you not to touch that.
ANGELICA: I thought it was something to eat, but it's –
MILDA: Please. If you want something to eat, there's food in the cupboard. Just take something, comrade Angelica. Then I ask you to leave. I have no time.
ANGELICA: Oh? Piss off, in other words?
MILDA: Why be so unpleasant? I didn't say that. I just said politely that I was busy. I'm expecting guests.
ANGELICA: I'm tired. Could I take forty winks here behind the screen?
MILDA: No, Angelica, it's not convenient.
ANGELICA: Not convenient? I don't understand. (*A knock on the door.*)
MILDA: Come in. (*Yakov enters.*)
YAKOV: Hello. Here I am. Am I late?
MILDA: No, you're just in time. Please meet –
YAKOV: I came straight here from the building site. I haven't even washed my hands.
MILDA: Well, there's a basin. Do it here if you want, comrade.
YAKOV: Your communal kitchen is filled with women, all making one hell of a noise.
MILDA: Comrade Angelica, it'll be very remiss of you not to attend that event in the club.
ANGELICA (*as if she hasn't heard*): Comrade, why do you speak of the women's noise so spitefully?
YAKOV: Spitefully? I'm just a simple bloke, but they make so much noise you can hear it from outside. You know, women's noise.
ANGELICA: You're a bit anti-women, then, are you, comrade?
YAKOV: How should I speak about them, then?
ANGELICA: You don't need to be so snooty about them. Haven't you ever needed a better way to treat women? Like, if you had a woman in your –
YAKOV: You're talking about love now, eh?

ANGELICA: Um, love, if you like. But do you treat a woman tenderly then?

MILDA: Comrade Angelica, you promised me.

ANGELICA: I did nothing of the sort.

MILDA: Well, I'm asking you now, please –

ANGELICA: But it's much more interesting to me to carry on this conversation with the comrade here.

MILDA: Comrade Angelica.

ANGELICA: Okay. Finish what you have to do with this comrade. I can wait. Then we can leave together and I can carry on with him. Okay?

YAKOV: Fine. With pleasure. (*To Milda*) Did you want me to answer some questions?

MILDA: I need you a little longer than that, comrade.

ANGELICA: Carry on, I've got plenty of time. (*To Yakov*) So you think it's acceptable to treat women so off-handedly?

MILDA (*to Angelica*): You think it should be different?

ANGELICA: Actually, I can't understand why people have to create so many problems, why they have to make things so awkward in their relationships. They should be much lighter, much less serious, more casual.

MILDA: Oh, it's casual and light-hearted, is it? That sounds like a good approach. But the trouble is that kind of approach usually leads to unwanted consequences.

ANGELICA: Comrade Milda, what's wrong with you tonight?

MILDA: When you had gonorrhoea, was that the result of one of these light-hearted, casual affairs?

ANGELICA: You're out of your mind, I got rid of it! What's up with you? How dare you! In front of this comrade!

MILDA: Why shouldn't he hear that? You want to look at things more light-heartedly and casually.

ANGELICA: You're jealous. This is stupid. You could just tell me straight out.

MILDA: I've been telling you for the last half hour.

ANGELICA: Hmm. This is a case of still waters running deep. Down with romance, eh, down with romance. But it's a bit different when it's in your own little place. Gonorrhea. Bitch! (*She goes out.*)

MILDA: Hold your tongue, Angelica! (*Milda falls silent and looks towards Yakov.*)
YAKOV: She got you annoyed all right.
MILDA: Not at all. I just couldn't organise what I wanted to say, and I felt you wanted to be off.
YAKOV: I've only got half an hour.
MILDA: It won't take more than that.
YAKOV: It's just that I promised a comrade I'd meet her in the park.
MILDA: What do you like doing? Going for a drink?
YAKOV: No, I don't drink. I like listening to music. Or going to the films. Actually you were asking about my grandfather. On the way here, I was thinking about him. Do you know he was so strong physically that he was a wrestler in the circus. Then in the end he went off his rocker somehow.
MILDA: Mentally unbalanced?
YAKOV: Not really. Just uncontrollable.
MILDA: Ill?
YAKOV: Not exactly that. He wasn't ill. How should I put it? He had a surplus of health. His wife was, you know, not very faithful to him, and one day he had an absolute fit and grabbed her, and after that she couldn't get up for a long time. Well, he was put in a straightjacket. I remember it, it had huge long sleeves. And you, comrade, are you a writer?
MILDA: No.
YAKOV: On my way here I was trying to think what else I could tell you about my grandfather. Are you getting together material for some kind of a report?
MILDA: I think I can explain it to you now, comrade. Will you listen carefully, please. I'm not a very good speaker, but it's rather a difficult thing anyway.
A VOICE: Citizen, there's someone for you at the door.
MILDA: Have a heart. Please, will you open the door, and say I'm not in. (*To Yakov*) Um, you know what's going on in our country now, all this national construction? You know we're setting up co-operatives, and building schools, hospitals, everything to improve people's lives?
VOICE: They don't believe you. It's somebody from the club, saying they know you're here. They've been sent by your friend.

MILDA: Close the door. Forget them. They'll soon go away. All the same, I'll lock this door. (*She does so.*)

YAKOV: You're very busy.

MILDA: Yes. Now, where did I get to? Yes, that's right. You see, comrade, I don't know how to put it simply, but you know we support all kinds of production. You know, factories produce goods, and farms produce, er, vegetables, and of course there is reproduction as well. That is, when people participate in the reproduction process, or to put it more simply, when they give birth to children.

YAKOV: Yes, I see.

MILDA: But when production isn't properly planned, the results can be rather low grade quality. And when you don't properly plan the reproduction of human beings, you get poor quality people. For example, children of sickly parents are usually rather weak. From drunkards we get mentally retarded children. And from mentally retarded parents, we get children with suicidal tendencies.

YAKOV: Yes, I see.

MILDA: And more than this, you take the family. Quite often, the in-laws bring up the child, and quite often very badly, in accordance with their own ideas and make the child into exactly what they are themselves.

ANOTHER VOICE: Citizeness! I think a letter was delivered here when it should have come to me in E 42.

MILDA: Leave me alone, please. I don't know anything about a letter.

VOICE: Oh, I see. You speak to me politely when you want me to go to the door for you, but when it's me wants you, then you change your tune.

MILDA: Sorry. I'm busy. (*A silence. Somewhere a baby can be heard crying.*) Listen. Crying. It's probably got a tummy ache.

YAKOV: No, it's probably just after a bit of tit. That's all babies are interested in.

MILDA: Yes. And that brings me to what I wanted to say, comrade. I, comrade, want to have a baby, but I want it to be a special baby. I need a father who's healthy and strong, and of course one who comes from the working class. Well?

YAKOV: Mm, yes, I get it. Not a bad idea.

MILDA: Yes. So – would you agree to be the father?

YAKOV: Me? Father?

MILDA: You. Father.

YAKOV: You must be out of your mind, comrade.

MILDA: I'm absolutely normal.

YAKOV: First of all, comrade, I already have, er, how shall I put it, a woman. And I'll probably go with her to the registry office. It's what I want. You want a bit of a fling, eh, but I'd have to pay for it.

MILDA: Comrade, wait a minute. You haven't heard the details yet. Sometimes with a woman it's as if something took her by the throat, she can't even concentrate on her job properly. I don't want a husband, I just want a baby. It's not you yourself I need, it's your function – as a male. As for me, I'm absolutely healthy, I even have a doctor's note here, dated yesterday. So you won't be taking any risks, you won't get any diseases from me. And I'm not going to interfere with your relationship with another woman. And there's no obligation on your side, there won't be any maintenance money to pay, I've taken care of all those problems. I've got a document here where I state that I have no claims on you whatsoever. In other words, to cut it short, the idea is for you to come here regularly till the doctor confirms I'm pregnant, and after that we'll just part – no claims on each other, no responsibilities towards each other.

YAKOV: I understand you, comrade. But why me? There are plenty of guys around.

MILDA: I've been looking for a long time, comrade. You see, I needed a man who was not only healthy and strong himself, but his father and grandfather were, too.

YAKOV: Oh, so that's why you were asking about my granddad?

MILDA: Yes. Besides, I wanted my baby's father to be one hundred per cent proletarian.

YAKOV: Well, you should have chosen Grinko. He took a shine to you.

MILDA: Ah, but he'd be more cautious than you are. And I'm cautious, too. And cautiousness multiplied by cautiousness gives a multi-cautious product.

YAKOV: So it's got to be me who's the father?

MILDA: Yes, you.

YAKOV: This is amazing! You're really odd! (*He laughs.*)

MILDA: Comrade, you still think I'm joking, don't you?

YAKOV: Some joke! You're an odd woman! No, stop kidding me!

MILDA: Comrade, I'm quite serious. I'm not going to repeat it. I think you understand it perfectly well.
YAKOV: Oh yes, I understand it okay.
MILDA: So – what?
YAKOV: What what?
MILDA: Do you agree?
YAKOV: Look, I don't get it. There's some kind of muddle.
MILDA: There's no muddle. You're going to stay here tonight.
YAKOV: Tonight?
MILDA: Why not?
YAKOV: Look, it doesn't make sense. How can you just set about making babies like that?
MILDA: What's the problem?
YAKOV: I don't know how to say it, comrade.
MILDA: I know, I'm not an attractive woman.
YAKOV: Why not attractive? A wench is a wench.
MILDA: I'm not a wench, I'm a woman.
YAKOV: Well, okay, a lass is a lass.
MILDA: So what's the problem?
YAKOV: Well, er, how can I put it? It's just that, well, I haven't got the appetite for it.
MILDA: I see.
YAKOV: Well, you know, when people are attracted to each other, they go mad, it all happens – I don't know, music, a good time. But here, it's like I was in a courtroom.
MILDA: I know. I thought of that. Just a minute, please, comrade. (*She goes behind the screen. Yakov fidgets uncomfortably.*) What's your name, by the way?
YAKOV: Yakov. Yakov Nikitich Kichkin. What's yours?
MILDA: Milda.
YAKOV: That's not a Russian name.
MILDA: I'm Latvian.
YAKOV: Ah. They're good snipers, Latvians. Good workers, too. They don't hide from work. No. They've got plenty of stamina for work, too. (*Walking up and down.*) Comrade.
MILDA: Yes?
YAKOV: Comrade. Look, you know what I think? It's not right, this, what you're thinking about. I mean, first of all, I feel a swine to

Olympia – Lipa, you know. And then, I don't know what you take me for. What do you think I am? – some kind of stallion? – some kind of buck? It's okay for you, but I don't want to.

MILDA: Comrade, just a minute.

YAKOV: What am I waiting for? We're not going to agree. I've got to go, comrade. I'm sorry. Could you open the door, please? You've got the key, comrade.

MILDA: Just wait.

YAKOV: But I don't want to wait. Give me the key. I'm off. I've got to go. Bye!

MILDA Stay! (*Somebody knocks on the door. Milda dashes to it, knocking the screen down as she does so. She is changed – her hair looks permed, she's wearing make-up and a low-necked dress.*) Who do you want?

LIPA (*outside*): Is Kichkin there? Yakov Kichkin?

(*Yakov makes a sign to Milda, urging her not to give him away.*)

MILDA: No no.

LIPA: You're lying. He is there!

MILDA: Nobody's here.

LIPA: Open the door.

MILDA: I won't.

LIPA: Yakov, I heard your voice. Answer me. You promised you'd see me in the park. I've been waiting there a bloody hour. Yakov! Where are you? Will you answer?

MILDA: Comrade, nobody's here.

LIPA: I don't believe you. You watch it, Yakov! Okay, stay there, okay!

(*She goes away. A long pause. Yakov stares at Milda.*)

YAKOV: Bloody hell! What a change!

MILDA: You mean her?

YAKOV: No, you. Where've you come from?

MILDA: Where've I come from? The hairdresser's, the perfume shop ... Yakov!

YAKOV: Ah.

MILDA: Come here. Don't think of anything else. Listen – you're strong, you've got nice eyes. We're bound to have a good baby between us.

YAKOV: You're okay. I like your hands, they're strong.

MILDA: Yes, and I'm going to hold the baby with them.

YAKOV: You're a funny woman. You don't know how to use make-up properly, your lips are all smudged.

MILDA: I'm going to sing lullabies to our little chucky baby.
YAKOV: Mm, you have good breasts, firm.
MILDA: They'll produce sweet milk for the little chucky baby.
YAKOV: Your hips are big.
MILDA: There's enough room for a baby inside me. You'll give me a good baby, Yakov.
YAKOV: Closer, come closer.
MILDA: Turn off the light.
   (*He puts out the light.*)

* * *

OLD WOMAN (*walks purposefully*): I won't die, I won't die, till I've seen what's going on here, what all this fornication's about. Number 32. They say it's along the corridor. She's said to have seduced just about everyone in the whole house. No, I won't die ... I've got to see this. I won't die, not till I've seen how these Bolsheviks fornicate. (*She enters the construction site.*)
WORKER (*from scaffolding*): Take care! Eh, granny, take care.
OLD WOMAN: Where are these bastard Bolsheviks fornicating round here?
WORKER: There are no bastards here. It's a construction site. Take care.
OLD WOMAN: Well, my neighbour told me ...
WORKER: Be careful. You could get killed here. Get away from the construction site.

SCENE EIGHT: VITRIOL

Milda's room. Yakov, with a few nails in his mouth, is hanging up a curtain and singing softly.

YAKOV:　　Our women in the health resorts
　　　　　　Get larger round the girth;
　　　　　　When they come back, you find out why:
　　　　　　They'll all be giving birth.
　　　　(Lipa enters quietly, stands in the doorway. Her hand is in her pocket. Thinking she is Milda, Yakov carries on without turning round.)
　　　　You see how nice it is with the curtain up. Your room always looked to me like the inside of a garage – no curtains, nothing, all bare. And by the way, I've mended the side of the bed, too. And I've made the table legs level, so it won't wobble any more. So there you are, comrade Milda – I've made your place comfortable and liveable-in. See?

LIPA: Yes, I see.

YAKOV: Lipa.

LIPA: Well?

YAKOV: Bloody hell! What are you doing here?

LIPA: That doesn't matter. Is the citizen who lives here in?

YAKOV: What do you want?

LIPA: I've brought a Recorded Delivery for her.

YAKOV: Put it on the table. She'll be here in a minute.

LIPA: Yes, but it needs her signature.

YAKOV: I can sign it.

LIPA: No – we can't trust the signatures of liars or deceitful people.

YAKOV: Listen, Lipa …

LIPA: Excuse me, citizen, would you mind not calling me Lipa? Just carry on with what you're doing. Where did those curtains come from? They say there are lovely bed clothes, too, in Smolensky Market.

And have you got a chamber pot? Oh, and by the way, do take care of your key – we wouldn't want any old person coming in in the middle of the night, would we?

YAKOV: Lipa, stop being a fool.

LIPA: Who's a fool? Who told me – 'Come at ten o'clock'? And who was hiding with the door locked? And who spent a whole fortnight avoiding me? Tell me.

YAKOV: It's not that important.

LIPA: Of course – what's important is who's got a room and who hasn't. She's got a room – though without curtains, of course.

YAKOV: Please, Lipa, don't. (*He tries to take her hand which is in her pocket.*)

LIPA: Get your hands off! Do you hear? Get your hands off! I'll scream! Get away!

YAKOV: Why are you being like this to me? Am I different?

LIPA: You're different to me. You're like a used stamp – somebody else has licked you! You weren't addressed to me. And the children'll have a different address, too. (*Milda enters.*)

YAKOV: Lipa.

MILDA: Yes.

LIPA: Ah, citizen, I've got a Recorded Delivery for your signature.

MILDA: Yes? Thanks.

LIPA: But him ...

MILDA: What?

LIPA: You can get without a signature.

MILDA (*looks at her carefully*): Hold on, comrade. Didn't I see you on the construction site?

LIPA: You may have seen plenty of people on the construction site.

MILDA: You think he's my husband?

LIPA: Oh no – he's your nephew. Or is it your grandfather?

MILDA: He's not my husband.

LIPA: Well, lover.

MILDA: And not my lover.

LIPA: Ah, he's come about the wallpapering – or to polish the floors ...

MILDA: He's the father of my baby.

LIPA: So he's not your husband.

MILDA: Certainly not. We made an agreement about a temporary liaison. It was for a fixed term – in a few days he'll leave me.

LIPA: He hasn't been a very successful stud, then?
YAKOV: Eh, eh!
LIPA: I'm not a brood mare. I've cried my eyes out because of you, so hold your tongue.
MILDA: Comrade, this is just absurd.
LIPA: Absurd! It's absurd to steal someone else's bloke and go to bed with him yourself? Not unlocking the door to me when he was here, that's not absurd?
MILDA: Comrade, this is just blind jealousy, it should be beneath us.
LIPA: Blind, am I? No, I'm not blind. But you will be blind!
MILDA: Calm down, comrade.
LIPA: Absurd! Lying! And you dare to laugh at me! You get stuffed, you dirty cunt! (*The hand in her pocket is trembling, and vitriol, is dripping out of it.*)
YAKOV: Lipa! Something's dripping.
LIPA: You dirty dog, keep away. I'll leave my mark here, I'll stamp your eyes. (*She takes out her hand.*)
YAKOV: Lipa!
LIPA: There! (*She splashes vitriol. Yakov manages to grab her by the hand so the vitriol splashes on the curtain. Only a drop lands on Milda.*)
YAKOV: Wipe it carefully. Don't smear it.
LIPA (*furiously*): Okay. Don't arrest me. I'll go myself. (*She tries to open a bottle of ammonia.*) I'll finish myself off without your help.
MILDA: She's going to poison herself. (*She throws herself on Lipa.*)
LIPA: Get away! Don't touch me! Don't dare! Don't dare! (*Milda holds Lipa's hands.*) This time you win, I'll get even with you. (*She spits in Milda's face.*) I don't want to be here. Don't touch me! I've got to get out. Let me go! Let me go, go, go! (*She is hysterical.*)
VOICES (*in the doorway*): – They're fighting!
  – Who killed who?
  – I'll call the police.
STRIPES'S VOICE: When I was in England ...
YAKOV: Give her some valerian drops.
MILDA: I haven't got any.
VOICES: – It's in the First Aid kit.
  – Carry her there.
  – Stop the show!

(*Milda and Yakov take Lipa out. She is still in hysterics. The crowd of neighbours burst into Milda's room. They mill about.*)

VOICES: – Look, this is her room.
- Her briefcase. She's a Party member.
- Lenin's works.
- (*reading the title of a book*) 'Mother and Baby'. Ah ha.
- A sausage. Look. Smoked sausages.
- To treat her fellow.
- A revolver. Take care of that revolver.
- She probably hasn't got a licence for it.
- It squeaks. (*About the bed.*)
- The blanket's threadbare. What about the pillow?
- The sheets haven't been washed for weeks.
- They probably still show where she had her last screw.
- Here's a bag.
- Dirty linen. Look. Her bra.
- Yes yes. And here – a box of powder, and a powder puff.
- And a bottle of scent. Violets. Hee hee.
- Would you believe it? Violets! And lipstick too!
- She's soliciting. It's obvious.
- This is her nightie.
- Have you found any of the fitter's underwear?
- Here it is. Here it is. It's here.
- An electric point. For boiling water.
- But this is supposed to be available for everybody.
- She's stealing electricity.
- What do you expect? She's got to make tea for her man.
- She'll have to answer for that.

STRIPES: When I was in England – this kind of lady was thrown out.

MILDA (*entering*): Citizens, have I invited you in here? (*She grabs the revolver, points it at them.*) Stand back from the door! Put everything back. You forgot the nightie. Tidy the bed. Put it back. Everything back where it goes.

A VOICE: – I'm not going to.
- It's against the rules of the House Association.
- You've got no right.
- You haven't got a private meter, but you're using electricity.

MILDA (*pointing the revolver*): All of you, stand in a line. Don't push each other. Now – run! One, two, three! (*They run out, one after another. During this, Yakov enters.*) Why aren't you with her?
YAKOV: They didn't let me anywhere near her. There were so many women there, and they wouldn't let me get to her. They were all talking together. Dynda or somebody is talking to her now. Never mind.
MILDA: Yakov, that's impossible. She's bad, her nerves are completely shattered.
YAKOV: But she tried to splatter vitriol in your face.
MILDA: You must take care of her. (*She starts muttering numbers.*)
YAKOV: What are you counting?
MILDA: At the end of the month, I usually have ten roubles left out of my salary, sometimes less. And now I've got to start getting things ready for the baby.
YAKOV: What baby?
MILDA: My baby. Have you forgotten? All that row was because of this baby.
YAKOV: Never mind the row.
MILDA: And out of my ten roubles, I've got to give something for Lipa, so she can get a doctor.
YAKOV: Why the hell should you do that?
MILDA: I feel myself responsible for her hysterics. I should have known, and stopped it happening.
YAKOV: She wouldn't take money from you.
MILDA: No, but you will. You'll buy whatever she needs, and take her to the doctor.
YAKOV: I have my own money for that. Don't be so petty.
MILDA: Go home. These scandals are no good for anybody.
YAKOV: Okay.
MILDA: You can come again ... (*She looks in her diary.*) ... the day after tomorrow.
(*Yakov goes out. The hysterics heard outside come closer and closer. Milda dashes to lock her door. But the key is not there. She rushes about, looking for it. Enter Stoneturner with a whirligig. He makes the noise of hysterics.*)
STONETURNER: It sounds very real.
MILDA: What? That's Lipa.
STONETURNER: No, it came from the window, didn't it?

MILDA: That was you, Stoneturner.
STONETURNER: Me? But listen. And the illusion is complete.
MILDA: You're mad.
STONETURNER: I took a bet. I was told that true hysteria could only be performed when you were really overwrought, and your nerves absolutely taut. Otherwise you can't reproduce hysterics. But I said you could. Who's right? Only listen.
MILDA: Stoneturner, tell me, what sort of a background do you come from?
STONETURNER: Very mixed, Milda. There are five nations in my blood which took part in the construction of me. I have 50 per cent Ukrainian blood – that's where I get my musicality from; 25% Russian – which gives me my Tartar wildness; 12 and a half per cent Tartar – which gives me my Great Russian obstinacy; 6 and a quarter per cent German blood – that's where my diplomatic skills come from; and 6 and a quarter per cent gypsy – which is where my originality comes from.
MILDA: Stoneturner, you know what? You could develop for me, instead of that stupid noise you produced, something like an electric rattle that'll make a two month old baby laugh and giggle. Can you do that?
STONETEURNER: I can.

SCENE NINE: A FATHER IS UNNECESSARY

Milda is sitting in her room, very tired. There is medicine on the table. Yakov dashes in with a pram.

YAKOV: Milda. You look really down.
MILDA: Yakov, how many times have I told you - they can't get me down?
YAKOV: Has there been another row? Did they swear at you, comrade? Please don't say they can't hurt you.
MILDA: If they'd hurt me I'd have gone to Court, don't worry about that. But look – I'm sitting here in my room.
YAKOV: Your face is as pale as whitewash. I can smell valerian drops. You're pretending. Aren't you?
MILDA: It's the baby, Yakov.
YAKOV: What's the baby?
MILDA: The baby is here.
YAKOV: That's just you. Eh? What a tale! When?
MILDA: I'm pregnant.
YAKOV: So I guessed right, (*He points to the pram.*) Look. I was going through Sukharyovka – it was standing there. It's as good as a bus. The wheels will last fifteen years. It's brand new, and look how well made. And you've got the baby to go in it?
MILDA: Yes.
YAKOV: Oh, fantastic. Just imagine! (*Fantasizing*) Here he is. Ask him – how are you, little one? Please, comrade baby, get your toes out of your mouth. Look, comrade baby, birds in the big sky. We're pushing the pram along the street. Clear the way, citizens, please, here comes comrade baby! He's coming up the street. You, old woman, please give way. A new citizen is here. Cars, stop! Make way! Comrade son, don't cry, we'll cross the road okay. Policeman, please clear the way for us. Hold up your truncheon. Stop, bus.

Stop, motorbike. A new citizen is on his way. (*He takes Milda in his arms.*) Milda!

MILDA: Yakov, don't life me, please.

YAKOV: I'm not lifting you, I'm lifting my baby. What are you? You're only the packaging. You're wrapping paper. You're wrapping paper. You're wrapping paper, wrapping paper, wrapping paper. Hold tight! We've done it!

MILDA: Put me down! You bastard! (*He puts her down.*) Well, Yakov, thank you very much.

YAKOV: For what?

MILDA: You worked for it too.

YAKOV: What's that mean? You make it sound as if I'd been building something.

MILDA: Do you think it was easy? I'm knocked out with tiredness and worry.

YAKOV: What are you worrying about?

MILDA: Well, you, but you can keep an eye on your own life now. And me I was worrying about – will I have a period, or no period? – period, no period? – Now it's clear. So – once again, thanks very much, Yakov. You can go now.

YAKOV: Okay. I'll see you this evening.

MILDA: No, there's no need. There's no need for you to come back.

YAKOV: What? There's no need? I don't understand.

MILDA: It's obvious. We agreed.

YAKOV: Agreed what?

MILDA: That when the baby was conceived our relationship would come to an end, and we wouldn't have any claim on each other.

YAKOV: What? No claims?

MILDA: Yes. No claims.

YAKOV: Well, am I his father or not?

MILDA: You are.

YAKOV: Then I have rights.

MILDA: None whatsoever. When the baby's born, I may show it to you. But you have no rights whatsoever.

YAKOV: Ah, so I've done my job. It's all done now. I'm just a bloody stud. A few fucks, that's it. Yes?

MILDA: Yakov, don't get so cross. (*Voices are heard off stage.*) Here she is again. Let her in, let her in.

YAKOV: Don't be stupid! It's on my head – (*Lipa is in the doorway.*)
MILDA (*to Lipa*): He won't go.
LIPA: Please, darling. (*Hearing laughter in the crowd, she turns to them.*) What's funny?
A VOICE: Watch it – you don't live here.
YAKOV: You watch it ... (*Yakov grabs the pram as if about to hit someone with it. Milda intercepts him.*)
MILDA: Comrade, please stop it. I'll have to pay. You can't behave like that.
YAKOV: Goodbye. (*He goes quickly, taking Lipa by the hand and leaving with her.*) Come on, Lipka. (*They go. Milda feels sick. She is restless. Then the Lad and Ivan Baran enter.*)
LAD: Hello. I came to town to get a white doe, so I thought I'd call on you. He came, too. I couldn't get rid of him. So he's here as well.
IVAN BARAN: I've got things to do, too. Look. Gherkins.
MILDA: They're early.
IVAN BARAN: From the greenhouse. But the Ermilovs ...
LAD: ... Cabbages planted on some peat.
IVAN BARAN: Just taste it. Go on, have a taste. It's delicious.
LAD: Comrade agronomist, look. I did the breeding by selection, and they're all the same. (*He shows his baby rabbits.*)
IVAN BARAN: You should come back and see.
MILDA: How far have you got with the mechanisation now?
IVAN BARAN: Oh, some bloody kulak wants to take all our farm machinery for himself.[103]
LAD: But we're not going to let him have it.
MILDA: Have you repaired the seeding machine?
IVAN BARAN: No, it's still at the smithy.
LAD: We shall get it mended.
IVAN BARAN: You must come and see us. I'll give you plenty of milk – look at you, you look as if your face had been whitewashed.
LAD: Yes, we'll cure you.
IVAN BARAN: Listen, I've got something to boast about. (*He takes out a small piglet.*) Yorkshire!
MILDA: What a beauty!

---

103   *Kulak*: Kulaks were rich peasants accused of standing in the way of collectivisation.

IVAN BARAN (*to the Lad*): It's better than what you've got.
MILDA: What's his name?
IVAN BARAN: Yes. I've called him Peasant's Moneybox. I know it's a bit long, but it's a very honourable name.
LAD: It's a bit like Ivan Evseyevich Baran, isn't it?
IVAN BARAN: Shut it, you. When he gets a bit bigger, I'm going to show him.
MILDA: You'll get a gold medal for him.
LAD: So long. I'll call another time.
MILDA: Please do.
IVAN BARAN (*in the doorway*): And if he gets a gold medal, who should wear it – him or me?
MILDA: Who do you want to?
IVAN BARAN: Me! Then everyone would know. Should Ivan Baran promote a pig to the status of a human being? Why the hell should a pig wear a medal? He's not responsible for the fact that he turned out such a fine specimen.
MILDA: True.
LAD: We could argue about that. I don't agree. Let's go on about it.
   (*They go. Yakov, drunk, enters.*)
YAKOV: Aha!
MILDA: What's up with you?
YAKOV: Yes, with me. Am I the father or not?
MILDA: Yakov, go now.
YAKOV: You don't want to say. Right, now listen to me. I know why you kicked me out. Because you found another bloke. Listen, I don't want anybody else looking after my son.
MILDA: You're drunk.
YAKOV: So what if I am drunk? It wasn't on your money. You get out now. I'm going to sleep here tonight.
MILDA: Yakov, don't be funny.
YAKOV: It's my baby. I'm its owner. Give me the baby back. I'll cut you up.
MILDA: Yakov, don't touch the baby!
YAKOV: I'll kill you!
MILDA: Yakov! Don't!
YAKOV: Agh! (*He kicks her in the stomach.*)
MILDA: Yakov! (*She hits him on the head with her revolver. Yakov falls down.*)
LIPA (*in the doorway*): You've killed him.

MILDA: My baby. He kicked it.
LIPA: Help. Let's put him on the bed. Give him the smelling salts. We'd better bandage his forehead.
MILDA (*gives her a cloth.*): You can tear that up. (*They bandage him up.*)
YAKOV (*tossing about*): Oh, my head. Milda ... Lipa ... my head.
LIPA: You needn't have done it so hard.
MILDA: It's over and done with. Just apply water. Take him away now. And don't ever let him come back.
LIPA: So that's it. (*Milda offers her hand. Lipa refuses to take it.*) I'm not going to be all friendly with you just like that.
MILDA: Oh.
LIPA: What name have you chosen?
MILDA: What for?
LIPA: Can't you see beyond your own belly?
MILDA: See what?
LIPA: I'm expecting Yakov's baby, too. Imagine. Some time in the future, they'll meet, get close. Then what? Brother can't marry sister. That's incest. So what name are you going to give it? Just so I know.
MILDA: What name? If it's a boy – Yasnich. A girl – Yuna.
LIPA: Yasnich? That's a funny sort of a name. What is it? We'll have to swap addresses, you know. When you have the baby, write and let me know, and I'll do the same for you. We've got to keep in touch, so we know where the little brother and sister are. That's what I wanted to say.
MILDA: Listen, you're being stupid, Lipka.
LIPA: I'm stupid?
MILDA: Don't interrupt, let me finish. (*Stoneturner enters with a long bundle.*) The time will come when all this building work will be finished. There will come a time when there won't be household chores any more, but that won't mean people being unemployed, just that nobody will be a housewife full time. People will have recovered from all the devastation and trauma of social upheaval, and there will be nurseries, kindergartens, crèches, everywhere. There'll be palaces for babies. We'll take our babies there, you and me, we'll just be two friends. That's how it will be.
LIPA: That'll never happen.
MILDA: Remember what I've said. Do you want a bet?

LIPA: Over my dead body.

MILDA: And I say, we shall! (*They shake hands. Stoneturner breaks the shake.*)

STONETURNER: I'm witness to the bet.

LIPA: And by the way, I'm only giving you my hand because of the bet, not because I want to make friends.

MILDA: Okay. (*Lipa goes out. Milda counts on her fingers.*) April, May, June, July, August, September, October, November, December, January. Ah, good. In December Milda will have leave. (*To Stoneturner*) Where've you come from?

STONETURNER: When a person has had a bath, he has more of the milk of human kindness.

SCENE TEN: EXHIBITION OF CHILDREN

Three years hence – i.e. 1930. A gallery, with a line of children's cots on each side. Posters on the walls. Some mothers are feeding their babies. Nurses walk up and down in the aisle. Stoneturner, now bearded, is doing something by one of the cots: it makes a rattly noise. The public is milling about.

SHE: Look, this baby is sucking his toe.
HE: But this one's even better. Look how lively it is. (*He reads the card on the cot.*)
SHE: I'd like to have a baby like that.
HE: Well, why not? When we've finished at the Institute, why not? (*She takes him by the hand affectionately.*)
SHE: This whole place smells of milk and manure.
STRIPES (*in a fur coat, also bearded, but looking rather lost*): When I was in England, I never had any difficulty in getting information. (*To Stoneturner*) Excuse me, are you a local?
STONETURNER: I'm the director of the dispensary here.
STRIPES: Would you be so good as to tell me what happened to the communal flat that used to be here? Actually, where is the whole building?
STONETURNER: The communal flat? Have you fallen out of the moon?
STRIPES: No, but I've been out of Moscow.
STONETURNER: How long for?
STRIPES: Er, three years. From 1927. It's 1930 now. Yes, three years.
STONETURNER: Did you go far?
STRIPES: Through Siberia. To the Narymsky region.[104]

---

104   *Narymsky region*: Narym in the Tomsk region, was notorious as a destination for prisoners exiled to Siberia. Among those sent there were Shostakovich's grandfather and Joseph Stalin.

STONETURNER: What did you go there for?
STRIPES: I've got something wrong with my lungs. But imagine – I don't recognize Moscow any more. So many new buildings, whole new streets have appeared. Such fine edifices. Cabbies are probably extinct, it's not a poor version of London any more.
STONETURNER: The communal flat you're looking for is certainly extinct.
STRIPES: I'll go to the Information Bureau.
STONETURNER: No need to. Just phone for information.
STRIPES: These children – are they orphans?
STONETURNER ; Not exactly.
STRIPES: I meant – are they homeless?
STONETURNER: Quite the contrary.
STRIPES: That is, no family?
STONETURNER: This is our district Children's Home. Today is the Exhibition of Children. It's the Carnival of Motherhood today, and these are the final selection of children, those from the best blood.
STRIPES: When I was in England ...
(*Two people, arguing, come in front of them.*)
FIRST ARGUER: You're talking rubbish.
SECOND ARGUER: Nonsense upon nonsense!
FIRST ARGUER: It's only heredity that's important. Only what's inherited.
SECOND ARGUER: It's only environment. Only the social environment.
FIRST ARGUER: Absurd! You're removing biology entirely.
SECOND ARGUER: And you're advocating counter-revolution.
FIRST ARGUER: So you think you could create another Pushkin just by how you brought him up?
SECOND ARGUER: Why not? In socialist society, an ordinary man is worth five Pushkins.
STONETURNER: Don't shout.
BOTH: Comrade, is it heredity or environment that's important?
STONETURNER: Both heredity and environment.
BOTH: Rubbish. Either environment or heredity. Either or, either or.
STONETURNER: Both, both.
BOTH: Either or, either or.
STONETURNER: Both, both.

NURSE: Please be quiet. I'll have to turf you out.
FIRST ARGUER (*whispers*): Don't you finds this data enlightening?
(*Both start reading the notes attached to the cot.*)
NURSE: All mothers, please come over here. (*Yakov tries to push his way through the crowd.*) You're not allowed in here. Only mothers.
YAKOV: I've got to do something.
NURSE: Are you one of the cleaners?
YAKOV: I'm much more important.
NURSE: The cook?
YAKOV: More important.
NURSE: Oh, you're a paramedic?
YAKOV: More important. I'm a most important person. I'm a father.
NURSE: You may think you're important, but you're not allowed here.
YAKOV: I'm bringing my baby's bib.
NURSE: Oh, all right then.
(*Doctors appear. Everybody shushes everybody else.*)
DOCTOR: Let me announce the results of the competition for children in the three year old's section. The following factors have been taken into account: the children's weight, their diets, the volume of their ribcages, their digestion, the composition of their blood, their reflexes, temperaments, conditions of conception, and the mother's condition during pregnancy and birth. Our Commission has decided to give the first prize jointly to two children – numbers 17 and 5 – and the second prize to number 8.
VOICES: – Let the mothers come over here.
    – And prize babies! Let's see the prize babies.
STONETURNER: The prize winners are on the third floor.
(*On the platform from opposite ends, enter Milda and Lipa. They stare at each other in amazement. Each holds a child by the hand.*)
LIPA: Milda.
MILDA: Lipa.
LIPA: A boy.
MILDA: A girl.
LIPA: Ah ha. What I thought.
MILDA: It's fine. Do you remember?
LIPA: What?
MILDA: Our bet.
LIPA: Well?

MILDA: I lost.

LIPA (*giving her child to Milda*): Take her. And give me yours. (*They exchange children.*)

MILDA: Yakov's?

LIPA: Yes.

MILDA: It's obvious. She's got his eyes and his forehead, but her mouth is yours.

YAKOV: Lipka, you look like a princess.

LIPA: Yakov, look.

YAKOV (*to Milda*): Ah. We meet again. You still working?

MILDA: I'm still an agronomist.

YAKOV: Dealing with piglets?

MILDA: Wheat, actually. On the Dnieper.

YAKOV: Your child's with you there?

MILDA: No.

YAKOV: He's here?

MILDA: I'm not saying.

YAKOV: So, he doesn't know the word 'daddy', only 'mummy'.

MILDA: No, he doesn't know the word 'mummy' either.

YAKOV: How come? Have you given him away?

MILDA: Not quite. I visit him, but as if I'm just an acquaintance.

YAKOV: What the hell for?

MILDA: When I die, he won't cry for me. Let him live his life strong and happy.

YAKOV: So you had a son? You blabbed it out! And why the hell can't I be with my son? What's wrong with me?

MILDA: That's enough of that. You built an impressive place here. Do you remember when you were working? – Dadadada … (*repeating the noise he made when demolishing the night club in scene 6.*)

YAKOV: Comrade.

MILDA: No sentimentality! Don't think those thoughts. Just imagine – now we have collective farms, villages, towns, megatowns. Pay no attention to the adult noise. Listen. Children's voices. Soviet children, growing up. And these are the best Soviet children. Twenty years ago, out of every hundred children born, fifty would die. Five years ago, thirty would die. And ten years from now, all one hundred will survive. And all of them will be as good as our best are today. We shall have children just like we have wheat

on the Dnieper now – strong and vigorous. (*Yakov turns away.*) Where are you going?
YAKOV: To the third floor.
MILDA: You don't need to. Listen.
LIPA (*gives Yakov the child*): Yazha, take it, I'm tired.
STONETURNER: Can I ask all mothers, expectant mothers and all members of the section for 'Rational Conception' –
VOICE: And fathers.
STONETURNER: – and all male stock providers to go through now to hear the doctor's lecture.
IVAN BARAN (*entering*): Excuse me!
VOICE: You're not allowed!
IVAN BARAN (*getting through*): Who's not allowed? I've only just found the bloody place. Sorry, comrades, but there's only an hour before my train, and my business is urgent. (*He is wearing a medal.*) Look at this. I've got it. (*He holds a piglet in his arms.*) On our collective farm, they're nearly all like this. (*He points to the piglet.*) But I'd like to talk about the feeding problems.
MILDA: Why, what's the matter? Stoneturner! Come on!
STONETURNER: I'm just doing this electric rattle.
YAKOV: He's not allowed. Only male stock providers are allowed here.
STONETURNER: What's that?
YAKOV: What's that? What's not that? You've no right to be here.
STONETURNER: This is our place. You'd better take that back. Or I'll – one ... two ... three ... four ...
YAKOV: I won't take it back.
MILDA: Are you swearing or trying not to lose your temper?
STONETURNER: Five ... six ... seven ... eight ... (*He takes out of his pocket a flash card with the number 8 on it.*) Number eight – what is it, eh? Not a number? And what am I? Not a father?
MILDA: Come on, the baby isn't called Stoneturner.
STONETURNER: She forbade it. So it has its mother's name.
MILDA: Who is the mother?
STONETURNER: She'll come over. (*Shouts.*) Mother! (*Out of the crowd, a woman approaches.*)
YAKOV: Look, they're all moving.
STRIPES: When I was in England, they had nothing like this.
STONETURNER: Those who would like to give their best babies to

the Soviet Union, not deformed or abnormal little monkeys, but healthy, bouncing, beautiful, Soviet babies, follow me. (*Rattling his electric rattle, he goes into the heart of the kindergarten, and the crowd follows him.*)

ALTERNATIVE ENDING

SCENE TEN: EXHIBITION OF CHILDREN

A gallery with a line of children's cots on each side. Posters on the walls. Some mothers are feeding their babies. Nurses walk up and down in the aisle. Stoneturner, now bearded, is doing something by one of the cots: it makes a rattly noise. The public is milling about.

STRIPES: When I was in England, I was never in such an idiotic place. (*To Stoneturner*) Excuse me, are you a local?
STONETURNER: I'm a chemist at the laboratory. You're not local?
STRIPES: No, I'm local, but I've been away for a while.
STONETURNER: How long for?
STRIPES: Three years.
STONETURNER: To the north pole?
STRIPES: No, through Siberia –
STONETURNER: Siberia? I was born there. That's a long way.
STRIPES: – to the Narymsky region.
STONETURNER: What did you go for?
STRIPES: Er, I've got something wrong with my lungs.
STONETURNER: Have you got a kid here?
STRIPES: I left a light overcoat here, but I can't find it.
STONETURNER: You dropped it?
STRIPES: There was a three story building here, and in it was Flat 14, and in Flat 14 my friend lived, and at my friend's was my suitcase, and in my suitcase was my light overcoat. I was looking for the caretaker, but he's not here, his wife's here instead. I was looking for her – I'm moving here. (*Noticing the children.*) Are these orphans?

STONETURNER: Not exactly.
STRIPES: I meant – are they homeless?
STONETURNER: Quite the contrary.
STRIPES: That is, no family.
STONETURNER: This is our district Children's Home. Today is the Exhibition of Children. It's the Carnival of Motherhood. The caretaker's wife's over there, see, feeding her baby. Wait – she's taking care of it, then she'll come over.
STRIPES: When I was in England ...

(*Two people, arguing, come in front of them.*)

FIRST ARGUER: This place is depriving these children of love. In two years they'll be neurotic.
SECOND ARGUER: But these are your celebrated infants, cooked up in advance, well thought-out, everything planned ... And they're simply dull.
FIRST ARGUER: You're talking rubbish!
SECOND ARGUER: Nonsense upon nonsense!
FIRST ARGUER: It's only heredity that's important, only what's inherited.
SECOND ARGUER: It's only environment. Only the social environment in which the child grows up.
FIRST ARGUER: You're going against biology, you're against eugenics, you're against medical controls over conception.
SECOND ARGUER: You're advocating counter-revolution.
FIRST ARGUER: So you think you could create another Pushkin just by how you brought him up?
SECOND ARGUER: Why not? In socialist society, an ordinary man is worth five Pushkins.
STONETURNER: Don't shout.
BOTH: Comrade, is it heredity or environment that's important?
STONETURNER: Both heredity and environment.
BOTH: Rubbish. Either heredity or environment. Either or, either or.
STONETURNER: Both, both.
BOTH: Either or, either or.
STONETURNER: Both, both.
NURSE: Please be quiet. I'll have to turf you out.
FIRST ARGUER (*whispers*): Don't you find this data enlightening?

(*Both start reading the notes attached to one of the cots. They continue their quarrel. Supervisor and Milda enter.*)

SUPERVISOR: Who's responsible?
MILDA: Yes! Who's responsible for the badly-fixed wash basin? It's come loose.
SUPERVISOR: Well, please don't start giving orders.
MILDA: No, I will give an order. We don't bring our children here to have them injured. Anyone can see it should be removed.
SUPERVISOR: If every mother was to worry about an injury to her child – life here would be impossible.
MILDA: In this case it's not mine, but it could be mine.
SUPERVISOR: Well, if it's not yours, why are you getting worked up?
MILDA: It's good. Getting worked up. And why for heaven's sake is the mother's co-operative in existence at all? With an attitude like yours, it's impossible for anyone to say anything about the Children's Home. I want to be happy I can be away from here for six months.
SUPERVISOR: For six months you can take a rest from giving orders.
MILDA: You see, to be easy in my mind, it would be helpful to know there are a few nails for the wash basin. And what about the dust under the wardrobe?
SUPERVISOR: I don't intend to answer in this environment.
MILDA: You find it difficult to answer, but I'm putting these questions on behalf of the co-operative.
SUPERVISOR: You're just getting excited, for goodness' sake.
CARETAKER'S WIFE: Excuse me. Stop shouting, please. The children get upset by loud voices. (*To Milda*) Thank you for coming, but we can't have loud voices like that in this place.
STONETURNER (*to Milda*): There's no point in killing yourself. The home isn't that bad. To a sensible person, it's a detail.
MILDA: No, it isn't. After that, how can people be taught to approve of this place?
STONETURNER: Take a second look.
MILDA: You opportunist. If it's such a model place, you shouldn't need to shout just to get a nail.
STONETURNER: What are you driving at?
MILDA: Driving at? My paper on agronomics is going for nothing – I have to consult this doctor. But they're dragging out these proceedings – it's time to decide on the prizes for the children. Wait! It looks like they're going to make an announcement.

STRIPES (*to the caretaker's wife*): Madam caretakeress, I understood that you'd fed your baby and were now ready to pass on to your social function.

CARETAKER'S WIFE: Move on, shaggy, you're in the way.

STRIPES: When I was in London ...

DOCTOR: Silence, please. Comrade chemist, stop the yelling. Let me announce the results of the competition for children in the two to three year old age group. The following factors have been taken into account: the children's weight, their diets, the volume of their ribcages, their digestion, the composition of their blood, their reflexes, temperaments, conditions of conception, and the mother's condition during pregnancy and birth. Our commission has decided to give first prizes to children numbers 5, 17 and 33, and second prizes to numbers 8, 11 and 60.

VOICES: – Let the mothers come over here!

– And the prize babies! Let's see the prize babies!

STONETURNER: The prize winners are on the third floor.

CARETAKER'S WIFE: Well, get them here for their prizes. Where's the assistant? Make way!

ASSISTANT'S VOICE: What are you shoving for? Wait a minute.

CARETAKER'S WIFE: No, we can't wait all day. You over there, you have to pull in your paunches so the children can line up. Actually it's not my concern now.

(*The competing mothers pass through the crowd. Yakov forces his way through to where the doctor is standing.*)

NURSE: You're not allowed in here, only mothers.

YAKOV: I've got to do something.

NURSE: Are you one of the cleaners?

YAKOV: I'm much more important.

NURSE: The cook?

YAKOV: More important.

NURSE: Oh, you're a para-medic?

YAKOV: More important. I'm a most important person. I'm a father.

NURSE: You may think you're important, but you're not allowed here.

YAKOV: I'm bringing my baby's bib. It's a bib.

(*He goes through. The mothers are greeted with a buzz of approval.*)

DOCTOR: Mothers will please not disperse. Those who want to see the prize-winning children, please come with me. (*The doctor leads out the crowd, including most of the mothers. In the midst of the mothers, Lipa, with her baby in her arms, and Milda see one another.*)

MILDA: Comrade Lipa.

LIPA: Oh, hello.

MILDA: I recognized you.

LIPA: That face.

MILDA: Well, here we are, with your prize-winner. Congratulations. (*She holds out her hand.*)

LIPA: I've got my hands full here.

MILDA: You're still angry. Have you been coming here long?

LIPA: Four months.

MILDA: This is your second?

LIPA: So we're not playing dollies.

MILDA: A boy?

LIPA: No. She's a girl. (*Looking round*) Where's Yakov?

MILDA (*nervously*): Is Yakov here?

LIPA: Worried? We've been together ... about four years.

MILDA: You're not sure?

LIPA: Why wouldn't I be sure?

MILDA: I heard from him for a few months. 'Where's the baby? Show me the baby.'

LIPA: And how did you answer?

MILDA: I didn't. I don't want him to see the child. I don't want him to see me. I'm going.

LIPA: Stay. You can meet him. He's somewhere about. You must meet him, he's here in the the Home.

MILDA: Let me hold your little girl for a minute while you look for him.

LIPA: Okay. (*She gives over her baby and goes. Milda stands with the child. Yakov, not recognizing her, tiptoes up with his daughter's bib.*)

YAKOV: Here you are, princess. (*Milda turns round. They look at each other, dumbstruck.*) So. You got in ... Do you work here?

MILDA: I'm not stopping. I work on the Dnieper.

YAKOV: Dealing with piglets?

MILDA: Wheat, actually.

YAKOV: Your child's here?

MILDA: I'm not saying.

YAKOV: Of course he's here. What are you doing here otherwise?
MILDA (*looking at the baby*): Your daughter has your eyes.
YAKOV: So he doesn't know the word 'daddy', only 'mummy'.
MILDA: No, he doesn't know 'mummy' either. He says 'nanny'.
YAKOV: How come? Have you given him away?
MILDA: Not quite. I visit him, but as if I'm just an acquaintance.
YAKOV: What the hell for?
MILDA: When I die, he won't cry for me. Let him be secure and happy.
YAKOV: He's here. Now. Where? Tell me, where?
MILDA: I'm not saying.
YAKOV: Just a glimpse. He's my son, you know. We know who's the father, and the father has rights in the lad. Even if I'm a bourgeois – I'm a thief – I'm a flea.
MILDA: Stop, comrade Yakov.
YAKOV: You threw him into the Children's Home like a bag of rubbish. Even when he really needed you. You don't love him, so don't stop someone else loving him.
MILDA: D'you think I don't love him?
YAKOV: All you love is your wheat.
MILDA: Both the wheat and him.
YAKOV: Like tablets from a chemist's. You're dried up. Four years ago I wrote you a letter ... and ...
MILDA: You have a family. You have Lipa and your daughters. You will have a son.
YAKOV: He should have known me from the start. He should know me now.
MILDA: He will know you. I'll tell him.
(*Noise gets louder. The doctors and the whole crowd enter with several three year olds running about among them. Lipa rushes in. She confronts Yakov and Milda.*)
LIPA: Yakov! (*Yakov doesn't hear. With wide eyes, he is watching intently the group of children running about.*)
YAKOV: Milda. This one here, yes? No, he's not got your eyes. That one's pretty lively, maybe ... Or that one, Milka, eh? Where's my son?
MILDA: Yakov, don't be so self-centred.
YAKOV: There, there, that blue-eyed one, that's him, definitely! Look, look! (*Milda tries to restrain him.*) Listen, little one. Is this your mum? This one? No?

MILDA: Mine ...

YAKOV: That is, mine ...

MILDA: ... doesn't know the word 'mum'. Comrade Yakov – they're all yours. Love them all. They're all healthy and sturdy, like the wheat on the Dnieper.

YAKOV: I'll find him. (*He wants to run to the group.*)

MILDA: Lipa, help me! (*She passes the baby back to Lipa. Lipa gets in Yakov's way.*)

LIPA: Yasha, will you hold her? I want to put her bib on.

YAKOV: I get it. Skirts ...

LIPA: Yasha, I'm tired.

YAKOV (*among the children*): I'm not talking to him, I'm talking to you – my eyes can't fail me, I'll discover your brother.

DOCTOR: I'm asking the comrade mothers to hear the report and to join us for a cup of tea.

CARETAKER'S WIFE: And the fathers.

DOCTOR: And the male stock providers.

IVAN BARAN (*entering with a piglet under his arm*): Excuse me!

SUPERVISOR: Unbelievable!

IVAN BARAN: Let me through. Time's short.

SUPERVISOR: He's in galoshes. And he's got a piglet! You'll have to leave that with the caretaker.

IVAN BARAN: The caretaker's not there. And you can't hang a piglet on a cloakroom peg.

SUPERVISOR: I can't let you in.

IVAN BARAN: Oh, this is impossible. I've got to see her. (*He points at the group where Milda is.*)

SUPERVISOR: They can't be doing with trivialities. This brute'll be the death of me. It's not allowed!

IVAN BARAN: Never mind what's allowed. (*To Milda*) I've only just found the bloody place. Sorry, comrades, but there's only an hour before my train, and my business is urgent. (*He is wearing a medal.*) Look at this. I've got it. (*He holds out the piglet.*) On our collective farm, they're nearly all like this. (*He points to the piglet.*) But I'd like to talk to you about the feeding problems.

MILDA: Why? What's the matter? (*To Stoneturner*) Stoneturner, come on.

STONETURNER: I'm just doing this electric rattle.

CARETAKER'S WIFE (*points at Stoneturner*): He's not allowed. Only male stock providers are allowed here.
STONETURNER: What's that?
CARETAKER'S WIFE: What's that? What's not that? You've no right to be here.
STONETURNER: This is our place. You'd better take that back. Or I'll – one ... two ... three ... four ...
CARETAKER'S WIFE: Don't imagine –
MILDA: Are you swearing, or trying not to lose your temper?
STONETURNER: Five ... six ... seven ... eight ... (*He takes out of his pocket a flash card with the number 8 on it.*) Eight – what is it, eh? Not a number? And what am I? Not a father?
MILDA: When did you –
(*Enter a woman with a baby.*)
CARETAKER'S WIFE: This mother, here – ?
MILDA: It's like you.
STONETURNER: I don't think so.
MILDA: Why?
STONETURNER: Because they parked it on me. And I adopted it.
IVAN BARAN: They paired you off, like with my pigs.
STRIPES: When I was in England, they had nothing like this.
IVAN BARAN (*to Stoneturner*): So it's not your own production?
STONETURNER: Correct. But if I imagine production, then I'm okay – I give the Soviet Union not a deformed or abnormal little monkey, but a true Soviet baby who will crack open the world!
(*Rattling his electric rattle, he goes into the heart of the Children's Home, and the crowd follows him.*)

Nikolai Gumilev's Africa

Gumilev holds a unique position in the history of Russian poetry as a result of his profound involvement with Africa. He extensively wrote both poetry and prose on the culture of the continent in general and on Ethiopia (Abyssinia, as it was called in Gumilev's time) in particular. During his abbreviated lifetime Gumilev made four trips to Northern and Eastern Africa, the most extensive of which was a 1913 expedition to Abyssinia undertaken on assignment from the St. Petersburg Imperial Museum of Anthropology and Ethnography. During that trip Gumilev collected Ethiopian folklore and ethnographic objects, which, upon his return to St. Petersburg, he deposited at the Museum. He and his assistant Nikolai Sverchkov also made more than 200 photographs that offer a unique picture of the African country in the early part of the century.

This volume collects all of Gumilev's poetry and prose written about Africa for the first time as well as a number of the photographs that he and Nikolai Sverchkov took during their trip that give a fascinating view of that part of the world in the early twentieth century.

Buy it > www.glagoslav.com

Forefathers' Eve
by Adam Mickiewicz

Forefathers' Eve [*Dziady*] is a four-part dramatic work begun circa 1820 and completed in 1832 – with Part I published only after the poet's death, in 1860. The drama's title refers to *Dziady*, an ancient Slavic and Lithuanian feast commemorating the dead. This is the grand work of Polish literature, and it is one that elevates Mickiewicz to a position among the "great Europeans" such as Dante and Goethe.

With its Christian background of the Communion of the Saints, revenant spirits, and the interpenetration of the worlds of time and eternity, *Forefathers' Eve* speaks to men and women of all times and places. While it is a truly Polish work – Polish actors covet the role of Gustaw/Konrad in the same way that Anglophone actors covet that of Hamlet – it is one of the most universal works of literature written during the nineteenth century. It has been compared to Goethe's Faust – and rightfully so...

Buy it > www.glagoslav.com

Acropolis – The Wawel Plays
by Stanisław Wyspiański

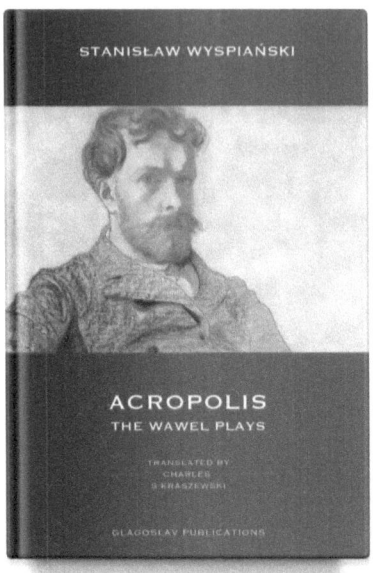

Stanisław Wyspiański (1869-1907) achieved worldwide fame, both as a painter, and Poland's greatest dramatist of the first half of the twentieth century. *Acropolis: the Wawel Plays*, brings together four of Wyspiański's most important dramatic works in a new English translation by Charles S. Kraszewski. All of the plays centre on Wawel Hill: the legendary seat of royal and ecclesiastical power in the poet's native city, the ancient capital of Poland. In these plays, Wyspiański explores the foundational myths of his nation: that of the self-sacrificial Wanda, and the struggle between King Bolesław the Bold and Bishop Stanisław Szczepanowski. In the eponymous play which brings the cycle to an end, Wyspiański carefully considers the value of myth to a nation without political autonomy, soaring in thought into an apocalyptic vision of the future. Richly illustrated with the poet's artwork, *Acropolis: the Wawel Plays* also contains Wyspiański's architectural proposal for the renovation of Wawel Hill, and a detailed critical introduction by the translator. In its plaited presentation of *Bolesław the Bold* and *Skałka*, the translation offers, for the first time, the two plays in the unified, composite format that the poet intended, but was prevented from carrying out by his untimely death.

Buy it > www.glagoslav.com

Dear Reader,

Thank you for purchasing this book.

We at Glagoslav Publications are glad to welcome you, and hope that you find our books to be a source of knowledge and inspiration.

We want to show the beauty and depth of the Slavic region to everyone looking to expand their horizon and learn something new about different cultures, different people, and we believe that with this book we have managed to do just that.

Now that you've got to know us, we want to get to know you. We value communication with our readers and want to hear from you! We offer several options:

– Join our Book Club on Goodreads, Library Thing and Shelfari, and receive special offers and information about our giveaways;

– Share your opinion about our books on Amazon, Barnes & Noble, Waterstones and other bookstores;

– Join us on Facebook and Twitter for updates on our publications and news about our authors;

– Visit our site www.glagoslav.com to check out our Catalogue and subscribe to our Newsletter.

Glagoslav Publications is getting ready to release a new collection and planning some interesting surprises — stay with us to find out!

Glagoslav Publications
Email: contact@glagoslav.com

Glagoslav Publications Catalogue

- *The Time of Women* by Elena Chizhova
- *Andrei Tarkovsky: The Collector of Dreams* by Layla Alexander-Garrett
- *Andrei Tarkovsky - A Life on the Cross* by Lyudmila Boyadzhieva
- *Sin* by Zakhar Prilepin
- *Hardly Ever Otherwise* by Maria Matios
- *Khatyn* by Ales Adamovich
- *The Lost Button* by Irene Rozdobudko
- *Christened with Crosses* by Eduard Kochergin
- *The Vital Needs of the Dead* by Igor Sakhnovsky
- *The Sarabande of Sara's Band* by Larysa Denysenko
- *A Poet and Bin Laden* by Hamid Ismailov
- *Watching The Russians (Dutch Edition)* by Maria Konyukova
- *Kobzar* by Taras Shevchenko
- *The Stone Bridge* by Alexander Terekhov
- *Moryak* by Lee Mandel
- *King Stakh's Wild Hunt* by Uladzimir Karatkevich
- *The Hawks of Peace* by Dmitry Rogozin
- *Harlequin's Costume* by Leonid Yuzefovich
- *Depeche Mode* by Serhii Zhadan
- *The Grand Slam and other stories (Dutch Edition)* by Leonid Andreev
- *METRO 2033 (Dutch Edition)* by Dmitry Glukhovsky
- *METRO 2034 (Dutch Edition)* by Dmitry Glukhovsky
- *A Russian Story* by Eugenia Kononenko
- *Herstories, An Anthology of New Ukrainian Women Prose Writers*
- *The Battle of the Sexes Russian Style* by Nadezhda Ptushkina
- *A Book Without Photographs* by Sergey Shargunov
- *Down Among The Fishes* by Natalka Babina
- *disUNITY* by Anatoly Kudryavitsky
- *Sankya* by Zakhar Prilepin
- *Wolf Messing* by Tatiana Lungin
- *Good Stalin* by Victor Erofeyev
- *Solar Plexus* by Rustam Ibragimbekov

- *Don't Call me a Victim!* by Dina Yafasova
- *Poetin (Dutch Edition)* by Chris Hutchins and Alexander Korobko
- *A History of Belarus* by Lubov Bazan
- *Children's Fashion of the Russian Empire* by Alexander Vasiliev
- *Empire of Corruption - The Russian National Pastime* by Vladimir Soloviev
- *Heroes of the 90s: People and Money. The Modern History of Russian Capitalism*
- *Fifty Highlights from the Russian Literature (Dutch Edition)* by Maarten Tengbergen
- *Bajesvolk (Dutch Edition)* by Mikhail Khodorkovsky
- *Tsarina Alexandra's Diary (Dutch Edition)*
- *Myths about Russia* by Vladimir Medinskiy
- *Boris Yeltsin: The Decade that Shook the World* by Boris Minaev
- *A Man Of Change: A study of the political life of Boris Yeltsin*
- *Sberbank: The Rebirth of Russia's Financial Giant* by Evgeny Karasyuk
- *To Get Ukraine* by Oleksandr Shyshko
- *Asystole* by Oleg Pavlov
- *Gnedich* by Maria Rybakova
- *Marina Tsvetaeva: The Essential Poetry*
- *Multiple Personalities* by Tatyana Shcherbina
- *The Investigator* by Margarita Khemlin
- *The Exile* by Zinaida Tulub
- *Leo Tolstoy: Flight from paradise* by Pavel Basinsky
- *Moscow in the 1930* by Natalia Gromova
- *Laurus (Dutch edition)* by Evgenij Vodolazkin
- *Prisoner* by Anna Nemzer
- *The Crime of Chernobyl: The Nuclear Goulag* by Wladimir Tchertkoff
- *Alpine Ballad* by Vasil Bykau
- *The Complete Correspondence of Hryhory Skovoroda*
- *The Tale of Aypi* by Ak Welsapar
- *Selected Poems* by Lydia Grigorieva
- *The Fantastic Worlds of Yuri Vynnychuk*

- *The Garden of Divine Songs and Collected Poetry of Hryhory Skovoroda*
- *Adventures in the Slavic Kitchen: A Book of Essays with Recipes*
- *Seven Signs of the Lion* by Michael M. Naydan
- *Forefathers' Eve* by Adam Mickiewicz
- *One-Two* by Igor Eliseev
- *Girls, be Good* by Bojan Babić
- *Time of the Octopus* by Anatoly Kucherena
- *The Grand Harmony* by Bohdan Ihor Antonych
- *The Selected Lyric Poetry Of Maksym Rylsky*
- *The Shining Light* by Galymkair Mutanov
- *The Frontier: 28 Contemporary Ukrainian Poets - An Anthology*
- *Acropolis: The Wawel Plays* by Stanisław Wyspiański
- *Contours of the City* by Attyla Mohylny
- *Conversations Before Silence: The Selected Poetry of Oles Ilchenko*
- *The Secret History of my Sojourn in Russia* by Jaroslav Hašek
- *Mirror Sand: An Anthology of Russian Short Poems in English Translation* (A Bilingual Edition)
- *Maybe We're Leaving* by Jan Balaban
- *Death of the Snake Catcher* by Ak Welsapar
- *A Brown Man in Russia: Perambulations Through A Siberian Winter* by Vijay Menon
- *Hard Times* by Ostap Vyshnia
- *The Flying Dutchman* by Anatoly Kudryavitsky
- *Nikolai Gumilev's Africa* by Nikolai Gumilev
- *Combustions* by Srđan Srdić
- *The Sonnets* by Adam Mickiewicz
- *Dramatic Works* by Zygmunt Krasiński
- *Four Plays* by Juliusz Słowacki
- *Little Zinnobers* by Elena Chizhova
- *We Are Building Capitalism! Moscow in Transition 1992-1997*
- *The Nuremberg Trials* by Alexander Zvyagintsev
- *The Hemingway Game* by Evgeni Grishkovets
- *A Flame Out at Sea* by Dmitry Novikov
- *Jesus' Cat* by Grig
- *Duel* by Borys Antonenko-Davydovych
- *Mikhail Bulgakov: The Life and Times* by Marietta Chudakova

More coming soon...

www.ingramcontent.com/pod-product-compliance
Lightning Source LLC
Chambersburg PA
CBHW031054080526
44587CB00011B/673